TRUE CRIME

CASE HIS

VOL. 16

CW01499370

12 DISTURBING TRUE CRIME STORIES

JASON NEAL

TRUE CRIME CASE HISTORIES - VOLUMES 16, 17, & 18

36 DISTURBING TRUE CRIME STORIES

JASON NEAL

JASON NEAL BOOKS

More books by Jason Neal

Looking for more?? I am constantly adding new volumes of True Crime Case Histories. The series **can be read in any order,** and all books are available in paperback, hardcover, and audiobook.

Check out the complete series at:

https://amazon.com/author/jason-neal

All Jason Neal books are also available in **AudioBook format at Audible.com.** Enjoy a **Free Audiobook** when you signup for a 30-Day trial using this link:

https://geni.us/AudibleTrueCrime

FREE BONUS EBOOK FOR MY READERS

As my way of saying "Thank you" for downloading, I'm giving away a FREE True Crime e-book I think you'll enjoy.

https://TrueCrimeCaseHistories.com

Just click the link above to let me know where to send your free book!

CONTENTS

TRUE CRIME CASE HISTORIES - VOLUME 16
12 DISTURBING TRUE CRIME STORIES

Introduction	3
1. Friendly Reminders	5
2. The Highway of Tears	13
3. The Christadelphian	25
4. It's Done	43
5. No Body, No Crime	55
6. Apartment 9	67
7. Sacred Trust	81
8. The Krug Park Killers	91
9. The Bedroom Basher	105
10. Five Fatal Minutes	117
11. The Frankston Serial Killer	131
12. The Mission Valley Mall Murders	147
13. Bonus Chapter: The Gift Shop Murder	163

TRUE CRIME CASE HISTORIES - VOLUME 17
12 DISTURBING TRUE CRIME STORIES

Introduction	177
1. The Butcher of Aberdeen	179
2. The House on Langworthy Road	193
3. The Pizza Bomber	207
4. The REDRUM Murder	219
5. A Strange Case	233
6. The Vanishing	245
7. The Night Shift	261
8. The Killer Poet	279
9. The Bathtub Killer	293
10. Child of Chaos	307
11. He Needed Killing	319

12. The Millionaire   335
13. Bonus Chapter: A Familiar Face   347

TRUE CRIME CASE HISTORIES - VOLUME 18
12 DISTURBING TRUE CRIME STORIES

Introduction   359
1. The Unraveling   361
2. Shared Psychosis   377
3. The Stanford Cold Case   393
4. The Trainspotter   413
5. The Dark Web Assassin   433
6. The Waterbed   451
7. The Second Chance   469
8. The Greek Pilot   487
9. Count to Three   507
10. The Pink Notebook   525
11. Bail Granted   541
12. The Hudson Murders   559
13. Bonus Chapter: The Caldwell Farmhouse   575

Online Appendix   593
Also by Jason Neal   595
Free Bonus Book   597
About the Author   599

INTRODUCTION

Truth is darker than fiction.

This volume of *True Crime Case Histories* presents twelve chilling cases that defy belief—crimes so unsettling they could be mistaken for fiction.

Meet a woman who reinvented herself under eighteen aliases across fourteen states, all while meticulously researching murder and body disposal—until she put her knowledge to use. Discover how a broken-down motorcycle on Christmas Eve triggered a deadly chain of events that shattered two families forever.

Uncover the truth behind a trusted priest who hid a terrible secret for half a century until a deathbed confession exposed his sins. Follow the twisted path of teenage lovers whose obsession with demons and ritual sacrifice led them to lure in an innocent victim through social media.

Step inside the case of the *Bedroom Basher*, a serial predator whose crimes sent an innocent man to prison for sixteen years while he continued his reign of terror. Learn how forensic science unraveled the carefully crafted identity of a corrections officer to reveal a predator hiding beneath his badge.

Travel to Australia, where a seemingly ordinary young man terrorized an entire community with his calculated brutality. And in Colorado's high country, see how a Craigslist ad—live for just five minutes—led to an unthinkable contract killing.

Each case is meticulously researched using court documents, police records, and forensic reports, revealing the raw, unfiltered truth of true crime. Unlike sanitized television dramas, these stories expose the real horrors that haunt small towns and ripple through entire communities.

Though gripping, many of these cases have remained largely unknown, shared by readers who remember them from their home-towns. They serve as stark reminders of the darkness lurking in everyday life.

A word of caution: This book contains graphic details that may be disturbing. They are included not for shock but to provide a full understanding of these crimes' devastating impact. If you're ready to confront the realities of human nature's darkest side, read on.

For case photos, documents, and bonus materials, visit TrueCrime-CaseHistories.com/vol16. Join my mailing list for updates and a free e-book.

Let's begin.

CHAPTER 1
FRIENDLY REMINDERS

I n late July 2013, Jamie Parsons made a disturbing report to the Rowan County Sheriff's Office. His adoptive sister, thirteen-year-old Erica Parsons, hadn't been seen since December 2011, and no one outside the family had even noticed. The timing wasn't a coincidence; Jamie had just been kicked out of his home after a fierce argument with his adoptive parents, Casey and Sandy Parsons. He sought revenge and made a chilling accusation to the authorities. He claimed Erica was missing and suspected his parents were behind her disappearance. This sparked an investigation that would expose a web of lies and shocking family secrets. It would lead investigators to one haunting question: What happened to Erica Parsons?

———

To understand the circumstances that led to Erica's disappearance, we have to go back to her beginnings. Born on February 24, 1998, Erica Lynn Parsons entered a world of instability. Sandy's sister-in-law, Carolyn, found herself pregnant, alone, and fearful for her unborn child's future. Sandy and his wife Casey stepped forward, deciding to adopt the baby. The adoption was finalized in the spring of 2000 when Erica was two years old. To the outside world, it appeared that Erica had found her forever home with a couple willing to open their hearts to a child in need. Unfortunately, as the years passed, the reality behind the Parsons' front door would prove to be far from the loving home anyone had envisioned for her.

The Parsons lived in a modest home in Salisbury, North Carolina. From the outside, their house looked like any other on the street. Casey and Sandy raised their biological children there alongside Erica and, at times, took in foster children. To neighbors, they seemed like generous people willing to give needy children a chance at a better life.

But behind the family's carefully maintained façade, a different reality was unfolding. The other Parsons children went to public school and lived normal lives, while Erica was kept isolated. Casey withdrew all her children from public school early on and registered for homeschooling. This cut Erica off from the outside world. It also removed her from the watchful gaze of teachers who might have noticed something was wrong.

As investigators would later discover, Erica's isolation wasn't about education—it was about control. Family members eventually revealed that she was an outcast at home. She was punished far beyond typical discipline. While her siblings slept in beds, Erica was forced to sleep on the floor "like a dog," according to Casey's own mother. When she was allowed to eat at all, she was often forced to stand alone in a corner, separate from the family table.

But these indignities were just the beginning. What happened within the walls of that ordinary house in Salisbury was unimaginable. The truth would only emerge after Erica vanished.

After Erica's disappearance, investigators interviewed her family. They found a horrifying pattern of abuse. Jamie Parsons revealed how Casey would punish Erica with what she called "friendly reminders," bending her fingers back until they nearly snapped. Family members described her as being forced to stand in corners for hours, even days, as punishment.

Casey's mother provided investigators with devastating details. She described witnessing her daughter's cruelty firsthand, watching helplessly as Erica was either confined to a closet or forced to stand in a corner by the television. Casey's mother admitted to leaving the house because the abuse was too difficult to watch. Casey would openly beat and choke Erica in front of others. She said Erica always smelled horrible because they refused to let her bathe.

Erica's adoptive sisters tried to help in small ways, sneaking her scraps of food when they could. However, their attempts at kindness often resulted in more punishment for Erica if they were caught. The sisters later revealed that Erica was so desperate for food that she would resort to eating from dog and cat food cans.

While Casey was the primary abuser, Sandy Parsons was far from innocent. Family members described him delivering blows to Erica's face and head. The abuse was so severe that, at one point, Erica's arm was broken. Instead of taking her to a doctor, Casey had the children go to Walmart for first aid supplies to make a makeshift cast. The improper setting left Erica's arm permanently disfigured.

What made the abuse even more shocking was how long it continued without intervention. Despite multiple complaints filed with Social Services over the years, Erica always ended up back in the Parsons' custody. Their promises of reform were taken at face value, and each time, the abuse would resume behind closed doors. The system designed to protect children like Erica failed her repeatedly, and the consequences proved devastating.

By late 2011, something sinister was brewing in the Parsons household. According to Jamie, he last saw his adoptive sister on December 17, 2011. Her condition was alarming—she was stuffed inside the bedroom closet, covered in infected wounds. She was pale, weak, and struggling to breathe. When she told Casey she couldn't breathe, she only screamed at her to go back to the corner.

The next morning, Erica was gone.

———

For the next year and a half, Casey and Sandy Parsons carried on as if nothing had happened. They kept getting monthly checks of $634 for adoption assistance. They also collected Erica's Social Security benefits and claimed her on their taxes. When relatives or neighbors asked about Erica, the Parsons had a quick answer: She had gone to live with her grandmother, "Nan," in Asheville, North Carolina.

When investigators began looking into Erica's disappearance in July 2013, they faced significant challenges. It had been eighteen months since anyone had seen her, and that time could have been spent gathering evidence or interviewing witnesses while memories were fresh. However, as detectives dug deeper into the Parsons' story, red flags began emerging at an alarming rate.

In their first police interviews, the Parsons repeated their story that Erica had gone to live with her grandmother, "Nan," in Asheville. They claimed this mysterious woman—whose full name they said was Irene Goodman—had reached out on Facebook, expressing an interest in getting to know her granddaughter. According to their story, Nan owned a large farm where Erica could indulge in her love of horses. When asked about ongoing contact, Casey's explanations grew increasingly convoluted. She claimed she had been messaging Erica on Facebook but couldn't locate her profile. She said she had spoken with Erica by phone, but the number had been mysteriously disconnected. Most bizarrely, she claimed Erica had invited the family to her fourteenth birthday party, only to uninvite them all at the last minute.

The investigation took a dramatic turn when police executed a search warrant at the Parsons' home. Inside the bedroom closet where Erica had reportedly spent so much time, investigators found large blood-stains soaked into the carpet. DNA analysis would later confirm what many had feared: The blood belonged primarily to Erica, with traces of both Casey's and Sandy's DNA also present. Additional bloodstains were found on the bedroom wall, though investigators couldn't determine the primary donor of those stains.

Still, the Parsons maintained their innocence. In their boldest move, they appeared on the Dr. Phil show. They thought they could convince the nation of their innocence; it would prove to be a devastating miscalculation. The show's production team thoroughly investigated the Parsons' claims about Nan and found no trace of an Irene Goodman living in Asheville—because she didn't exist. The real Irene Goodman had died in 2005, years before Erica supposedly went to live with her.

During the show, Casey refused to take a polygraph examination, citing severe pain. When offered the chance to take her medication and complete the test the following day, she declined. Sandy agreed to take the test. He scored a negative nine when asked about Erica's disappearance. This score was much lower than the negative four that would suggest deception. The Parsons refused to continue with the show after these developments and returned to North Carolina—where federal agents were waiting.

———

On July 30, 2014, Sandy and Casey were arrested in Fayetteville and charged with seventy-six counts of federal fraud. The charges included theft of government funds, mail fraud, tax fraud, conspiracy to defraud the government, and identity theft. Of course, as investigators dug deeper, they uncovered a pattern of deception that went far beyond stolen benefits.

They discovered that Casey had run an adoption scam, posting ads online offering to give up her unborn baby for $10,000. After one hopeful couple paid her the money, Casey claimed she had miscarried. She refused their calls and sent hateful emails when they tried to contact her. Casey was indeed pregnant and would go on to attempt selling the baby to her sister for $110,000. The first couple eventually obtained a court order granting them legal custody of the child. The Parsons had also maintained an eBay scam for years, with Casey listing items for sale and then either never shipping them or severely misrepresenting what buyers would receive.

Casey pleaded guilty to multiple fraud charges and received a ten-year sentence. Sandy opted for a jury trial and was found guilty of forty-three counts, receiving an eight-year sentence. But even as the judge handed down these sentences in 2015, he made it clear that there were serious doubts about whether Erica was still alive.

The breakthrough came in August 2016, when Sandy finally broke under the pressure of repeated visits from his sister, Angela, and his daughter, Robin. With Casey serving her sentence in Texas, he sent word through Robin to the FBI: He was ready to reveal what had really happened to Erica.

Sandy led investigators to a rural property in Chesterfield County, South Carolina, owned by his family. There, he broke down in tears—though investigators noted they seemed to be tears for himself rather than for Erica. He described how, on December 18, 2011, Casey had told him Erica was dead, claiming she had overdosed on sleeping pills. Sandy admitted to helping conceal the crime, folding Erica's frail body into garbage bags, and placing her in a plastic tub. Casey had poured bleach over the body to mask any odors. After keeping the tub in their house for a day while their other children walked past, unaware, they drove to South Carolina to bury her. Sandy disposed of the tub and Erica's clothes in a dumpster at a local gas station before they returned home to begin crafting their story about Nan.

When confronted with the evidence from Erica's remains, Casey abandoned the Nan story entirely. She now claimed that on the night of her death, Erica had threatened to hang herself and asked for a rope. According to Casey, when she refused to provide one, Sandy had told Erica to "shut up, or he would go and get her a rope himself." Casey claimed she later found Erica hanging from a dog leash in a closet. Neither version—the tale about Nan or the suicide story—matched the evidence itself or Sandy's account of Casey's claim that Erica had overdosed.

The medical examiner's findings revealed the true horror of what Erica had endured. Her autopsy showed evidence of chronic, devastating abuse. She had suffered broken bones throughout her body, including a broken nose, broken teeth, and numerous broken ribs on both sides. Her fingers showed signs of repeated breaks, confirming the accounts of Casey's "friendly reminders." The childhood arm break that had been "treated" with a homemade cast was evident in her bones; her upper left arm had never properly healed. Her shoulder blade was also broken, and she had suffered fractures to her back.

Most disturbing was the medical examiner's conclusion about her death. While the exact cause couldn't be determined due to the condition of the remains, the manner of death was ruled "homicidal violence of undetermined means." The examiner noted that they couldn't exclude the possibility of "a terminal blunt force injury, suffocation, or strangulation."

In 2019, both Casey and Sandy Parsons faced murder charges in Rowan County. Casey maintained her defiance until the end but ultimately agreed to a plea deal. She pleaded guilty to first-degree murder, child abuse, and concealment of a death. At her sentencing hearing, she made only a brief statement, saying she was "sorry" and had "failed Erica terribly."

The judge showed no mercy. Casey received life in prison without the possibility of parole for the murder charge. Sandy's fate was different. In 2016, he had led investigators to Erica's body with no deal in place, yet three years later, his cooperation was considered in his murder trial. In December 2019, prosecutors let him plead guilty to second-degree murder, not first-degree. The judge accepted the plea agreement and sentenced him to serve a minimum of thirty-three years and a maximum of forty-three years in a North Carolina state prison.

The sentencing marked the end of a six-year investigation. It began with a son's report to the police and revealed unimaginable cruelty. But for many, the question of "why" remained unanswered. Why had Casey singled out Erica for such brutal abuse while her other children lived normal lives? Why had so many adults who witnessed the abuse remained silent for so long? And how had a system designed to protect children failed so completely?

CHAPTER 2
THE HIGHWAY OF TEARS

The snow was falling lightly across northern British Columbia that November night in 2010, dusting the dense forests that bordered Highway 27. At nearly 10:00 p.m., the remote stretch of road was pitch black except for the occasional sweep of headlights piercing the darkness. The highway branched off from the infamous Highway 16, known throughout British Columbia as the "Highway of Tears"—a 450-mile stretch where women had been vanishing for decades. The numbers told a grim story: The Royal Canadian Mounted Police counted eighteen victims, while aboriginal organizations estimated more than forty women had disappeared along this lonely road that cut through some of the most isolated territory in Canada.

———

A young RCMP officer was patrolling the darkness when movement caught his eye—a pair of headlights in the distance bobbing erratically as they emerged from an unused logging road. Through the gentle snowfall, he watched as a black pickup truck burst onto the highway, fishtailing on the slick pavement before the driver regained control.

Something about the scene struck the officer as deeply wrong. There was no reason for anyone to be on that logging road at this hour, especially not someone in such a hurry to leave it.

Following his instinct—the kind that experienced officers say you should never ignore—he called for backup. When his fellow officer was approaching from the opposite direction, he flipped on his emergency lights, red and blue flashing against the falling snow, and briefly hit his siren. The black truck continued for several hundred meters before finally pulling over to the side of the road. As the officer approached, his flashlight beam revealed the driver: Cody Legebokoff, a young man in his early twenties, wearing only shorts and a long-sleeve sweater despite the freezing temperatures. However, it was what the officer saw next that made his pulse quicken: a small red smear on the left side of his chin and what appeared to be drops of blood on his thigh.

"Just on my way to my grandfather's house," the young man explained when questioned about his presence on the logging road.

When the officers searched Legebokoff's truck, the situation grew even more disturbing. A multi-tool and wrench covered in blood. A pool of blood on the floor mat. In the back of the truck was something that seemed bizarrely out of place—a backpack with a monkey design, the kind a young girl might carry. Inside, they found a wallet containing a children's hospital card with the name "Loren Leslie."

When questioned about the blood on his face and legs, Legebokoff remained unnervingly calm. He explained that he and a friend had been poaching in the woods. Since they didn't have a hunting license, he told the officers that they'd had to club the deer to death instead of shooting it. His tone was almost casual as he added,

 "I'm a redneck. That's what we do for fun."

The story made little sense. There was no deer carcass in the truck. The officers pressed him further, questioning why someone would

beat a deer to death rather than shoot it. They asked him where this friend was now. Legebokoff's response only raised more suspicions—he claimed his friend had already left with the deer's body, but he couldn't provide a clear explanation of why they would have separated or where his friend had gone.

———

Earlier that evening, fifteen-year-old Loren Leslie had told her mother she was going to meet a friend for coffee. It was the kind of reassuring detail parents wanted to hear—it suggested this was someone Loren knew, someone trustworthy. Unbeknownst to her parents, Loren spent much of her free time on the internet. Like many teenagers, she had created a life online that her family knew nothing about, chatting with people from all over and making connections her parents couldn't see. There was no friend waiting to meet her that night. Instead, she had arranged to meet a stranger—someone she knew only through their online conversations.

Cody Legebokoff

The officers arrested Cody Legebokoff under the Wildlife Act and called for Conservation Officer Cameron Hill to investigate the alleged poaching. Hill arrived and began retracing the truck's path back up the remote logging road. There were about eight to ten inches of snow on the ground, with roughly an inch of fresh snow covering the tire tracks he was following.

A few hundred meters ahead, Hill noticed the truck marks came to a stop. He pulled over his vehicle and got out into the frigid night air. His flashlight beam cut through the darkness to illuminate two sets of footprints in the snow leading toward a dense area of brush. As he followed the prints, he discovered blood splattered across the pristine white snow. Then he noticed something else—drag marks in the snow as if something heavy had been pulled through it.

Following these disturbing signs, Hill weaved through the dark forest branches until his flashlight beam revealed something that made his blood run cold. There, partially buried in the snow near a gravel pit, lay the body of a young woman. Her pants had been pulled down around her ankles, and her face was so badly beaten it was unrecognizable.

It was Loren Leslie. She had been murdered just hours before.

Loren Leslie was just fifteen years old, a student at Nechako Valley Secondary School in Vanderhoof. Despite being legally blind—she had no vision in one eye and only fifty percent vision in the other—she had never let her disability define her. Loren was known for her compassion and had dreams of becoming a forensic pathologist. Her family and friends described her as a kind and thoughtful girl who always wanted to help others.

Like many teenagers, Loren lived part of her life online, particularly on a Canadian social networking site called Nexopia. There, she had begun chatting with Cody Legebokoff, who used the username "1CountryBoy." Their online exchanges would later reveal a troubling pattern. From the very beginning, he had sent her sexually explicit messages, but Loren had either ignored them or tried to change the subject. Her responses made it clear she was looking for friendship, not romance. Just before they met, he told her not to tell anyone they were going to hang out. Her reply was firm: "Well, we're just hanging out, right, nothing inappropriate."

Before meeting with Loren, Legebokoff had made a stop at the store. He bought four packs of alcohol—Kahlua Mudslides and White Russians—despite knowing she was only fifteen. As she waited at the school, she texted him to hurry because she was cold waiting outside. Around 8:20 p.m., a witness saw Loren sitting alone on the swings in the gathering darkness. A black pickup truck pulled into the parking lot, and a man wearing shorts stepped out and walked toward her.

It was the last time anyone would see Loren alive.

Less than four hours later, Conservation Officer Hill's flashlight beam would illuminate her body in the snow, and investigators would begin piecing together the events of that terrible night. The brutality of the scene suggested a level of violence that seemed impossible to reconcile with the quiet town of Vanderhoof. However, as investigators would soon discover, this was not an isolated incident.

———

Nothing in Cody Legebokoff's background suggested the violence of which he was capable. Born in 1990, he was raised in Fort St. James, a small town just off the Highway of Tears. Standing at six feet two inches tall and weighing 225 pounds, he cut an imposing figure, but by all accounts, he had a normal childhood in a loving, respectable family.

His grandfather, Roy Goodwin, had taught him to hunt and fish from an early age. "I hunted with him. I fished with him. We did everything together, and he was a perfectly normal child," Goodwin would later say. "He was no different than you or I when we were younger." But there were hints, even then, of something darker. As a hunter, Legebokoff showed a disturbing tendency to maim deer first, then finish them off with his hands—behavior that experts would later identify as a warning sign for violence against humans.

In school, he excelled in sports, particularly ice hockey, though his aggressive playing style raised concerns. He was also a member of his high school's snowboarding team. Despite his rough demeanor on the ice, he was well-liked among his peers and showed no clear signs of the brutality to come.

After graduating from Fort St. James Secondary School, Legebokoff lived briefly in Lethbridge before moving to Prince George. There, he quickly established what appeared to be a stable life. He found work as a mechanic at a Ford dealership and shared an apartment with three female friends from his hometown, occupying the basement level while they lived upstairs. These living arrangements would later seem chilling given what investigators would find in that basement.

He began dating Amy Voell, who was studying psychology at the College of New Caledonia. To all outward appearances, it was a serious relationship, and they talked about spending their lives together. However, Legebokoff was living a double life that even Amy knew nothing about. When she wasn't around, he was developing a serious cocaine habit, using sex workers to obtain drugs, and spending hours on the social networking site Nexopia under the username "1CountryBoy."

———

Three hundred miles away in Prince George, British Columbia, investigators had been quietly working on a disturbing series of cases, each bearing brutal similarities. The first victim had vanished more than a year before Loren Leslie's murder.

Jill Stuchenko was thirty-five years old and a mother of five children. She battled a cocaine addiction, a demon she had tried repeatedly to overcome but which kept pulling back in. Despite her struggles, friends described her as well-liked and lovely to talk to, with a beautiful singing voice. On October 9th, 2009, she disappeared from Prince George. Her body was found four days later, half-buried in a gravel pit on the outskirts of town. The autopsy revealed she had been sexually assaulted and died violently—massive blunt force trauma to her head and face, with injuries suggesting she had tried to defend herself from her attacker. The amount of blood loss was so extreme that the pathologist had difficulty obtaining samples during the autopsy.

Less than a year later, twenty-three-year-old Natasha Montgomery vanished. She was last seen leaving a friend's house in the north end of Prince George on August 31, 2010. Natasha, a mother of two young children, had been recently released from the Prince George Regional

Correctional Centre. She had been a skilled figure skater and musician in her youth, playing both clarinet and trumpet, before becoming addicted to crystal meth at age seventeen. She had managed to break that addiction and graduate high school, but after the birth of her youngest child in 2006, she developed a cocaine habit that led to her incarceration. When she was released in August 2010, she told her mother she was excited to be home in time for her daughter's birthday. Her mother never heard from her again. Despite extensive searches, Natasha's body has never been found.

Just days after Natasha Montgomery disappeared, thirty-five-year-old Cynthia Maas went missing. Known to her family as "Cindy," she was described by her sister as having had struggles since birth, born with an unspecified disability that made her vulnerable to those who might take advantage of her. A cousin introduced her to hard drugs at a young age, and she quickly became addicted. However, even while living on the streets, she continued to call her family and made efforts to attend AA and NA meetings. She was a mother working to get clean and regain custody of her child when she disappeared on September 10, 2010. Her body was found in L.C. Gunn Park on October 9, 2010. The autopsy revealed horrific injuries: a hole in her shoulder blade, a broken jaw and cheekbone, and injuries to her neck consistent with someone stomping on it. Like Jill Stuchenko, she had died from blunt force trauma to the head and penetrating wounds.

At first, nothing connected these cases to the murder of Loren Leslie. Then, when investigators began searching the young man's apartment in downtown Prince George, they discovered something that would crack all four cases wide open. Under the stark blue light of their forensic equipment, the apartment told a horrific story.

Forensic experts used specialized chemicals and black lights to expose cleaned blood stains, uncovering evidence of extreme violence throughout his basement unit. Blood spatter on the dining room ceiling told a gruesome story, with more than 100 stains marking a chilling pattern of events. A footprint in the middle of a bloodstain on the floor added another sinister detail to the narrative. Natasha Montgomery's DNA was found in over thirty locations, including the walls, floors, and even the box spring mattress. The most damning discovery was an ax stored in a linen closet; it carried nine separate blood stains matching Natasha's DNA. Despite her body never being found, the blood evidence painted a clear picture of her brutal death.

Jill Stuchenko's blood was soaked into the cushions of a couch that Legebokoff had moved between apartments months after her murder. A former roommate recalled helping him relocate the couch, unaware of its dark significance. The carpet in his previous apartment also held traces of Jill's blood, further tying Legebokoff to her killing.

Cynthia Maas's DNA appeared on a pickaxe stored in the apartment, along with evidence on a sock found in his truck and on the sweater he wore on the night of his arrest. Forensic tests pieced together a haunting chain of events that underscored Legebokoff's calculated brutality.

The cumulative evidence left no room for doubt. Each discovery in his apartment added another layer of horror, linking Legebokoff to the murders with a precision that only forensics could provide. The sheer volume of blood evidence revealed a pattern of unimaginable violence that prosecutors would later use against him in court.

———

The trial began in June 2014. Over thirteen days, the court would hear testimony from ninety-three Crown witnesses and the defendant himself. However, it was Legebokoff's testimony that would prove the most bizarre aspect of the trial.

Taking the stand in his own defense, Legebokoff spun an extraordinary tale. He admitted he was "involved" in three of the deaths but claimed he wasn't the actual killer. Instead, he blamed the murders on three other people whom he would only identify as "X," "Y," and "Z." When pressed by the judge to name these alleged accomplices, Legebokoff refused, claiming he didn't want to be labeled a "rat" in prison.

His stories about each murder strained credibility. He claimed that after a house party, drug dealers had shown up at his apartment and killed Jill Stuchenko because "she owed a lot of money." According to Legebokoff, he had merely handed one of them a pipe from his toolbox, then watched as they killed her. He admitted to helping carry her body and clean up the blood, then claimed he went to Thanksgiving dinner with his family the next day as if nothing had happened.

Similar stories followed for Natasha Montgomery and Cynthia Maas —in each case, Legebokoff insisted that mysterious drug dealers were the real killers, and he was merely present. Yet, he could provide no explanation for why these dealers would repeatedly choose his apartment as their killing ground or why they would trust a relative stranger to witness multiple murders.

The forensic evidence told a different story. RCMP Sergeant Beverly Zipperzian, a blood spatter expert who had worked previously on the notorious Robert Pickton serial murder case, took the court through the extensive blood evidence found throughout Legebokoff's apartment. During thirteen days of trial, the prosecution presented over six thousand pages of forensic evidence linking him conclusively to all four murders. Throughout the proceedings, Legebokoff refused to answer eighty of the questions posed to him by the prosecution. The Crown also revealed that he had used his computer to search for information about the difference between murder and manslaughter while in custody, suggesting he was already planning his defense strategy from his cell.

After fourteen hours of deliberation, on September 11, 2014, the jury returned their verdict: guilty on all four counts of first-degree murder. The courtroom was packed five days later when British Columbia Supreme Court Justice Glen Parrett delivered the sentence. Legebokoff would serve life in prison with no possibility of parole for twenty-five years.

During sentencing, Justice Parrett's voice broke with emotion. He had to pause and reach for water before continuing. Looking directly at Legebokoff, he dismissed the stories about mysterious accomplices as pure fabrication. "Nothing is ever his fault," the judge declared. "These are not the actions of a simple killer but of something infinitely worse." He noted that Legebokoff "lacks any shred of empathy or remorse" and stated firmly that "he should never be allowed to walk among us again."

The impact on the victims' families was devastating. Robert Donovan, Natasha Montgomery's grandfather, spoke about sitting through the testimony detailing how his granddaughter was murdered. "I couldn't take it," he said outside the courthouse. "I thought I was a big tough guy, but big tough guys fall apart too."

Natasha's mother, LuAnn Montgomery, made an emotional plea to the public. "It's not over for me. I still don't have Natasha back," she said, asking people to keep looking for her daughter's remains. Years later, Legebokoff still hasn't revealed what he did with Natasha's body, adding another layer of torment to the family's grief.

Judy Maas, Cynthia's sister, described the verdict as "bittersweet." She emphasized that the victims shouldn't be defined by their struggles.

 "They weren't 'just' a drug addict, and they weren't 'just' a sex trade worker," she said. "They were loved. They're missed."

Doug Leslie, Loren's father, had mixed feelings about the outcome. While grateful for the conviction, he was troubled by Canada's "faint hope clause"—a provision that could allow Legebokoff to apply for parole after just fifteen years. Although this clause was repealed in 2011, it still applied to crimes committed before that date. "I just bit my lip," Leslie said when hearing about this possibility. He was seen outside the court with a bruised lip from biting it so hard during the sentencing.

Given the sexual nature of the attacks, Legebokoff was added to the national sex offender registry. His sentences would run concurrently, meaning he would be eligible to apply for parole in November 2035.

The families' pain was compounded in 2019 when Legebokoff was transferred from a maximum-security prison in British Columbia to a medium-security facility in Ontario. Grand Chief Stuart Phillips of the Union of British Columbia Indian Chiefs called the move "absolutely shocking" and "a slap in the face to the missing and murdered indigenous women and girls movement." The families weren't even notified of the transfer before it happened.

In February 2015, Legebokoff filed an appeal, claiming that the denial of his request to change trial venues from Prince George to Vancouver had put him at a disadvantage due to extensive local media coverage. But in September 2016, all three judges of the British Columbia Court of Appeal endorsed the original judge's decision, noting that media coverage had been widespread throughout the province. The appeal, like his stories about mysterious accomplices, was seen by many as just another attempt to avoid responsibility for his crimes.

CHAPTER 3
THE CHRISTADELPHIAN

I n the summer of 1979, the small town of Springfield, Vermont, seemed like any other peaceful New England community. Nestled along the Connecticut River, with its characteristic covered bridges and rolling green hills, Springfield embodied the quintessential charm of rural Vermont life.

However, beneath this serene exterior, a darkness was about to descend upon the town that would haunt its residents for years to come.

————

On the evening of August 28, 1979, thirteen-year-old Sherry Nastasia was doing what many local kids did on warm summer nights—spending time outside with her younger brother. The siblings had recently moved to Springfield that July to live with their father, John Nastasia, while their mother remained in Florida. John worked as a truck driver for an oil company, which meant he was often on the road, leaving the children to look after themselves or stay with neighbors.

That night, Sherry and her brother were shopping at the Springfield Shopping Plaza, a routine activity for the pair. At some point, Sherry split off from her brother to go out on her own—something that wasn't entirely unusual for the independent teenager. Local police had even grown accustomed to seeing Sherry and her eleven-year-old brother outside after dark, though recently, she had been seen with her brother less frequently.

But this night would prove different from all the others. When darkness fell and Sherry hadn't returned home, her absence was particularly concerning. This wasn't like her at all—despite her independent nature, she had always been responsible, especially when it came to watching out for her younger brother. The Nastasia house at 43 River Street remained dark and eerily quiet that night, missing the usual sounds of Sherry and her brother's evening routine.

The next day, with still no sign of Sherry, her increasingly worried family reported her missing to the police. Springfield Police investigators were immediately concerned about her disappearance; this behavior was completely out of character for Sherry. While some local residents had grown accustomed to seeing her out after dark and whispered that this might just be more of the same, her family and close friends vehemently disagreed. They knew a different Sherry— one who had never simply vanished before, one who understood the importance of checking in and keeping her commitments.

They spoke with various witnesses, including a renter who lived in the same house as the Nastasias. He provided what seemed like a promising lead: Around midnight, he had observed Sherry walking along River Street when a dark green car, possibly a Pontiac Firebird, had slowed beside her. After a brief interaction, the vehicle had stopped, and Sherry had gotten in.

It was the last time anyone would see her alive.

———

For three and a half months, Sherry's disappearance cast a shadow over Springfield as investigators pursued every possible lead. The police focused heavily on interviewing people who frequented the seedier parts of town, areas where they had occasionally spotted Sherry in recent months. They meticulously tracked down and questioned anyone who might have seen her that night.

The only solid lead remained the dark green Pontiac Firebird. Local newspapers printed official police reports describing the vehicle as a 1970–74 model, but despite the distinctive description, no one came forward with information about the car or its driver. Investigators conducted numerous interviews and administered polygraph tests to various men in the area. Curiously, many of these subjects failed their polygraph tests despite having solid alibis. This suggested they might have been hiding other secrets, though likely none related to Sherry's disappearance.

Missing person flyers began to yellow on Springfield's bulletin boards and storefront windows as fall turned to early winter. Investigators continued following up on tips, but the trail was growing increasingly cold. Then, on December 13, 1979, during one of those bitter Vermont winter days when darkness comes early and the mercury barely rises above freezing, a truck driver pulled into a rest area along Vermont Route 103 in Rockingham. The location was just a short distance from the state police barracks, though the building was barely visible through the swirling snow. As he stepped from his truck into the biting cold, something caught his eye: a dark shape protruding from a snowbank that didn't look quite right. Drawing closer, he made a horrifying discovery—human remains, partially buried in the frozen ground and dusted with fresh snow.

Within days, dental records confirmed what many had feared: The body was Sherry Nastasia. The state medical examiner's findings painted a grim picture of Sherry's final moments. Her body showed signs of a violent struggle. Multiple ribs had been shattered, and one leg was broken with such force that it suggested she had fought desperately against her attacker. Unfortunately, the three-and-a-half months of exposure to the elements had taken their toll, leaving much of the evidence degraded and parts of the body missing. This made determining a definitive cause of death challenging.

Nonetheless, the medical examination revealed crucial details. The damage to her throat area was particularly telling—specifically, the hyoid bone, a delicate U-shaped bone that sits just above the larynx, was missing. This small but significant detail pointed toward strangulation as the likely cause of death, as this bone typically fractures during such an assault. The extensive damage to her body suggested this was no random act of violence but a deliberate, brutal murder.

Despite a thorough examination of the area, investigators found no additional evidence in the snow-covered ground. The pristine white powder that had blanketed the region in the days since the body's discovery had erased any trace of the killer's presence. The rest stop, normally a place of brief respite for weary travelers, had become a grim crime scene that yielded few answers.

A team of seasoned investigators worked through the bitter winter days, methodically interviewing anyone who might have information about Sherry's final moments. They focused particularly on the rougher areas of Springfield where she had been spotted in recent months, questioning the locals and regular visitors who frequented these neighborhoods. Unfortunately, every promising lead seemed to dissolve upon closer inspection. Witnesses' stories contradicted one another, and suspicious behaviors turned out to have innocent explanations. Each dead end only added to the investigators' growing frustration, knowing that somewhere in Springfield, a killer walked free.

———

The investigation into Sherry's murder gradually grew cold, but Vermont's nightmare was far from over. In May 1981, the state was rocked by another tragedy when twelve-year-old Melissa Walbridge was murdered in Essex Junction after being attacked along a wooded path with her friend. Though her teenage killers were quickly caught, the incident—combined with the still-unsolved murder of Sherry—shattered any remaining sense of security in Vermont's small communities.

By August 29, 1981, almost exactly two years after Sherry's disappearance, Springfield's parents had grown hypervigilant about their children's safety. Twelve-year-old Teresa Fenton lived in this atmosphere of heightened fear and caution. Parents who had once let their children roam freely now kept them close, watching anxiously whenever they ventured outside. The Fentons were particularly careful, having established strict protocols for their daughter's activities, including carefully planned routes and precise timings for her bike rides. Every outing was treated like a military operation with designated check-in times and clearly defined boundaries.

That evening, during a car ride home, Teresa asked her parents if she could go on a quick bike ride before dinner. Her mother's first instinct was to say no. Teresa had originally wanted to make a four-mile round trip to the Cheshire County toll bridge, but her parents negotiated it down to a shorter, safer route: a two-mile round trip along Old Connecticut River Road, where houses were more frequent and neighbors could keep watch. Before setting off, Teresa tied a bandana over her hair and had a final conversation with her father, Richard. The family's safety code included specific timings—Teresa had forty minutes to complete her ride with a ten-minute grace period. "We would challenge her to do a length in a certain amount of time," her mother Barbara would later explain. "That was planned to help us pinpoint problems if things went awry."

When Teresa missed her 6:30 p.m. return window, her parents felt the first cold tendrils of fear. They didn't wait for the full grace period. Within minutes, they were in their car, searching their daughter's planned route. Richard Craig, a neighbor, joined the increasingly frantic search effort. While scanning the roadside with his flashlight,

Craig's beam caught something reflective in the growing darkness. His heart sank as the light revealed Teresa's bicycle, carefully propped up against a tree, but no sign of Teresa herself. The empty road stretched out before him, dark and accusing in the fading light.

By 8:30 p.m., a full-scale search was underway involving family, friends, police, firefighters, and volunteers. The next morning, diving teams searched the river while a helicopter surveyed from above. Bloodhounds initially picked up Teresa's scent where her bike had been found but lost the trail, suggesting she might have left the area in a vehicle.

Approximately twenty hours after her disappearance, Torrey Walters took his children fishing, hoping to enjoy a peaceful morning in the Vermont woods. Instead, they became part of Springfield's darkening story. As they walked through a remote section off Mile Hill Road, five miles from the Fenton home, they heard something that seemed out of place in the morning quiet—a soft, barely audible moaning sound coming from beneath a pile of brush and debris.

What they found was the stuff of nightmares. Teresa lay half-buried in the earth, with only a single arm visible through the carefully arranged cover of leaves and branches. She was still alive, but barely. Her skull had been brutally beaten, with dark blood matting her hair and staining the ground beneath her. The careful arrangement of debris covering her body suggested her attacker had taken time to conceal his crime, leaving her to die alone in the woods.

Despite being rushed to medical care, Teresa never opened her eyes again. She clung to life for another day but finally succumbed to her injuries almost exactly forty-eight hours after she had set out on her bike ride. The autopsy findings painted a picture of unimaginable brutality. Her killer had struck her head repeatedly—six distinct blows, each delivered with devastating force. The fatal strike had been precisely placed at the base of her skull. Her face also bore evidence of the attack: bruises on her right cheek and lower lip, a broken tooth, and abrasions consistent with being struck multiple times.

But the violence didn't end there. The medical examination revealed extensive evidence of sexual assault, and the bruising patterns on her neck told their own horrifying story. On the right side of her neck was a deep bruise, while the left side showed distinct abrasion marks —injuries consistent with manual strangulation. The killer had used his hands, making the attack intensely personal.

What disturbed investigators most wasn't just the brutality of the assault but the eerily controlled behavior that followed. After committing such savage violence, the killer hadn't fled in a panic. Instead, he had taken his time. Each article of Teresa's clothing had been carefully replaced and adjusted with unsettling precision. Her shoes had been tied, and her shirt had been properly buttoned. It was as if the killer had been trying to restore a semblance of dignity to his victim—or perhaps, more disturbingly, trying to cover his tracks with methodical attention to detail.

The single leaf found in Teresa's waistband would prove to be one of the most telling pieces of evidence. To investigators, its presence was a crucial discovery; this wasn't debris from the surrounding area where she was found but could only have gotten trapped in her clothing during the process of redressing. This small detail confirmed their suspicions about the methodical nature of their killer. Even more chilling was the way Teresa had been positioned and partially buried. The debris hadn't been frantically scattered over her body; instead, it had been arranged with what one investigator described as an almost ritualistic care.

The criminal profiler brought into the case, John Philpin, saw these details as crucial indicators. This wasn't the work of someone who had lost control in a moment of passion. The careful redressing, the methodical burial, the attention to detail—all this suggested a killer who derived satisfaction not just from the violence but from the complete control he exercised over his victims. The ritualistic aspects pointed to someone who might have been moved by religious symbolism, who might have seen these acts as a sort of twisted ceremony. Most worryingly, this level of controlled behavior typically indicated an experienced killer—someone who had refined his methods through practice. Someone who, without intervention, would almost certainly strike again.

————

Philpin developed a detailed portrait of the killer. He believed they were looking for someone who was moved by religion, touched by ritual, and likely a regular churchgoer. The perpetrator would probably have changed their behavior after the murders, either through increased substance use or by throwing themselves into work and church services.

Philpin suggested that someone close to the killer likely suspected their involvement. He described the perpetrator as someone who lived with family and had an immature personality, possibly coddled by their mother and either neglected or oppressed by their father. The killer's strong need to impress others would be a defining characteristic.

The profiler's assessment differed from some law enforcement theories. Police Captain Richard Speer, head of the state police criminal division, believed the killer was someone Teresa knew—someone with some standing in the community and who had made an advance that was rebuffed. This assumption would prove to be a critical misstep in the investigation.

————

In November 1982, seventeen-year-old Deanna Buxton thought nothing of hitchhiking; it was something she did often enough without incident. On November 12, she set out mid-morning, hoping to visit her boyfriend Jerry Twitchell at the prison in Rutland, about fifty miles from her home in Brattleboro. Her journey began innocently enough with two short rides: First, a man in a green van took her north on Route 5 to Putney, dropping her near the interstate along the Connecticut River. Within five minutes, she caught another ride in a blue Nova to Rockingham, just south of Springfield.

Her third ride would prove nearly fatal. A man in a red car with Vermont plates pulled over, appearing helpful and harmless. He seemed average in every way—about five foot eight, in his early forties, and wearing a checkered flannel shirt and wire-framed glasses. His short brown hair was parted to the side in an old-fashioned style, and his face bore distinctive moles. He introduced himself as Stan and engaged her in friendly conversation, asking questions about her life. When Deanna mentioned she was a ward of the state, he filled the silence with his own story. He claimed to be divorced with three daughters and a Navy veteran who had been shot in the shoulder, ankle, and left hand.

The façade of normalcy shattered less than an hour into the drive. They had just passed a highway sign reading "Rutland 13 Miles" when "Stan" pulled into a rest stop, saying he needed to use the restroom. But instead of getting out, he reached behind the driver's seat. Deanna's heart stopped as he produced a shotgun and pointed both barrels directly at her. "Don't try to run away or scream," he growled, "or I'll kill you." To prove he wasn't bluffing, he opened the bolt and showed her the two green shells loaded inside. "You know I'm not fooling around," he said. "It only takes one trigger, and you'll be dead. So do what I say, or I'll kill you."

What followed was a nightmare of escalating terror. He forced her to drink from a bottle of Colt 45 malt liquor, saying with chilling casualness, "We'll get drunk, and then we'll have some fun." He ordered her to remove her undergarments but put her outer clothing back on. As they drove, he kept the shotgun trained on her head while subjecting her to a stream of vulgar commentary about sexual acts, using the crudest terms possible. When he wasn't talking, he was reaching over with his free hand, groping and violating her.

At one point, he forced Deanna to take over driving—a move that gave him both hands free to continue his assault. The horror intensified when he began talking about war, specifically about what fighting men did to women in their power. He boasted about enjoying rape and claimed she wasn't his first victim; he'd done this before and had been forced to kill two others. His casual tone while discussing murder sent ice through Deanna's veins.

During a stop at a liquor store in White River Junction, Deanna saw her first chance. With "Stan" momentarily distracted while making his selection, she desperately tried to signal the store clerk, mouthing "please help me" and gesturing to her captor. However, the clerk didn't understand, and Deanna found herself back in the car, her hope fading.

Then came a moment of clarity through her fear and the forced alcohol—if she didn't act soon, she would become his third victim. When they stopped at another small store, she made her most dangerous gamble. Complaining of nausea, she convinced him to let her go inside for Rolaids. His warning rang in her ears as she walked away: He would be watching, and he had a gun.

Inside the store, Deanna counted the customers—three men, one woman, plus the woman behind the counter. "Help me," she cried out, her voice shaking. "He's going to kill me!" One man who had just finished paying heard her plea. Thinking someone inside the store was threatening her, he moved to the doorway and beckoned her over. When Deanna rushed to him and pointed to "Stan" waiting in the car outside, the man's expression darkened. This guardian angel glared down at "Stan" and shouted, "What the fuck are you doing to her?"

The predator's response was telling. "I don't even know her," he called back, already preparing his defense, but Deanna wasn't letting this chance slip away. She ran back into the store, begging the clerk to call 911 and warning them about the man with the gun who was trying to kidnap her.

Officer John Halpin arrived within three minutes, but in all the chaos, her attacker had fled. Yet Deanna's powers of observation would prove remarkable. Despite her ordeal, she provided investigators with an extraordinarily detailed description of both her attacker and his vehicle. She remembered everything: the pink inspection sticker dated July 24, 1982, the Playboy bunny sticker on one window, and the sheepskin cover on the driver's seat. She even recalled seeing a blanket in the back seat. Her precise recollections would later prove crucial—though, at the time, no one realized just how important they would become.

———

The spring of 1983 brought no relief to Springfield's fears. On April 9, eleven-year-old Katie Richards was living the kind of Saturday that meant everything to a young girl; she'd attended two dance rehearsals for an upcoming recital where she would wear a special sequined tutu her mother had lovingly made for her. Later that afternoon, she and her best friend Rachel Zeitz, also eleven, begged Rachel's mother, Judy, for permission to visit Athens Pizza and play arcade games. Initially, Mrs. Zeitz said no—the murders of Sherry and Teresa still haunted every parent's decisions. However, the girls pleaded their case: It was just a ten-minute walk, they'd stay together, and they'd come straight back. Finally, she relented.

The girls arrived at the arcade just before 5:00 p.m., but their anticipated fun dissolved when some schoolmates wouldn't give them a turn at Ms. Pac-Man. Disappointed but not discouraged, they bought two small bags of Doritos and started their walk home. That's when Rachel's instincts began screaming that something was wrong. A light blue J2000 Pontiac kept appearing on their route—once, twice, three times, then a fourth and fifth pass. Each time, the driver seemed to be watching them.

Finally, around 5:15 p.m., the car stopped alongside them on Peddan Road. They had wandered into the perfect trap—a curved section of road invisible from both Vermont 106 and the nearby Peddan Acres development. No witnesses and no escape route. Katie, always friendly, asked if the driver was lost. He claimed to be looking for the house of someone named Joe Serniglia. When the girls couldn't help, he switched tactics, asking for directions to the Springfield racquet-ball club instead.

As Katie began giving directions, the man stepped out of his vehicle. Rachel's blood ran cold when she noticed the bulge in his pocket—unmistakably the shape of a gun. Her fear was confirmed when he threatened to kill them if they didn't get into the car. In that moment of terror, the girls' reactions split: Rachel turned and ran for her life, her heart pounding in her ears. However, when she glanced back, she saw a sight that would haunt her forever: Katie, tears streaming down her face, climbing into the driver's seat of the Pontiac.

What followed would become one of the darkest chapters in Springfield's history, not just for the crime itself but for the inexplicable response of law enforcement. Rachel ran straight home, and her parents immediately contacted Katie's mother, Rose Elise Thayer. The Thayers' desperate pleas for help were met with a response that defied all logic and human decency. The police chief didn't just refuse to mount a search—he actively prevented one. "Searches destroy evidence," he told Mrs. Thayer with cold detachment. Then came words that would haunt the community for years to come:

> "We know who he is. After we find her body, we'll get him."

The police chief's actions grew increasingly bizarre and cruel. When Katie's father Charlie—desperate to do something, anything, to find his little girl—prepared to conduct an aerial search in his private plane, the police chief sent officers to stop him. They stationed a patrol car in the Thayers' driveway, effectively imprisoning the family in their own home. An officer was posted inside to monitor their phone calls, preventing them from organizing a private search. Meanwhile, Springfield Police waited over an hour before even notifying state police of the abduction. No roadblocks were established. No comprehensive search was organized. It was as if they had already decided Katie's fate.

Nineteen hours later, around noon on Sunday, their worst fears were confirmed. Katie's body was found in a wooded area just 2.2 miles from where she was taken, yet even this devastating discovery was handled with shocking insensitivity. No one came to inform the Thayers. Instead, after hours of agonizing silence, Mrs. Thayer had to call the police herself. The response she received was brutally cold:

> "We have found the deceased body of a young girl wearing her clothes on the Baltimore Road. You cannot go there."

Katie would never perform her dance recital. Instead, she would be buried in the sequined tutu her mother had so carefully made, a final testament to dreams that would never be realized. The community's grief quickly turned to rage as the details of the police department's handling of the case became public. How could they have simply waited for a body to be found? Why had they prevented any rescue attempt? And, most disturbing of all, if they truly knew who the killer was, why hadn't they stopped him before he had claimed another victim?

The medical examination revealed the full horror of Katie's final moments. Unlike Teresa Fenton, who had received multiple blows, Katie had been killed by a single, devastating strike to her head with a stone. Before her death, she had been sexually assaulted and forced to perform sexual acts. Her body was so badly beaten that investigators could only identify her by her dental braces and the pattern of freckles on her skin. She had been found partially undressed, once again indicating the methodical nature of her killer—a signature that linked this murder to the others.

———

The breakthrough in the case came through Rachel Zeitz's remarkable eye for detail. She perfectly recalled the killer's yellow-tinted wire-frame glasses, and most crucially, she noticed that he wore a distinctive bright red sweatshirt with lettering across the front. "I thought it was some kind of football shirt," Rachel later explained. "I thought it said the Dolphins." But then she remembered her friend, Joel de Lorenzo, had one just like it.

This seemingly minor detail would crack the case wide open. When investigators visited the de Lorenzo home, they discovered the sweatshirt wasn't for a football team at all—it was branded with "Christadelphians," associated with a local church that had only sixty members. As police began calling church leaders that Sunday, word spread quickly through the close-knit congregation that investigators were looking for one of their own.

James Malay, one of the church leaders contacted by police, recalled seeing church member Gary Lee Schaefer driving near the area close to the time of Katie's abduction. Meanwhile, Schaefer himself arrived at Sunday services shortly after 9:00 a.m. A teenager who had grown close to him—he had been especially "friendly" with the church's youth, even writing them letters with biblical references and song lyrics—greeted him with an innocuous joke: "Hey, are the police after you too?" She explained that police were asking about the sweatshirts. Schaefer excused himself to the bathroom, where he vomited.

While this occurred, Detective Mike LeClair met with James Malay and showed him the composite sketch made from Rachel's description. Malay took one look and said, "Oh sure, that looks just like Gary Schaefer"—who, it turned out, was Malay's own cousin. He confirmed Schaefer had been wearing his Christadelphian sweatshirt and driving a light blue vehicle.

Instead of fleeing, thirty-one-year-old Schaefer returned home. When detectives arrived, they were led upstairs by his mother, with whom he still lived. Schaefer's first words were telling: "I've been sick." He excused himself to vomit again while officers listened through the door. When questioned about his whereabouts that Saturday, Schaefer claimed he had been with his boss, Thomas Soucy, picking up cars for the dealership where he worked as a mechanic. His mother, hovering nearby like a protective shadow, confirmed he had left around 2:00 p.m. wearing blue pants and his red Christadelphian sweatshirt. He hadn't returned until 9:15 p.m.

The officers let Schaefer finish his story before informing him they had already spoken with his boss. Schaefer had not been with him that day. When confronted with a witness placing him in town during Katie's abduction, Gary Lee Schaefer was arrested without resistance.

The search of Schaefer's home yielded damning evidence: the Christadelphian sweatshirt Rachel had described and blue pants with a hair matching Katie's dusty blonde color. He was held at the Woodstock Community Correctional Center on $50,000 bail for kidnapping a minor. As the investigation deepened, the bail would rise to $75,000 when charges expanded to include murder and rape.

But Katie's murder wasn't the only crime that would be laid at Schaefer's feet. The composite sketch of Katie's killer bore a striking resemblance to the man who had attacked Deanna Buxton. When police finally located Schaefer's crashed red Pontiac at a junkyard in Rutland —where it had sat untouched for months—Deanna confirmed it was the same vehicle. Her denim jacket and red and blue vest were still inside, overlooked when Schaefer had drunkenly tried to clear evidence from the car after his crash.

A darker pattern began to emerge. Investigators learned that during Schaefer's ten years in the Navy, he had faced trouble with military police. More disturbingly, they discovered that at each base where he had been stationed, young girls had gone missing or been murdered. Though these cases were investigated, no definitive connections were ever established.

As the case moved toward trial, Schaefer's emotional state deteriorated. Prosecutor William S. Bos noted he was so severely depressed that he was considered a suicide risk. He was placed in maximum security, away from the general prison population and under close watch. In early October, Schaefer allegedly wrote to the prosecutor stating he believed he had murdered Teresa Fenton as well.

On December 5, 1983, Gary Lee Schaefer said through his attorney that he wished to "clear himself in the eyes of God." He changed his plea from innocent to no contest on charges of second-degree murder, sexual assault, and kidnapping in Katie's death. The plea bargain included a crucial stipulation: No charges could be filed against him for Teresa Fenton's murder, provided he wrote a detailed confession about her death.

His attorney argued that Schaefer had been temporarily insane when he killed Katie, claiming he had no recollection of trying to harm her. The lawyer suggested Schaefer's actions had "an interrelationship with things that happened to him as a child," though this was never elaborated upon. He insisted that Schaefer would "feel more pain from his sense of guilt and sense of confusion than from any sentence."

Rose Elise Thayer, Katie's mother, spoke powerfully at sentencing:

> "As long as this man lives, he will feel compelled to destroy the lives of innocent children by his odious and obscene means as he can devise. I don't want any child so tortured such as she was ever again. He must never be allowed near another young child."

In January 1984, Schaefer received the maximum term for murder at that time in Vermont: thirty years to life with the possibility of parole. He would serve his time at the Kentucky State Penitentiary in Eddyville.

The case of Sherry Nastasia took one final, tragic turn. In May 1984, Schaefer was charged with her murder, but he pleaded not guilty. His lawyer produced naval records suggesting he wasn't in Springfield when she disappeared. When Detective Michael J. LeClair offered to conduct a new interview with Schaefer about the case, he was denied. The charges were eventually dropped after a judge ruled Schaefer's confession had been obtained illegitimately through hypnosis. To this day, Sherry's murder officially remains unsolved.

Gary Lee Schaefer's reign of terror ended on November 26, 2023, when he died in prison at age seventy-one after an unremarkable medical event. He had served less time behind bars than some drug offenders, a fact that continues to anger many in the Springfield community.

The tragic events in Springfield serve as a haunting reminder that evil can lurk in the most unexpected places—even in a trusted church member who worked with youth, even in a quiet mechanic who lived with his mother, and even in the heart of a peaceful Vermont town. The cases highlighted the devastating failures in law enforcement response and the crucial importance of taking every lead seriously—lessons learned at an unthinkable cost to three families and an entire community.

The memories of Sherry Nastasia, Teresa Fenton, and Katie Richards live on in the hearts of Springfield's residents. Their cases led to important changes in how missing children cases are handled in Vermont, ensuring that no other family would ever be told to wait while their child's killer roamed free. Their stories, though tragic, have helped shape modern investigative procedures and serve as a sobering reminder of the importance of community vigilance and proper law enforcement response.

CHAPTER 4
IT'S DONE

I owa stretches out like a patchwork quilt of farmland and small towns, each square telling a story of resilience and dreams both realized and forgotten. Agency was one such square—a mere dot on the map of Wapello County, a place where generations had put down roots so deep they seemed almost impossible to disturb. But on May 26, 2012, those roots would be violently, irrevocably torn.

The town of Agency had a population of just 629, making it the kind of place where everyone knew the rhythm of their neighbors' lives. Pickup trucks lined dusty streets, local diners hummed with morning conversations, and the horizon seemed to extend forever as a canvas of corn fields and possibility. This community prided itself on stability—on knowing exactly who belonged and who didn't.

———

Lisa Marie Caldwell, born on May 7, 1989, in nearby Ottumwa, was a hometown success story. From her earliest years, she carried a spark that set her apart. The bowling alley became her first arena of triumph, where she discovered a competitive spirit that would define her life. As a member of her high school bowling team, she helped secure three state titles—no small feat in a state where sports were a fundamental language of community pride.

Her father, Todd Caldwell, was a deputy sheriff who represented everything noble about local law enforcement. Respected, steady, and committed to serving his community, Todd saw in Lisa not just a daughter but a kindred spirit. She inherited his sense of purpose, his belief that one person could make a difference.

After graduating from Ottumwa High School in 2007, Lisa pursued her passion methodically. She earned a degree in Criminal Justice with a minor in psychology, splitting her studies between Indian Hills Community College and Buena Vista University. Along the way, she gained hands-on experience through an internship with the Iowa Division of Criminal Investigation (DCI). Each step was calculated, each choice bringing her closer to her dream of becoming a criminal investigator.

The Champion Bowl in Ottumwa was where Seth Techel and Lisa's paths first crossed. Despite both teenagers working part-time at the bowling alley owned by Seth's father, they seemed an unlikely match at first. Lisa was driven and focused, while Seth was more laid-back, though he shared her interest in law enforcement. Their early courtship played out like many small-town romances—stolen moments between shifts and casual dates that slowly transformed into something more serious.

Over seven years of dating, they grew from teenagers to young adults, supporting each other's dreams. Lisa pursued her criminal justice studies while Seth explored various career options, from firefighting to law enforcement. Their families became intertwined, with Todd Caldwell viewing Seth almost as a second son, while Seth's fascination with law enforcement and public service seemed to make him a perfect match for the deputy's daughter.

Their wedding on October 15, 2011, was a celebration that reflected everything about their shared history. Held locally, with friends and family from Ottumwa and Agency in attendance, it was the perfect representation of their journey. The wedding photos told a story of pure joy—Lisa, beautiful and beaming, and Seth looking at her with a mixture of love and something akin to awe.

They decided to start their life in a trailer—it was both practical and typical of young couples in their community who were building their joint futures step by careful step. By early 2012, everything seemed perfect. Lisa was pregnant, a development that brought joy to both families. She was working at the Washington County Jail while serving as a reserve deputy in Wapello County. Seth had secured a position as a security officer at Job Corps and was about to begin training as a jailer in the same county where Lisa's father worked.

Their excitement and hope for the future seemed boundless. No one could have anticipated the darkness that was gathering just beyond their carefully constructed horizon.

———

By spring 2012, Lisa was seventeen weeks pregnant, and the first visible signs of motherhood were beginning to show. Lisa's natural competitiveness had been channeled into planning for the baby's arrival. She and Seth had already chosen a name for their daughter, Zoe Maria, and they were preparing the spare room of their trailer as a nursery.

Though modest, their home represented the beginning of their dreams. The trailer, owned by Seth's father, was on a plot of land he had given them—a temporary residence while they planned to build something more permanent. On the surface, their future seemed secure, their path clear.

———

5:00 a.m., May 26, 2012. The world was still dark, the Iowa landscape hushed and waiting.

According to Seth's account, he woke up early that morning and decided to take a shower while Lisa continued sleeping. The trailer was quiet, the kind of peaceful morning that seemed unremarkable in every way. He would later tell investigators that while in the shower, steam filling the small bathroom, he heard what sounded like a loud noise—a sharp sound that cut through the steady rhythm of water against tile. Concerned, he said he quickly finished and began to investigate, moving through the small space of their home.

What he found would change everything.

Lisa was in their bedroom, unresponsive. The amount of blood was shocking. Panic rising, Seth made the 911 call. His words came out fragmented, urgent, a mix of confusion and terror.

 "My wife," he stammered, "she's been shot. She's not breathing."

His voice cracked, alternating between a whisper and a near-shout. In the background, the dispatcher could hear his ragged breathing, the sound of someone struggling to maintain composure.

"Is she conscious?" the dispatcher asked.

"No," Seth responded, his voice breaking. "I just got out of the shower and heard something. She's just… There's blood everywhere."

The call lasted three minutes and seventeen seconds. Each second was filled with a raw, visceral desperation—the sound of a man who seemed caught between disbelief and horror. His words tumbled out in fragments, circling back to the same details over and over: the sound he'd heard, the blood he'd found, his wife who wouldn't respond.

When deputies arrived, the trailer's interior told a stark story of sudden violence. The small space felt charged with an immediate sense of wrongness—something fundamental had been disrupted.

Lisa's lifeless body lay on the bed, positioned in a way that suggested she had been sleeping. Her body was positioned on her back, one arm slightly askew, as if she had been abruptly interrupted mid-rest. The bedding was saturated with blood, deep crimson spreading in a grotesque pattern across the light-colored sheets. Her seventeen-week pregnancy was visibly apparent, the slight swell of her abdomen a painful contrast to the violent scene.

The initial assessment was grim. A single gunshot wound was evident on her upper left side, the trajectory suggesting a close-range shot. Forensic investigators would later note the precise nature of the wound, a shotgun blast that had caused catastrophic internal damage. Blood spatter patterns told their own silent story—a quick, decisive act of violence that left little room for struggle.

———

Seth's behavior in those initial moments caught the attention of the first responding officers. He was shirtless, wearing only a pair of loose-fitting cargo shorts, his body language a mixture of apparent shock and something else—a nervous energy that seemed out of place. He moved repeatedly between rooms, his movements quick and somewhat erratic. Deputies would later note how he seemed to be talking constantly, his words tumbling out in a stream of explanation and disbelief.

"I was in the shower," he kept repeating. "I heard a noise. I don't understand."

His physical appearance was carefully noted. No visible signs of injury. No obvious indications of a physical struggle. His skin was damp, consistent with his claim of having just finished showering. But there was something else—a tension in his movements, a tightness around his eyes that seemed at odds with pure grief.

The trailer itself showed no signs of forced entry. No broken windows, no damaged door locks. Everything was in its place, with the exception of the bed where Lisa lay. Personal items were arranged neatly—a baby book on the nightstand, a sonogram photo tucked into its pages. The contrast between these symbols of hope and the violent reality was devastating.

Preliminary forensic team members began their careful documentation. Photographs captured every inch of the scene. Measurements were taken. Each piece of evidence, no matter how small, was cataloged. The bedroom told a story—but it remained unclear what exactly that story was.

When Todd Caldwell received the call that something had happened to his daughter, he rushed to the scene. A deputy himself, he couldn't be stopped from running inside the house. Those who watched could see the moment he realized the full extent of what had happened—a physical transformation of grief that seemed to age him instantly.

The medical examiner would later confirm what everyone already knew—a single shotgun blast had ended two lives that morning. A mother-to-be and her unborn child, gone in an instant.

When investigators asked Seth if he could think of anyone who might want to harm his family, his response was immediate and forceful. "Tate," he told them, "my crazy ass neighbor." Seth's voice tightened with apparent certainty as he added,

 "Because of the things he's been saying and doing to us. I honestly think the guy's off-his-rocker crazy."

Todd Caldwell quickly echoed his son-in-law's accusations. "Get him," he urged the officers, his voice carrying the weight of both a grieving father and a fellow deputy. "Get him now."

———

The Iowa Division of Criminal Investigation responded with swift action. Armed with rifles and wearing full tactical gear, officers surrounded Tate's property, prepared for a potentially volatile confrontation with the man Seth had described as dangerous and unstable. However, what they found surprised them.

Brian Tate welcomed them calmly into his home, displaying none of the erratic behavior Seth had described. Though diagnosed with PTSD and schizophrenia, Tate was clear-headed and cooperative, a stark contrast to the unstable figure Seth had portrayed. "I was Mr. Nice Guy for a long time," Tate explained to investigators, discussing the harassment he'd endured. "It done me no good. People took advantage of me."

The feud had indeed started over something as trivial as a dead deer. Seth Techel had found a deer carcass in the middle of the road and, rather than disposing of it properly, had dragged it onto Tate's property. When Tate discovered it and moved it back, a petty war of territorial aggression began. According to Tate's reports to local law enforcement, Seth and his friends had escalated to vandalism, even dumping buckets of dog waste on his car.

The situation had become serious enough that Tate had made multiple complaints to the sheriff's office. Ironically, it was Todd Caldwell himself who had responded to these calls. Tate had no way of knowing that the responding deputy was his neighbor's father-in-law, a fact that would later raise questions about the handling of his complaints.

But on the morning of Lisa's murder, Tate had a solid alibi. His mother and brother both confirmed he had been sleeping soundly at home until 10:30 a.m., hours after the shooting. Recent changes in his antipsychotic medication had been helping him sleep better than he had in years. When questioned directly about Lisa's death by the sheriff, Tate firmly denied any involvement.

The careful investigation of Tate revealed something unexpected—rather than the aggressor Seth had portrayed, Tate appeared to be the victim of targeted harassment. After speaking with Tate and corroborating his alibi, the sheriff was definitive: They were "100 percent confident it wasn't him."

But by then, in the small community of Agency, the damage to Tate's reputation had been done already. Seth's accusations had painted a target on his back, marking him as a killer in the eyes of many locals who would hold on to their suspicions long after investigators had cleared him.

———

During a thorough search of the property surrounding the Techels' trailer, investigators uncovered a critical piece of evidence: a Mossberg 500 shotgun. The weapon had been carefully wiped clean of fingerprints and hidden in tall grass approximately ninety feet from the home. Despite the lack of fingerprints, ballistics testing confirmed it was the murder weapon.

Investigators noted that Seth had failed to mention this particular shotgun when providing a list of firearms in the home despite having specifically requested that it be left behind by a former roommate just days before the murder. Suspiciously, Seth had also insisted the gun remain loaded.

On May 27, 2012, the day after Lisa's murder, Seth was allowed to return to the property under police surveillance. Officers observed him walking directly to the area where the shotgun had been discovered, appearing to search for something. This behavior further raised suspicions, as he seemed unusually aware of the weapon's location.

Later that same day, Seth approached deputies with a curious question: "Were you watching my house?" This query struck investigators as highly calculated, suggesting he might be trying to gauge whether his movements had been observed. At this point, their suspicions were mounting, but there was still no direct evidence tying him to the crime scene beyond the gun.

———

On May 28, investigators uncovered another piece of critical evidence: Seth's prepaid phone hidden in his truck. This device contained thousands of text messages exchanged with Rachel McFarland, a coworker from Job Corps, revealing an affair that had begun almost immediately after Seth and Lisa's wedding. Rachel had given Seth an ultimatum just weeks before Lisa's death: leave his wife or lose her. Seth had promised Rachel that everything would be resolved soon.

> Just give me two weeks

he had texted her. On the night before Lisa's murder, he sent Rachel another message:

> It's done.

Rachel assumed this meant Seth had finally ended his marriage.

When confronted by investigators, Rachel initially tried to downplay the nature of their relationship, but the overwhelming evidence in the messages left no room for doubt. She admitted to the affair and shared that Seth had confided in her about his dissatisfaction with his marriage and his plans for their future together. Her testimony added critical context to the events leading up to Lisa's murder and provided the investigators with a clear motive.

The combination of the phone's contents and Seth's behavior around the murder weapon solidified the case. Investigators pieced together a narrative of a man trapped between the life he had built and the one he secretly desired. This duplicity, combined with the physical evidence, pointed toward premeditation.

———

With mounting evidence, law enforcement made their move. On May 30, 2012, Seth Techel was arrested and charged with first-degree murder and nonconsensual termination of a human pregnancy. The arrest was particularly symbolic: Seth was handcuffed using Lisa's own set of handcuffs, a poignant reminder of the life he had taken.

———

The path to justice would prove long and complex. Seth's first trial in Wapello County in 2013 ended with a hung jury, and the community was divided over the guilt of a man many had known since childhood. A second trial that same year, which was moved to Henry County due to media coverage, produced the same result—another deadlocked jury, another failure to reach a consensus.

Seth Techel

The prosecution's case was strong but circumstantial, built on the foundation of secret text messages, suspicious behavior, and a hastily hidden murder weapon. They painted a picture of a man trapped between the life he had chosen and the one he wanted—a man who saw murder as his only escape from a marriage complicated by pregnancy and small-town expectations.

By the third trial in 2014, moved to Scott County, prosecutors had refined their approach. The prosecution methodically laid out their case: The affair that began the same month as the marriage, the ultimatum from Rachel, Seth's promise that things would be better "in two weeks," the suspicious shower story that conveniently explained away any gunshot residue, and the hidden weapon found on his own property.

The defense tried multiple strategies. First, they had pointed to Brian Tate, the convenient scapegoat. When that narrative crumbled, they attempted to paint Lisa as unfaithful, revealing she had her own relationship with a married colleague, Jason Tennis. However, this last-ditch effort failed to gain traction—DNA testing had already confirmed Seth was the father of Lisa's unborn child, and Tennis had a solid alibi for the morning of the murder.

In September 2014, after careful deliberation, the jury reached their verdict. Seth Techel was found guilty of first-degree murder and nonconsensual termination of a human pregnancy. The sentence was unequivocal: life in prison without the possibility of parole.

———

The ripples of violence spread far beyond the immediate tragedy. Brian Tate, the neighbor whose reputation had been savaged by false accusations, died on September 30, 2012, just months after the murder. His family believed he died of a broken heart, the strain of being falsely labeled a killer proving too much to bear.

The Caldwell family's loss was immeasurable—not just a daughter but a grandchild who would never draw breath. The pregnancy that had complicated Seth's plans had been a source of joy for Lisa's family, making the double loss even more devastating.

The tight-knit community of Agency found itself forever changed. The story of the Techels had been one of small-town success—the local business owner's son and the deputy's daughter, high school sweethearts building a life together. Its tragic end shattered not just two families but the community's sense of security, its belief that such violence happened elsewhere and to other people.

Seth Techel remains in Anamosa State Penitentiary, his appeals exhausted. The young man who once dreamed of following his father-in-law into law enforcement now views the world through prison bars, his life sentence a daily reminder of the choices he made.

CHAPTER 5
NO BODY, NO CRIME

The children waited.

It was Mother's Day 2018 in Yulee, Florida, and Joleen Cummings' three kids sat by the window, eagerly watching for their mother's beige Ford Expedition to pull into the driveway. Joleen, a thirty-four-year-old hairstylist known for her radiant smile and perfect timing, was never late—especially not for her children. But as minutes stretched into hours, their excitement faded to confusion, then fear.

Anne Johnson, Joleen's mother, was the first to sound the alarm. When her daughter failed to pick up the children from her ex-husband Jason's house, somewhere deep within her, she knew something was terribly wrong. Calls to Joleen's phone went straight to voicemail. Texts remained unanswered. As the day meant for celebration turned to dusk, the first ripples of panic spread through the family.

At work that Monday, one of Joleen's close friends was scrolling through Facebook when her heart stopped. There on her screen was a missing person post—with Joleen's smiling face staring back at her.

She immediately called another friend, her hands shaking as she dialed. "Have you heard from her? What's going on?" Unfortunately, nobody knew anything. A group of Joleen's friends gathered quickly, their worry turning to panic as they realized no one had heard from her since Saturday.

Anne Johnson reported her daughter missing to the Nassau County Sheriff's Office that Monday morning. The community of Yulee, a close-knit town in Florida's northeastern corner just above Jacksonville, mobilized quickly. Friends and family began organizing search parties, driving down unfamiliar dirt roads with binoculars, desperately looking anywhere they could think of. They gathered at Tangles Hair Salon, where Joleen worked, leaving flowers and messages of hope. "We were all in shock," one friend said as they organized their search efforts. "No one knew if she was dead or alive. You'd be at the grocery store and think you saw her—you were looking everywhere because you just didn't know."

As investigators began piecing together Joleen's last known movements, they learned she had been seen on Saturday, May 12th, leaving her shift at Tangles Hair Salon. The quiet beauty shop had been more than just Joleen's workplace—it was where she had built a loyal clientele through social media and her natural talent for brightening people's days.

Among her coworkers was Jennifer Sybert, a reserved stylist who had only been working at the salon for about two and a half months. When detectives first arrived at Tangles to interview the staff, the salon's owner was on the phone with Jennifer, telling her that investigators wanted to speak with her since she had been one of the last people to see Joleen. Jennifer, who was pulling into the Tangles parking lot during the call, spotted the investigators' vehicles. She immediately turned around and drove away. She then texted the owner that she was quitting and would mail back her salon key.

During these initial interviews, Joleen's coworkers told detectives about growing friction between Joleen and the new stylist in recent weeks. They learned that Joleen had confronted Sybert about her identity—a detail that would take on new significance as the investigation unfolded.

Two days into their investigation, on May 16, detectives found Joleen's Ford Expedition in the parking lot of a Home Depot in Yulee. The discovery sparked an immediate review of the store's surveillance footage. The grainy video revealed someone dressed in black parking the SUV at 1:17 a.m. on Sunday morning, May 13—Mother's Day— and walking away into the darkness. Following the figure's path through various security cameras in the area, investigators watched as the person stopped at a gas station to buy a bottle of water with a credit card, then called a taxi.

The footage led investigators back to Tangles Hair Salon, where the mysterious figure had retrieved another vehicle. It was time for a closer look at the premises. At first glance, the salon appeared normal —chairs neatly arranged, magazines fanned out in the waiting area table, the faint scent of hairspray still lingering in the air. However, when forensics investigators dimmed the lights and began spraying Luminol, a different story emerged.

The chemical reaction revealed what someone had tried desperately to hide. Blood residue lit up the darkness—not small spots, but massive amounts splashed across the walls. It was on the chairs where clients sat for their weekly styling. It had seeped into the cabinets where hair products were stored. Most tellingly, traces were found in the sink drain, suggesting someone had tried to wash away evidence of violence. The salon that had once been filled with the friendly chatter of stylists and clients had become an eerie crime scene, its cheerful façade masking a darker truth.

That same day, May 16, investigators received word that a black Kia Soul had been spotted at a rest stop in St. Johns County. Inside, they found the woman who called herself Jennifer Sybert asleep between two semi-trucks. She appeared to be living out of her car, and when officers approached, they noticed something peculiar—her face and hands were covered with bandages. When questioned about a prominent scratch below her left eye, she blamed it on a collision with a tree branch while riding her bike.

Initially arrested for stealing and abandoning Joleen's Ford Expedition, the woman's true identity began to unravel during a videotaped interview forty-eight hours later. Seated casually in an orange jumpsuit, she made a startling admission:

 "When you run my fingerprints through, they come up as Kimberly Lee Kessler," she said with an unsettling lightheartedness. "I am fifty years old, and I've been running for over twenty-five years."

For two hours, Kessler spoke freely about her past—until the questioning turned to Joleen Cummings. Her demeanor shifted instantly, and she uttered the words that experienced detectives knew all too well: "You may not like the answer, but I would like to retain legal counsel."

Kimberly Kessler

As investigators dug into Kimberly Kessler's background, they uncovered a labyrinth of deception spanning decades. The name Jennifer Sybert, they discovered, belonged to a thirteen-year-old girl who had died in a car crash in Germany in 1987 and was buried in a Butler, Pennsylvania cemetery—the same state where Kessler was born. She had stolen the identity from a tombstone.

Kessler's own family had reported her missing in 2012, eight years after she had vanished from Pennsylvania in July 2004. Of course, local law enforcement had already figured out the truth. She wasn't missing—she simply didn't want to be found. Her car held the evidence of an elaborate life on the run: Multiple false documents and identification cards revealed that Kessler had used eighteen different aliases across thirty-three cities in fourteen states since 1996.

But it was the digital breadcrumbs that truly revealed the calculated nature of what had happened to Joleen Cummings. Detective Charity Rose would later testify about the thousands of disturbing searches found on Kessler's phone. In the weeks leading up to the murder, she had searched for terms including "autopsy," "cadavers," "postmortem bodies," "murderpedia," "victimpedia," "female murderers by country," and "Florida female murderers." Two weeks before the murder, she specifically searched for "coworker guilty of murder missing person body not found." Then, in the forty-eight hours after Joleen disappeared, Kessler obsessively searched her victim's name 457 times, including the telling phrase "Joleen Cummings no body no crime." Strangely, there were further searches for "Satanist," "witch," and "evil murderous gang."

Surveillance footage from the night Joleen vanished painted a disturbing scene. Behind Tangles, cameras recorded Kessler wrestling with heavy trash bags, staggering as she hoisted them into a dumpster. Hours later, Walmart security footage caught her buying thirty-gallon trash bags, rubber gloves, an electric carving knife, and a bottle of ammonia. She then returned to the salon, discarding more overstuffed trash bags in the same dumpster. Their contents, hauled away by a garbage truck, were lost forever.

The investigation took a crucial turn when investigators discovered Kessler had rented a storage unit in the area. When questioning employees at the facility, they learned that Kessler had been particularly interested in the security measures, specifically asking whether the facility had live video surveillance and if it was recorded—questions that immediately raised red flags. When investigators searched Kessler's rented unit, they discovered a damning collection of evidence: Kessler's boots—the same ones she had been wearing the day Joleen disappeared—stained with dried blood that would later be confirmed as Joleen's. Inside a blue bin, they found one of Joleen's fingernails. The unit also contained blood-stained scissors—a hairstylist's tool turned murder weapon—and socks with blood on them.

However, the storage unit revealed more than just evidence of violence; it offered a glimpse into Kessler's life of deception. Six wigs were carefully stored away, along with multiple cell phones—tools of her trade in identity theft. These wigs, investigators would learn, were part of her elaborate scheme to create new identities, complete with practiced changes in her walk and speech patterns to fully embody her various personas.

As the investigation continued, Kessler's recorded jail phone calls to her mother revealed a mind more preoccupied with conspiracy theories than the serious charges she faced. "I'm all over the news," she told her mother during one call, seeming almost pleased with the attention. When her mother confirmed that she was indeed front-page news, with outlets like Dateline reaching out to the public defender's office, Kessler had her own explanation for the media coverage.

"I think that her people definitely are fucking seriously involved in it," Kessler ranted, referring to the Illuminati. "I mean, again, I can't prove it, it's just my opinion and what a little bit I've seen on YouTube… nobody gets even five minutes' worth or five seconds worth of airtime unless they have some sort of connection."

Her paranoid musings extended to the legal system itself. "The prosecutors are just a giant weenie," she declared in another call. "I'm not gonna say, well, maybe there's some that are good, no, 'cause they all— oh, we need you to put on a suit, and you turn into a weenie." She seemed more focused on these conspiracy theories than on the mountain of evidence building against her.

On September 7, 2018, a grand jury indicted Kessler for first-degree murder. However, the path to trial would be long and marked by increasingly erratic behavior. Her mental state became a central issue as she engaged in extreme acts of self-sabotage. What began as a weight of nearly 200 pounds dropped precipitously to a life-threatening seventy-four pounds through an extended hunger strike. The situation became so dire that Nassau County Sheriff Bill Leeper was forced to file a civil suit requesting permission to force-feed her, as it appeared she was trying to starve herself to death.

Kessler's disruptive behavior wasn't limited to self-starvation. She would strip naked in her cell and smear the walls with feces. These actions led to frequent hospitalizations and raised serious questions about her competency to stand trial. In July 2019, after multiple mental evaluations, a judge ruled her not competent for prosecution. She was committed to Florida State Hospital in Chattahoochee to "restore competency" with a planned reevaluation in six months.

But even as questions swirled about her mental state, investigators couldn't help but remember the calculating nature of her previous deceptions—how she had methodically created and maintained multiple identities across more than a dozen states, carefully crafting each persona. Was this just another performance from a woman who had spent decades playing different roles?

By October 2020, after a second mental evaluation, a judge reversed the earlier decision and ruled Kessler competent to stand trial. This ruling was reaffirmed following a third mental evaluation in June 2021. As her trial finally began in November 2021, Kessler's theatrical disruptions continued. During jury selection, she was promptly removed from the courtroom after shouting, "Jordan Beard is Joleen's cousin!"—a false accusation about one of her former defense attorneys that she would repeat at nearly every court appearance.

Throughout the trial, Kessler was largely absent from the proceedings, sequestered in a separate room due to her outbursts. Meanwhile, prosecutors methodically laid out their case. They presented the surveillance footage of Kessler disposing of evidence, her suspicious purchases at Walmart, and the damning DNA evidence found throughout the salon and in her storage unit. The scissors from her car, they argued, had been the murder weapon.

The defense offered little resistance to the mountain of evidence. They suggested there had been a violent conflict between the two women, implying self-defense. Still, they could not explain away the premeditated internet searches or Kessler's calculated actions after Joleen's disappearance. They pointed to a baggie with a chalky substance found in the salon, suggesting an argument over drugs in the workplace, but this theory gained little traction.

After just over an hour of deliberations on December 9, 2021, the jury returned with their verdict: guilty of first-degree murder. Kessler, watching from her separate room, remained unmoved. She was also found guilty of theft for abandoning Joleen's vehicle in the Home Depot parking lot.

After the guilty verdict, Joleen's mother made an emotional plea to Kessler: "If you could find it in your heart to tell us the remains of my daughter, where are the remains of my daughter? Give us some closure. I am asking you from one mother to another." But Kessler remained silent.

———

Kimberly Kessler's sentencing hearing was held on January 27, 2022. She was wheeled into the courtroom wearing a dark green suicide smock and strapped to a chair due to her disruptive behavior and refusal to appear voluntarily. True to form, she began shouting and was again removed to a separate room where she could watch the proceedings via video. The real emotional weight of the day came from those left behind to speak about the devastating impact of her crimes.

Joleen's mother, Anne Johnson, stepped forward to read what she called the hardest thing she'd ever had to write.

 "When my precious daughter was murdered, part of us died. Our family has struggled to make some sort of semblance of life ever since,"

she told the court, speaking not just for herself but for Joleen's three children and her brother, who couldn't attend because he was serving in the military.

 "We are still waiting for Joleen to walk through that door. But Joleen is never coming home. Not only are we traumatized, but this is a never-ending nightmare."

She spoke of all the moments stolen from her daughter—the chance to watch her children grow up, to share their most important milestones like birthdays and graduations, and to see them have their own children someday.

 "We suffered the greatest nightmare of all," she said. "Her beautiful soul was taken from us. The only thing that keeps us together is faith that one day we will be reunited."

Judge James Daniel sentenced Kessler to life in prison without the possibility of parole, plus a concurrent five-year sentence for the theft of Joleen's vehicle. Nassau County Sheriff Bill Leeper didn't mince words after the sentencing:

 "She is evil. She is evil in the flesh." But he voiced an even more chilling suspicion: "I don't believe for one second that Kimberly Kessler, or whatever name she is going by today—I don't believe this is her first murder. I don't at all."

The case, however, wasn't quite finished. In July 2024, Kessler filed a 224-page handwritten motion asking for her life sentence to be overturned. In the filing, she submitted twenty-seven grounds for appeal, claiming everything from prosecutorial misconduct to violations of due process. Despite the overwhelming physical proof that had convicted her, she argued there was "no case" and "no evidence." She maintained her innocence and claimed she had been framed, writing that she did nothing to Joleen.

Perhaps most telling was her continued insistence that she had "never been disruptive or disrespectful" during the proceedings—a claim that stood in stark contrast to her documented outbursts, hunger strikes, and other erratic behavior. The Florida Supreme Court dismissed her appeal in March 2024.

———

Today, Tangles Hair Salon is out of business, a quiet reminder of the tragedy that unfolded within its walls. The community of Yulee continues to grapple with the impact of Kessler's crimes. As one friend of Joleen's reflected, "You're always looking. You're always wondering when someone goes missing."

CHAPTER 6
APARTMENT 9

The autumn wind in New Salem, North Dakota, carried the scent of harvest across the Morgensterns' farm. There, young Mindy felt most at home. Behind the wheel of the family tractor, she embodied the strong work ethic her parents had instilled in her. Larry Morgenstern had taught his daughter to handle the massive machine with confidence, and he watched with pride as she tended to the endless tasks of farm life.

Mindy's journey to the Morgensterns' farm began in Bogotá, Colombia. There, Larry and Eunice Morgenstern saw their future daughter for the first time. They had a beautiful family with their daughter, Rebecca, and their son, Michael, whom they had adopted, but their hearts had more love to give. They knew their family wasn't complete when they learned of two sisters in Colombia who needed a home— April, a toddler, and baby Mindy. The moment Eunice first held baby Mindy, those big, dark brown eyes captured her heart.

From her earliest days on the farm, Mindy's personality was impossible to contain. She was loud and happy, constantly moving, with her infectious laugh echoing across the farmyard. In rural North Dakota, her caramel skin set her apart, but Mindy's charm and caring nature won over even the most reluctant hearts. When other kids teased her about her looks, Mindy would say, "Jesus made me that way." She was confident and comfortable in her skin.

The farm became Mindy's training ground for life. Tending to gardens, caring for animals, and helping with the harvest, she developed a strong work ethic and a tender heart. She would adopt every stray cat or dog that crossed her path, nurturing them with the same love her parents had shown her. At family dinners, Mindy sat at the head of the table, where she commanded attention with her story-telling and joy.

Basketball became Mindy's true passion. She idolized Michael Jordan and would practice his moves late into the night, often joined by her sister, April. However, she wasn't content with just athletics; she also played the clarinet in the marching band and performed as a cheer-leader, refusing to be limited to any one role.

Of those who knew Mindy best, most would say her greatest quality wasn't any talent or achievement. Rather, it was her ability to make everyone feel special and included. Whether singing in the church choir, lifeguarding at the local pool, or sharing coffee with friends, she had a way of turning ordinary moments into cherished memories.

———

By 2006, Mindy was twenty-two years old, in her final year at Valley City State University, and living 200 miles away from the farm where she had grown up. Majoring in physical education, she had already faced more adversity than most people her age, yet her resolve was unshakable. Mindy had been diagnosed with multiple sclerosis recently, which could have derailed her. Instead, she channeled her energy into her studies. She was determined to live life on her terms.

She was even participating in a clinical trial for an experimental drug designed to manage her symptoms. To further protect her health, Mindy decided to move into an off-campus apartment away from the crowded dorms. This apartment was more than a retreat; it was a haven chosen for its protected neighborhood with nearby law enforcement officers. The presence of the officers gave Mindy a sense of security, a feeling that she was safer living alone, particularly in light of her condition.

Despite the daily challenges of managing her illness, Mindy felt optimistic. Her relationship with her boyfriend, Jordan, was blossoming, and she was thinking ahead to life after graduation. Whether that meant pursuing a career in sports medicine or coaching, she was ready to take the next step. With her health stabilizing and a strong support system in place, Mindy felt ready for anything. Then, everything changed in an instant.

———

An unusual quietness marked the autumn evening of September 13, 2006—a calm that would soon be broken. Mindy's friend Toni glanced at her phone screen, which displayed a dozen missed calls to Mindy—all unanswered. So unlike Mindy. Everyone who knew her could always count on her to pick up, to return a call, and to be there when needed. Always.

By 9:00 p.m., that gnawing worry drove Toni and her friend Danielle to Mindy's apartment at 515 8th Street. The sight of Mindy's white car still parked outside offered momentary relief. While Danielle waited in the car, Toni climbed the stairs to Apartment 9, each step echoing in the night air.

The silence that answered her knocks felt wrong. When Toni tried the handle, it turned easily—unlocked. Darkness greeted her as she stepped inside, her hand fumbling for the light switch. Two steps into the hallway, her foot caught on something. In the sudden flood of light, Toni struggled to process what she saw before her.

Mindy Morgenstern was sprawled diagonally across the entry hallway, her dark hair splayed out on the floor. A belt was pulled tight around her neck, and a knife—its handle broken away from the blade —protruded from her throat. Her white, long-sleeved top had ridden up slightly, exposing her midriff. Her arms lay at her sides, her right arm still threaded through her purse straps. A pool of blood had formed beneath her head, stark against the gray carpet.

The overwhelming smell of Pine-Sol filled the air. An empty bottle, with its cap nearby, lay tucked between Mindy's right arm and her body. A coral and white striped shirt lay inside out across her right arm, her wallet open beside it. Her cell phone rested nearby, silent now after hours of missed calls.

Toni fled down the hallway screaming, the image seared into her memory. Her cries drew the attention of Danielle and a neighbor, Robert Lind, who lived nearby. Danielle ran up to see for herself, taking those same few steps inside before reality hit her. She backed away with such force that she slammed into the hallway wall.

Robert Lind entered and checked for signs of life, but the stillness of Mindy's body, the positioning, and the blood all spoke of an awful finality. He approached with caution. He used the back of his hand to check for a pulse he knew he wouldn't find. Later, he explained he didn't want to leave fingerprints. That detail would raise investigators' eyebrows.

When Sergeant Dave Swenson arrived minutes later, the Pine-Sol scent struck him first. It was sharp and chemical, almost masking the metallic smell of blood. His flashlight beam revealed more details. Clothes were scattered from the hallway to her bedroom. A second bloody knife lay near her head. When investigators moved the Pine-Sol bottle, they revealed her keys lay beneath it. The rest of the apartment was untouched and tidy except for a trail of clothes that led to her bedroom. It was like breadcrumbs marking a path of violence.

Outside, Valley City's quiet night dissolved into a chorus of sirens and murmuring neighbors. In Apartment 9, police flashlights revealed a haunting scene. It was a glimpse of evil that had no place in this small college town. People still left their doors unlocked in this building. It was the home of a young woman loved by all who knew her.

————

The deputy's cruiser cut through the darkness toward New Salem, his headlights illuminating mile after mile of empty road. Every minute that passed was another minute closer to destroying a family's world. Around 11:00 p.m., he pulled up to the home of Mindy's oldest sister, Rebecca, and her husband Jason, a local pastor. The deputy's boots crunched on the gravel driveway as he approached their door.

Rebecca's heart dropped the moment she saw him standing there, his face cast in shadow and hat in his hands. No one came that late with good news. When he told Rebecca that her sister was dead, her legs gave way. The wooden floor rushed up to meet her as the words echoed in her ears, impossible words that couldn't be true.

The deputy accompanied Rebecca and Jason to tell their parents. The 200-mile drive to the family farm felt endless. Dried corn stalks whispered in the night breeze as they pulled up to the farmhouse where Mindy had spent so many happy years. Rebecca walked through the door, hearing her father call out, "Who's there?"

"It's me, Dad." Her voice cracked. "I've got some bad news." Rebecca looked at her mother's face, untouched by grief for the last time. "Mindy's dead."

The sound that came from Eunice Morgenstern wasn't quite human. She ran to Mindy's bedroom, her feet carrying her instinctively to this last piece of her daughter. The room was as Mindy had left it. Photos on the dresser, her old stuffed animals on the bed, and her perfume lingering in the air. Eunice grabbed a sweater from Mindy's closet. She pressed it to her face and inhaled deeply, desperately. She hoped to hold on to her daughter through this small piece of fabric. Through her sobs, she could still smell Mindy. It was the same sweet scent she'd known since Colombia, when she had first held her baby girl.

On that farm, Mindy had learned to drive a tractor and care for animals. Her laugh had once echoed across the fields. Now, her family huddled together in her bedroom. The deputy said only that she had died under "suspicious circumstances." Those words would torture them until dawn. Eunice clutched Mindy's sweater. Larry held Eunice. Together, they weathered the first hours of a nightmare from which they would never truly wake.

————

Back in Valley City, the news reached Mindy's childhood best friend, Ashley. They had grown up together in New Salem, and both had chosen to attend Valley City State. Her hands trembled as she drove to Mindy's apartment building, now transformed by the rotating lights of police cars. Yellow crime scene tape fluttered in the breeze. Through the second-floor window, she could see Mindy's curtains moving gently, the light still burning inside. It felt surreal. Any moment, Mindy might appear at the window. She would wave, laugh that infectious laugh, and say this was a mistake.

Inside Apartment 9, investigators worked quickly. Their cameras flashed like lightning in the dark. Friends arrived from across town, drawn by urgent late-night calls and texts. They huddled in small groups, voices low, some crying and others standing in shocked silence. Many still wore their work uniforms or pajamas, having rushed over the moment they heard. These were people who shared classes with Mindy, worked beside her, and sang with her in church. Now they stood in the growing September chill, staring up at her window, trying to comprehend how someone so vibrant, so loved, could be gone.

Special Agent Mark Sayler watched the gathering crowd carefully. Experience told him that killers sometimes returned to the scene, wanting to witness the chaos they had created. The killer could be anywhere, maybe even among the onlookers.

As investigators worked through the night, the brutal nature of the crime became clear. The medical examiner would find that Mindy had died from asphyxiation and deep neck cuts. It was a savage attack that showed both rage and grim determination. Her clothing was intact. There were no signs of sexual assault. However, the violence of the scene suggested something personal. The lack of robbery, coupled with the unforced entry, pointed to someone Mindy may have known, someone she might have trusted enough to open her door. Still, it was beneath Mindy's fingernails that investigators found their most telling clue. They found traces of her attacker's tissue. It was evidence that Mindy had fought back.

Investigators knew the first forty-eight hours would make or break the case. The team began methodically building their list of suspects, starting with those closest to the scene. James Robinson quickly emerged as a person of interest. He was dating Mindy's friend Toni, and Mindy hadn't approved of the relationship. Things had "gotten pretty scary" between Toni and James at times, and Mindy had been trying to get Toni to stop seeing him.

Ironically, it was this tension that had led Toni and Danielle to Mindy's apartment that night. They had been planning to use Mindy as an alibi to go out without James knowing, calling her repeatedly to coordinate their story. When questioned, Robinson admitted to his drug-related criminal record, but he said he was trying to clean up his act. He explained he had done court-ordered community service before Mindy's murder and then spent time with a friend. The alibi checked out, but investigators still took a DNA sample to be sure.

Investigators also found their attention drawn to Robert Lind, who lived in the apartment building. His behavior at the crime scene raised red flags for investigators. He had heard the screams and checked Mindy's pulse, but he had used the back of his hand to avoid leaving fingerprints. This forensic awareness made investigators take note.

Ralph Walters, who lived near the restaurant where Mindy worked, emerged as another person of interest. Investigators learned from her coworkers that Mindy had been troubled by his behavior. He would request to sit in her section, making her uncomfortable enough to complain about him. When questioned, Walters denied harassing anyone or having any issues at the restaurant, claiming he didn't even know who Mindy was. This contradicted the accounts of her coworkers, drawing further investigative scrutiny.

Another lead that demanded investigators' attention came from one of Mindy's own police reports. Three weeks before her death, she had reported a frightening encounter. A man in a blue car had pulled up asking for directions, then gotten out and chased her to her apartment. In her report, she had described him as a heavyset white man, around sixty years old, and driving what appeared to be a Ford Taurus. The incident had scared her enough that she reported it to both the police and her family.

Yet another puzzling figure emerged: Rodney Kuznia, father of Mindy's ex, Kyle. Even after Mindy and Kyle's breakup, Rodney had maintained unusually close contact with her. After learning of her death, he began leaving emotional messages on her voicemail: "I know what happened to you… I just love hearing your voice," he said in one message, crying. "I can't take it. I love you, kid. God picked a beautiful flower." The nature and timing of these post-mortem messages troubled investigators.

———

Crime scene analysts concentrated on the physical evidence. Tucked between Mindy's arm and body was the Pine-Sol bottle with her keys underneath. Then, there was the scattered clothing that led them to her bedroom. However, the most promising discovery was the DNA from beneath her nails. It was 41.2 nanograms of genetic material that revealed a desperate struggle.

The investigation spread across the apartment complex. Every resident was asked for DNA samples. It was a routine request, but it would prove crucial.

A week into the investigation, the DNA results arrived, and with them came a shocking revelation. The tissue under Mindy's fingernails matched an unsolved case—a brutal sexual assault from 2004 in nearby Fargo. The victim had been drugged at a bar, taken to an unknown location, and assaulted. Medical staff called it the worst case they'd ever seen. She had described her attacker as a muscular Black male standing at more than six feet tall and over 200 pounds.

Several law enforcement officers lived in the building, which was one reason Mindy had chosen to live there. She felt safer knowing officers were nearby. One of these was Moe Gibbs, a corrections officer at Barnes County Jail, who lived in a downstairs apartment with his pregnant wife, Christina. When asked to provide a DNA sample, Gibbs complied willingly. A week later, the results stunned investigators: The tissue under Mindy's fingernails matched Moe Gibbs.

———

Moe Gibbs, the man at the center of the Mindy Morgenstern murder investigation, had a dark and twisted past that he had gone to great lengths to conceal. Beneath his façade as a correctional officer, Gibbs was a predator. His violent nature had been brewing for years.

Moe Gibbs

Born Glenn Dale Morgan Jr., Gibbs had a troubled youth marked by violence and criminal behavior. In 1994, he was convicted in military court of attempted premeditated murder and sentenced to ten years in prison at Fort Leavenworth. After serving five years of that sentence, Gibbs was released. He then changed his name to Moe Gibbs to distance himself from his past.

Gibbs's criminal behavior escalated over time. He built a shocking record of sexual assaults and abuses of power. Court records revealed Gibbs's involvement in multiple paternity cases, with at least two women accusing him of fathering their children during his marriage.

One of Gibbs's ex-wives, Tasha, remained with him for several years after his release from prison and even had a child with him. However, she eventually divorced him before he went on to marry another woman, Melissa, a few years later. That marriage also ended in divorce after just three years—the same year Gibbs changed his name.

Amid personal chaos, Gibbs landed a job as a correctional officer at Barnes County Jail. Remarkably, his violent criminal past and allegations of sexual misconduct didn't raise red flags. The required background checks, shockingly, only scrutinized local records. This oversight gave him power over vulnerable inmates despite his dark past.

Mindy's murder investigation exposed Moe Gibbs as a ruthless predator hiding behind a polished façade. He easily infiltrated trusted positions, and this revealed a disturbing truth: The system failed to protect vulnerable women. Moe Gibbs was a wolf in sheep's clothing, thriving on deception while darkness lurked beneath the surface.

———

Detectives called Moe Gibbs to the station on September 20, 2006, claiming it was just a routine follow-up. Gibbs didn't suspect a thing, casually arriving with his fifteen-month-old stepdaughter, Tiana, perched on his hip. As investigators escorted him to the interview room, cameras rolled, capturing a crucial moment. Here was Gibbs, a respected corrections officer and pillar of the community, soothing a tiny tot who gazed up at him with total trust.

As investigators dug deeper into Moe Gibbs, pressure mounted, closing in. His carefully spun tale began to unravel thread by thread. Just after 12:35 p.m. on the day of the incident, he dropped his wife off at work. This brought him near Mindy's apartment when her phone went dark at 12:47 p.m.—the tragic moment her life ended.

Faced with damning evidence, Gibbs fumbled for a plausible explanation. How did his DNA end up under Mindy's fingernails? He insisted he had only helped her carry laundry days prior. Yet, investigators were not buying this excuse. Gibbs's hands bore fresh cuts and scratches, silent witnesses to a fierce struggle.

Five days later, he pleaded not guilty.

Then came the avalanche of revelations. As whispers of Gibbs's arrest spread, five brave women from Barnes County Jail emerged. They accused him of assault. One woman recounted the harrowing encounter, claiming Gibbs attacked her at dawn, mere hours before Mindy's tragic murder.

————

The first trial in the death of Mindy Morgenstern began in July 2007. Prosecutors painted a clear picture: Gibbs saw Mindy return with laundry. He followed her inside and tried to assault her. When she fought back, scratching him deeply enough to leave tissue under her fingernails, he killed her to prevent exposure—not just of the attack but of his entire carefully constructed life.

The defense focused on reasonable doubt. They questioned the DNA evidence, suggesting an innocent transfer when Gibbs helped Mindy with her laundry. They pointed to two unidentified male DNA profiles found on the murder weapons. Furthermore, a delivery man had reported seeing two men running from the building on the day of the murder. The defense also questioned how Gibbs could have murdered Mindy while caring for his toddler stepdaughter.

After twenty-three grueling hours, the jury in Moe Gibbs's first trial was hopelessly deadlocked. Six jurors were convinced of his guilt, but the other six just couldn't bring themselves to declare him guilty beyond a reasonable doubt. With no unanimous decision reached, the judge had no choice but to declare a mistrial.

The outcome was utterly devastating for the Morgenstern family. Mindy's father, Larry, was angry and disbelieving. He told reporters,

"The DNA didn't seem to mean anything to the jurors. It seemed pretty simple to me."

———

The second trial began in October 2007. This time, the prosecution was better prepared. Forensic experts found 41.2 nanograms of DNA under Mindy's fingernails. Out of this, 30.8 nanograms came from Gibbs. This suggests a violent struggle occurred, not just casual contact. They also detailed Gibbs's texting patterns, showing how they stopped completely during the murder and then resumed immediately afterward.

After twenty-seven hours of deliberation, the jury returned with a verdict: guilty.

At sentencing, Mindy's mother, Eunice, faced her daughter's killer.

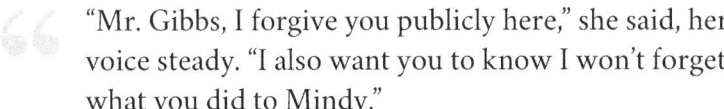 "Mr. Gibbs, I forgive you publicly here," she said, her voice steady. "I also want you to know I won't forget what you did to Mindy."

Then, in an extraordinary moment of grace, she extended sympathy to Gibbs's family and children.

Moe Gibbs maintained his innocence in Mindy's murder even as he pleaded guilty to the Fargo rape and the sexual assaults at the jail where he worked.

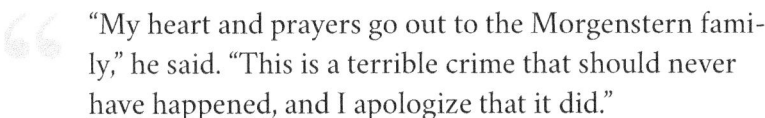 "My heart and prayers go out to the Morgenstern family," he said. "This is a terrible crime that should never have happened, and I apologize that it did."

Gibbs received life without parole to be served at the North Dakota State Penitentiary in Bismarck. However, the case prompted changes beyond his conviction. North Dakota strengthened criminal background check rules for corrections officers, combatting the rule that had allowed Gibbs to hide his violent past.

Meanwhile, in the wake of tragedy, the Morgensterns chose grace. They channeled their grief into forgiveness and kept Mindy's memory alive. A heart-shaped memorial stands at the corner of 9th Street Northeast and 5th Avenue Northeast in Valley City. It celebrates how Mindy lived, not how she died.

CHAPTER 7
SACRED TRUST

I n the industrial town of Springfield, Massachusetts, during the early 1970s, the Croteau family lived a modest but fulfilling life. The city sprawled along the Connecticut River, its character shaped by both bustling factories and quiet residential neighborhoods. Amid the industrial rhythm of Springfield, Catholic churches stood as pillars of the community, their towering spires rising above the streets where factory workers' children played. On Sundays, church bells echoed across town, their chimes weaving through the fabric of daily life—a sound that resonated deeply with the Croteau family.

Carl and Bernice "Bunny" Croteau were raising seven children—five sons and two daughters—in this deeply Catholic environment. Carl worked tirelessly, often holding down two jobs to support his large family, while Bunny managed their busy household with equal measures of love and discipline. As devoted members of St. Catherine of Siena parish, they attended Mass regularly, their faith forming the cornerstone of their family life. The church's stone façade and vivid stained-glass windows created a kaleidoscope of colors during services, bathing the pews where the Croteaus knelt in prayer.

Among their children was thirteen-year-old Daniel Thomas Croteau, known to all as Danny. He was a force of nature within the family—a quick-witted, mischievous boy whose talent for making others laugh brightened even the darkest days. His mother often likened him to Huckleberry Finn, for Danny shared that character's restless spirit and appetite for adventure. Yet beneath his playful exterior lay a deeply compassionate soul. The elderly residents of their street particularly cherished him; Danny would shovel their snow or run errands, usually refusing payment unless it came in the form of milk and cookies.

Danny's world revolved around motion and exploration. When not organizing impromptu street hockey games with neighborhood kids, he could be found along the banks of the Chicopee River, fishing rod in hand. The river became his sanctuary, its flowing waters and secluded spots offering endless possibilities for adventure. Fishing wasn't merely a hobby for Danny but his passion, his escape. It was a world where his imagination could run wild beyond the pressures of school and adolescence.

In the classroom, Danny's academic performance often fell short of expectations. Teachers noted his tendency to daydream, his thoughts clearly drifting to his next outdoor expedition. Yet they couldn't help but be charmed by his quick wit and natural ability to connect with others. While his report cards may not have reflected his full potential, his character left an indelible impression on everyone who knew him.

Father Richard Lavigne, a charismatic priest at St. Catherine of Siena, became an integral part of the Croteau family's life. His warm demeanor and apparent dedication to his parishioners earned him the trust of many parents, including Carl and Bunny. He frequently joined the family for meals and often took the boys on outings, creating what seemed to be a wholesome bond between priest and parish children. During difficult times, he would appear at the Croteau doorstep with food and offers of support, his actions painting a picture of genuine care and concern.

Yet beneath Father Lavigne's affable exterior lay hints of a darker nature. There were whispers within the parish about his temper, stories of sudden outbursts and clashes with church officials over progressive views. However, these rumors remained largely overshadowed by his visible acts of kindness and the deep relationships he cultivated with families like the Croteaus. His connection to the family strengthened over time, with Bunny and Carl viewing him as both a mentor and moral compass for their children.

———

April 14, 1972, dawned with the kind of bright promise that heralded spring's full arrival in Springfield. The morning air carried winter's last crispness, tempered by hints of warming earth and budding trees. In the Croteau household, the day began with its familiar rhythm—Bunny preparing breakfast amid the cheerful chaos of children getting ready for school, Carl gathering his things for work, and Danny practically vibrating with excitement about the approaching fishing season.

After school, Danny began his mile-and-a-half journey home, following his usual route through the neighborhood's familiar streets. A fifth-grade teacher offered him a partial ride, as sometimes happened. He waved to Mrs. Kline, the elderly widow who lived two doors down, and he lingered briefly at the corner store, pressing his nose against the glass to admire the new baseball cards on display.

Back home, Danny helped his mother move a rug in the sunroom, his endless energy making quick work of the task. Then he was outside again, joining the neighborhood kids for a quick game of kickball. The steady thump of the ball against the pavement echoed down the block as shadows lengthened across neat lawns. When asked about his evening plans, Danny mentioned skipping his Boy Scout meeting, possibly to attend a party, though the details remained vague. Bunny, absorbed in household tasks, didn't press for more information; Danny had always been reliable about coming home.

As twilight settled over Springfield, porch lights began their nightly vigil, casting pools of warmth onto darkening sidewalks. Inside the Croteau home, dinner plates were cleared away, and the family settled into their evening routine. However, Danny's place remained empty. Initially, his absence raised little concern—perhaps he'd stayed late at scouts after all, or maybe he'd lost track of time at a friend's house. Yet as evening deepened into night, worry began to gnaw at Bunny's composure.

She started calling Danny's friends, her voice growing tighter with each call that yielded nothing. No one had seen him since the afternoon's kickball game. Carl, sensing the growing urgency, grabbed a flashlight and headed to the Chicopee River. He knew his son's fascination with the spot, especially with fishing season so close. The beam of his light cut through the darkness as he searched the riverbanks, calling Danny's name into the void. The quiet lapping of water against the shore offered no answers.

By midnight, desperation had replaced worry. Bunny's trembling fingers dialed the Springfield Police Department only to face frustrating bureaucracy—officers wouldn't file a missing person report until Danny had been gone at least twelve hours. The Chicopee Police finally took an official report at 2:11 a.m., though their assurances that Danny had likely wandered off rang hollow to his increasingly fearful parents.

————

The morning of April 15, 1972, cast long shadows across Springfield, the day's first rays illuminating a community already in motion. Search parties moved through streets and fields, their calls for Danny growing hoarse in the crisp morning air. Among them was a local handyman preparing for a weekend fishing trip at the Chicopee River, unaware he was about to make a discovery that would haunt the community for decades.

He parked his truck near Robinson Bridge and walked toward the water. The river flowed quietly, its surface catching the morning light in gentle ripples, but the scene's serenity shattered as his eyes fell upon a sight no one should ever witness. The unmistakable form of a young boy was floating face-down along the banks of the river. Stumbling back to his truck, he rushed to a nearby junkyard to call the police.

When police retrieved the body, they carefully searched the pockets of the bloodstained clothes. Among the items they found was a piece of yellow exam paper with "Daniel Croteau, Grade 7, Our Lady of Sacred Heart School" written neatly at the top. It was a cruel twist of fate that would quickly confirm the victim's identity. The investigation would reveal other puzzling details: several wads of chewing gum in Danny's stomach and mysterious red fibers clinging to his underwear and socks as though he had been walking on red carpet before his death.

The scene that greeted responding officers told a story of brutal violence. Danny's body, retrieved from the water, still wore his school clothes, now heavy with river water and stained with blood. Beneath the bridge's shadow, investigators found evidence of the attack—a large pool of blood on the gravel and drag marks leading to the water's edge, signs of a desperate struggle preserved in the disturbed earth and vegetation.

Forensic experts documented every detail, from blood spatter patterns to scattered personal effects. A piece of rope and a plastic straw, both bloodstained, were carefully collected and labeled as evidence.

The autopsy findings painted an even darker picture. Danny had suffered multiple blunt-force injuries to his head, including a fractured skull and severe brain lacerations. Signs of strangulation marked his neck. Most disturbing was his blood alcohol level—0.18, nearly twice what would have been the legal limit for an adult. This detail raised haunting questions: How had a thirteen-year-old boy consumed so much alcohol? Had it been forced on him or used to lower his defenses?

When news of Danny's discovery reached the Croteau home, it shattered the family's last hopes. Carl and Bunny, who had clung to the possibility of finding their son alive through the long night, collapsed under the weight of unimaginable grief. Their home, usually alive with the sounds of seven happy children, fell into a silence broken only by sobs and whispered prayers.

————

Danny Croteau's murder transformed a once-tranquil community into a landscape of suspicion and fear. The Chicopee Police Department assembled their most experienced detectives, knowing every hour that passed could mean vital evidence lost. They began their work methodically, piecing together the final hours of a thirteen-year-old boy's life.

Door by door, investigators moved through the neighborhood. They filled their notepads with fragments of information—a child who had seen Danny at kickball, a neighbor who had noticed unfamiliar cars near Robinson Bridge, a crossing guard who remembered Danny walking home from school. Each detail, no matter how small, was carefully logged and cross-referenced, building a mosaic of Danny's final day.

The physical evidence told its own stark story. Under the bridge, where Danny's life had ended so violently, investigators found not only his blood but also traces of type B blood, suggesting his attacker had been injured in the struggle. The drag marks leading to the water spoke of calculated efforts to conceal the crime. Each piece of evidence pointed to a killer who was both violent and methodical.

Danny's elevated blood alcohol level became a central focus of the investigation. Detectives believed someone Danny trusted had provided the alcohol, perhaps to gain his compliance or render him vulnerable. This theory narrowed their focus to adults who had access to both alcohol and Danny's trust, a line of inquiry that would prove crucial as the investigation progressed.

As detectives dug deeper, attention increasingly turned to Father Richard Lavigne. His initial interview raised subtle red flags. While maintaining he hadn't seen Danny for days before the murder, Father Lavigne asked investigators about tire impressions being found near the bridge—details that hadn't been released to the public. His demeanor during questioning struck investigators as carefully controlled, his responses seemingly rehearsed. While this alone was not enough to accuse him, it placed him firmly on the radar as someone who knew more than he was admitting.

The church's influence posed significant challenges to the investigation. Attempts to search the rectory or access Father Lavigne's personal belongings were met with institutional resistance. Warrants were delayed or denied, and potential evidence remained frustratingly out of reach. The Diocese of Springfield had close ties to local law enforcement and political figures, which made aggressive investigations into clergy members highly sensitive. Yet detectives persisted, convinced that somewhere in their growing case file lay the key to solving Danny's murder.

———

Months stretched into years as Danny's case grew cold, yet it never fully faded from the minds of investigators or the community. Then came a breakthrough: In 1993, after seeing Lavigne's picture in the newspaper, a witness finally came forward with a crucial recollection.

They had seen a man in his thirties wearing a priest's collar driving out from under the Governor Robinson Bridge between 12:30 and 1:00 a.m. that April night in 1972. The car matched one of the two vehicles Lavigne was known to drive at the time. The driver had looked directly at the witness before speeding away.

When questioned again, Father Lavigne's carefully maintained composure showed cracks. His eyes darted nervously during interviews, his answers became increasingly vague, and his previous confidence wavered. Meanwhile, former altar servers began sharing troubling accounts of inappropriate behavior by Father Lavigne, including instances where he provided alcohol to minors during outings—a detail that resonated ominously with the circumstances of Danny's death.

The evidence continued to mount. Lavigne's blood type matched the type B blood found at the crime scene, and his left-handedness aligned with the attack pattern determined by investigators. But perhaps most damning was a phone call received at the Croteau household shortly after Danny's funeral. Danny's oldest brother, Carl Jr., answered, hearing an unidentified caller say,

 "We're sorry about what happened to Danny. He saw something he shouldn't have behind the circle. It was an accident."

Weeks later, Carl Jr. became convinced the voice belonged to Father Lavigne.

As whispers of misconduct spread, the community's perception of Father Lavigne shifted dramatically. Parents who had once entrusted their children to his care now questioned their judgment. The parish itself became divided, with some defending their priest while others began to voice long-held suspicions.

———

Nearly fifty years passed before the case reached its final chapter. In the years following Danny Croteau's murder, an unsigned letter was mailed to law enforcement, appearing to be an anonymous reflection on the crime. The letter, which surfaced in the early 2000s, described the emotions the writer believed Danny's killer must have felt, speaking of guilt, inner turmoil, and the weight of carrying such a secret. At the time, the letter was noted but not acted upon, as it did not contain direct evidence identifying the author. However, in 2021, as investigators reexamined the case, they applied forensic linguistics to analyze the letter's phrasing, sentence structure, and unique linguistic patterns. The results matched the known writing style of Father Richard Lavigne, suggesting with a high degree of certainty that he had written the letter himself.

As Father Lavigne's health failed, detectives conducted a series of revealing interviews. Though he never made a full confession, he spoke of being at the river with Danny and of seeing the body in the water. His statements, while contradictory and incomplete, added weight to decades of circumstantial evidence.

In May 2021, Hampden County District Attorney Anthony Gulluni prepared to announce what many had long suspected: Father Richard Lavigne had killed Danny Croteau. However, justice had one final cruel twist in store. On May 21, 2021, less than forty-eight hours after prosecutors received approval to seek an arrest warrant, Lavigne died from COVID-19 complications at age eighty.

For the Croteau family, the news brought bittersweet closure. Carl and Bunny had already passed away, never knowing the full truth, but their surviving children found some solace in the official confirmation of their suspicions. "We're disappointed that he's not being brought to justice," one of Danny's brothers stated, "but we believe there's a higher power, and he will face that now."

Although he was never convicted, the Diocese of Springfield had already paid out millions in settlements to victims of clergy abuse, many of whom had been harmed by Father Richard Lavigne. In 2004, the diocese reached a $7 million settlement with forty-six victims, and in 2008, it agreed to an additional $4.5 million settlement with multiple claimants. By 2019, reports indicated that since 1992, the diocese had paid approximately $14.9 million to settle 147 abuse claims.

Danny's story became a catalyst for change in Springfield and beyond. His case highlighted the devastating consequences of the institutional protection of abusers and the importance of believing victims. While Lavigne escaped earthly justice, the truth about Danny's murder finally emerged from the shadows, offering some measure of peace to a community long haunted by the loss of a bright, mischievous boy who loved to fish.

CHAPTER 8
THE KRUG PARK KILLERS

"I'm pretty sure I just ran right across a dead body." The jogger's voice trembled as he spoke to the 911 dispatcher early on Sunday morning, October 16, 2016.

"I wasn't sure if it was a mannequin… but I stood there for two minutes trying to take everything in. I'm pretty sure it's real."

The morning run through Krug Park's wooded trails in St. Joseph, Missouri, had led to a discovery that would haunt the community for years to come. The park, known for its picturesque trails, rustic stone bridges, and old amphitheater, was a place where families gathered for picnics and children played without fear. On this crisp autumn morning, however, its serene atmosphere was shattered by a scene of unimaginable horror.

"It's actually like right in the middle of the trail," the jogger continued, his voice growing more uncertain with each detail he shared.

"It's a young lady, completely like her clothes are all ripped off, her shoes right next to her... The eyes were wide open, they're brown... I didn't touch it, but it looked like a hole, like, in the middle of the chest and then a cut by her neck, like maybe her neck was cut or something."

St. Joseph Police Department officers responding to the scene found exactly what the jogger described. A young woman's body lay exposed on the trail, her clothes carefully cut away and arranged beside her in an almost ritualistic manner. The violence inflicted upon her was evident—multiple stab wounds, a slashed throat, and signs of strangulation. Blood stained the fallen autumn leaves beneath her, but curiously, there was little blood on her discarded clothing, suggesting she had been disrobed before the stabbing.

Despite the brutality of the crime, the scene yielded few immediate clues. There were no weapons present, and the victim carried no identification. Her press-on fingernails were mostly broken off, found scattered underneath her body and in her hair, suggesting a desperate struggle. Beyond these sparse details, investigators had little to work with. The pristine arrangement of her clothing stood in stark contrast to the violence inflicted upon her body, a detail that suggested to investigators a level of ritual or ceremony in the killing.

———

The first break in identifying the victim came from an unlikely source: her t-shirt. Among her carefully arranged clothes was a Central High School shirt. With no matches in the fingerprint database or missing person reports, detectives brought crime scene photos to the school's administrators. They knew time was critical; the sooner they could identify the victim, the better their chances of finding her killer.

The assistant principal and school resource officer recognized her immediately. The young woman was seventeen-year-old Kaytlin Root, a former sophomore at the school. However, identifying the victim only deepened the mystery. No one had even reported Kaytlin missing yet—the murder had been discovered before anyone knew she was gone.

As detectives began unraveling the threads of Kaytlin's life, they found a story more complex than initially imagined. They learned she hadn't been living at home. Instead, she had been couch-surfing between friends' houses, primarily staying with a friend named Crystal and Crystal's grandmother, Sheila. Her home life had imploded after a devastating betrayal—her mother had chosen her boyfriend over Kaytlin after he had allegedly sexually assaulted her, leaving the teenager essentially homeless. Despite these challenges, those who knew her described someone who maintained a friendly disposition and an ability to connect with others, perhaps because she understood struggle firsthand.

———

The medical examiner's report painted a brutal picture of Kaytlin's final moments. She had been strangled, her throat had been slashed twice, and she had sustained two stab wounds to her torso from a single-edged knife. One of these wounds had damaged her liver, causing her to bleed out internally. The various wounds suggested an attack that was both frenzied and methodical—an unsettling combination that hinted at multiple attackers or a killer of an unusual temperament.

Initial interviews led investigators down several promising paths. Through conversations with those close to Kaytlin, including Crystal and Crystal's family, detectives learned of a concerning incident involving a young man named Kevin. Just two days before her death, Kaytlin had accused Kevin of physically assaulting her, claiming he had given her a bloody nose.

Kevin's reaction to these allegations caught investigators' attention. He had taken to Facebook on Saturday, tagging Kaytlin and insisting, "I don't hit women." This sparked what detectives described as "social media chaos" that spilled into Sunday, with Kevin and his supporters launching a social media campaign assailing Kaytlin's character and reputation. Even more disturbing, after Tabitha (a neighbor of Crystal's grandmother) informed the Facebook thread on Monday that Kaytlin was dead and police were at her house, Kevin responded by writing, "Take me to court because the truth will come out."

When a witness claimed to have seen a car associated with Kevin at Krug Park around 10:30 p.m. on the night of the murder, he quickly became the investigation's first serious person of interest. Detectives brought him in for questioning, noting he had collected some minor injuries in recent days.

"Got a little scratch there," they observed during the interview. Kevin had an explanation ready: "I caught the edge of a metal bar with my arm, and it cut me."

Under questioning, Kevin admitted to picking up Kaytlin on Thursday night, two days before the murder, but insisted his friend Chris had been with him the entire time. "We've literally been with each other all day every day for like the past month," he told detectives. He claimed everything was fine when he dropped Kaytlin off, and it wasn't until Saturday morning that he received strange phone calls about allegedly assaulting her.

Kevin told investigators that Kaytlin's ex-boyfriends had reached out to him since his Facebook post, saying she had "been known to play these games in the past." However, as detectives dug deeper, they found that Kevin's alibi for Saturday night was airtight. His story checked out, and the witnesses he named confirmed his whereabouts.

Meanwhile, another person of interest emerged. A young man named Adam had reportedly been one of the last people to see Kaytlin alive. According to witnesses, Kaytlin had been with Adam at a party on

Saturday night. The story went that Adam and Kaytlin had walked off into Krug Park's woods together, but only Adam had returned, claiming she had "gone off by herself." Adding to the suspicion, Adam had allegedly posted on Facebook that he "wished he would have never done that." The investigation seemed to be stalling until forensics made a crucial breakthrough.

On October 20, five days after the murder, investigators conducting a grid search of Krug Park found the main section of Kaytlin's damaged cell phone. This discovery would prove crucial to solving the case. Forensic investigators purchased a similar phone model to facilitate data recovery, and what they found inside Kaytlin's damaged device painted a chilling picture of her final hours.

The last photograph on Kaytlin's phone showed the front of a convenience store, timestamped from the night of her murder. More crucially, investigators discovered Facebook Messenger conversations from her final evening. At 9:30 p.m. on Saturday night, Kaytlin had received messages from someone using the screen name "Amanda Panda" that invited her to hang out and smoke marijuana. The invitation came with an ominous instruction:

Don't tell anyone it's me.

Kaytlin's last message indicated she was walking down the street to meet this person. She would never send another text.

————

Police began searching for "Amanda Panda" among Facebook's many users with that screen name. Meanwhile, surveillance footage from the convenience store showed a young man in a green Hyundai Santa Fe arriving around the time of Kaytlin's final photograph. He went inside, bought snacks, and returned to the car. Though they couldn't see the driver or get a license plate, this seemingly mundane piece of evidence would soon prove crucial.

Through Facebook, investigators identified their person of interest as Amanda Bennett, a seventeen-year-old who lived just a short distance from the convenience store. When detectives drove past her house on King Hill Avenue, they found a green Hyundai Santa Fe identical to the one in the surveillance footage parked in the alley. The pieces were starting to fall into place.

Amanda Bennett

On Saturday, October 22, exactly one week after Kaytlin's murder, police made their move. They located Amanda and her boyfriend, eighteen-year-old Sebastian Dowell, at a local parade and took them into custody. It was Amanda's seventeenth birthday. Officers arrested her first, approaching from behind as she walked with her mother and best friend.

———

The interrogations that followed would reveal a story more disturbing than investigators could have imagined. Amanda's demeanor immediately unsettled the detectives. While most murder suspects show fear, anger, or distress, Amanda appeared almost jovial, occasionally giggling during questioning. When confronted about her unusual behavior, she simply smiled and continued to deny any involvement.

Her story began to unravel quickly in the interrogation room. She claimed she'd been at a movie theater watching "The Girl on the Train" on the night of the murder, but there was something off about how she described the experience. When detectives asked her about the film's plot, Amanda was surprisingly vague. "It was weird," she said, "just weird. It was, like, kind of a plot twist." When pressed about the movie's central mystery, she admitted, "I don't know, I wasn't paying attention." The detectives found it peculiar that someone would use a movie as an alibi yet be unable to describe even its basic plot.

Theater surveillance footage confirmed their suspicions, showing no sign of Amanda or Sebastian that night. When confronted with this evidence, she stubbornly maintained her false alibi: "We were at the movies." Even when shown proof that she wasn't at the theater, she doubled down, insisting with surprising defiance, "You better watch it again because I was there." Throughout the interrogation, Amanda alternated between giggling and making strange jokes, a behavior that unsettled even veteran detectives. At one point, when cornered about inconsistencies in her story, she deflected by asking if she could "get a cupcake or something" for her birthday.

Sebastian, interviewed separately, displayed an equally disturbing but markedly different demeanor. Calm and detached, he seemed unbothered by his arrest. "Whatever's going to happen is going to happen," he said with unnerving serenity. "I know I didn't do anything." More tellingly, when detectives mentioned Amanda's movie alibi, Sebastian appeared genuinely confused. "Did you maybe go to a movie or something Saturday?" they prompted. "The Girl on the Train?" Sebastian's brow furrowed as he replied, "I don't recall seeing it." The detectives pressed harder: "I mean, you should remember going to the movies," the detective pressed. Sebastian's continued confusion about the movie only highlighted the lies in Amanda's story.

The contradictions didn't stop there. When questioned about their other activities that night, Sebastian mentioned they were supposed to visit his father—something Amanda had also included in her alibi. However, unlike Amanda's confident assertion that they'd made the visit, Sebastian admitted, "I don't think he answered the phone when we were supposed to go there."

What struck the detectives most wasn't just the obvious lies but how both suspects behaved when caught in them. Most people, when their alibis fall apart, show signs of stress or anxiety; Amanda simply continued her inappropriate giggling and jokes while Sebastian maintained his unnervingly calm demeanor. It was as if neither of them grasped the gravity of their situation—or perhaps they simply didn't care.

———

As investigators dug deeper, they discovered that Amanda Bennett's public persona stood in stark contrast to her private life. She was a straight-A student, a cheerleader, and actively involved in church activities. She volunteered at soup kitchens and ran children's church programs. Her name regularly appeared in local newspapers for her achievements and community involvement.

But behind this carefully crafted image lay a troubled teenager who had been battling depression since age eight. Following a miscarriage with another boy, she had found herself drawn to Sebastian Dowell, a high school dropout whose own life was marked by instability.

Sebastian had been kicked out of his mother's house and was living with his father in what was described as a "trap house" with no electricity or running water. Amanda would visit him there, claiming she wanted to ensure he wasn't using drugs. When rumors of an impending SWAT raid began circulating, Amanda convinced him to move in with her at her mother's house.

Their relationship quickly became all-consuming and dangerously codependent. "If you messaged one of us, the other one probably answered," Amanda would later explain. "We sounded exactly the same when we talked… we went to the bathroom together, it was like we were conjoined at the hip." She described their bond as complete enmeshment: "We were one person."

––––––

But their relationship wasn't just intense—it was toxic, infused with dark spirituality and violent fantasies. Sebastian practiced what Amanda described as his own religion centered around demon worship. He had created an entire notebook documenting his beliefs, rituals, and supposed communications with demonic entities. According to Amanda's later testimony, Sebastian claimed to have made a pact with a specific demon who controlled a section of Hell dedicated to torture. In exchange for human sacrifices, Sebastian believed he would be granted special privileges in the afterlife—specifically, upon his death, he would bypass judgment and be given a position as a torturer in Hell.

The couple kept journals in their room at Amanda's mother's house filled with detailed instructions for inviting demonic possession, guides for offering souls to demons, and disturbing proverbs like "bleed for those who only love the taste of your blood." Amanda, raised Christian but receptive to supernatural ideas, rationalized this by comparing it to "yin and yang," telling her mother, "Where there's good, there's evil."

––––––

Under continued questioning, both suspects eventually broke. The truth of what happened to Kaytlin Root proved even more horrifying than investigators had imagined. Amanda admitted to messaging several people she believed were "depressed" on Facebook that night, searching for someone to meet up with. Kaytlin was simply the one who responded.

After picking her up, they drove to Krug Park. As they walked deeper into the wooded area, Sebastian pulled Amanda aside and whispered, "We're running out of time." What followed was a sequence of events so brutal that investigators found themselves disturbed by the details.

Amanda struck first, hitting Kaytlin with a large stick. When Kaytlin turned, confused and asking, "What the fuck?" Sebastian tackled her to the ground and began choking her. Then, in a particularly disturbing detail, Sebastian produced a syringe filled with a mixture of bleach and water and injected it into Kaytlin's neck, causing her to seize.

Death did not come quickly or easily. Even after being injected, Kaytlin managed to stand and attempt to walk away. Sebastian tackled her again, and what followed was a prolonged ordeal involving multiple stab wounds. Throughout the attack, Sebastian remained eerily calm, as if "just making breakfast," according to Amanda's testimony. They stripped off Kaytlin's clothes, claiming "they wouldn't accept it if she had clothes on." The "they" referred to the demons Sebastian believed he served.

———

During interrogation, Sebastian introduced a disturbing new element to his story—an alternate personality he called "Drake." He described Drake as "the more violent, evil part" of himself, claiming that at certain times, "this state of my consciousness just kind of goes away for a bit, a different kind of consciousness comes away." According to

Sebastian, Amanda was well aware of Drake's existence and could even distinguish between the two personalities.

Meanwhile, Amanda displayed an unsettling and extensive knowledge of demonology. In an unguarded moment while waiting to be transported to juvenile detention, she spent nearly twenty-five minutes describing her supposed experiences with demons and Hell. Her description wasn't the typical fire-and-brimstone imagery most people associate with Hell. Instead, she painted a picture of a disturbingly bureaucratic underworld.

> "Hell's way more complex than what everyone says," she explained. "There's no fire for one. It's not hot, it's normal. It's kind of like an office building, there's different sections and each demon has like a secretary who goes out and collects like debts and souls from people."

She went on to describe an intricate system of supernatural transactions and demonic hierarchy.

Amanda claimed to have her own supernatural abilities: "I can manipulate like fire… I made a lighter explode one time and stuff like that. I can make it go in different spots." She warned about the permanent nature of demonic possession, explaining,

> "Whenever you reach out to a demon and you accept them into your body…you can't ever get rid of them again. They have a connection and a tie to you where they want you, they will find you, and they will put thoughts in your head to make you go somewhere and do something and make it think that it's your idea."

Her beliefs extended into past lives and reincarnation. "I was born in the 1200s," she stated matter-of-factly, though she offered no additional details about this supposed past life. She explained that one of her demonic "deals" involved taking a secretary position in Hell's hierarchy in exchange for memories from her past lives. She described a system where souls could be traded like currency: "What you can do is you can sacrifice souls to people… when someone dies or whatever you give their soul to them."

Perhaps most chilling was her understanding of the demons' indifference to human consequences: "They are getting stuff no matter what, so they don't care what happens to you… If you get arrested for, like, killing and murdering, they're not going to stop that. You're going to spend your time in jail." She added with a touch of bitterness, "Which is bull crap because they should help you."

These weren't just the ramblings of a scared teenager trying to deflect blame. The level of detail and consistency in their supernatural beliefs suggested a complex shared delusion that had apparently motivated the murder. This was further evidenced by Sebastian's description of chanting during the murder. When asked about Amanda's behavior at the crime scene, he mentioned that "she chanted something" that had been written down. Amanda later confirmed this, describing a paper with words she couldn't understand.

Their dark beliefs were also documented in physical evidence. Investigators found journals in their room filled with writings about demon interactions, including guides for inviting possession, instructions for offering souls to demons, and disturbing proverbs. While Amanda claimed Sebastian had burned the paper containing the chant used during Kaytlin's murder, the remaining writings painted a picture of two individuals deeply immersed in a dark and elaborate belief system—one that ultimately led them to murder in service of what they believed were supernatural obligations.

———

In May 2017, both Amanda Bennett and Sebastian Dowell pleaded guilty to second-degree murder despite clear evidence of premeditation—they had brought weapons, selected a victim deliberately, and planned the crime in advance. The resolution came down to prosecutorial strategy and plea negotiations. Amanda's lawyer presented her with two stark options: She could go to trial, where prosecutors would pursue first-degree murder charges and seek the death penalty under the Armed Criminal Action statute, or she could accept a plea deal for second-degree murder.

The prosecution's willingness to accept a plea to a lesser charge likely stemmed from several factors. Both defendants were young—Amanda was still a juvenile at the time of the crime—and both were blaming each other for the murder, which could have complicated a trial. Sebastian claimed Amanda was the driving force, while Amanda insisted she was under Sebastian's influence. This conflicting testimony, combined with their strange supernatural beliefs and Amanda's apparent mental health issues, might have made securing a first-degree murder conviction more challenging than it appeared.

When Amanda called her mother to discuss these options, her mother's response was unequivocal: "Anything but the death penalty." Amanda agreed to the plea deal, though she displayed a disturbing naïveté about the process. She thought sentencing would work like an auction where she could negotiate terms with the judge. This misunderstanding became painfully clear during sentencing when she tried to reject the life sentence, telling the judge, "I don't accept that." The judge had to explain that she didn't have a choice.

Sebastian, following similar legal advice, also accepted the plea deal. For the prosecution, these pleas guaranteed life sentences while avoiding the cost and uncertainty of a trial, as well as sparing Kaytlin's family from having to endure lengthy court proceedings.

Their behavior during the legal proceedings continued to disturb everyone involved in the case. While in jail awaiting sentencing, Amanda wrote several letters that revealed her continued obsession with violence and the occult. She mused about getting away with murder and described in graphic detail how she would torture future victims. Most disturbing was her attempt to manipulate the case by sending Sebastian a vial of her own blood, accompanied by messages about its supposed demonic significance.

The judge, observing Amanda's behavior throughout the proceedings and reviewing the evidence of her continued fascination with violence, labeled her a psychopath before delivering his sentence. Both Amanda and Sebastian received life sentences with the possibility of parole after thirty years. For Kaytlin's mother, even this felt insufficient.

The randomness of Kaytlin's selection haunted everyone involved in the case. She hadn't been specifically targeted—she was simply the one who responded to Amanda's messages that night. Four other people had received similar invitations to hang out. Had any of them responded instead of Kaytlin, they might have been the victim of the couple's twisted ritual.

In the years following her incarceration, Amanda Bennett's behavior has suggested little remorse or rehabilitation. Fellow inmates report that she proudly refers to herself as the "Krug Park Killer," seemingly reveling in her notoriety. Sebastian, meanwhile, maintains his story about alternate personalities and demonic influences. Though both will be eligible for parole after serving thirty years, Amanda herself acknowledges this is unlikely. She understands that the heinous nature of the crime, combined with her young age at the time of the murder, will likely count against her in any parole hearing.

CHAPTER 9
THE BEDROOM BASHER

The September air in 1979 carried a crispness that hinted at the approaching autumn. For Kevin and Dianna Green, a young couple living in Tustin, California, the season seemed to promise something more—the excitement of new beginnings. Kevin, a twenty-year-old Marine, was stationed at El Toro Air Base, a position that brought pride but also the weight of responsibility. Dianna, his twenty-one-year-old wife, had grown up in a small Midwestern town and was known for her kind demeanor and love of family. She was eagerly awaiting the birth of their first child, a moment she had dreamed about since they had gotten married.

Life wasn't perfect, but it was full of hope and potential. Their modest apartment complex, nestled within the suburban sprawl, was a hub of activity, with neighbors exchanging pleasantries and children playing in the courtyards. Kevin and Dianna were known in the community as a friendly, approachable couple. Kevin's easygoing charm and Dianna's warmth made them popular among their peers, though Kevin's long hours and the stresses of military life sometimes created tension at home.

Like many young couples, Kevin and Dianna were learning how to build a life together amidst the pressures of military life and impending parenthood, but their relationship wasn't without its darker moments. Kevin's long hours at El Toro Air Base often left Dianna feeling lonely and frustrated, and her excitement about their baby sometimes clashed with his concerns about their readiness—financially and emotionally—for the changes ahead. Their arguments could turn volatile, with shouting matches that drew concerned glances from neighbors. More than once, these conflicts escalated to physical confrontations that left both of them shaken. Despite these struggles, they always seemed to find their way back to each other, bound together by their shared dreams of a bright future and determination to make their marriage work.

———

On the evening of September 30, 1979, Kevin and Dianna Green's apartment became the setting of an unimaginable horror. The night had already been tense—another argument had erupted between them, their voices carrying through the thin apartment walls. Frustrated and needing space, Kevin decided to step out for a late-night snack, leaving Dianna alone. The quiet hum of the suburban night provided no hint of what awaited him upon his return.

When Kevin came back, the sight that greeted him was beyond comprehension. The apartment door was ajar—a subtle but sinister detail that immediately raised the hairs on the back of his neck. Pushing it open, he stepped into a scene of chaos and violence. Dianna lay sprawled on the bed, unconscious, her body battered and bloody. The bedding beneath her was soaked with blood, and the room bore signs of a desperate struggle. Overturned furniture and scattered belongings told a silent story of brutality.

Kevin's breath hitched as he dropped the bag of food he was carrying and rushed to her side. Her face was swollen and bruised, almost unrecognizable, and the faint rise and fall of her chest was the only indication that she was still alive at all. The air in the apartment was heavy with the metallic tang of blood, and an eerie silence hung over the scene, broken only by Kevin's frantic breaths.

Shaking, Kevin scrambled for the phone and dialed 911. His voice trembled as he spoke.

> "My wife," he stammered. "She's been attacked. She's pregnant. Please, send help."

The dispatcher's calm voice guided him through the call, but Kevin's mind was a blur of fear and disbelief.

When paramedics arrived, they worked quickly to stabilize her, checking her vital signs and preparing her for transport. Kevin watched helplessly as they loaded her onto a stretcher, his heart sinking further when he overheard one of them mutter, "It doesn't look good."

At the hospital, the reality of the situation became even grimmer. Doctors discovered that Dianna had been sexually assaulted and had suffered severe head trauma caused by multiple blunt force blows. The most horrifying detail was that the injuries were so severe they had exposed part of her brain, leaving her clinging to life. As if the physical devastation weren't enough, Dianna slipped into a deep coma, her body's way of shielding itself from the trauma. Despite the surgeons' tireless efforts, they delivered devastating news: Their unborn child had not survived the attack. The loss of their baby was an emotional blow that compounded the horror of the night. Kevin sat in the sterile waiting room, his mind awash with guilt, grief, and a relentless torrent of questions. Why had he left the apartment? Could he have prevented this?

At the apartment, investigators worked methodically to piece together what had happened. The scene presented a chilling puzzle. Blood spatter on the walls and floor hinted at the ferocity of the attack, while the disarray in the bedroom suggested that Dianna had fought back against her assailant. Yet, there were no signs of forced entry—no broken locks and no shattered windows. This troubling detail led detectives to wonder if the attacker had been someone Dianna knew, someone she might have willingly let inside.

The lack of obvious leads only deepened the mystery. Detectives photographed every inch of the apartment, collected samples of blood and fibers, and bagged potential evidence. Although DNA technology was a long way off, evidence from semen left at the scene indicated that the assailant had type O blood. Investigators noted the half-eaten hamburger Kevin had brought home, now abandoned on the kitchen counter, and the faint scent of Dianna's perfume lingering in the air. These details, though seemingly mundane, painted a haunting picture of a life violently interrupted.

The community of Tustin, a quiet suburb where violent crime was rare, was shaken to its core. Neighbors whispered about the attack, their fear palpable. How could something so horrific happen in their seemingly safe neighborhood? Speculation ran rampant. Some wondered if a stranger had broken in while Kevin was gone, while others couldn't help but cast suspicion on Kevin himself. After all, in cases like this, the husband was often the first suspect.

As Dianna lay in a coma, fighting for her life, the investigation intensified. The police's task was daunting: unraveling the events of that night, finding a suspect, and bringing justice to a case that already felt deeply personal to the shaken community.

———

Tustin Police quickly began piecing together the events of that night. Kevin's account of leaving to get food was corroborated by an employee at the Jack in the Box restaurant who remembered seeing him. However, the lack of forced entry into the apartment still raised suspicions. Investigators wondered: Could the assailant have been someone Dianna knew? Or was it possible that Kevin himself was involved?

The small community buzzed with speculation. Neighbors described Kevin and Dianna as a seemingly normal couple, though some mentioned hearing arguments in the weeks leading up to the attack. Kevin's demeanor during questioning was scrutinized. While he appeared distraught, detectives noted that his behavior also seemed inconsistent—a subjective observation that would later become a key point of contention.

Dianna's condition remained critical for weeks, and when she eventually regained consciousness, the true extent of her injuries became apparent. The severe head trauma she had sustained caused retrograde amnesia, erasing her memories of the events leading up to and during the attack. Her brain's ability to form and retain new memories had been profoundly compromised, leaving her unable to recall even basic details of what had happened.

Doctors revealed that the blows to her head had caused such extensive damage that the area of her brain responsible for speech and motor functions was also affected. Dianna was temporarily unable to speak, a devastating complication that further hindered her ability to communicate with investigators. Flashes of violence occasionally surfaced in her fragmented recollections, but these were vague, disjointed, and offered little clarity. Attempts to piece together a coherent narrative from her memories proved futile, as the neurological damage rendered her statements contradictory and unreliable.

———

The police's focus on Kevin intensified as investigators struggled to find other viable suspects. Dianna, still in recovery and under immense pressure, began to recall vague and fragmented details about the attack. These recollections—shaped by her trauma, repeated questioning, and the suggestions of those around her—eventually included statements that seemed to implicate Kevin. Detectives seized on these statements, interpreting them as proof of his guilt despite her significant neurological impairments and inability to provide a consistent account.

Forensic analysis at the time offered little clarity. DNA testing was still decades away from being a reliable tool, and the physical evidence was inconclusive. Investigators zeroed in on the lack of forced entry, which they argued indicated that Dianna's attacker must have been someone she trusted—someone like her husband.

The mounting pressure to resolve the case led to Kevin's arrest. He was charged with the murder of his unborn child and the attempted murder of Dianna. At trial, prosecutors painted a damning picture of Kevin as a volatile and controlling young man prone to anger and violence. They argued that the couple's recent arguments over intimacy and finances provided a motive for the attack. Dianna's testimony, though riddled with inconsistencies due to her injuries, was presented as a central piece of evidence. Her inability to recall the events of the attack clearly was overshadowed by the emotional weight of her words and the narrative crafted by the prosecution.

The trial was swift and emotionally charged, with public opinion largely turning against Kevin. In 1980, the jury convicted him, and he was sentenced to fifteen years to life in prison. For Kevin, the verdict was a devastating blow, as he maintained his innocence and struggled to understand how he had become the primary suspect in such a horrific crime.

———

For Kevin, prison was nothing short of a waking nightmare. Branded as a baby killer by both inmates and guards, he became a target of scorn and violence within the prison system. Convicted of a crime so heinous, his fellow inmates saw him as the lowest of the low, and the stigma attached to his conviction followed him relentlessly. Threats and physical assaults became a regular part of his existence, forcing him to remain constantly vigilant and isolated. He spent many days in fear for his life, knowing that even the smallest lapse in awareness could make him a victim of prison justice.

Despite these hardships, Kevin steadfastly maintained his innocence. Each parole hearing became another agonizing ordeal. The parole board made it clear: Admitting guilt and expressing remorse were prerequisites for any chance of release, yet Kevin refused. "I can't admit to something I didn't do," he said often, his voice unwavering even in the face of a prolonged incarceration. By clinging to the truth, Kevin knowingly prolonged his own suffering, but he could not bring himself to confess to a crime he had not committed.

The years passed slowly. Kevin's days were filled with monotony and quiet endurance. He found solace in writing letters to the outside world, seeking support from advocacy groups as he maintained a fragile connection to the hope that, someday, the truth would come to light. Meanwhile, Dianna's life was irrevocably altered. Her injuries left her with permanent disabilities, and the emotional trauma of losing her child created a void that could never be filled. Believing in Kevin's guilt, she cut ties with him completely, further isolating him from the life he had once known.

Kevin often replayed the events of the night in his mind. One detail stood out, haunting him: He recalled seeing a man outside his apartment shortly before he left to grab food. Though he couldn't remember the man's face, the memory lingered like a nagging puzzle piece that didn't fit. Could this shadowy figure have been the true perpetrator?

The knowledge that the real attacker was still out there, free to harm others, added another layer of torment to Kevin's incarceration. This unanswered question fueled his determination to hold on to his innocence, even when it meant enduring brutal conditions and constant danger. His resilience was remarkable, driven by a deep conviction that the truth, no matter how delayed, would eventually prevail. The thought that justice had not yet been served—for Dianna, for their unborn child, and for himself—gave him a purpose that carried him through the darkest moments of his imprisonment.

———

By the mid-1990s, advancements in DNA technology began to revolutionize criminal investigations. Around this time, Tustin Police were also reexamining five brutal unsolved murders that had haunted the region since the late 1970s. These cases, collectively attributed to a predator known as the "Bedroom Basher," involved a chillingly similar modus operandi: Women attacked in their homes, often late at night, and sexually assaulted before being killed. The brutality of these crimes sent shockwaves through the area, and their unresolved nature left a deep scar on the community.

In 1996, forensic analysts tested DNA evidence collected from one of the Bedroom Basher's crime scenes using California's newly established offender DNA database. The results were groundbreaking: The DNA matched Gerald Parker, a former Marine who was already serving time in prison for unrelated crimes. Parker's background and military training added a sinister layer to his profile, as he had used his skills to evade detection for years.

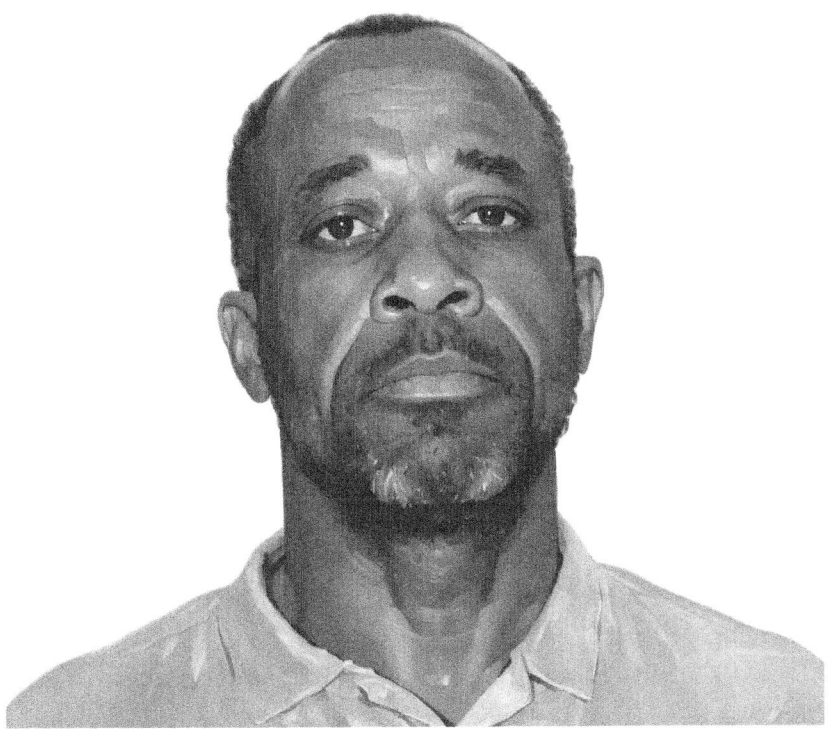

Gerald Parker

When investigators confronted Parker with the DNA evidence, he not only confessed to the Bedroom Basher murders but also revealed chilling details about the attack on Dianna Green. Parker admitted that he had been outside the Greens' apartment that night and over-heard Kevin and Dianna arguing. Watching from the shadows, he waited until Kevin left for hamburgers before making his move. He simply walked through the unlocked front door, catching Dianna completely off guard. Once inside, he brutally attacked her with calculated precision, beating her head with a wooden beam and leaving her unconscious, near death. Parker also admitted that he had learned from news reports that Kevin was a Marine, a detail that had stuck in his mind and made him feel untouchable; the blame fell squarely on Kevin. His knowledge of these specific details, including the layout of the apartment, left no doubt about his guilt.

———

Gerald Parker was born in 1955 and grew up in Southern California, where his early years were marked by a seemingly normal upbringing. He joined the Marine Corps as a young man, a decision that gave him access to specialized training and structure. However, Parker's military career masked a darker side. While he served honorably on paper, his personal life was riddled with disturbing behaviors that hinted at his violent tendencies.

In the late 1970s, Parker's name became associated with a series of unsolved rape-murders in Orange County, later attributed to the predator known as the "Bedroom Basher." His crimes followed a chilling pattern: He would break into the homes of women late at night, often targeting those who appeared vulnerable or lived alone. Once inside, Parker would attack with brutal efficiency, sexually assaulting and bludgeoning his victims to death. His opportunistic approach and use of blunt objects to inflict fatal injuries left investigators baffled, and the community was terrified.

Between 1978 and 1979, Gerald Parker attacked six women, killing five of them, and left a trail of terror throughout Southern California. His victims ranged in age and background, but all shared one tragic similarity: They were attacked with a brutal ferocity that left investigators stunned. Among his earliest known victims was Theresa Bunn, a twenty-four-year-old woman who was found murdered in her Santa Ana apartment in March 1978. That same year, in December, Parker struck again, taking the life of seventeen-year-old Cynthia Lynn Kibble, a high school student whose body was discovered in a Westminster home.

The following year saw an escalation in his crimes. In April 1979, Sandra Fry, 20, was attacked and killed in her Costa Mesa residence. Just two months later, in June, Deborah Kennedy, a twenty-four-year-old living in Buena Park, was brutally murdered. The reign of terror continued with Carolyn Kastner, a thirty-one-year-old Tustin resident who was killed in the summer of 1979. Then came the attack on Dianna Green in September 1979—which, though she survived, claimed the life of her unborn child. The following month, on October 20, Parker struck again, taking the life of seventeen-year-old Debra Lynn Senior.

Parker left more victims in his wake, though some lived to tell their harrowing stories. In early 1980, two survivors emerged: Aida Demirjian, who was attacked on February 2, and just two weeks later, a thirteen-year-old girl known as Paula S. Four years later, on February 13, 1984, David Feurtadot became Parker's final known victim when he survived a brutal attack—the last before Parker's eventual capture.

―――――

On June 20, 1996, Kevin Green walked out of prison, a free man, after sixteen years of wrongful incarceration. The emotional weight of his release was overwhelming. He expressed gratitude to those who had fought for his exoneration but also anger at the system that had stolen so many years of his life. His journey, however, was far from over. Kevin faced the challenge of rebuilding his life in a world that had moved on without him. He received $620,000 in compensation from the state of California, but no amount of money could make up for the lost time, the damage to his reputation, or the emotional toll of being branded a murderer.

For Dianna, the revelation of Gerald Parker's guilt did not bring the closure many expected. Despite the DNA evidence and Parker's confession, she continued to believe Kevin had played some role in the attack. Her long-held conviction of his guilt remained unchanged, and she later sued him for the wrongful death of their child, leading to an out-of-court settlement. The trauma of that night, her lasting injuries, and the loss of her baby were wounds that Parker's conviction could never erase.

Gerald Parker faced justice for his heinous crimes. He was convicted of multiple murders and sentenced to death in 1999. His capture and conviction brought closure to many of the families of his victims, but it also underscored the devastating consequences of the failures in the investigation of Dianna's attack. Parker's confession revealed just how close he had come to escaping accountability entirely, his crimes nearly buried beneath the weight of Kevin's wrongful conviction.

CHAPTER 10
FIVE FATAL MINUTES

Broomfield, Colorado, was not the kind of place where people expected tragedy to unfold. Nestled between Denver and Boulder, this suburban enclave of 73,000 residents was a patchwork of manicured parks, tree-lined streets, and the distant silhouette of the Rocky Mountains. It was a community where neighbors waved from front porches, children played in well-maintained parks, and the most exciting event was typically a high school football game or community barbecue.

But on a cold December morning in 2017, the veneer of suburban tranquility cracked, revealing a story so bizarre, so heart-wrenching, that it shook the community to its very core. At the center of this unfolding nightmare was Natalie Bollinger—a nineteen-year-old with dreams, struggles, and a life cut tragically short in a way no one could have anticipated.

———

Born on February 24, 1998, in Westminster, Colorado, Natalie Bollinger entered a world already marked by complexity. Along with her twin sister Alicia, she was born to Rose—a mother barely nineteen herself—and Ted Bollinger. The twins' early years were marked by change and disruption as they moved between their parents; circumstances beyond their control shaped their childhood.

Despite these challenges, Natalie developed into a young woman of remarkable resilience. Art became her sanctuary. She began drawing as soon as she could hold a crayon, creating works that captured not just images but emotions. This creative spirit, combined with an almost inexhaustible capacity for compassion, defined her character and ultimately played a crucial role in the events that unfolded.

————

At seventeen, Natalie's path intersected with that of Shawn Schwarz, a homeless man she encountered on the streets of Boulder. What began as a simple act of kindness—offering rides, sharing meals, lending an ear—spiraled into a nightmare of obsession that shadowed the final year of her life.

Their initial connection seemed almost predestined. Both were artists; Schwarz possessed a talent for photorealistic drawings that impressed Natalie. Both understood the weight of mental health struggles; Schwarz dealt with Asperger's and Tourette's syndromes and a lifetime of challenges, while Natalie carried her own burdens of depression and substance abuse. She saw in him someone society had overlooked, and her natural impulse was to help.

But compassion proved a dangerous gift.

What started as gratitude from Schwarz transformed into an overwhelming fixation. As Natalie attempted to create distance between them, his behavior grew increasingly erratic. He created multiple fake social media profiles to contact her after she blocked him. His Facebook videos became a disturbing chronicle of deteriorating mental health—rambling monologues that oscillated between praise and threats, self-pity and rage.

"I'm at war with all of you," he ranted in one particularly disturbing video. "You are my enemies. I didn't choose this!"

———

By December 2017, the situation turned unbearable. Natalie, now living with her boyfriend Joey, faced constant harassment. Her social media became a battleground, with Schwarz launching tirades against her from an ever-growing collection of fake profiles. When she blocked one account, three more appeared. His emails arrived daily, filled with alternating pleas for attention and dark threats.

On December 13, Natalie made a public Facebook post that served as both a warning and a cry for help:

> "There is a man named Shawn Schwarz… When I told him I didn't want to see him anymore, he sent me hundreds of texts and calls. He sent emails for over a year close to every day harassing me… threatening my family, telling me he'd kill himself in front of me."

The situation grew so dire that Natalie obtained a restraining order. It was a piece of paper that offered little real protection, but it marked her first official attempt to create a legal barrier between herself and her tormentor. Her messages to friends during this period painted a portrait of escalating fear.

> "If I ever go missing, he did it," she wrote to her friend Tim B. "If I end up dead, tell the cops it was him."

The weight of constant vigilance took its toll. Natalie slept with a loaded gun nearby, its presence both a comfort and a reminder of her vulnerability. Her boyfriend's Glock 9mm became a constant companion, always within reach and always loaded with a round in the chamber.

———

Behind Natalie's bright smile and artistic talent lay a complex world of untold stories. In the summer of 2016, she allegedly wrote an email to Shawn Schwarz that offered a glimpse into her past.

> "My mom left when Alicia and I were three," it read. "She was 19 and married to my father. He was cheating and beating her. My dad told her that he would kill her if she didn't leave, so she left us as well and moved to Rhode Island."

The email continued with darker revelations:

> "He had us selling drugs for him, he was hitting us and doing drugs with us while being a little too friendly, so my sister told on him, and we were put into foster care."

While the email's authenticity was never verified, public records confirmed that the twins' childhood had indeed been marked by separation, upheaval, and their father's recurring legal troubles.

These experiences left Natalie with deep scars and complex coping mechanisms. Her extraordinary capacity for empathy seemed to grow from these wounds—she understood pain so intimately that she couldn't help but recognize and respond to it in others. This same sensitivity that led her to reach out to Shawn Schwarz also made her vulnerable to darker influences.

Substance abuse became another shadow in her life. Her struggle with heroin developed alongside her dreams of becoming a trauma nurse—perhaps an attempt to transform her pain into purpose. The contrast defined her: a young woman caught between extraordinary potential and overwhelming demons.

———

In the early hours of December 28, 2017, while most of Broomfield still slept, an invisible clock began ticking. Joey Marino left for work at 6:30 a.m., bidding Natalie a quiet goodbye. She was still in bed, her phone within easy reach, as always. Neither could have known that these ordinary morning moments were the beginning of something extraordinary.

The day unfolded in fragments. A text exchange at 9:00 a.m., normal and routine. Another at 1:30 p.m., still nothing unusual. Then came the last message, four simple words that later haunted Joey:

> Someone's at the door.

Then, nothing.

When he arrived home at 3:00 p.m., the first wrong note struck him immediately: The apartment door was unlocked. Inside, the silence felt heavy. Natalie's phone lay abandoned on their bed—a detail that raised the hair on the back of his neck. She never went anywhere without it. Never.

But it was the open bottom drawer of their dresser that turned unease to dread. His Glock 9mm was missing.

The next hour became a desperate chess game against an invisible opponent. Joey's calls went out in rapid succession: to Natalie's mother, Rose, who lived in Virginia. She said Natalie had tried to call her at 2:00 p.m., but she had missed the call. Natalie's friend, Tim, who was supposed to take her motorcycle riding that day, hadn't heard from her since the morning.

Each dead end amplified the silence of the apartment. Each unanswered call made the missing gun weigh heavier on Joey's mind. Just days earlier, Natalie had obtained a restraining order against her stalker. Her words about Shawn Schwarz echoed in his memory: "If I ever go missing, he did it. If I end up dead, tell the cops it was him."

Broomfield Police Department's response was initially measured. A missing adult, gone only a few hours, was not normally cause for immediate alarm. However, as Joey described the restraining order, the missing firearm, and the threatening messages that had terrorized Natalie for months, the tenor of their questions changed.

Within hours, social media blazed with speculation. A Facebook group materialized, its members playing detective as they shared clips of Shawn Schwarz's erratic videos and threatening posts. The online mob had found its villain.

Then came the strangest twist of all. Schwarz himself joined the search efforts online. He posted on Facebook, sharing the police department's contact information and begging for help in finding her. To many, it seemed like the ultimate act of deception—a stalker hiding in plain sight among the searchers.

But as the sun set on that December day, no one had yet realized that the truth about Natalie's disappearance was far stranger than anything they could imagine.

———

On December 29, 2017, two hikers taking a morning drive along Riverdale Road made an unexpected discovery. After turning onto a gravel road near Macintosh Dairy, they spotted something near the road—a body partially concealed among the winter-bare trees.

They immediately contacted the Adams County Sheriff's Office. The scene they'd stumbled upon was stark: a young woman dressed entirely in black, fallen leaves scattered over her head and hair, the morning frost still clinging to the ground around her. Officers arriving at the scene recalled a recent BOLO alert from the Broomfield Police Department issued just the day before about a missing nineteen-year-old named Natalie Bollinger.

The physical description matched precisely: Natalie was 4'11" and about 102 pounds, with maroon-colored hair, hazel eyes, and piercings on her lip and nose. A distinctive tattoo on her left forearm—a red and black yin-yang symbol surrounded by a turquoise flower—confirmed her identity beyond any doubt.

The forensics team worked methodically in the cold morning air. They discovered a 9mm bullet casing near Natalie's body. She had died from a single gunshot wound to the temple. Despite searching the area thoroughly, including beneath her body, no firearm was found at the scene. That ruled out suicide.

A toxicology report uncovered another chilling truth—Natalie had a potentially fatal dose of heroin in her system. Whether by bullet or overdose, death had already marked its claim. If the gun hadn't ended her life, the heroin almost certainly would have.

As news of the discovery spread through the community, the case's direction shifted dramatically. The online community that had been convinced of Shawn Schwarz's guilt would soon learn that the truth behind Natalie's death was far darker and more complex than anyone had initially suspected.

————

While the online community rushed to condemn Shawn Schwarz, detectives from the Adams County Sheriff's Office pursued a more methodical approach. Their breakthrough came from the painstaking analysis of Natalie's phone records. On the day she vanished, she exchanged 111 messages with an unknown number—a number that had never appeared in her contact history before that day.

The messages began shortly after 6:30 a.m. and continued until just after noon. The number belonged to Joseph Michael Lopez, a twenty-two-year-old who lived in Thornton, Colorado. On paper, he seemed remarkably ordinary: a pizza delivery driver at Domino's, married with a seven-month-old infant, his criminal record was limited to a single seatbelt violation.

Investigators approached the case with subtle precision. They went undercover at Lopez's workplace posing as Domino's corporate executives. Through careful interviews with his colleagues, they learned that Lopez had left work early on December 28, claiming illness. His manager recalled him vomiting in the bathroom—a detail that initially seemed irrelevant but later took on darker significance.

The investigation gained sudden momentum when detectives first approached Lopez. Before they could explain their presence, he asked a question that shifted the entire trajectory of the case: "Is this about the girl from Craigslist?"

Joseph Lopez

With those six words, the investigation veered in an unexpected direction, away from the obvious suspect and toward a truth stranger than fiction.

———

What Natalie's boyfriend, Joey, didn't know was that, while he lay asleep in the stillness of that morning before Natalie vanished, she was wide awake. At 6:25 a.m., she opened her laptop and logged in to Craigslist, her fingers hovering over the keys before typing out a message that would set an unstoppable chain of events into motion. In just five minutes, everything changed. Her ad was brief, stark, and hauntingly clear: "Can you put a hit out on yourself?"

The post itself was equally direct:

> "I need someone to do this for me. I'm not trying to be saved. Not a cry for help. I've made this decision. I don't need to be talked down. I just want someone to do it for me. I'm seriously asking. This isn't a ****ing game. I just need help doing it."

Within five minutes, the post was flagged and removed from the site. However, in that brief window, it caught the attention of a twenty-two-year-old pizza delivery driver whose outwardly normal life masked impulses darker than anyone might have suspected.

———

Joseph Lopez's initial account painted him as an unlikely savior. He claimed he responded to Natalie's Craigslist post out of concern, hoping to talk her out of her suicidal intentions. His story emerged in careful layers during interrogation, each version more revealing than the last.

"I'm the type of person who will do anything to help someone stay alive," he told detectives, describing himself as an online role-player who saw an opportunity to prevent a tragedy. Cell phone GPS data told a different story, placing him exactly where Natalie's body was found.

Confronted with this evidence, Lopez's narrative shifted. First, he claimed Natalie had shot herself. When forensics proved this impossible—the bullet's trajectory clearly indicated it came from someone standing over her—his story changed again. In his final version, Lopez described a chilling scene: Natalie kneeling in the woods, a shared prayer, and him closing his eyes as he pulled the trigger.

Investigators, however, noted not only that Lopez's story had changed multiple times but also that contradictions plagued his statements. At one point, he insisted he had tried to convince Natalie not to go through with her plan. In another version, he claimed she had already injected herself with heroin before insisting that he complete the act. While forensic evidence confirmed a potentially lethal dose of heroin in Natalie's system, it remained unclear whether she had taken it voluntarily or whether it was part of Lopez's plan.

As investigators dug deeper into Lopez's background, they found disturbing details that further contradicted his claims of innocence. Years earlier, during his high school days, he had left behind a personal journal filled with stories about kidnapping, torture, and murder. While dismissed at the time as dark teenage fiction, those writings now took on an unsettling significance. The man who claimed he was trying to save a life had spent years imagining how to take one.

———

On February 8, 2018, detectives arrested Lopez at his workplace. The evidence was overwhelming: cell phone records, GPS data, and the murder weapon found in his truck alongside Natalie's purse. His shifting stories only strengthened the case against him.

The legal proceedings that followed sparked controversy. On December 14, 2018, Lopez accepted a plea deal that divided the community and devastated Natalie's family. In exchange for pleading guilty to second-degree murder, he received a forty-eight-year sentence instead of life in prison.

The courtroom on sentencing day crackled with raw emotion. Ted Bollinger, speaking from a place of barely contained rage, condemned not just Lopez but the justice system itself. "You took advantage of my daughter," he declared, his voice breaking. "She was vulnerable and drugged. You premeditated, brutally shot, and killed my baby."

Rose Bollinger clutched a framed photo of her daughter throughout the proceedings, her hands trembling with grief and anger. Beside her stood Alicia, Natalie's twin, her silence more powerful than any words —a living reminder of what was lost.

———

As public interest in Natalie's murder grew, so did speculation—and not just about the crime itself but about her family. In particular, Natalie's father, Ted Bollinger, found himself at the center of online scrutiny.

Ted had a criminal history, including past arrests and jail time, and internet sleuths quickly unearthed his record. While there was no evidence whatsoever connecting his past to Natalie's murder, it became a frequent topic in online discussions. Some questioned whether his history of legal troubles made him an unreliable figure, while others speculated about his motivations, especially after he set up a GoFundMe campaign for funeral expenses within days of Natalie's death.

The fundraising efforts sparked further controversy. Over a short period, multiple GoFundMe pages appeared under different names, each with varying monetary goals. Some saw it as a grieving father trying to cover funeral costs, while others viewed it as opportunistic.

The debate intensified when Natalie's funeral was abruptly canceled due to a dispute between Ted and his estranged wife, Rose. Critics questioned what would happen to the donations, while supporters defended Ted against what they saw as unfair assumptions.

Ultimately, no wrongdoing was ever proven regarding the fundraisers, and law enforcement never considered Ted a suspect in Natalie's murder. However, his past, coupled with the fundraising controversy, kept him at the center of speculation and further complicated an already tragic case.

————

Even after Lopez's conviction, shadows of doubt lingered. The Craigslist post—visible for just five minutes before being flagged and removed—seemed an improbable catalyst for such a tragedy. That Lopez happened to see it in that brief window strained credibility, yet investigators confirmed its existence.

The heroin in Natalie's system raised other questions. While her history with substance abuse was known, the circumstances surrounding this final, near-fatal dose remained unclear. Had she taken it voluntarily? Was it part of Lopez's plan? These questions joined others in the growing list of mysteries that survived the investigation.

Meanwhile, Shawn Schwarz, the man initially vilified by online vigilantes, retreated further into his world of social media rants and conspiracy theories. Though cleared of involvement in Natalie's death, his obsession continued. His Facebook page remained a shrine to Natalie even as he denied ever stalking her.

————

The community struggled to reconcile the various versions of Natalie they encountered through the investigation: the compassionate artist who dreamed of becoming a trauma nurse, the troubled young woman battling addiction, the frightened stalking victim sleeping with a loaded gun, and the person driven to post that fatal Craigslist ad.

In the end, she was all of these and more—a complex young woman whose life was cut short at the intersection of compassion and cruelty, hope and desperation, trust and betrayal. Her story became not just a cautionary tale about digital dangers but a reminder of how quickly and irrevocably lives can change in our interconnected world.

CHAPTER 11
THE FRANKSTON SERIAL KILLER

The seaside suburb of Frankston lies roughly twenty-five miles southeast of Melbourne, Australia. With its mix of coastal charm and suburban comfort, it was the kind of place where people left their doors unlocked and children played freely in the streets. In the winter of 1993, that sense of security would be shattered.

———

February 1993 brought the first whispers of unease to the area. Donna Vanes returned home one evening to a scene of inexplicable horror. Her cat lay dead on the laundry room floor, its body mutilated. Above it, written in what appeared to be blood, were the words, "Donna you're dead." The home had been ransacked, with drawers pulled out and cupboards opened. In the bathroom, two kittens had been killed, their bodies arranged with clinical precision. On the mirror, someone had written "Donna and Robin" in shaving cream—though Donna knew no one by that name.

The incident left Donna terrified. She moved in with her sister Tricia, where she found an unexpected source of comfort. Julia, one of Tricia's neighbors, had experienced something similarly disturbing. While away on holiday, someone had broken into her unit and methodically slashed every photograph she owned. Her engagement party dress had been cut to ribbons. Like Donna, Julia had no enemies and couldn't imagine who would harbor such malice.

Neither woman could have known then just how fortunate they were.

————

Elizabeth Stevens was eighteen years old when she arrived in Victoria from Tasmania in January 1993. She moved in with her aunt and uncle, Rita and Paul, in Patterson Avenue, Lang Warren, part of the greater Frankston area. Elizabeth was quiet and shy but unfailingly friendly to those she met. Having grown up in Tasmania, she had few friends in the area and spent most of her time reading or studying at the local TAFE college.

On Friday, June 11, Paul and Rita returned home from work to find a note on the kitchen bench. Elizabeth had gone to the TAFE library to study and expected to be home around 8:00 p.m. She was always conscientious about letting them know her whereabouts, which made her absence all the more concerning when 10:00 p.m. came and went without her return.

Paul drove out into the night, searching the streets between their home and the TAFE. The weather worked against him, with heavy rain and strong winds making visibility poor. He drove past the bus stop on Cranbourne Road where Elizabeth would have alighted, then expanded his search to the surrounding streets. By 1:00 a.m., with no sign of his niece, Paul and Rita contacted the police.

Sergeant Webster, who took the initial report, immediately sensed something was wrong. In his experience, there were missing person cases where young people had simply lost track of time while partying with friends or teenagers who had run away after an argument at home, but Elizabeth wasn't like that. She was reliable, well-behaved, and had left a clear note about her plans. She didn't have a boyfriend or many friends, and she wasn't the partying type.

The next day, a local man named Rod ventured into Lloyd Park, located on Cranbourne-Frankston Road. He was searching for a small pine tree to use as decoration for an upcoming mid-year Christmas party. As he walked along one of the tracks that wound through the scrub and trees, he made a discovery that would change everything.

————

Elizabeth Stevens' body lay in a secluded area of Lloyd Park, only a short walk from her usual bus stop. The scene confronting investigators was brutal. She had been the victim of a frenzied knife attack, with multiple stab wounds and a disturbing crisscross pattern carved into her chest. The killer had stomped on her face with such force that it broke her nose. While her top had been removed, her lower clothing remained intact. There were no signs of sexual assault.

The post-mortem would reveal a crucial detail: Elizabeth had been choked unconscious before the stabbing began. It was a detail that would later prove significant, but at the time, it was just another piece in a puzzling and horrific crime.

The heavy rain that had hampered the search for Elizabeth continued to work against investigators, washing away potential evidence. A piece of a broken knife blade was recovered—such was the force of the attack that the killer's weapon had shattered. However, it yielded no prints or other forensic evidence. Elizabeth's bag and the top half of her clothing were found nearby, soaked through and similarly devoid of clues.

Detectives began the painstaking process of interviewing everyone who might have crossed paths with Elizabeth that evening. Every student at her TAFE was checked. Some names emerged that raised eyebrows based on prior criminal history, but all were eventually eliminated from the investigation. The bus driver couldn't remember Elizabeth, and the librarians had no recollection of seeing her. Appeals for other bus passengers to come forward produced no witnesses.

In an attempt to jog memories, police set up a roadblock near Elizabeth's bus stop. They displayed a mannequin dressed in clothes similar to those Elizabeth had worn that night, hoping it might trigger recollections from passing motorists who had been in the area. They handed out pamphlets seeking information, and while people came forward with tips, none led anywhere concrete.

The investigation seemed to have hit a wall. There was no forensic evidence, no witnesses, no suspects, and no leads at all. Elizabeth Stevens' murder had all the hallmarks of a random attack—the kind that's notoriously difficult to solve.

———

Four weeks passed. On Thursday, July 8, 1993, at 5:50 p.m., forty-one-year-old Rosza Toth stepped off a train at Seaford station. She began walking along Railway Parade, past Seaford North Reserve—another grassy area surrounded by scrub and trees, not unlike Lloyd Park.

Rosza noticed a man standing near the toilet block. She didn't think much of it; there were other people around, including other passengers from the train still in the car park and the occasional car passing by. But within moments, her world would turn upside down.

The man suddenly ran up behind her, covered her mouth, and forced her to the ground. He dragged her from the footpath, past the toilet block, and into the grass. In the gathering darkness, the train station suddenly seemed impossibly far away. Rosza kicked and struggled, fighting desperately against her attacker's grip. He pressed something against her head, threatening to "blow her head off" if she didn't stop fighting.

But Rosza could tell it wasn't a real gun—the object felt wrong. When her attacker relaxed his grip, thinking his threat had worked, Rosza seized her chance. She broke free and ran straight out onto the road, screaming as loudly as she could. Her attacker fled in the opposite direction through the reserve. A passing car stopped, and the driver gave Rosza a lift home.

She survived with a badly grazed right leg, torn clothing, and some of her hair pulled out. She described her attacker as male, eighteen to twenty years old, wearing a black jacket and beanie, just under six feet tall, and with a round face and blue eyes.

That same night, only a short distance away in Cannons Creek Avenue, Seaford, twenty-two-year-old Debbie Fream was cooking dinner for a friend. Debbie had just given birth to a son twelve days earlier. Her boyfriend, Gary Blair, was at work, and she was preparing an omelet for their mutual friend, Russell Hayes, who hadn't seen her since the baby's birth.

Realizing she needed milk, Debbie told Russell she would quickly drive to the shops. She said she would be gone for only two minutes. Her son was asleep, so she left him in Russell's care. It was 7:00 p.m. when she walked out the door.

As five minutes turned to ten, then ten to twenty, Russell grew increasingly concerned. He didn't know which shop Debbie would have gone to, and he couldn't leave to look for her—not with the baby asleep inside. After an hour passed with no word from Debbie, he called the police and local hospitals to check if there had been any accidents. There hadn't been.

He called Gary Blair at work. Gary arranged to leave early, and one of Debbie's friends came to look after the baby while Gary and Russell drove around searching for Debbie or her gray Pulsar. They checked the local shops where she might have gone and drove through surrounding streets, but they found no trace of her or the car. Finally, they headed to Frankston Police Station to report her missing.

They waited anxiously throughout the night, hoping to hear from Debbie or receive some information about her whereabouts, but there was nothing. Debbie Fream had vanished into thin air.

———

Police didn't wait long to link the attack on Rosza Toth with Debbie Fream's disappearance. The timing was too close to ignore—the incidents occurred within an hour of each other. Debbie lived near Cannons Creek train station, just one stop south of Seaford station where Rosza was attacked. Both locations were only a short drive from Lloyd Park, where Elizabeth Stevens had been found just weeks before.

Even without connecting these incidents, Debbie's disappearance raised immediate red flags. She had dinner cooking on the stove, a guest waiting, and a twelve-day-old son at home. Nothing about her vanishing made sense.

A search was organized along nearby Cannons Creek. Divers probed the waters while teams combed through the thick bush surrounding the area. Their efforts yielded nothing, but witness reports started painting a disturbing picture. Several people came forward describing a gray Pulsar—the same as Debbie's car—driving erratically through the streets of Frankston that night, swerving and flashing its lights at passing cars. Was Debbie trying to signal for help?

The next day, detectives working the case drove past a gray Pulsar parked outside a Christian Center on Madden Street in Seaford, just over a mile from where Debbie had disappeared. A quick check confirmed it was her car. The front passenger door was unlocked, and there was a fresh dent in the center of the hood—damage that Gary Blair later confirmed hadn't been there before.

The forensic examination of the car revealed ominous signs. Traces of Debbie's blood were found inside. However, what caught investigators' attention was the driver's seat—it was pushed all the way back. Debbie was a small woman; there was no way she would have had the seat in that position. Someone else had driven her car there.

———

Four days after Debbie's disappearance, a local farmer was checking the fence line on his property along Taylor's Road in Carrum Downs. The area was pure farmland, a quiet and isolated spot about a fifteen-minute drive from where Debbie had vanished. Under some large fern trees along his fence line, He spotted what he initially thought was illegally dumped rubbish. As he got closer, he thought he was looking at a mannequin—perhaps someone's idea of a practical joke. The reality was far worse.

That morning, the farmer had read a front-page newspaper article about Debbie Fream's disappearance. Now, he stood frozen, knowing he had found her. Police arrived and secured the scene. The similarities to Elizabeth Stevens' murder were impossible to ignore. Debbie had been subjected to a brutal knife attack with no signs of sexual assault. Like Elizabeth, she had been strangled before being stabbed. Debbie's arms and hands bore numerous defensive wounds—evidence of her desperate fight for survival.

Just as with the Elizabeth Stevens crime scene, not a single piece of forensic evidence was found. The killer was either extremely lucky or extremely careful. Or both.

———

The media coverage was relentless. The Frankston area was completely gripped by fear. Two young women had been brutally murdered, another attacked, all within weeks of each other. The randomness of the attacks was perhaps the most terrifying aspect.

These weren't crimes of passion or revenge; they appeared to be the work of someone choosing victims simply because they were in the wrong place at the wrong time.

People began changing their habits. Many wouldn't venture out at night, and most wouldn't go anywhere alone. Suspicious glances were cast at strangers—was that person the killer? Some residents put their houses on the market, desperate to leave the area. However, sales dried up; nobody wanted to move into a community stalked by what the media was now openly calling a serial killer.

Women started arming themselves with makeshift weapons—hockey sticks, cricket bats, even carrying oven cleaner in their handbags to spray in the eyes of potential attackers. Enrollment in self-defense classes skyrocketed. The fear was palpable, hanging over the community like a dark cloud.

In response to the growing hysteria, police launched Operation Reassurance. The Frankston area was flooded with extra officers—a high-visibility operation designed to make the public feel safe and hopefully deter further attacks. Unfortunately, the killer wasn't finished.

———

On Friday, July 30, just three weeks after Debbie Fream's murder, a postal worker was delivering mail on her motorbike along Sky Road in Frankston. Around 2:30 p.m., she noticed an old, rusted yellow Toyota Corona with no number plates. It was parked opposite the entrance to a bike track that ran between two golf courses—a shortcut frequently used by local students.

The track was overgrown, with a high wire fence running down each side. Thick scrub and trees pressed against the fence, making it invisible from both the road and the golf courses. The postal worker observed a man with a chubby face sitting in the driver's seat wearing a dark-colored cap. As she rode past, he slouched down as if trying to avoid being seen.

Something about the scene bothered her. Given recent events in the area, she decided to call the police. She pulled into a nearby driveway and asked to use the phone. As she did so, she noticed a schoolgirl walking along Sky Road headed toward the track.

The girl was seventeen-year-old Natalie Russell, a Year 12 student at John Paul College located just off Sky Road. Natalie had finished the day with a free period and was heading home early to study for an upcoming exam. Just two days earlier, her school's principal had warned students at an assembly to avoid shortcuts home, specifically mentioning the bike track. But Natalie, like many others, continued to use it. It was a much quicker route home to Frankston North.

What neither Natalie nor the postal worker could know was that they were being watched. The man in the yellow Toyota had been waiting for just such an opportunity.

———

Police responded to the postal worker's call about the suspicious vehicle on Sky Road, but by the time they arrived, the yellow Toyota was empty. They conducted a quick door knock of nearby houses but got nothing useful. The afternoon was drawing to a close, and students were starting to stream out of school, scattering in all directions. When a call about an armed robbery came over the radio, the officers had to leave.

A few students ventured down the bike track that afternoon. One noticed a shoe lying in the middle of the path. It was right next to a hole cut in the fence that led into the thick scrub. Another student recalled seeing a man walking hurriedly toward him along the track, head down, hands thrust deep into his pockets. The fear that initially gripped the young witness quickly passed when the man continued walking by without a word.

At 8:00 p.m. that night, Natalie Russell's family reported her missing. The report was treated with immediate urgency—Natalie was always home before dark and called her parents unfailingly if her plans changed. She had never run away before. When police learned about the bike track she used to walk home, they quickly organized a search.

They found several holes cut into the wire fence along the track. Through the third hole, deep in the scrub and trees, they discovered Natalie's body. Like Elizabeth Stevens and Debbie Fream before her, Natalie had been the victim of a relentless knife attack. She had numerous defensive injuries—evidence, like the others, that she had fought desperately for her life. Once again, there were no signs of sexual assault.

But this time, the killer had made mistakes.

————

The crime scene examination the next morning proved crucial. Blood was found on the outline of the hole cut in the fence. A small piece of skin, which appeared to be from someone's finger or hand, was located at the scene. About ten small dark hairs that didn't belong to Natalie were found clutched in her hand—she had managed to grab some of her attacker's hair during the struggle. Two leather straps stained with blood were also found at the scene.

Perhaps most importantly, the cuts in the fence could potentially be matched to whatever tool had been used to make them. For the first time, investigators had substantial physical evidence to work with.

As the forensic examination continued, the two police officers who had responded to the suspicious vehicle call the day before approached detectives. Though the car had no plates, they had recorded the registration number from the sticker on the windshield. That number led them to Paul Charles Denyer.

————

Detectives arrived at Denyer's Frankston North home that afternoon. The small apartment on Dandenong Road was sparsely furnished and cluttered, but what struck them most was Denyer's demeanor. Here was a man being questioned about brutal murders in his community, yet he displayed an unnerving calm, almost an eagerness, to speak with them.

Paul Charles Denyer

At first glance, Denyer seemed unremarkable. Overweight, with a baby face that made him look younger than his twenty-one years, he wasn't what most would picture when imagining a killer. He sat casually in his messy apartment, his girlfriend Sharon by his side, and began methodically answering their questions with an air of someone discussing the weather rather than multiple homicides.

The first red flags appeared when they noticed his hands. Fresh cuts marked his fingers and palms, including significant gashes on his middle finger and thumb. When questioned, Denyer launched into a detailed explanation about car repairs, describing work on the fan and alternator. His story was precise—too precise, as if rehearsed.

But it was his next responses that truly chilled the detectives. Without prompting, Denyer began placing himself at or near the scenes of both Elizabeth Stevens' and Debbie Fream's murders. For Elizabeth's murder, he described walking in the rain that night, searching for a spare car battery, coincidentally near Lloyd Park. For Debbie's murder, he volunteered that he had been at Cannons Creek train station, just around the corner from where she had disappeared.

Most suspects, when questioned about murders, try to distance themselves from the crimes. Denyer was doing the opposite. It was almost as if he was playing a game, seeing how close he could step to the truth without crossing the line. His eyes showed not fear or concern but something closer to satisfaction, perhaps even enjoyment.

When detectives suggested continuing their conversation at the police station, Denyer readily agreed. He didn't ask for a lawyer. He didn't seem worried. If anything, he appeared almost eager to accompany them, as if he had been waiting for this moment. As they left the apartment, one detective later recalled that it felt less like they were leading a suspect to questioning and more like they were being led themselves—straight into the mind of a killer who had been yearning to tell his story.

————

The interview room at Frankston Police Station felt charged with tension as two homicide detectives began their questioning at 9:20 p.m. on July 31. They advised Denyer of his right to remain silent and his right to legal representation. He waved these off with unsettling casualness. "I'm happy to talk," he said, as if settling in for a friendly chat rather than an interrogation about three brutal murders.

For hours, the detectives methodically dismantled Denyer's story. His timeline of car troubles didn't add up. His explanations for his injuries grew increasingly convoluted. Yet through it all, he maintained an almost surreal calm—until they mentioned DNA testing.

The mere suggestion of blood and hair samples cracked his composed façade. During a break in questioning, Denyer noticed one detective's cross visible beneath his shirt. What followed was a bizarre conversation about religion followed by pointed questions about DNA evidence. How long would the tests take? Had they found anything at the scenes? The detectives could almost see the calculations running behind his eyes.

Then, without preamble or drama, Denyer simply said,

"Okay, I killed all three of them."

What followed was one of the most chilling confessions in Australian criminal history. For five hours, Denyer recounted each murder with the detached precision of someone describing a mundane task. He didn't just confess; he seemed to savor each detail, speaking without emotion or remorse.

He described making a crude gun from an aluminum pipe to threaten Elizabeth Stevens, forcing her into Lloyd Park. "I started choking her with my hands," he explained, demonstrating the grip position as casually as if teaching a sports technique. He recounted waiting in Debbie Fream's car at the milk bar, forcing her to drive when he revealed himself. He detailed how he had pre-cut the holes in the fence along Natalie's track, lying in wait with obvious premeditation.

The investigators had heard many confessions over their careers, but this was different. Most killers show something during confession—remorse, anger, fear. Denyer displayed nothing. When asked why he killed these women, his response was devastating in its simplicity:

"I just wanted to."

He explained that he had fantasized about killing since age fourteen, stalking his potential victims for years while waiting for what he called "that silent alarm to trigger me off."

Even more disturbing was his demeanor when describing the victims' final moments. He recalled Elizabeth's death tremors, Debbie's desperate offers of money, Natalie's final screams—all with the same flat affect one might use to describe yesterday's breakfast. The only time he showed any animation was when he described his own cleverness in evading detection or the techniques he used to kill.

When he finished his confession in the early hours of the morning, he appeared almost relieved, as if he had unburdened himself of a secret he'd been eager to share. The investigators, hardened by years of police work, were shaken. They had sought justice for three grieving families and a terrified community. Instead, they had stared into an abyss of pure evil, one that wore an unremarkable face and spoke in measured tones about unspeakable acts.

Their only consolation was that Paul Charles Denyer would never walk the streets of Frankston again—or so they thought.

———

Paul Charles Denyer was charged with three counts of murder and one count of abduction. While awaiting trial, he underwent extensive psychological evaluation. The clinical psychologist who examined him observed something particularly disturbing—not only did Denyer show no remorse, but he appeared to take pleasure in discussing the murders in detail. He showed behaviors consistent with what they called sadistic personality disorder at the time, demonstrating a pattern of cruel, aggressive behavior and deriving satisfaction from others' suffering.

On December 15, 1993, Denyer appeared before the Supreme Court of Victoria. He entered guilty pleas to all charges. During the proceedings, the court heard expert testimony about his psychological state and the calculated nature of his crimes. The prosecution detailed how his murders had escalated in both violence and premeditation, from the opportunistic attack on Elizabeth Stevens to the carefully planned murder of Natalie Russell.

On December 20, 1993, the court handed down its sentence. Denyer received three terms of life imprisonment plus eight years for the abduction charge. The judge, describing him as a danger to society, ordered that he serve his sentence without the possibility of parole.

However, this wasn't the end of the legal process. In July 1994, Denyer's lawyers successfully appealed the no-parole aspect of his sentence. In a controversial 2-1 decision, three appeal court judges overturned the original no-parole period, instead setting a minimum term of thirty years. This meant Denyer would become eligible for parole at age fifty-one in 2023. When that time came, he did apply for parole but was denied.

———

In a cruel twist that emerged years later, investigators learned that Denyer had been living next door to Tricia Vanes, whose sister Donna had experienced the terrifying break-in and cat mutilation in February 1993. Denyer admitted to those crimes as well, saying he had intended to kill Donna that night, but she hadn't been home. Denyer had even told Donna afterward that if police found who was responsible, he would "take care of them" for her.

In 2003, ten years into his sentence, Denyer began identifying as transgender, asking to be called Paula and requesting gender reassignment surgery at the taxpayer's expense. This development raised eyebrows, particularly given that his supposed hatred of women had been his claimed motive for the murders. In letters from prison, Denyer attempted to reframe his crimes, suggesting that his murders were an attempt to "destroy" his suppressed feelings about his gender identity. However, investigators noted this explanation contradicted his original confessions and psychological evaluations, where gender identity had never been mentioned. The prison system rejected his requests for hormone therapy and gender reassignment surgery. By 2014, Denyer had reverted to identifying as Paul and no longer maintained claims of being transgender. Some experts, including Dr. Darren Russell (brother of victim Natalie Russell), who coincidentally was a leading expert in transgender health, found this reversal highly unusual, noting that it is very uncommon for truly transgender individuals to revert to their birth gender.

CHAPTER 12
THE MISSION VALLEY MALL MURDERS

C hristmas in San Diego carries its own particular magic. While other parts of the country might be blanketed in snow, in Southern California, the holiday season brings mild temperatures and palm trees wrapped in twinkling lights. In December 2013, the Westfield Mission Valley Mall embodied this Southern California holiday spirit. Located in a sprawling commercial district nestled between highways and hills, the mall was a cornerstone of local life, its parking lots filling each day with shoppers hunting for last-minute gifts.

For twenty-two-year-old Ilona Flint, the extended holiday hours at the Cathy Jean shoe store meant extra shifts but also extra pay. She didn't mind; she and her fiancé, twenty-eight-year-old Gianni Belvedere, were building their future together. Their story had begun seven years earlier in Provo, Utah, when Ilona was just fifteen, newly arrived from Russia. In Gianni, she found not just love but a sense of belonging in her adopted country. When Gianni and his family moved to San Diego to open an Italian restaurant, Ilona followed, unable to imagine life without him.

The Belvedere family had welcomed her completely. Gianni's younger brother, twenty-two-year-old Salvatore—known to everyone as Sal—had become like her own brother. The three were inseparable, sharing Sunday dinners where the musically talented brothers would perform for the family, filling the house with laughter and song. They worked together at the family restaurant, dreaming of expanding the business, while Ilona took retail jobs to help save for their future.

None of them could have known that on this mild December night, as holiday music played softly through the mall's speakers and the last shoppers hurried through decorated corridors, their lives were about to intersect with a troubled stranger whose motorcycle had just broken down in the parking lot outside.

———

At 12:22 a.m. on December 24, 2013, Ilona clocked out from her shift. The mall was finally winding down for the truly last-minute Christmas shoppers. She stepped into the cool night air, automatically reaching for her phone to check in with Gianni, who always picked her up after work.

But tonight, something was different. Gianni wasn't answering.

The sprawling parking lot, still dotted with cars but growing emptier by the minute, suddenly felt vast and exposed. After several unanswered calls, each one increasing her sense of unease, Ilona did what had become second nature when she needed help—she called Sal.

The close-knit nature of the Belvedere family meant that Sal didn't hesitate. He jumped into his black sedan and headed to the mall immediately. This behavior was completely out of character for his brother. Gianni was reliable and responsible—the kind of person who always answered his phone and never left anyone waiting, especially not Ilona.

As the early hours of Christmas Eve set in, Sal and Ilona sat in his car, methodically calling hospitals and even local jails. Each dead end only heightened their anxiety. The festive lights that still illuminated the mall's exterior now cast strange shadows across the parking lot, and the holiday music drifting faintly from the building seemed increasingly divergent with their growing sense of dread.

At 1:14 a.m., Ilona made what would be her final phone call. The 911 dispatcher's question was simple: "Where are you?"

"I've been shot," Ilona managed to say, her voice already fading. "Mission Valley Mall."

Then silence.

———

When police arrived minutes later at the 1600 block of Camino Del Rio North, the scene they encountered would haunt even veteran officers. Sal's black sedan sat under the harsh glare of parking lot lights, its windows reflecting the still-blinking Christmas decorations. Inside, they found Ilona slumped in the passenger seat, a single gunshot wound to the back of her head having ended her young life. Sal, grievously wounded with shots to his head and torso, clung to life as paramedics rushed him to the hospital.

The crime scene told a puzzling story. Shell casings from a .22 caliber weapon were found in the car, but strangely, no witnesses reported hearing gunshots—an odd detail that would later prove crucial to solving the case. A mall employee who later spoke to police reported seeing a man of average height standing by the driver's side window. The witness described watching this figure walk away and drive off in a vehicle that matched the description of Gianni's dark green 2004 Toyota Camry.

———

The shootings cast an immediate pall over San Diego's holiday season. In a city known for its gentle weather and easy lifestyle, such violence felt particularly jarring. The Mission Valley area, with its mix of retail centers, restaurants, and office complexes, had always represented the comfortable heart of middle-class San Diego life. Now, yellow crime scene tape and police floodlights cast harsh shadows across its familiar landscape.

For the Belvedere family, the nightmare deepened with each passing hour. While Sal fought for his life in the intensive care unit, Gianni's continued absence defied explanation. The family's Italian restaurant, usually filled with the warmth of holiday celebrations, stood dark and silent. Regular customers called constantly, offering help, seeking updates, and sharing in the family's anguish.

Three days after the shooting, on December 27, the family's hopes were dealt another crushing blow. Despite the doctors' best efforts, Sal succumbed to his injuries. The loss of the younger brother was devastating enough, but Gianni's unknown fate added an almost unbearable weight to the family's grief.

Lieutenant Mike Hastings, a twenty-year veteran of the San Diego Police Department's homicide unit, found himself increasingly troubled by the case's peculiarities. In a press conference held in the mall's parking lot, now crowded with news vans instead of holiday shoppers, he shared what little they knew: Gianni's last known contact had been a phone call with his cousin at 11:45 p.m. on December 23, in which he said he was headed to pick up Ilona. His phone had gone dark immediately after, never to be activated again. His credit cards remained untouched. The dark green Toyota Camry, with its distinctive Utah license plates, had vanished as completely as its owner.

The investigation began with the obvious questions. Could this have been a robbery gone wrong? But nothing had been taken from Ilona or Sal. A drug deal, perhaps? However, background checks showed no history of drug involvement. A love triangle? Those who knew the victims scoffed at the notion. Ilona and Gianni's relationship

150

was rock-solid, and their future plans were already taking shape. Plus, Sal had been protective of both his brother and future sister-in-law, considering Ilona family from the moment she entered their lives.

———

As December gave way to January, the case took on an almost mythic quality in local media. The timing—Christmas Eve—and the victims' youth and innocence made the story impossible to ignore. The mall itself became a sort of macabre tourist attraction, with people driving slowly past the spot where Sal's car had been found, trying to make sense of the senseless.

The police investigation continued methodically, but each new lead seemed to end in frustration. Surveillance cameras that might have captured crucial evidence were discovered to be malfunctioning that night—a detail that would later spark legal action against the mall's management. Witnesses described seeing a man wearing tan pants and a black hoodie with distinctive white bands around the bicep area, but these descriptions led nowhere.

The Belvedere and Flint families held vigils. On December 28, over 150 people gathered at La Jolla Shores, one of Ilona's favorite places, to remember the young woman who had crossed an ocean to find love, only to have it ended by violence. "We're all on this boat of we don't know what's going on," one friend told the assembled crowd. "We just don't know, and it is mind-blowing how little information there is out there."

A few days later, on New Year's Day 2014, another hundred mourners assembled at Crystal Pier in Pacific Beach to honor Sal. The location had been chosen because it was his favorite surfing spot, a place where he had found joy in San Diego's endless summers. The contrast between the beautiful setting and the harsh reality of his death seemed to emphasize the senselessness of it all.

Through it all, the family maintained hope for Gianni. They announced a $10,000 reward for information leading to his safe return. His uncle, Paul Donato, made public pleas:

> "If you've seen the car, seen him, think you've seen him, please report it to Crime Stoppers, San Diego PD, to the news media, anybody. We need any clues we can get our hands on to bring him home, to put a little closure to this whole nightmare that we're living right now."

———

January 17, 2014, dawned cool and clear in Riverside, California. The city, some 100 miles north of San Diego, had no apparent connection to the Mission Valley case. However, at 11:45 a.m., local police received a call about a foul odor emanating from a green Toyota Camry parked outside a fast-food restaurant.

The responding officers immediately noticed the blood staining the passenger seat. When they opened the trunk, they found what everyone had feared but no one had wanted to believe: Gianni's decomposing body, identified later through dental records. He had been shot behind the left ear—an execution-style wound that spoke of close-range brutality.

The killer had attempted to mask the evidence of their crime. Cans of Febreze air freshener were found in the trunk, their triggers taped down in a crude but methodical attempt to continuously emit scent. Boxes of Arm & Hammer baking soda had been scattered around the body. The attention to these details suggested both planning and a desperate attempt to buy time.

Forensics teams processed the scene meticulously. They collected a single black hair from the tape used on the air fresheners and dusted the gas cap for fingerprints, knowing the killer must have refueled during the journey to Riverside. Each piece of evidence was carefully cataloged and sent to the lab, where it lay waiting for the final piece of the puzzle—a match that would come from an unexpected source.

For the Belvedere family, this discovery marked the end of hope but not the end of questions. Who could have done this? Why? How had their sons, raised in a close-knit family and pursuing their American dream through hard work at their restaurant, become victims of such calculated violence? And how had Ilona, who had found her own American dream in their family, been caught in the same web of violence?

The answers would come, but not from any of the usual sources. No eyewitnesses would step forward with crucial information, and no confession would suddenly break the case. Instead, the key to unlocking the mystery of the Mission Valley Mall murders would emerge from a routine traffic stop, an illegal weapons charge, and a DNA database that finally connected the seemingly random dots of this tragic puzzle.

———

On January 18, 2014, just one day after the discovery of Gianni's body, a white Ford Explorer approached the Border Patrol checkpoint near San Clemente. The checkpoint, a familiar sight to Southern California drivers, sits along Interstate 5 about halfway between San Diego and Los Angeles. On this particular day, an agent noticed something unusual about the driver—a sort of vacant, emotionless demeanor that raised immediate concerns.

The driver, when questioned, said he was headed to a shooting range in San Bernardino. It might have been an innocent enough explanation, but something about his affect prompted the agent to look closer. In the back seat lay a suspicious weapons case.

What they found inside the vehicle would later prove to be key to unlocking the Mission Valley Mall murders, though nobody knew it at the time. The arsenal was disturbing: an AR-15-style assault rifle equipped with three fully loaded ten-round magazines and two fully loaded thirty-round magazines, a .45 caliber semi-automatic handgun with three fully loaded magazines and a spare barrel, a .22 caliber semi-automatic handgun with two loaded magazines, and perhaps most tellingly, a homemade silencer hidden in the SUV's center console.

The driver was identified as twenty-nine-year-old Carlo Mercado. While two of the weapons were legally registered to him, the modifications and unregistered firearms—particularly the homemade silencer—resulted in their immediate confiscation. Yet, without any obvious connection to the Mission Valley case, Mercado was released. The California Department of Justice began building a case regarding the weapons violations, but it seemed, at first, to be an entirely separate matter from the triple homicide that had shocked San Diego.

———

As investigators would later discover, Carlo Mercado's path to violence had begun long before that December night at Mission Valley Mall. Born and raised in San Diego to what was described as a traditional family, Mercado had struggled with emotional issues from an early age. Former schoolmates remembered him as a shy, introverted child who frequently found himself the target of bullies. These early experiences seemed to shape his personality in troubling ways, leading to episodes of aggressive and paranoid behavior that would only intensify with time.

Carlo Mercado

In early adulthood, Mercado began showing more pronounced signs of mental health issues. He was diagnosed with schizoaffective disorder, a complex condition that combined symptoms of schizophrenia —including hallucinations and delusions—with severe mood disorders like depression or mania. Despite the diagnosis, reports indicated that he rarely adhered to recommended treatments. This was a decision that would have devastating consequences.

Between 2012 and 2013, Mercado's mental state deteriorated significantly. He lost his job at a convenience store due to conflicts with coworkers and faced mounting financial difficulties. It was during this period that he began actively collecting weapons, a behavior that caught the attention of acquaintances but somehow failed to prompt serious intervention.

His interactions with others grew increasingly erratic. In August 2012, when he rear-ended a truck, he then sent what was described as an "aggressive" email to the other driver, meticulously listing motorcycle parts and their prices and demanding over $2,000 in compensation but offering to settle for half that amount. When the other driver, after consulting with his insurance company, ignored these demands, Mercado's response was a series of increasingly hostile messages.

Perhaps most tellingly, Mercado's digital footprint began to reflect his darkening mindset. He set his iPhone's display name to "Assassin," his computer searches focused increasingly on movies about hitmen and professional killers, and in what would later prove to be a chilling detail, his calendar entry for December 24, 2013, contained a single, ominous notation: "RIP."

The break in the case came through modern forensic science and, ironically, Mercado's own legal troubles. In April 2014, as part of a plea deal related to the illegal silencer found at the Border Patrol checkpoint, Mercado's DNA was collected and uploaded to CODIS, the Combined DNA Index System. Within twenty-four hours, investigators received the match they had been waiting for.

The DNA found on the tape used to secure the air fresheners in Gianni's trunk matched Mercado's profile perfectly. Suddenly, investigators had a solid lead. When they began digging deeper, other pieces fell into place quickly. Cell phone records placed Mercado's phone in the vicinity of the mall on the night of the murders. The .22 caliber handgun confiscated at the checkpoint matched the ballistics from all three shootings. The homemade silencer explained why no witnesses had heard gunshots during Ilona's 911 call.

Yet one question remained maddeningly elusive: Why? Despite an exhaustive investigation, no connection could be found between Mercado and his victims. Their paths had never crossed in the year leading up to the killings. The randomness of the violence made it all the more terrifying—these were truly victims of circumstance, in the wrong place at the wrong time.

————

On June 20, 2014, Carlo Mercado was arrested and charged with three counts of first-degree murder. What followed was nearly three years of legal proceedings complicated by questions about Mercado's mental competency to stand trial.

The proceedings revealed more about Mercado's troubled state of mind. On July 26, 2016, he attempted suicide in his cell at San Diego Central Jail, overdosing alongside his cellmate. He survived and was hospitalized for about a month before returning to custody.

His defense team argued strenuously that he was incompetent to stand trial. In November 2014, Judge Joseph P. Brannigan agreed, ordering Mercado to be treated at Patton State Hospital until he could assist in his own defense. The decision was later reversed, with another judge ruling in December 2015 that Mercado was indeed competent to face the charges against him.

Throughout the proceedings, Mercado's behavior remained eerily consistent with witness descriptions from the Border Patrol checkpoint: emotionless, vacant, and disconnected from the gravity of his actions. During hearings, he would stare blankly ahead or look down at the table, showing no reaction as evidence of his crimes was presented.

Finally, on January 12, 2017, Mercado changed his plea to guilty, accepting three consecutive life terms without the possibility of parole in exchange for avoiding the death penalty.

————

Only after Mercado's guilty plea did investigators finally piece together the complete sequence of events from that December night. The tragedy began with something as mundane as a broken-down motorcycle in the parking lot of Mission Valley Mall.

Around 11:30 p.m. on December 23, Carlo Mercado's motorcycle broke down near the Mission Valley Mall. At the same time, Gianni Belvedere was in the parking lot outside Macy's. Deputy District Attorney Brian Erickson would later explain that Mercado approached Gianni's car and may have attempted to carjack him. The confrontation ended with Mercado shooting Gianni. After shooting him, Mercado pushed Gianni's body into the trunk, where he bled out in his own car.

Mercado then drove Gianni's car to Mira Mesa to fill it with gas before returning to the mall to retrieve his motorcycle. Meanwhile, unaware of what had happened to Gianni, Ilona finished her shift at the Cathy Jean shoe store at 12:22 a.m. When she couldn't reach Gianni by phone, she called his brother Sal for help.

Sal came to the mall, and together, they sat in his car, calling hospitals and jails, desperately trying to locate Gianni. Around 1:14 a.m., their search took a fatal turn. They spotted Gianni's car returning to the parking lot—Mercado had come back to retrieve his abandoned motorcycle, never expecting to encounter anyone who would recognize the vehicle. When they confronted the unfamiliar driver, Ilona quickly realized something was terribly wrong and dialed 911. She only managed to give her location before Mercado opened fire with his .22 caliber weapon —the same gun that had killed Gianni now claimed two more victims in the darkness of what should have been a festive holiday night.

The silencer on Mercado's gun explained one of the case's early mysteries—why no gunshots were heard on Ilona's call to emergency services. After shooting both Sal and Ilona, Mercado fled the scene again in Gianni's car.

In the days that followed, Mercado's actions revealed both calculation and increasing desperation. He attached fake license plates to Gianni's car and parked it near his home and workplace in Mira Mesa. While Gianni's body decomposed in the trunk, Mercado went to the Target store where he worked and purchased Febreze air fresheners to mask the growing odor. At one point, he even tried to sell the stolen vehicle.

Finally, he drove the car to Riverside and abandoned it in a shopping center parking lot more than 100 miles from the scene of his crimes. In a final attempt to cover his tracks, he rented a U-Haul truck with a trailer to retrieve his motorcycle from the mall parking lot. The motorcycle fell off during transport, leading him to file an insurance claim—one more seemingly ordinary action that would later help investigators establish the timeline of events.

———

On January 12, 2017, in a San Diego courtroom, Judge Frederic Link prepared to pass sentence on Carlo Mercado. The families of the victims were present carrying photographs of their loved ones. The judge ordered Mercado to look at each image, to face the full weight of what he had taken from the world.

When given the opportunity to address the families, Mercado glanced at his lawyers and uttered a single word: "No." His affect remained flat, his expression blank as Judge Link handed down three consecutive life sentences without the possibility of parole, telling him simply, "Sir, you will never get out of prison."

Antoinette Belvedere, sister to Sal and Gianni, read a letter from their mother that laid bare the family's devastation:

> "The unbearable pain is to stay, for all of these difficult and heartbreaking years—three years that feel like thirty. May God continue to grant me the grace and courage and strength to somehow endure."

The letter spoke of Sunday night family dinners, once filled with the brothers' musical performances and laughter, now marked by silence and empty chairs. Ilona's mother, Inga, spoke of her daughter's promise, of dreams cut short just as they were beginning to take shape.

———

San Diego County Deputy District Attorney Brian Erickson emphasized the random nature of the crimes, a fact that made them all the more terrifying.

 "Gianni, Salvatore, and Ilona had nothing to do with their demise," he stated. "And I know people have a hard time accepting that because they think, 'Oh, they must've done something.' They didn't. They didn't do anything. This could have been any one of us in that parking lot that night."

The case raised difficult questions about mental health intervention and public safety. Mercado's diagnosed schizoaffective disorder, his increasing isolation, and his weapons collecting were all warning signs that somehow failed to trigger meaningful intervention. The legal proceedings, with their back-and-forth over his competency to stand trial, highlighted the challenges of addressing mental illness within the criminal justice system.

The Westfield Mission Valley Mall became the target of legal action by the victims' families, who questioned the property's security measures. Why weren't the surveillance cameras working on such a busy holiday shopping night? Why wasn't there better lighting in the parking lots? These questions led to calls for legislation mandating improved security measures at shopping centers.

———

The Mission Valley Mall murders changed how many San Diegans viewed their city. In a place known for its easy lifestyle and year-round sunshine, the case served as a stark reminder of how quickly violence can shatter the illusion of safety. The holiday season, in particular, would never be quite the same for those who remembered the events of 2013.

CHAPTER 13
BONUS CHAPTER: THE GIFT SHOP MURDER

April 15, 1992. While most Americans were rushing to mail their tax returns, life in Agawam, Massachusetts, moved at its usual steady pace. Located just south of Springfield, where the Connecticut River curved through the valley, Agawam was a working-class town of 27,000 people carving out their piece of the American dream. The streets told the story of a place caught between old New England charm and modern suburban growth—colonial homes shared neighborhoods with newer developments, while shopping plazas and small businesses served the community's changing needs.

Main Street reflected this blend of old and new. Mom-and-pop shops operated alongside chain stores, and neighbors still greeted each other by name even as the town grew with an influx of new residents drawn to its convenient location. The shopping plaza on Springfield Street exemplified this evolution, housing a collection of local businesses that served as gathering spots for the community. Among them was Brittany's Card and Gift Shop, a practical space wedged between a sandwich shop and other local stores.

Brittany's was a staple of daily life in Agawam. Its aisles were lined with greeting cards for every occasion, seasonal decorations, and small gifts. In spring 1992, the shelves brimmed with Easter merchandise, pastel-colored cards, stuffed bunnies, and ceramic eggs filling the displays. The store's reliable presence in the community was matched by its staff, who knew many customers by name and kept track of local birthdays and anniversaries.

————

Among those who worked at Brittany's was Lisa Ziegert, a twenty-four-year-old teacher's aide at Agawam Middle School. Lisa had the kind of presence that made an impression, with curly brown hair, bright blue eyes, and a laugh that could lift anyone's spirits. She was small in stature but carried herself with warmth and purpose, especially when working with her special education students.

Teaching was more than a job for Lisa; it was her calling. She worked part-time as an aide while pursuing her dream of becoming a full-time special education teacher. Her colleagues noted her natural ability to connect with students, particularly those who needed extra attention and care. To supplement her income while working toward her goals, she took the evening shift at Brittany's, where her friendly demeanor and helpful nature made her a favorite among regular customers.

————

April 15 began like any other Wednesday. Lisa finished her day at the middle school, where she had spent hours helping students with their coursework and providing the individual attention they needed. By 5:00 p.m., she had arrived at Brittany's to begin her evening shift, settling into the familiar routine of straightening merchandise and greeting customers.

At 5:30, Lisa's sister Lynn stopped by the store. The sisters shared a close relationship, and these casual visits were common. They talked about Lisa's aspirations, her work with the students, and her plans for the future. Lynn would later recall how ordinary the conversation felt —two sisters chatting about life's everyday moments and dreams yet to be realized.

The evening continued at its normal pace. Customers came and went, purchasing last-minute greeting cards and small gifts. A receipt time-stamped at 8:20 p.m. showed a routine transaction, and the customer who made the purchase later confirmed that everything had seemed normal during their visit. Lisa had been her usual friendly self, helping them find what they needed with her characteristic attention to detail.

But something changed in the following hour. At 9:00 p.m., as the store was preparing to close, another customer entered Brittany's. The lights were still on, and the door was unlocked, but Lisa wasn't visible in the main area of the store. The customer, feeling uneasy about the empty shop floor, heard an unusual banging noise coming from the storage area. Uncertain what to make of it and not wanting to investigate, they left without making a purchase.

———

The next morning dawned crisp and bright as Sophia Maynard pulled into the parking lot of Brittany's to open the store. Her routine morning shift took an immediate turn when she spotted Lisa's familiar car, still parked where it had been the evening before. The sight stopped her cold. Lisa was meticulous about her responsibilities, never leaving work unfinished. The morning sun glinted off the car's empty windows, and Sophia felt the first ripple of unease course through her.

Inside, the store felt wrong. The fluorescent lights that should have been dark hummed overhead, casting their harsh glow over the silent aisles. The front door had been unlocked all night. At the counter, Lisa's personal belongings lay exactly where she always kept them during her shift—her purse and car keys tucked beneath the register. A radio played softly somewhere in the background, its cheerful morning show creating an eerie contrast to the untouched scene before her.

The wrongness of it all intensified as Sophia approached the storage room. Here, the careful order of the store dissolved into chaos. Boxes lay toppled and scattered, their contents spilled across the floor like evidence of a struggle no one had witnessed. The back door hung open, creaking softly in the morning air. The familiar scent of the store—paper, ink, and birthday cake candles—now seemed to carry an undertone of something ominous. Sophia backed away from the scene, her instincts screaming that something terrible had happened in this room. Without touching anything else, she fled to the sandwich shop next door and called the police.

———

Law enforcement responded quickly, transforming the quiet shopping plaza into a hive of activity. Officers cordoned off the store with yellow crime scene tape while investigators began their methodical work inside. They discovered scuff marks on the back door, suggesting a struggle. More ominously, they also found small amounts of blood on some of the scattered boxes.

Meanwhile, at Agawam Middle School, Lisa's absence from her morning shift had already raised alarms. She was known for her reliability and dedication to her students. When calls to her home went unanswered, concerned colleagues contacted her family. The Ziegerts rushed to the gift shop only to find the police presence and a growing sense of dread.

As investigators pieced together the timeline, they learned of the customer who had entered the store at around 9:00 p.m. the previous night. The witness's account of the banging noise from the storage room took on new significance. Another key detail emerged from a woman who had been driving home around 9:15 p.m. While stopped at the intersection of Route 75 and Adams Street, she had noticed a Ford Bronco pulled over near a wooded area, with a man in the front seat and what appeared to be someone in the back. The vehicle had then driven into the woods.

———

The next four days saw an unprecedented mobilization of law enforcement and community resources. Multiple agencies converged on Agawam—local police, Massachusetts State Police, and the FBI joined forces in what became one of the area's largest missing persons investigations. Volunteers from Agawam and the surrounding communities formed search parties that methodically combed through wooded areas, fields, and back roads. Posters with Lisa's photo appeared in shop windows and on telephone poles throughout the region. Each passing hour weighed heavily on the searchers, but the community refused to give up hope.

Easter Sunday, April 19, 1992, began like the previous three days— with determination and dread. That morning, a resident decided to take his dog for a walk in the woods near Route 75. The area was rural and isolated, with no houses nearby. It wasn't a visible turn-off from the main road; someone would need to know the area to find it. As he walked deeper into the wooded area, he discovered something that would shatter the community's last hopes.

Investigators quickly secured the scene. They found Lisa's body in a clearing, partially concealed. The location itself spoke volumes to investigators—this wasn't a random spot chosen in panic. Whoever had left Lisa here was intimately familiar with the area, comfortable enough with these backwoods to navigate them in darkness. The scene held crucial evidence: Lisa had been sexually assaulted and stabbed approximately six times. Despite the devastating nature of the discovery, investigators were meticulous in processing the scene, collecting DNA evidence from Lisa's body—biological evidence left behind by her attacker during the sexual assault.

That evening, a detective from the Agawam Police Department made the hardest walk of his career: up the front steps of the Ziegert family home.

Lisa's mother would later recall the moment. "He said we found her, and I went, 'She's dead, isn't she?' And he had tears in his eyes." The detective's emotional response spoke to how deeply Lisa's case had affected everyone in the community.

In 1992, DNA technology was still in its early stages. While investigators could develop a profile from the evidence they had collected, there was no database to match it against. The evidence would wait years for science to catch up, but its preservation would prove crucial to eventually solving the case.

———

The impact of Lisa's murder rippled through Agawam with devastating force. The comfortable assumption of safety in this suburban community evaporated overnight. Women began taking self-defense classes and applying for firearm permits, while parents kept closer watch over their children. Brittany's Card and Gift Shop, once a cheerful fixture of daily life, stood empty and dark, its windows covered with brown paper.

The investigation generated hundreds of leads. Residents called in tips about suspicious vehicles and unusual behavior. Men throughout the community voluntarily provided DNA samples for testing. Local investigators worked tirelessly, conducting interviews and following up on every possible lead. Yet, despite their efforts, the case grew cold.

In the vacuum of concrete answers, rumors flourished. The community's need to make sense of the senseless led to speculation and finger-pointing. Ed Bugatti, a friend of Lisa's sister, found himself under particular scrutiny. Despite having a solid alibi—he had been working at his restaurant that night, witnessed by family and friends —the cloud of suspicion would hang over him for years.

———

As months turned into years, Lisa's case remained active, but progress was slow. Investigators had their most promising piece of evidence— the killer's DNA—but in the 1990s, this was like having a key without knowing which lock it might fit. Hundreds of men in the community voluntarily provided DNA samples, each test raising hopes only to dash them again when no match was found.

Throughout these years, the Ziegert family kept Lisa's memory alive. They established a scholarship in her name at Agawam High School to help future teachers pursue their dreams as Lisa had pursued hers. Her desk at the middle school became a memorial, a reminder of the vibrant young woman who had touched so many lives.

The investigation files grew thick with witness statements, tips, and leads that went nowhere. Among them was a statement from Joyce McDonald, the estranged wife of a local man named Gary Schara. In the years following Lisa's murder, McDonald had contacted police through her attorney, claiming that Schara had been unusually obsessed with the case. She mentioned that he had purchased a music box from Brittany's shortly before the murder. However, McDonald was in the midst of a bitter custody dispute with Schara and struggled with alcohol dependency. Her claims, like many others, were filed away.

———

By 2015, DNA technology had advanced dramatically. The Hampden County District Attorney's office learned of a cutting-edge technique called DNA phenotyping—a process that could predict a person's physical characteristics from their genetic material. The DNA sample from Lisa's case, carefully preserved for twenty-three years, might finally have a story to tell.

Gary Schara

Working with a Virginia laboratory, investigators used this technology to create a composite image of the killer. The analysis predicted a man with a fair to very fair complexion, brown or hazel eyes, and brown or black hair. When the composite was released to the public, it renewed interest in the case and prompted investigators to revisit old files with fresh eyes.

This revival of the investigation led to a new strategy. Rather than waiting for a match in DNA databases, investigators compiled a list of persons of interest who had refused to provide DNA samples over the years. Through a novel legal approach, they obtained court orders compelling these individuals to submit samples.

The list contained eleven names. Among them was Gary Schara, who had refused to provide a DNA sample in 2008, claiming a fear of being cloned. He had maintained a low profile in the community, leading an apparently normal life; he had worked various jobs, dated, and even attended his high school reunion in 2015.

————

September 13, 2017, marked the beginning of the end. When Massachusetts State Police investigators arrived at Gary Schara's residence with a court order for his DNA, they found he wasn't home. His roommate was there alone and promised to relay their message: State troopers had been by and were looking for him. When Schara later received this simple message from his roommate, it must have carried the weight of inevitability. After twenty-five years of keeping his secret, the moment he had dreaded had finally arrived.

That evening, Schara reached out to his girlfriend, Noel Delaurier, asking to spend the night at her house. Nothing in his manner betrayed the turmoil within. This was the same man who had recently decorated Christmas cookies with her, who drove a shuttle for a rental car company, who shared her love of dogs and Agatha Christie novels. The man who wore Batman t-shirts and identified with Bruce Wayne had seemed, to all outward appearances, utterly ordinary.

The next day, Schara disappeared, but not before leaving three carefully composed letters at Noel's home. The first letter, addressed to Noel herself, began as a love letter but quickly turned dark. He told her she was about to learn awful things about him—specifically, that he had murdered a woman twenty-five years ago. In his detailed confession, he acknowledged his complete guilt while claiming he hadn't initially intended to kill. The letter laid bare his lifelong struggles, describing disturbing fantasies of abduction and bondage that had haunted him since childhood—thoughts he claimed he could never escape. Looking back on the decades since the murder, he wrote about his self-hatred and admitted to considering turning himself in hundreds of times, but he also confessed that cowardice had always held him back.

The second letter contained his last will and testament, a final accounting of a life about to end. The third letter was perhaps the most poignant—an apology to Lisa's family that attempted to address twenty-five years of their pain and loss.

For Noel, finding these letters shattered the image of the man she had known. This was someone who had seemed thoughtful and romantic, who had never shown her anything but kindness. Yet here in her hands was evidence that he had lived a double life for decades, carrying the weight of an unspeakable crime while going about his daily routine. She didn't hesitate long with her decision. Despite their relationship, despite the complex person she had known, she gathered the letters and took them to the nearest State Police barracks.

———

Police tracked Schara's cell phone to a Connecticut hospital, where he had gone after attempting suicide with ibuprofen. He was arrested and extradited to Massachusetts. DNA testing confirmed what his letters had confessed—he was Lisa's killer. The composite generated through phenotyping had proven remarkably accurate.

In 2019, twenty-seven years after Lisa's death, Gary Schara stood before a judge and pleaded guilty to first-degree murder. He was sentenced to life in prison without the possibility of parole. In the courtroom, Lisa's family finally had the opportunity to face the man who had haunted their lives for so long.

The resolution brought complicated emotions to Agawam. For Ed Bugatti, it meant the end of decades of undeserved suspicion. For Gary Schara's ex-wife, Joyce McDonald, it was validation of her early suspicions, though it brought no joy. For the investigators who had worked the case over the years, it demonstrated the value of persistence and advancing technology.

Yet questions remained. How had Schara managed to live among them for so long while carrying this terrible secret? He had walked the same streets and shopped in the same stores even as the community grieved. His letters spoke of remorse, but they offered no real explanation for why he had chosen Lisa, why that night, or why at all.

———

Lisa's family continued the scholarship program they had established in her name, ensuring that her dream of teaching lived on through others. The middle school where she had worked created a memorial garden, a peaceful space where students and staff could reflect on her impact on their lives. Her passion for special education inspired others to enter the field, creating a legacy of caring and dedication that extended far beyond her brief time as a teacher's aide.

For Lisa's sister Lynn, the case's resolution brought an end to decades of wondering every time she passed someone on the street—could that person be the killer? For her parents, it meant no more anxious calls every time a news report mentioned a breakthrough in the case. The community could finally lay to rest the suspicions that had damaged relationships and trust.

The gift shop where Lisa worked never reopened. The space was eventually renovated and became something else entirely, but long-time residents still referred to it as "Brittany's" —a linguistic reminder of how deeply the case had embedded itself in the community's consciousness. The wooded area where she was found was cleared and developed, erasing the physical reminder of the tragedy while symbolizing the town's determination to move forward.

Gary Schara's guilty plea meant there would be no trial, no lengthy appeals process, and no need for Lisa's family to relive their pain in court. His confession letters, while providing closure, offered little comfort. They revealed a man who had lived for decades with the weight of his crime, yet he had chosen silence while a community suffered and an innocent man endured suspicion.

The case files, stretching back to 1992, tell a story of persistence. They document the evolution of criminal investigation from an era of paper files and basic DNA testing to the age of genetic phenotyping and digital databases. But beyond the technological advances, they reveal the human element that never wavered—investigators who refused to let the case go cold, family members who kept Lisa's memory alive, and a community that never forgot.

TRUE CRIME

CASE HISTORIES

VOL. 17

12 DISTURBING TRUE CRIME STORIES

JASON NEAL

INTRODUCTION

If you've read the previous volumes of *True Crime Case Histories*, you already know what to expect—stories of real crimes, carefully reconstructed and presented without censorship or sensationalism.

If this is your first time, consider this a brief warning: These aren't dramatizations or sanitized summaries. These stories can be graphic and disturbing. Oftentimes, true crime television shows or news stories can gloss over the gruesome parts, but in my books, I do my best to give you every detail, regardless of how unsettling they may be.

I include these details not to sensationalize, but to provide readers with a deeper understanding of the killer's mind. Although it might be impossible for us to grasp their motives fully, the sheer magnitude of their depravity will keep you turning pages.

Each story in this book has been meticulously researched using court transcripts, police files, autopsy reports, and first-hand testimony. Many are little-known cases, long forgotten by the media but remembered all too vividly by the people they affected.

Many of the stories in this volume were suggested by readers who remembered them from their own hometowns or were personally affected by the events. Some are recent, others decades old, but all are shocking.

Each of these cases reveals something different: calculated cruelty, unchecked obsession, shattered families, and the staggering depths of human depravity. Some were solved by luck, others by science. A few almost got away.

For case photos, court records, and bonus materials related to this volume, please visit:

TrueCrimeCaseHistories.com/vol17

To join my mailing list for updates and a free e-book, visit:

TrueCrimeCaseHistories.com

Thanks for reading,

Jason Neal

CHAPTER 1
THE BUTCHER OF ABERDEEN

Aberdeen is a quaint coal mining town nestled in the fertile Hunter Valley of New South Wales, Australia. With a population of just under 2,000 people, it's the kind of place where everyone knows everyone else's business. This sleepy community sits about 180 miles north of Sydney among rolling hills and pastures dotted with cattle and sheep. Historic buildings dating back to the 1800s line its main street, giving it a charming old-world feel that masks the horror that would unfold there one fateful night.

Most residents work in the nearby coal mines or on surrounding farms. Life moves at a steady pace in Aberdeen—people wave to each other on the street, gather at the local pub after work, and generally keep to themselves. It's not the sort of place where you'd expect to find yourself at the center of national headlines.

That all changed on a late February night in 2000, when this peaceful town became the setting for one of the most disturbing crimes in Australian history—a horror so gruesome that it would make hardened police officers vomit at the scene.

In the late afternoon of February 29, John Price finished his shift at the local mines where he'd worked for seventeen years. The forty-five-year-old father of three had warned his coworkers earlier that same day, "If I'm not here tomorrow, it's because Kath killed me." Those ominous words would come to haunt everyone who knew him.

Just hours earlier, Price had appeared before a magistrate to take out a restraining order against his partner, Katherine Knight. The pair had been in a volatile relationship for five years, and Price had finally reached his breaking point. Katherine Knight had stabbed him in the chest during an argument a few days before, and although the wound wasn't severe, it served as a clear-cut warning—one that, unfortunately, came too late.

That night, Price stopped at a neighbor's house before heading home. During the visit, he seemed agitated but attempted to conceal it through casual conversation. As night came, he said goodnight to his friends. He walked home the short distance to his simple one-story house, not knowing it was his last night on Earth.

Meanwhile, Katherine Knight was on a path toward something unspeakable—an eruption of violence that would soon horrify the entire nation.

————

Katherine Mary Knight was born in October 1955 to a dysfunctional family in the small town of Tenterfield, about 270 miles north of Sydney. Her early life was marred by violence and instability. She claimed she had been sexually abused by several male relatives throughout her childhood, though her claims were never verified. Meanwhile, former classmates remembered her as a bully who exhibited aggressive behavior from an early age.

Katherine's adulthood followed the turbulent pattern of her childhood. At nineteen, she married David Kellett in 1974. This marriage set the tone for her future relationships. On their wedding night, an inebriated Kellett fell asleep after sex, and Katherine, in a rage at feeling ignored, tried to strangle him. This incident was a precursor to the violence to come.

Katherine's explosive outbursts punctuated their marriage. In one incident, while she was in the later stages of her pregnancy, she struck Kellett in the back of the head with a frying pan as he returned home after a darts competition. Kellett sought medical treatment for a fractured skull, but Katherine convinced him to drop the charges.

After their first child was born in 1976, Kellett left Katherine for another woman. Katherine's reaction was extreme: She kidnapped their infant daughter and placed the baby on railroad tracks before threatening a woman at knifepoint and taking a young boy hostage. Police subdued her and transported her to a psychiatric hospital. However, she was released shortly after. Remarkably, Kellett was so frightened by Katherine's actions that he returned to Aberdeen to support her. The couple had another daughter in 1980, but by 1984, Katherine had left Kellett for good.

Katherine's later relationships followed the same violent pattern. In the late 1980s, she lived with David Saunders, a local miner. Her jealousy manifested in horrifying ways. She wanted to teach Saunders a lesson about cheating, so she cut the throat of his two-month-old dingo puppy right in front of him. Then she knocked him unconscious with a frying pan. Despite this traumatic episode, they remained together and had a child in 1988. However, after Katherine attacked Saunders with an iron and stabbed him with scissors, he fled into hiding. Katherine then filed a police report claiming she was the victim of abuse and obtained a restraining order against Saunders.

After that relationship fell apart, Knight then took up with John Chillingworth, with whom she had a son in 1992. A few years later, she left Chillingworth for John Price.

Throughout these tumultuous years, Katherine built a career as a slaughterhouse worker at the local meat processing plant. She excelled in the environment and was known for her skill with knives and cleavers. She took pride in her work, decorating the walls of her home with animal skins, skulls, and butchering tools—a macabre foreshadowing of the horror to come.

By all accounts, Katherine Knight was a walking contradiction. She could be charming and hardworking, but she could also explode into violent rages at the slightest provocation. Psychiatric evaluations later revealed she suffered from borderline personality disorder, a condition often linked to childhood trauma and characterized by unstable relationships and impulsive aggression. However, experts emphasized that this condition did not render her incapable of distinguishing right from wrong.

John Price came into Katherine Knight's life around 1995. Born the same year as Knight, Price was well-liked in Aberdeen, described by friends as a "terrific bloke" who was generous and outgoing. After divorcing in 1988, he lived with two of his three children in the home where he would ultimately meet his tragic end.

When John and Katherine began dating, the locals expressed concern. Price knew about Knight's violent reputation but believed his love would change her. Price often described the early days of their relationship as "a bunch of roses," and his children reportedly liked Katherine. To outsiders, they appeared to be a normal couple despite the occasional argument.

Over time, however, the relationship deteriorated. In 1998, Katherine wanted to get married, but John refused. In retaliation, she sent a video to Price's employer showing items she claimed he had stolen from work—outdated medical kits he had scavenged from company trash. Despite their minimal value, Price was fired from his job of seventeen years. Furious at this betrayal, Price kicked Knight out of his house and ended the relationship.

Astonishingly, they eventually reconciled, but on Price's terms. He allowed Knight to spend time with him but refused to let her move back into his home or share his finances. This arrangement only increased Knight's insecurity and resentment, and their fighting intensified. Many of Price's friends avoided him whenever Knight was around, unwilling to tolerate the drama she brought.

By February 2000, their relationship had reached a breaking point. Katherine's erratic behavior had escalated, culminating in her stabbing Price in the chest during an argument. Though the wound wasn't fatal, it was the wake-up call Price needed. On February 28, 2000, he went to court and obtained a restraining order against Knight. That same day, he confided to coworkers that he feared for his life, even telling one colleague that if he didn't show up for work the next day, it would mean Knight had killed him.

Price went home that night, even with the restraining order and his fears; he worried that Katherine might hurt his kids if he stayed away. It was a decision that would cost him his life.

On the evening of February 29, 2000, John Price behaved as usual after work, spending time with neighbors before returning home around 11:00 p.m. Unknown to Price, Knight had already arranged for his two older children to stay at a friend's house that night, ensuring he would be alone. When Price arrived home, Knight wasn't there, and he went to bed just after 11:00 p.m.

Meanwhile, Knight was preparing for her final, gruesome confrontation. That afternoon, she had purchased a new black lingerie outfit and made strange comments to her children while videotaping them, almost as if recording a farewell message. She arrived at Price's house later that night while he was asleep. With chilling composure, she let herself in, watched television briefly, and took a shower before waking Price.

Wearing the black negligee, Knight initiated sex with Price, and he obliged. For a fleeting moment, the horrific events to follow were delayed by a façade of intimacy. Price then fell asleep, unaware that his partner was merely lulling him into a false sense of security.

In the early hours of March 1, 2000, Katherine Knight retrieved a large butcher's knife and attacked John Price as he slept. The first thrust pierced his chest, jolting him awake into a living nightmare. Blood evidence later showed that Price made a frantic attempt to escape. Injured and bleeding, he staggered out of his bedroom and down the hall, trying to reach either the front door or a light switch.

Knight pursued him through the house as he struggled to escape. Price made it to the front door and got outside, leaving a trail of blood in the doorway. However, he either collapsed from blood loss on the porch, or Knight dragged him back inside. He fell in the hallway just inside the house, where he bled to death from his numerous injuries. An autopsy would later reveal at least thirty-seven stab wounds to his front and back, with damage to several vital organs.

But Katherine Knight's night of horror had only begun. In the aftermath of the killing, she exhibited a level of calm, calculated butchery that defies comprehension. According to the investigation, Knight left the house shortly after the murder and drove into town to withdraw $1,000 from Price's bank account via ATM. She then returned to the blood-soaked home and set about mutilating Price's body with the expertise her career had afforded her.

Katherine Knight

Using her razor-sharp knives and years of meat-working experience, Katherine Knight skinned Price's entire corpse. She removed his skin in one piece with remarkable skill and a steady hand, achieving one full pelt that included the skin of his face, ears, nose, torso, genitals, and limbs. She then hung this skin on a meat hook affixed to the top frame of the lounge room door. The forensic pathologist later found that the skin was so intact that it could be re-sewn onto Price's body during the autopsy, demonstrating the precision of Knight's flaying work.

Knight then decapitated Price, cutting off his head and carrying it into the kitchen, before she proceeded to cook some of his body parts. She placed his decapitated head in a large pot on the stove, added vegeta-

bles—potatoes, pumpkin, cabbage, zucchini, squash, and beetroot—
and boiled them together to create a macabre stew.

She also sliced off strips of flesh from Price's buttocks and baked
them in the oven with more vegetables. Once these "roasts" were
done, Knight arranged the cooked meat and vegetables on dinner
plates as if serving a meal. She set two place settings at the dining
table, complete with notes beside each plate bearing the names of
Price's children. Knight intended to serve this horrific cannibal feast
to Price's son and daughter—a final act of perverse brutality.

Knight then took Price's head out of the pot and placed it in a serving
dish. She arranged what remained of his decapitated, skinless body on
the living room floor. In a final bizarre gesture of contempt, Knight
posed the body by crossing Price's legs and draping his left arm over
an empty soda bottle as if in a casual lounging position.

Near the body, Knight left a handwritten note atop a photograph of
Price, serving as a twisted justification for her actions. Scrawled with
blood and bits of flesh, the note accused Price of terrible crimes,
including raping her daughter and abusing his own children. The
accusations were entirely groundless, as investigators would later
confirm.

Having staged this grotesque scene, Knight attempted to take her own
life—or at least render herself unconscious by swallowing a large
number of pills. She later claimed this was a suicide attempt, but the
amount she took was not lethal. It caused her to lose consciousness
and slip into a comatose state on the floor of the home, which was
how the police would find her when they arrived.

At 6:00 a.m. on March 1, 2000, neighbors noticed something was
amiss at John Price's house. His work truck was in the driveway,
which was unusual because he usually left early for his job. Concerned
coworkers, remembering Price's ominous warning, sent a colleague to
check on him when he didn't show up for work. That colleague and a
worried neighbor met at the house. They knocked on the bedroom

window and called out, but there was no response. Through a door-way, they spotted what looked like blood smears on the front door and immediately contacted the police.

Local Aberdeen police arrived at the scene shortly after receiving the call. Two officers approached the front door, where they saw blood on the door frame. Receiving no answer, they forced entry into the house and encountered a scene so ghastly that many of the responding officers would later need counseling.

In the entryway and hall, they discovered Price's headless, skinned body lying on the floor, grotesquely draped over a bottle. His skin was hanging nearby. On the kitchen table, police found two place settings with meals prepared—plates of cooked meat and vegetables, each labeled with a note bearing Price's children's names. The food was still warm, with a pot on the stove gently simmering with the horrific stew.

Amid this carnage, officers found Katherine Knight unconscious on the floor in a bedroom, having overdosed on pills. Knight showed no immediate reaction as the officers secured the scene. They had to carry her out on a stretcher, given her comatose state, and an ambulance rushed her to the hospital for treatment.

With Knight in custody, investigators began the grim task of processing the crime scene. They took photographs, many of which authorities deemed so graphic that they sealed them from public access. Forensic examiners documented the extensive blood trails throughout the house, showing the path of Price's futile escape attempt and the struggle. A butcher's knife, one of Knight's own from her work kit, lay coated with Price's blood near the bed.

The autopsy confirmed the ferocity of the attack: at least thirty-seven stab wounds, deep and penetrating, including injuries to vital organs such as the lungs, liver, and aorta. Many wounds were on the front of the body, but numerous stab injuries were also found on his back, indicating he had been stabbed from behind as he tried to escape.

Defensive wounds on Price's hands and arms showed he had tried to ward off the knife. The pathologist also cataloged the post-mortem mutilations: the complete skinning, decapitation, and butchering of the body.

When Katherine Knight awoke from her drugged stupor at the hospital, she initially claimed to have no memory of what had happened the night before. She feigned confusion and amnesia when the police began questioning her. However, the evidence was overwhelming. On March 2, 2000, as soon as she was physically well enough, Katherine Knight was formally charged with the murder of John Price.

The brutality of Katherine Knight's crime posed a challenge to the New South Wales justice system. She was arraigned in March 2001 and, defying the evidence, entered a plea of not guilty. The trial was scheduled for July 2001 but had to be postponed when one of Knight's attorneys fell ill. It was rescheduled for October 15, 2001.

When the trial date arrived, the court took extraordinary precautions in anticipation of the graphic evidence to be presented. The presiding judge addressed the sixty potential jurors and gave them an unprecedented warning: Because of the extremely disturbing photographs and details they would see, anyone could opt out of serving on the jury if they felt unable to handle it. Five people accepted the excuse and were dismissed immediately.

To everyone's surprise, before any testimony was heard, Knight's defense team announced that she would change her plea to guilty. Knight had instructed her attorneys to seek a plea change after hearing the prosecution's opening statement, possibly realizing the futility of contesting the case. The trial was abruptly aborted on its second day.

The judge adjourned proceedings for the day and ordered a psychiatric evaluation to ensure that Knight was mentally fit to make a guilty plea and understood the consequences. Two psychiatrists examined her and found that while Knight did have borderline personality disorder, she was sane and knew right from wrong. They also noted Knight's claims of amnesia regarding the crime, but they did not find these claims credible enough to prevent her plea. Satisfied that the plea was voluntary, the judge reconvened the court. On October 18, 2001, Katherine Knight's guilty plea to the murder of John Price was formally accepted.

Knight never gave any official reason for her sudden reversal to a guilty plea. Some speculate that the mountain of evidence—and perhaps the prospect of seeing the photographic proof of her deeds displayed in court—prompted her to concede. Still, despite pleading guilty, she refused to fully accept responsibility for the act and continued to claim memory loss about the mutilation and cannibalism.

During the sentencing hearing in November 2001, Knight's lawyers petitioned to have her excused from hearing the gory details of her own crime, presumably to spare her feelings. The judge denied the request. When the pathologist took the stand and methodically described the condition of Price's body, Knight broke down in the dock, sobbing and wailing. She became so hysterical that the court adjourned, and she had to be sedated.

On November 8, 2001, the judge delivered a scathing sentencing judgment. He recounted the viciousness of the attack and the almost unimaginable defilement of Price's body. He noted that Knight had been motivated by spite and vengeance, essentially punishing Price for trying to leave her. The judge emphasized how meticulously and calmly Knight had committed the post-mortem acts, showing cognition, planning, and surgical precision. Far from an uncontrollable frenzy, her actions were calculated, indicating she took a form of satisfaction in them.

Given the extreme and unprecedented nature of the crime, the judge concluded that only the harshest penalty available was appropriate. Knight's history of violence and lack of remorse led him to deem her an ongoing danger to society. He sentenced Katherine Mary Knight to life imprisonment and refused to set any non-parole period, meaning there was to be no possibility of release. Furthermore, he ordered that her prison papers be marked "Never to be Released"—an order never before imposed on a woman in Australia. With that, Katherine Knight became the first Australian woman to receive a true life sentence without parole.

Knight showed little reaction to the sentence. Price's family expressed relief at the outcome, feeling that anything less than life without parole would not have been justice for John.

In 2006, Knight appealed her sentence to the New South Wales Court of Criminal Appeal. She did not contest her conviction, only the penalty. Her lawyers argued that a life sentence without parole was too harsh. They pointed out her plea and personal circumstances, and they also claimed the judge did not fully consider Knight's mental state. They noted her alleged psychotic episode during the crime and her history of trauma and abuse.

The Crown prosecutor argued that the sentencing judge had looked at all key factors. They stated that the sentence matched the crime's severity. In September 2006, the court dismissed Knight's appeal. The chief justice noted, "This was an appalling crime, almost beyond contemplation in a civilized society." The appellate court found no mistakes in the original sentence; they agreed that Knight's actions fell into the most heinous category imaginable.

Katherine Knight was moved to Silverwater Women's Correctional Centre in New South Wales to serve her life sentence. Her inmate file displayed "Never to be Released" in bold letters.

In prison, Knight has reportedly been a relatively compliant prisoner. She has taken on a "mother hen" role among inmates, working as a mentor and mediating minor disputes between other prisoners. By 2017, officials noted that Knight had a clean prison record with no violent incidents within the facility. Now in her late 60s, Katherine

Knight will die in custody, having exhausted her appeals and with no possibility of parole.

When details of the killing emerged in the media, news outlets struggled with how to report the extreme gore. Many included warnings due to the graphic content. The tabloids dubbed Katherine Knight "Australia's Hannibal Lecter" and called her a "cannibal killer"—although technically, there was no confirmed act of cannibalism since Knight didn't get to feed anyone the food. Still, the intended cannibalism cemented her infamy.

The police officers who worked the case were profoundly affected. The first officer on the scene knew John Price personally, making the discovery even more traumatic. Police officers who witnessed the scene required counseling and time off to recover from the psychological toll.

The Katherine Knight case prompted considerable analysis from psychologists, criminologists, and law enforcement professionals. It also challenged stereotypes about female offenders, as women rarely commit such savage acts of violence. Furthermore, Knight's borderline personality disorder, while significant, did not explain or excuse her behavior. Experts emphasized that Knight knew exactly what she was doing, noting that her actions demonstrated planning and goal-oriented anger, not psychosis or loss of reality.

Experts largely disregarded Knight's claims of amnesia. While memory can be unreliable during high stress or intoxication, most agreed she was neither in a fugue state nor hallucinating. The court psychiatrist and later commentators saw her "I don't remember it" defense as a convenient way to avoid talking about the gruesome details.

Criminologists have remarked on how rare it is for a female perpetrator to commit this kind of crime. Women commit a small fraction of homicides overall, and when they do, the circumstances are usually very different, often defensive or involving abuse or less violent methods like poison. Knight's case shattered assumptions about female killers.

Those who knew John Price quietly honor his memory. While Knight gained notorious headlines, Price's family sought privacy. At the sentencing, one of Price's relatives submitted a statement saying that John was a kind, loving man and that Knight had taken a father away from his children in an unimaginably cruel manner. Price's children expressed relief at the sentence through police representatives and asked others to remember their father not for how he died but for how he lived—as a hardworking man who loved his kids and helped others.

Many people in Aberdeen avoided the murder house for years. It stayed empty until it was renovated and got a new look. Residents say that, even decades later, the town hasn't forgotten what happened at that house on that leap day in 2000. It remains a grim point of local lore and a source of lingering sadness.

CHAPTER 2
THE HOUSE ON LANGWORTHY ROAD

The winter of 1992 in Manchester, England, was particularly cold. A bitter chill had settled over the industrial city's east side, where rows of modest houses lined narrow streets in the working-class neighborhood of Moston. The Christmas lights that decorated some of the homes created a cheerful veneer, but behind the doors of 97 Langworthy Road, a horror was unfolding that would shock even the most seasoned detectives.

On December 14, 1992, two men driving along a remote country lane near Werneth Low, about thirteen miles southeast of Manchester, noticed what appeared to be a badly injured person stumbling toward the road. As they approached, they were confronted with a sight that would haunt them for the rest of their lives.

A teenage girl—her body charred black, her skin peeling away in patches, and her hair completely burned off—was desperately waving her arm to flag them down. She was naked except for a thin skirt, and despite her horrific injuries, she managed to rasp out through scorched vocal cords: "Help me. I'm Suzanne Capper."

The motorists wrapped her shivering body in a jacket and called for an ambulance. Before losing consciousness, Suzanne made sure they knew exactly who had done this to her, naming each of her tormentors: "Bernadette, Jean, Glyn, Cliff, Jeff, and Anthony."

Suzanne Capper was sixteen years old. She had third-degree burns over eighty percent of her body, and doctors were astounded that she was still alive. But Suzanne was determined to tell her story—to ensure that the people who had kidnapped her, tortured her for a week, and set her on fire would not escape justice.

Four days later, despite the best efforts of medical staff, Suzanne Capper died from multiple organ failure. However, she had lived just long enough to identify her killers and set in motion a murder investigation that would uncover one of the most sadistic crimes in British history.

———

Suzanne Jane Capper was born in 1976 and grew up on Manchester's east side. Her early life was marked by instability. Her biological father left before she was born, and her mother, Elizabeth, struggled to provide a stable home. When Elizabeth's second marriage dissolved, fourteen-year-old Suzanne was briefly placed in local government care, feeling effectively abandoned.

Those who knew Suzanne described her as a gentle, timid girl desperate for acceptance. By her mid-teens, Suzanne had begun skipping school and drifting, seeking friendship wherever she could.

Unfortunately, her search for connection led her to the door of twenty-six-year-old Jean Powell's home on Langworthy Road in Moston. Jean was a single mother of three young children, and Suzanne sometimes babysat for her and even stayed overnight. To Suzanne, this arrangement provided the semblance of friendship and family she desperately craved.

What Suzanne didn't realize was that Powell's home was a hub for petty criminals and drug users. Living there, along with Jean and her kids, was twenty-four-year-old Bernadette McNeilly and her children. Jean's younger brother, eighteen-year-old Clifford Pook, and Bernadette's teenage boyfriend, sixteen-year-old Anthony Dudson, were frequent visitors. Jeffrey Leigh, a twenty-six-year-old ex-convict, also stopped by often to buy or use amphetamines. Finally, Jean's estranged husband, twenty-nine-year-old Glyn Powell, was another regular visitor.

This motley crew of adults and teenagers was essentially the only group of friends Suzanne had. In August 1992, alarmed by the "evil new friends" gathering at Powell's home, Suzanne's older sister Michelle moved out of the neighborhood. Suzanne, however, continued to spend time at the house on Langworthy Road, perhaps too naïve to recognize the danger.

———

By early December 1992, several trivial resentments toward Suzanne had festered within the Powell/McNeilly circle. Jean Powell had recently accused Suzanne of trying to push her into an unwanted sexual encounter with a man the group referred to as "the Arab." In late November, Jean and Suzanne had met a man named Mohammed Yussif in the town of Sale. He had allegedly propositioned Jean, and she later claimed that Suzanne had "tried to make me go with an Arab."

Around the same time, Bernadette McNeilly and Anthony Dudson had contracted pubic lice, which they concluded "had been caught from Suzanne," who often slept in their bed at the house. They seethed at her over this embarrassment. On top of it all, Bernadette also believed that Suzanne had stolen a pink coat worth £50 that belonged to her.

These absurdly small slights—a rejected sexual advance, a case of lice, and a missing coat—coalesced into a motive for revenge.

On December 7, 1992, Jean Powell and Bernadette McNeilly decided to act on their grudges. They showed up at the house of Suzanne's stepfather, where Suzanne was then living, and told her that a boy she had a crush on was at Powell's home and wanted to see her. This was a lie designed to lure out the love-struck teenager.

Suzanne went willingly with Jean and Bernadette, but when she stepped through the door at 97 Langworthy Road, the trap sprang. There was no boy waiting—instead, Anthony Dudson and Glyn Powell immediately ambushed Suzanne.

———

Almost as soon as she arrived, the group struck Suzanne with brute force. She was punched and beaten viciously and knocked to the floor. At one point, they struck her with a large wooden instrument—a three-foot-long wooden fork—as a weapon. They pinned the terrified girl down and crudely hacked off her long brown hair, even shaving her head and eyebrows completely bald.

After this initial beating and head-shaving, they stripped Suzanne naked to humiliate her further. Bruised, shorn, and terrified, she was then shoved into a narrow cupboard under the stairs. The group jammed the door shut, locking Suzanne in a dark closet overnight on December 7.

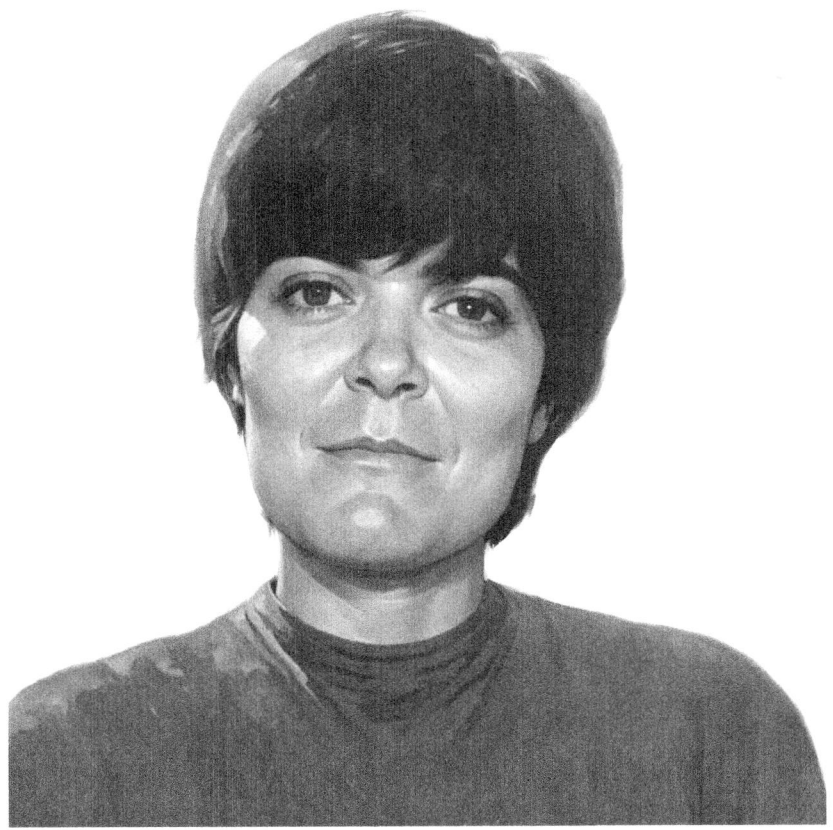

Bernadette McNeilly

The next day, her captors dragged her out and moved her to a different location to continue the abuse. They decided to use the house next door—91 Langworthy Road, which happened to be Bernadette McNeilly's former residence, and she still possessed a key. David Hill was the current resident at 91 Langworthy Road, but he lived alone and was acquainted with the group. They effectively took over his home for their gruesome purposes, and he was too intimidated to stop them.

In an upstairs bedroom, they bound Suzanne to an old bed frame so she could scarcely move. They tied her wrists and ankles with a cruel assortment of ligatures—cords, ropes, electrical cables, belts, even chains. Anything they could find to secure her limbs to the metal bed base. They also gagged her. In one instance, they shoved socks in her mouth and secured them in place so that her screams and pleas would be muffled.

What followed was seven days of systematic torture that would shock investigators. The group transformed into a gang of sadists, taking turns inflicting pain on the bound girl. They treated Suzanne not as a human being but as a plaything against which they could vent their rage and twisted urges.

From the outset, Bernadette McNeilly, in particular, took a leading role in tormenting Suzanne. What disturbed investigators and later the jury was how McNeilly didn't just participate in the torture; she transformed herself into a character to do it. At various points, McNeilly donned a creepy persona inspired by Chucky, the demonic doll from the horror film Child's Play. The group had in their possession an audio cassette with lines from the movie, and they played one line over and over through headphones placed on Suzanne's head: "I'm Chucky. Wanna play?"

McNeilly announced "Chucky's coming to play" at the start of each torture session, mocking Suzanne's terror. At times, Bernadette would lean in close to the helpless girl and hiss, "Chucky wants to play," while injecting her with drugs. Jean Powell later testified that McNeilly assumed the character of Chucky as she filled a syringe with amphetamine and jabbed it into Suzanne's arm. This ritualistic adoption of a sadistic fictional character revealed a disturbing psychological element that court psychiatrists later noted showed McNeilly wasn't just participating in violence. Rather, she was relishing a role that allowed her to detach from reality and her own humanity while inflicting pain.

Physical torture was constant and varied. The group beat Suzanne repeatedly with their fists and objects. At one point, they scrubbed her entire body with harsh, concentrated disinfectant and a stiff yard-bristle brush supposedly to "cleanse" her of the lice and filth. In truth, it was just to cause agonizing pain. They dumped undiluted household detergent and cleaning fluids into a bathtub and forced the girl into the caustic solution, scouring her raw skin. Her captors also burned her—a deep burn mark was seared between Suzanne's eyes, likely from someone stubbing out a cigarette on her face.

One of the most grotesque tortures involved pulling out Suzanne's teeth. Toward the end of her week in captivity, two of her front teeth were crudely extracted with pliers. This was done not only to cause excruciating pain but also with cold-blooded premeditation. The sadistic group was already planning to kill her, and by removing her teeth, they hoped to hinder the identification of her body. After yanking out her teeth, they laughed, saying that now she would be harder to recognize.

Through all of this, Suzanne's pleas and cries were largely silenced by the gag in her mouth. However, at times, her muffled screams could still be heard. David Hill later admitted he heard a female voice crying for help from the room. Paralyzed by fear of the violent gang, Hill did not rescue her.

By December 13, the group's energy for torment began to wane. They had to decide what to ultimately do with their victim. Suzanne was in awful condition: badly injured, weakened, and now a dangerous witness to their crimes if let go. On the seventh day of her captivity, the sadists formed a plan to commit murder.

––––––

In the early hours of December 14, 1992, Suzanne Capper's captors prepared to execute her. They untied her battered body from the bed and forced her into the trunk of a stolen white Fiat Panda. In the pre-dawn darkness, Glyn Powell drove out of Moston with his estranged wife, Jean Powell, as well as Bernadette McNeilly and Anthony Dudson. Suzanne lay crammed in the trunk, critically injured and likely drifting in and out of consciousness.

They drove thirteen miles to Werneth Low, a desolate hill and wooded area near Romiley in Stockport. At approximately 5:00 a.m., they arrived at a wooded stretch of remote land. The group dragged Suzanne out of the car and down an embankment, through thick brambles and brush on the hillside. She was so weak that she could barely stand or walk, so Glyn Powell and Anthony Dudson pushed her through the thorny undergrowth about forty yards from the road, where they dumped her on the cold ground.

Bernadette McNeilly had brought along a four-liter plastic canister filled with gasoline. In a final, macabre act, McNeilly doused Suzanne from head to toe with gasoline as she lay helpless in the grass. The group then stepped back for the final horrific act.

Later, each of the four would try to blame one of the others for what came next, but whoever it was, one of them pulled out a lighter. The testimony at trial varied significantly on this crucial point. According to some accounts, it was Glyn Powell who flicked the lighter first, while others claimed it was Dudson. McNeilly insisted she only poured the gasoline but didn't light it. The first attempt to ignite the gas failed, so someone tried again. In that confusing moment of finger-pointing and shared culpability, one of them deliberately set Suzanne on fire.

In an instant, Suzanne's gasoline-soaked body erupted into flames. The group watched as their victim burned alive, thrashing in the inferno. Her skin blistered and blackened; the fire was so intense that it caused severe burns to over eighty percent of her body.

Satisfied that their heinous task was done, the four murderers turned and headed back to their car, leaving Suzanne for dead. As they drove away from the scene, they did something almost as unfathomable as the act itself: They laughed and broke into song. Glyn Powell, Jean Powell, Bernadette McNeilly, and Anthony Dudson actually sang "Burn, baby, burn!" (the chorus from the song "Disco Inferno") as they departed.

———

Unbelievably, Suzanne Capper was not yet dead. After they left, Suzanne somehow clung to life. Engulfed in flames, she had rolled downhill. Perhaps the cold, wet winter ground helped douse the fire, or perhaps sheer willpower kept her alive a few minutes longer.

Once the flames subsided, Suzanne, horribly injured but still conscious, staggered through the woods. Incredibly, she managed to drag herself back up the embankment and onto a small rural lane sometime after the car had gone.

Around 6:30 a.m., two men driving along that quiet lane spotted her stumbling toward the road.

An ambulance was called, and she was rushed to the Burns Unit at Withington Hospital in south Manchester. Doctors were astonished to find Suzanne alive. In the burn unit, Suzanne remained conscious and coherent for several hours, and police officers were even able to interview her briefly despite her condition.

Suzanne recounted the nightmare she had been through over the past week. She not only identified her attackers by name, but she even gave the exact address—97 Langworthy Road—of where it had happened.

Despite the best efforts of the burn unit, Suzanne's injuries were too extensive. Four days after she was set ablaze, Suzanne Capper died at Withington Hospital on December 18, 1992, with her mother and sister by her bedside. She was just sixteen years old.

———

Greater Manchester Police, armed with the information Suzanne provided, acted swiftly on December 14, 1992. Just hours after Suzanne was found, police raided the house at 97 Langworthy Road in Moston at approximately 7:30 a.m. Jean Powell, Bernadette McNeilly, Glyn Powell, Jeffrey Leigh, and Clifford Pook were all present and promptly arrested. Anthony Dudson was picked up shortly thereafter.

The crime scenes themselves—both 97 and 91 Langworthy Road— yielded a trove of forensic and physical evidence corroborating Suzanne's account. In the upstairs bedroom at number 91, investigators found the makeshift restraints still attached to the bed: lengths of rope, electrical cords, and belts secured to the bed frame where Suzanne had been tied.

The floor and mattress were stained with blood, and clumps of Suzanne's hair were still scattered throughout the house. Police recovered the pliers that had been used to extract her teeth, with blood traces matching Suzanne's. One of her missing front teeth was discovered nearby.

At number 97, officers found the cupboard under the stairs where Suzanne had been imprisoned that first night—scratch marks and a few hairs inside attested to her desperate confinement there.

Investigators also seized the audio cassette tape that had been continuously playing the phrase "I'm Chucky, wanna play?" through headphones in the torture room. This tape was still in a cassette player, set to loop.

Physical evidence from outside the house also mounted. The Fiat Panda used to drive Suzanne to Werneth Low was found abandoned not far from the Powell residence. Forensic technicians matched tire tracks and trampled vegetation at the Werneth Low site to that vehicle and the suspects. Bits of melted plastic from a gas can were recovered from the burn site.

When confronted with the overwhelming evidence and Suzanne's dying testimony, the suspects began to turn on each other almost immediately. In police interviews and later in court, each tried to minimize their own role while pointing fingers at their accomplices.

By the time all evidence was gathered, the Crown Prosecution Service had prepared an extensive list of charges. In early 1993, murder charges were filed against Jean Powell, Glyn Powell, Bernadette McNeilly, Anthony Dudson, Clifford Pook, and Jeffrey Leigh. Additional charges included false imprisonment, conspiracy to cause grievous bodily harm, and attempted murder. The stage was set for a major trial that fall.

———

The trial of Suzanne Capper's killers opened on November 16, 1993, at Manchester Crown Court. In the dock were five defendants: Jean Powell (26), Bernadette McNeilly (24), Glyn Powell (29), Anthony Dudson (17), and Jeffrey Leigh (27), all charged with murder and other counts. The sixth person, Clifford Pook, was also in the courtroom, but partway through the proceedings, the judge directed the jury to formally acquit Pook of murder due to insufficient evidence of his intent in the killing.

The trial lasted twenty-two days, during which time the gruesome evidence reduced jurors to tears. Most harrowing of all, the jury listened to Suzanne's own deathbed statement, which was read into evidence: a calm, heartbreaking account of what each of the accused had done to her.

The jurors also saw photographs of the injuries Suzanne suffered and saw items like the charred brush and bloodstained bed frame recovered from the crime scene. Physical exhibits such as the "Chucky" tape were played in court, sending chills down the spines of those present.

One by one, the defendants took the stand in their own defense— except Bernadette McNeilly, who chose not to testify. Their testimonies largely mirrored what they had told the police, with each minimizing responsibility.

On December 16, 1993, after ten hours of deliberation, the jury returned with their verdicts. Jean Powell, Bernadette McNeilly, and

Glyn Powell were each found guilty of murder and other associated charges beyond any doubt. Anthony Dudson was also found guilty of murder despite his youth and his protests that he hadn't lit the fire.

Jeffrey Leigh, however, was acquitted of murder—the jury was not convinced that Leigh had intended or directly assisted in killing Suzanne. He was instead convicted of false imprisonment. Clifford Pook had already pleaded guilty to conspiracy to cause grievous bodily harm and false imprisonment.

The next day, December 17, 1993, Justice Potts pronounced sentences. His words in court were scathing. He said their actions had been "as appalling a murder as it is possible to imagine," emphasizing how they had tortured Suzanne for their own amusement and revenge, displaying cruelty beyond belief.

Jean Powell, Glyn Powell, and Bernadette McNeilly were each sentenced to life in prison for the murder of Suzanne Capper. The judge imposed a minimum sentence of twenty-five years. Anthony Dudson, being legally a juvenile, was ordered to be detained at Her Majesty's Pleasure—an indefinite sentence for young offenders convicted of murder. The judge set a minimum tariff of eighteen years for Dudson.

Clifford Pook was sentenced to fifteen years for his admitted role in the conspiracy to cause grievous bodily harm. Jeffrey Leigh was sentenced to twelve years in prison for false imprisonment.

As the sentences were announced, there was a sense in the courtroom that justice had been served, albeit for a crime almost too horrific for justice to encompass. Suzanne's mother and family reportedly expressed satisfaction that the murderers would "never see daylight for a long time."

———

News of the Suzanne Capper case sent shockwaves through the community and the country. Many struggled to comprehend how a group of relatively ordinary young people could commit acts reminiscent of a horror movie. Some investigators stated that "for sheer mindless brutality," this crime ranked alongside the Moors Murders committed by Ian Brady and Myra Hindley in the 1960s.

Headlines highlighted the utter senselessness of the motive, emphasizing how trivial the reasons were for such monstrous behavior. The public struggled with that notion—that a teen girl could be burned alive over lice and a borrowed coat.

In Manchester, Suzanne's murder prompted some introspection about social services and community interventions. How did a sixteen-year-old essentially slip through every safety net—school, social workers, neighbors—to end up in this deadly situation?

———

In the years following the trial, the perpetrators served their sentences, and the question of their possible release became a contentious issue. Suzanne's mother, Elizabeth Dunbar, remained an outspoken advocate for keeping the killers behind bars, along with local MP Graham Stringer.

Despite these efforts, over time, one perpetrator after another gained parole:

• Jeffrey Leigh was released in 1998.

• Clifford Pook was freed in 2001.

• Anthony Dudson was released in 2013 at the age of thirty-seven.

• Bernadette McNeilly was released in 2015 after serving only twenty-two years.

• Jean Powell was released in 2017 at the age of fifty.

• Glyn Powell, the last of the convicted murderers still behind bars, was reportedly slated for release in 2023.

Each release was met with disbelief and outrage from those who remembered the case. How could a justice system allow a group of killers who spent a week torturing a sixteen-year-old girl, then set her on fire while she was still alive, to ever walk free?

And yet, one by one, they did. As one headline bluntly captured it: "Gang who tortured and killed tragic teen all set to be released from prison." The very idea that such cruelty has a time limit defies reason.

The Suzanne Capper case remains one of the most harrowing in modern British history. Her final act of bravery—identifying her killers with her dying breath—ensured they were brought to justice. But justice in Britain, it seems, has an expiration date. That anyone involved in such a sadistic, prolonged campaign of abuse could one day be deemed fit for release is not just troubling: it's shameful. What happened inside the house on Langworthy Road should have meant life behind bars, no exceptions. Instead, it stands as a haunting example of a system more concerned with rehabilitation than remembrance.

CHAPTER 3

THE PIZZA BOMBER

O n a warm summer afternoon in Erie, Pennsylvania, television cameras captured what would become one of the most bizarre criminal cases in American history. Police officers surrounded a man sitting cross-legged on the pavement of a shopping center parking lot, his hands cuffed behind his back. Around his neck hung a strange, bulky device that resembled a homemade bomb. The officers maintained their distance as the man pleaded with them.

"I'm not lying," he begged. "I'm not doing this because I want to. I'm doing this because I have to."

For twenty-five minutes, news crews filmed as the man explained that someone had placed the device around his neck and forced him to rob a bank. Then, without warning, a shrill beeping sound emanated from the collar. The noise intensified, growing louder and faster.

"It's gonna go off!" the man cried just seconds before the device exploded.

As officers dove for cover, the man slumped forward, a gaping wound in his chest. The bomb squad, which had been summoned only minutes earlier, arrived too late. By the time they reached the scene, Brian Wells was already dead.

The date was August 28, 2003, and investigators were about to uncover one of the most elaborate and sinister criminal plots ever conceived—a deadly scavenger hunt, a group of twisted masterminds, and a pizza deliveryman caught in the middle.

————

Brian Douglas Wells was a quiet, unassuming man. At forty-six, he had been delivering pizzas for Mama Mia's Pizzeria for nearly a decade. His neighbors described him as trusting and kind. Certainly not the type to plan a bank heist.

That Thursday afternoon seemed routine when Wells left the pizza shop to make a delivery to an address near a remote television transmission tower on the outskirts of town. What happened during that delivery remains partially shrouded in mystery, but what is known is that at approximately 2:20 p.m., Wells walked into a PNC Bank branch in Millcreek Township, a suburb of Erie.

Bank surveillance footage showed Wells approaching the teller with an unusual calm, considering what he was about to do. He wore a plain white t-shirt with the brand name "Guess" printed across the front, under which a strange, boxy device protruded from his chest. In his hand, he carried what appeared to be a cane, though investigators later discovered it was actually a sawed-off shotgun that had been cleverly disguised. Wells slid a handwritten note across the counter.

The note was direct: He demanded $250,000. When the teller informed him she couldn't access that amount of money, he calmly accepted all the cash she could provide from her drawer—$8,702. Wells then walked out of the bank, sucking on a lollipop that had been given to him by his captors.

His strange demeanor caught the attention of a customer who followed him outside and jotted down his license plate number as Wells drove away in his car.

By 2:38 p.m., state troopers had spotted Wells in a parking lot near the bank. He was sitting outside his vehicle when officers approached with weapons drawn. They ordered him to the ground and hand-cuffed him. It was then that Wells began to plead with the officers.

"I don't have a lot of time," he said. "I'm not lying. I've been held hostage by people who had guns. There's a bomb around my neck."

With those words, the officers, following protocol for bomb threats, backed away and called for the bomb squad. Television news crews that had been monitoring police radio traffic arrived and began filming the scene. Wells sat cross-legged on the pavement, repeatedly asking officers to call his boss at the pizza shop—perhaps to verify his identity, or maybe to establish his role as a deliveryman.

At 3:18 p.m., with the bomb squad still en route, the device around Wells's neck began to beep. The sound quickened like a countdown, and before officers could react, it detonated. The explosion was powerful enough to tear a hole through Wells's chest, killing him instantly.

Inside Wells's car, investigators found several handwritten pages of instructions. It became clear that this was no ordinary bank robbery; it was the beginning of what investigators would come to call "a twisted treasure hunt."

———

The notes found in Wells's car revealed an elaborate scheme. They were addressed to the "Bomb Hostage" and contained detailed instructions for an elaborate scavenger hunt. After robbing the bank, Wells was supposed to follow a specific route to multiple locations around Erie. At each stop, he would find clues leading to keys or combination codes that would supposedly disarm the bomb around his neck.

Brian Wells

The first clue directed him to a McDonald's drive-thru, where a rock in a flowerbed concealed the next instruction. Other clues would lead him into the woods, where notes were taped under stones or hidden in jars. Investigators followed the trail and discovered several of these hidden messages, although some locations were empty, suggesting the perpetrators may have removed evidence after Wells's death.

The collar bomb itself was unlike anything law enforcement had ever seen. Constructed of metal, it had four padlocks and a three-digit combination lock. Inside the metal casing were two pipe bombs powered by commercial-grade smokeless powder. The device had been wired with three timers—two kitchen timers and one electronic timer—and included fake wiring and decoy stickers to confuse anyone attempting to disarm it.

Forensic analysis later revealed the bomb had been expertly crafted. It included sophisticated anti-tampering mechanisms that would trigger detonation if anyone attempted to remove it. The device was, in essence, a deadly puzzle with no solution.

The cane-shotgun found with Wells was equally sophisticated—a sawed-off shotgun disguised as a walking cane. The level of crafts-manship suggested that someone with mechanical expertise had built these devices.

As investigators pieced together the crime, they faced a central ques-tion: Was Brian Wells a willing participant in the robbery, or was he an innocent victim forced into a deadly game?

———

At the scene of his death, Wells had insisted he had been forced to rob the bank. He claimed that during his pizza delivery, armed men had ambushed him and locked the bomb around his neck. His final words to the police supported this narrative. He seemed genuinely fright-ened and repeatedly asked officers to help him.

Wells had no criminal record. His co-workers and neighbors described him as a timid, non-confrontational man who lived a modest life. Family members staunchly maintained that Brian would never willingly participate in a robbery.

However, as the investigation progressed, evidence emerged suggesting a more complicated story. The bomb's design was too sophisticated for Wells to remove on his own, but the timeline of events raised questions. The scavenger hunt was so elaborate that it would have been impossible to complete within the timeframe of the bomb's detonation. This led some investigators to believe Wells may have had prior knowledge of the plan, only to be double-crossed when he discovered the bomb was real.

Additionally, the "Guess" t-shirt Wells wore during the robbery was not his own. Some investigators speculated this might have been a cruel joke from the perpetrators—a taunt meaning "Guess who is behind this?" This level of sadistic calculation pointed to one or multiple minds far more twisted than Wells's friends and family believed him capable of.

————

On September 20, 2003, less than a month after the Wells incident, police received a bizarre letter. The handwritten note began, "This has nothing to do with the Wells case." The author, Bill Rothstein, went on to confess that there was a body in a freezer at his home.

When officers arrived at the address, they found William "Bill" Rothstein, a heavyset man with a long beard. True to the letter, police discovered the frozen body of James Roden in a chest freezer in Rothstein's garage.

Rothstein explained that he hadn't killed Roden—his ex-fiancée had. He claimed he was only helping to hide the body. The woman's name was Marjorie Diehl-Armstrong, and her connection to Rothstein would ultimately lead investigators to unravelling the pizza bomber case.

Marjorie Diehl-Armstrong was a study in contradictions. A former high school valedictorian with a master's degree, she possessed remarkable intelligence. Yet, by 2003, her life had spiraled into chaos. Her home was filled with thousands of pounds of rotting food and garbage—evidence of severe mental illness that included hoarding behaviors.

She also had a violent history. In 1984, she had shot a previous boyfriend but was acquitted on self-defense grounds. Her husband had died of a cerebral hemorrhage in 1992, ruled an accident at the time. And now, it seemed, she had killed James Roden, her latest boyfriend.

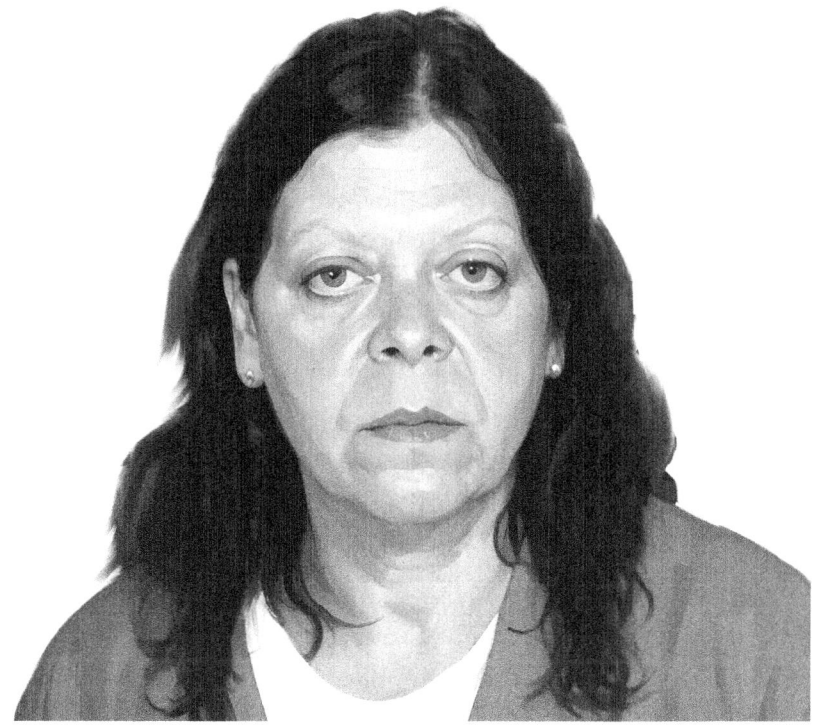

Marjorie Diehl-Armstrong

When questioned about Roden's death, Diehl-Armstrong admitted to shooting him during an argument. She eventually pleaded guilty but mentally ill to third-degree murder and was sentenced to seven to twenty years in prison.

As investigators explored the connection between Rothstein and Diehl-Armstrong, they began to suspect that these two eccentric individuals might have been involved in the Wells case, despite Rothstein's disclaimer in his letter.

———

Over the next four years, FBI agents conducted a meticulous investigation. They interviewed approximately 1,000 witnesses, analyzed every component of the bomb, and scrutinized the relationships between a growing cast of suspicious characters.

A break in the case came when investigators discovered that Diehl-Armstrong had provided kitchen timers to Rothstein—timers that matched those used in the collar bomb. Phone records showed she had been in contact with another man, Kenneth Barnes, about building explosive devices in the weeks before the bank robbery.

Barnes, a drug addict and friend of Diehl-Armstrong, eventually became a key witness. When arrested, he confessed that he had acted as a lookout during the bank robbery. According to Barnes, the original plan was for Wells to rob the bank with a fake bomb, but at the last minute, they switched it to a real one.

Barnes claimed that when Wells realized the bomb was real, he tried to back out. That's when another conspirator, Floyd Stockton—a roommate of Rothstein—allegedly pulled out a gun and forced Wells to go through with the robbery.

The puzzle pieces were falling into place. Investigators believed Diehl-Armstrong was the mastermind, motivated by a desire to secure money to hire Barnes to kill her father for inheritance. Rothstein, her former fiancée and a skilled handyman, had likely built the bomb using the timers she'd provided. Barnes served as a lookout during the robbery, while Stockton had helped secure the bomb around Wells's neck.

In July 2007, federal prosecutors announced an indictment against Diehl-Armstrong and Barnes for their roles in the deadly bank robbery. By this time, Rothstein had died of lymphoma in July 2004, never having been charged in the Wells case. Finally, Stockton received immunity in exchange for his testimony.

Barnes pleaded guilty in September 2008 to conspiracy and using a destructive device in a crime of violence. He was sentenced to forty-five years in federal prison.

Diehl-Armstrong's case moved more slowly. She was initially declared mentally incompetent to stand trial but later deemed fit to face charges. Throughout pretrial hearings, she maintained her innocence and blamed Rothstein for masterminding the plot.

In October 2010, Diehl-Armstrong's trial began. Prosecutors presented physical evidence linking her to the crime, including her purchase of the timers used in the bomb. Barnes testified against her, detailing meetings in which she discussed killing her father and using the bank robbery proceeds to pay for the hit.

The prosecution portrayed Diehl-Armstrong as a cold, calculating criminal who orchestrated the entire scheme. Her defense argued that she was mentally ill and incapable of planning such an elaborate crime.

On November 1, 2010, a federal jury found Marjorie Diehl-Armstrong guilty on all charges: conspiracy to commit armed bank robbery, armed bank robbery resulting in death, and using a destructive device in a crime of violence. In February 2011, she was sentenced to life in prison plus thirty years.

To her dying day, Diehl-Armstrong maintained her innocence in the Wells case, insisting that Rothstein was the true mastermind. She died of breast cancer in prison in April 2017 at the age of sixty-eight.

Barnes died in prison of liver cancer in June 2019. Stockton, who received immunity, has remained out of the public eye.

———

As the full story emerged, investigators were struck by the bizarre nature of the conspirators. A federal prosecutor described them as "a group of twisted, intellectually bright, dysfunctional individuals who outsmarted themselves."

Marjorie Diehl-Armstrong was perhaps the most complex. Despite her brilliant mind, she suffered from severe mental illness. Psychiatrists diagnosed her with bipolar disorder and narcissistic personality traits, documented in court records. She was described as manipulative, hostile, and grandiose, displaying a fear of abandonment and an inflated sense of her own intelligence. Her hoarding was so extreme that investigators found over 4,000 pounds of rotting food in her home.

William Rothstein was equally strange—a reclusive handyman who spoke multiple languages and had the mechanical skills to build sophisticated devices. Friends described him as meticulous and obsessive. Like Diehl-Armstrong, he was a hoarder, though his compulsion centered on tools and gadgets rather than food.

Kenneth Barnes was characterized by investigators as "brain-fried from drugs." His judgment was impaired by years of substance abuse, yet he was trusted with a significant role in the conspiracy.

Floyd Stockton, a convicted sex offender, was the man who allegedly forced the collar bomb onto Wells's neck. His full role remains somewhat mysterious, as he was granted immunity and has stayed out of public view since.

These four individuals, each damaged in their own way, came together to create one of the most bizarre crimes in American history. Their plot combined elements of hostage-taking, bank robbery, and cruel manipulation into a deadly game that claimed an innocent life.

———

Though the conspirators were eventually brought to justice, Brian Wells's family has continued to fight to clear his name. His sister, Jean Heid, has maintained for years that her brother was an innocent victim, not a willing participant in the robbery.

Federal prosecutors, however, have stated that Wells was aware of the bank robbery plan, though they believe he was told the bomb would be fake. According to their theory, Wells only became a true victim when he realized the bomb was real and was forced to go through with the robbery at gunpoint.

This characterization of Wells as partially complicit has been a source of pain for his family. Without Wells alive to tell his side of the story, the full truth may never be known.

———

Even after the convictions, several aspects of the case remain mysterious.

The elaborate scavenger hunt raises questions. Why create such a complex scheme when the timers on the bomb made it virtually impossible for Wells to complete it? Was it merely a cruel joke, or was there something else at play?

The true mastermind remains debated. Though Diehl-Armstrong was convicted as the ringleader, some investigators believe Rothstein was the actual architect. His mechanical skills made him the likely bomb builder, and his subsequent death before charges could be filed means he "had the last laugh," as one investigator put it.

Wells's level of involvement remains a subject of controversy. Was he truly an innocent deliveryman caught in a deadly trap, or did he agree to participate in what he thought would be a nonviolent crime, only to be betrayed?

The "Guess" t-shirt Wells wore, which wasn't his, remains a strange detail. Was it indeed a taunt from the perpetrators, a sick joke embedded in their deadly game?

Finally, there's the question of why the crime was documented so thoroughly. The handwritten instructions, the bomb design, the scavenger hunt—all of it seems unnecessarily complex. Some have suggested that Rothstein, in particular, may have engineered the crime simply to prove he could, a display of perverted genius that ultimately cost an innocent man his life.

———

The Erie pizza bomber case stands out as one of the most bizarre criminal conspiracies in American history. It combined elements of psychological torture, mechanical ingenuity, and lethal calculation in ways that continue to disturb investigators.

The case also exposed the dangerous capabilities of damaged minds working in concert. Diehl-Armstrong's mental illness, Rothstein's mechanical genius, Barnes's desperation, and Stockton's moral bankruptcy created a perfect storm that resulted in tragedy.

For law enforcement, the case represented a fact-finding challenge unlike any other. The seven-year investigation required extraordinary patience and attention to detail. FBI Special Agent Jerry Clark, who led the investigation, later called it one of the most complex cases of his career.

For the people of Erie, Pennsylvania, the case left a lingering shadow. The image of Brian Wells sitting on the pavement, pleading for his life moments before the collar bomb detonated, remains etched in the community's collective memory.

CHAPTER 4
THE REDRUM MURDER

Built in the 1700s, nestled between the lush forests of the Appalachian Mountains and the winding Schuylkill River, Reading, Pennsylvania, was a vibrant industrial city whose height of prosperity came during the railroad era. By the 1980s, however, the city had begun to fray around the edges as manufacturing declined.

In this working-class city of about 80,000 people, crime wasn't uncommon, but it typically consisted of petty thefts, bar fights, and the occasional domestic dispute. Violent crime existed, but rarely to the degree that it shocked the community. That changed dramatically in the summer of 1987, when a murder so gruesome and bizarre occurred that it sent shockwaves through the city and drew national attention.

On Saturday, July 25, 1987, David Lutz returned to his Fifth Street apartment around 3:30 a.m. after a night out partying. As he entered, he immediately knew something was terribly wrong. The apartment was eerily quiet, but evidence of violence was everywhere. Blood stained the carpet and walls. Trembling, he moved deeper into the apartment and discovered a sight so horrific that it would haunt him for years to come.

His roommate, forty-one-year-old Stanley Detweiler, lay on the floor, his body severed from his head. The decapitated head had been placed beside the body. Even more disturbing, someone had written the word "REDRUM"—"murder" spelled backward—on the wall in the victim's own blood. The killer had also scrawled "LSD" in blood on another wall.

Horror-struck and panicking, Lutz immediately called the police. When officers arrived, they were confronted with one of the most gruesome crime scenes any of them had ever seen. Reading Police Chief Rodney Steffy would later tell reporters, "What kind of lunatic would do something like this?"

The bloody writing on the wall provided an immediate, chilling clue. "REDRUM" was a direct reference to the horror film "The Shining," based on Stephen King's novel of the same name, which had coincidentally aired on television just a week before the murder. This suggested that whoever had committed this atrocity might have been inspired by fiction, blurring the lines between Hollywood horror and real-life terror.

———

Stanley Detweiler was not the type of person anyone would expect to fall victim to such violence. At forty-one, he was known throughout the community as a kind-hearted, gentle soul. He worked as a banquet setup staffer at a local Holiday Inn and played the organ at his church on Sundays.

Stanley, a talented pianist who sometimes tuned pianos for extra money, was described by those who knew him as generous to a fault— so much so that Stanley's good nature had occasionally placed him in risky situations before. On one occasion, he had picked up a hitchhiker who had repaid his kindness by threatening him with a knife and stealing his car.

Despite such experiences, Stanley remained trusting and quick to help others. He shared his Reading apartment with his younger roommate, David Lutz, and was looking forward to his forty-second birthday, which would have been just two days after his murder on July 27.

No one could have imagined that this gentle man would become the victim of one of the most brutal murders in Reading's history.

———

The events leading up to Stanley Detweiler's murder began innocently enough. On Friday evening, July 24, 1987, David Lutz went out partying in downtown Reading. While socializing on North 10th Street, twenty-year-old Lutz met sixteen-year-old Michael Boettlin Jr.

Lutz was attracted to the teenager and, hoping to impress him enough to continue the party back at his place, began boasting about his lifestyle. He told Boettlin that he and his roommate "had a lot of money and a nice stereo," and he even hinted that his roommate was wealthy and away on vacation. Lutz then invited Boettlin over to drink and party in private.

Initially, Boettlin agreed, and the two headed toward Lutz's home on South Fifth Street. But along the way, Boettlin changed his mind and decided to go to another party instead. Lutz, still hopeful, gave the teenager his address anyway in case he changed his mind before they parted ways.

What Lutz didn't realize was that his boastful comments had planted a seed in Michael Boettlin's mind—a tip about an apartment supposedly full of valuables and cash, sitting empty.

Shortly afterward, Boettlin ran into his old acquaintance, twenty-two-year-old John Calvaresi, at another party elsewhere in the city.

Calvaresi had actually been Boettlin's babysitter years earlier, when the teen was just a child. Now, Calvaresi gladly bought beers for the underage Boettlin, and as they drank into the late hours, the conversation turned to making some quick money.

Boettlin mentioned the boast he'd heard from Lutz: a "rich roommate" and "fancy stereo system" in an apartment that should be unoccupied. Lutz had said his roommate was on vacation, and Boettlin assumed Lutz himself wouldn't be back until nearly 4:00 a.m.

Calvaresi, who was nearly broke and always up for mischief, thought it sounded like an easy score. The pair formed a plan to break in and rob the place that very night, never imagining how horrifically wrong things would go.

———

As Friday night passed into the early morning hours of Saturday, John Calvaresi and Michael Boettlin set out to burglarize the Fifth Street apartment. Around 2:00 a.m., they arrived at the address David Lutz had given Boettlin. The pair was confident the apartment would be empty. They planned for a quick smash-and-grab of electronics and cash with no one home to stop them.

Calvaresi and Boettlin forced their way in, kicking open the apartment's front door with a loud crash. However, the noise woke someone inside. To their surprise, Lutz's roommate, Stanley Detweiler, was home after all, asleep in his bed until the commotion roused him.

Startled and still groggy, Detweiler hurried toward the source of the sound only to come face-to-face with the two intruders. A struggle ensued in the doorway. Calvaresi, taller and stronger, lunged at Detweiler and tackled him to the floor. The panicked victim tried to fight back, but Boettlin joined in, repeatedly kicking Detweiler in the face as Calvaresi held him down.

Together, the attackers brutally beat the man until he lay unconscious, his body half in the doorway and half in the building's entryway. During the vicious beating, Detweiler suffered five broken ribs among other injuries. The intruders then dragged the unconscious victim fully inside and shut the door behind them.

Michael Boettlin

Breathing heavily after the struggle, the two regrouped. Calvaresi stalked off to the kitchen while Boettlin began searching the apartment for valuables. The ransacking proved disappointing; Lutz's boasts had been greatly exaggerated. The modest apartment held little of worth, and Boettlin found only a glass coin bank containing about $22 in quarters and a checkbook.

Meanwhile, Calvaresi emerged from the kitchen armed with a ten-inch butcher's knife. What happened next would turn a simple burglary into an almost unspeakable horror.

———

Returning to the living room where Detweiler lay unconscious, Calvaresi—perhaps fueled by adrenaline or twisted curiosity—posed a shocking question to his young accomplice: "Should I cut his head off?"

Boettlin, in a moment of sheer panic and confusion, gave a short reply that he would regret forever: "Okay." The naïve teenager didn't believe Calvaresi would actually do it; he was in shock and simply blurted out a response, terrified that if he protested, the volatile older man might turn on him next.

"I remember thinking, 'I don't know this guy. What if I'm next?'" Boettlin later recalled, insisting he was traumatized by what followed.

As Detweiler began to regain consciousness on the floor, John Calvaresi moved in with the knife. He pinned the victim down, kneeling on the man's chest, while Detweiler weakly tried to fight back in terror. To keep the victim subdued, Boettlin stepped on Detweiler's arm, holding him in place.

Then, in an act of unfathomable brutality, Calvaresi began sawing at Stanley Detweiler's neck with the kitchen knife. The blade wasn't very sharp. Calvaresi had to work at the grisly task, slicing back and forth until the neck was nearly cut through. Then, using his bare hands, he twisted and pulled until he tore the head free from the remaining tissue. When the gruesome deed was done, he set Detweiler's severed head beside the lifeless body on the living room floor.

The nightmare was not over. Spattered in blood, Calvaresi grabbed a towel to wipe himself off. In a disturbing flourish, he then dipped his fingers in the victim's blood and began writing on the walls. On the kitchen wall, he scrawled the word "REDRUM"—a direct reference to a key scene in "The Shining." Unsatisfied, Calvaresi told Boettlin to smear the bloody letters to obscure any fingerprints and then wrote the word "REDRUM" again on another wall, this time more clearly. He also daubed the letters "LSD" nearby, joking that LSD was his favorite drug; he thought adding it would make it more interesting for whoever found the scene.

John Calvaresi

Throughout the ordeal, Michael Boettlin stood by in a state of shock. By his later account, he was frozen and horrified by what his friend had done, yet too afraid to intervene. Having committed an atrocity, the pair hurried to cover their tracks. They made only a cursory attempt to collect loot, notably failing even to take cash from the victim's wallet in their haste. Before leaving, however, Calvaresi and Boettlin took the time to clean up in the bathroom, washing off the blood before they fled into the night.

————

News of the crime spread quickly through Reading, leaving residents in disbelief. The sheer brutality of Detweiler's murder—a beheading in a home invasion—made headlines and drew national attention. Local authorities were shaken. Berks County District Attorney George Yatron struggled to find words to describe the crime scene's grotesque nature.

The bizarre "REDRUM" message immediately caught media attention; reporters seized upon it for headlines, dubbing it the "REDRUM Murder." The fact that a Hollywood horror motif had been recreated in a Pennsylvania apartment was morbidly fascinating to the public.

Reading suddenly found itself in the spotlight for a grisly murder rather than its industrial past or the Reading Railroad of Monopoly fame. To a community already struggling with rising crime, the Detweiler case was something entirely different, described by some as perhaps the most vicious homicide in the city's modern history.

In quiet suburbs and city row homes alike, residents double-checked their locks that weekend. Rumors swirled about cults or madmen on the loose, given the almost ritualistic mutilation and messages in blood. Some even drew comparisons to the Manson family murders of nearly two decades earlier—violent crimes marked by similar blood-written messages and a feeling of senseless evil. At Detweiler's church, fellow congregants wept and tried to make sense of the loss of a good man in such an evil act.

Local newspapers ran front-page stories on the murder for days as police worked feverishly to identify the perpetrators.

From the outset, detectives faced intense pressure to solve the case. The crime scene itself, while horrifying, yielded valuable clues. Bloody shoeprints and fingerprints were left throughout the apartment. The vandalized walls suggested the killer might have been inspired by the media, pointing to a young or at least psychologically disturbed suspect.

Crucially, David Lutz provided investigators with their first lead. In his initial interview, still dazed by shock, Lutz had not mentioned his encounter with the teenage stranger the night before. However, as police pressed him about anyone who knew he would be out that night, Lutz recalled his conversation with "Michael"—how he had bragged about the apartment and given Michael the address. However, Lutz didn't know Michael's last name.

That fragment of information was enough for detectives to start canvassing the area where Lutz met the youth. They learned of the party that had taken place that Friday night and began interviewing attendees. In short order, one attendee recalled that Michael was accompanied by an adult man in his early twenties named John Calvaresi. Another witness knew Michael Boettlin from the neighborhood, and they were able to provide his full name and even an address for his family's home.

Separately, investigators heard from at least one of Boettlin's friends that the teen had been bragging about the crime after it happened. This was the final piece of the puzzle that investigators needed.

Just four days after Stanley Detweiler's murder, on July 29, 1987, authorities moved to arrest Michael Boettlin Jr. They descended on the Boettlin home, where the sixteen-year-old lived with his mother and stepfather. Boettlin was taken into custody without incident and promptly arraigned as an adult on an array of charges, including criminal homicide, first-degree murder, second-degree murder, voluntary manslaughter, burglary, robbery, aggravated assault, and conspiracy.

The very next day, police tracked down John Calvaresi. The twenty-two-year-old was arrested in a rural area outside Reading on July 30, 1987. He, too, was booked on identical charges.

News of the swift arrests reassured the rattled community of Reading. Locals were stunned to learn the ages of the suspects—one barely old enough to drive, the other just a young adult. Both suspects had ties to Reading's youth social scene, and the fact that a teenager was involved particularly troubled residents.

Meanwhile, prosecutors signaled they would pursue the most severe penalties available. Boettlin, though a minor, faced the grim prospect of life in prison—or even a possible death penalty—given the first-degree murder charge.

———

Legal proceedings began to unfold in two separate tracks for the co-defendants. John Calvaresi, the older ringleader and the one who had physically committed the beheading, decided early on to cooperate with prosecutors. In March 1988, Calvaresi pleaded guilty but mentally ill to first-degree murder. As part of his plea deal, he agreed to testify against Michael Boettlin, effectively removing the possibility that Calvaresi himself might face the death penalty.

During his testimony, Calvaresi recounted the night of the murder in chilling detail, describing without emotion how he cut off Stanley Detweiler's head. Courtroom observers were struck by his flat, remorseless demeanor on the stand. Calvaresi attempted to explain his actions by pointing to his mental disturbances.

"There was something wrong because you just don't go around cutting people's heads off for nothing," he told the judge and jury.

A court-ordered psychiatric evaluation found that while Calvaresi did suffer from significant mental health issues, including epilepsy worsened by improper medication and drug abuse, he was legally sane and fit to stand trial. The diagnosis of "guilty but mentally ill" meant he would serve his sentence in state prison, albeit with access to psychiatric treatment. The judge accepted Calvaresi's plea and immediately imposed a sentence of life in prison for the first-degree murder, sparing him from execution.

With Calvaresi's fate sealed, attention turned to Michael Boettlin Jr.'s trial. Due to intense pretrial publicity in Berks County, the defense successfully moved for a change of venue. The trial was relocated across the state to Westmoreland County, Pennsylvania, in hopes of finding jurors who hadn't been tainted by the "REDRUM" media coverage.

In August 1988, one year after the crime, now seventeen-year-old Boettlin stood trial for murder before a Westmoreland County jury. Prosecutors presented a strong case, bolstered by physical evidence and, most damaging, John Calvaresi's firsthand testimony. Calvaresi took the stand and recounted the crime, placing blame on Boettlin as an eager participant. He testified that Boettlin had not only kicked Detweiler during the initial assault but also consented to the beheading by uttering "Okay" when prompted.

Boettlin's defense sought to minimize the teen's role. They painted him as a frightened boy under the sway of a deranged older man. Boettlin didn't deny being present, but he claimed he never believed Calvaresi would actually kill Detweiler. On the stand, Boettlin expressed remorse and insisted he was paralyzed by fear once the violence began. The defense highlighted that Boettlin had no history of violent crime and didn't start the more brutal acts.

Ultimately, however, the gruesome facts were inescapable. An innocent man had been killed in the course of a robbery that Boettlin helped plan and execute. The jury also heard about the chilling blood-scrawled messages on the walls and other disturbing details that underscored the depravity of the crime scene.

After deliberating, the Westmoreland County jury delivered its verdict on August 15, 1988. Michael Boettlin Jr. was found guilty of first-degree murder, second-degree murder, felony murder during a robbery, and related offenses. The teen stood quietly, showing no emotion as the forewoman announced the guilty verdict on all counts.

Given the first-degree murder conviction, a mandatory life sentence was imposed, meaning that Boettlin, at seventeen years old, would spend the rest of his natural life behind bars with no chance of parole. In addition, the judge sentenced him to an extra term of twenty to forty years for the robbery, burglary, and conspiracy charges—to be served consecutively.

As Judge Calvin Smith delivered the sentence, he admonished Boettlin for his role in the savagery, emphasizing that youth was no excuse for such cruelty. Boettlin's family quietly wept in the courtroom while Detweiler's relatives nodded somberly, feeling that justice had been served.

———

John Calvaresi was a troubled twenty-two-year-old with a history of mental health issues when he committed the brutal murder. Diagnosed with epilepsy as a child, Calvaresi had been prescribed anti-seizure medications but often mixed them with alcohol and illegal drugs, causing violent mood swings and erratic behavior.

According to psychiatric testimony presented at his sentencing, Calvaresi had attempted suicide multiple times and experienced psychotic episodes. He had once written a threatening letter to President Ronald Reagan, prompting a Secret Service investigation. Friends described him as a high school dropout and drifter who rode motorcycles and shot pool around town, with little direction in his life.

Despite his rough edges, he had once served as a babysitter for young Michael Boettlin, who was six years his junior. This early connection would later prove fatal for Stanley Detweiler, as it brought together two individuals who never should have reconnected.

Michael Boettlin Jr. was just sixteen at the time of the murder and about to enter the tenth grade that fall. By all accounts, he was an ordinary teenager who enjoyed partying and was flattered by the attention of Calvaresi, who now treated him like an adult by buying him beer.

Boettlin's background offered few clues to explain his participation in such a heinous crime. He came from a working-class family and had no significant criminal history before the murder. What might have seemed like a thrilling adventure—breaking into an apartment with an older friend—spiraled into a nightmare beyond imagination.

––––––

In the decades following 1988, both convicted perpetrators remained behind bars in Pennsylvania's state prison system. However, their stories did not end at sentencing.

John Calvaresi, inmate FD-2494, was sent to serve his life term. He spent years in various prisons and, according to records, struggled with his health. On July 31, 2015, after twenty-eight years of incarceration, John Italo Calvaresi died of natural causes at age fifty.

Michael Boettlin Jr. remained in prison as well, serving his life sentence. As years passed, Boettlin reportedly matured and made efforts at rehabilitation. He earned his GED diploma in 1994 while incarcerated and became an avid reader of books and newspapers, trying to educate himself. By his mid-forties, Boettlin had spent well over half his life in prison and had a spotless disciplinary record.

His case, along with those of many other juvenile lifers, took on new significance in light of evolving legal standards. In 2012, the U.S.

Supreme Court ruled in Miller v. Alabama that mandatory life-with-out-parole sentences for crimes committed by juveniles are unconstitutional. This landmark decision opened the door for Boettlin to receive a new sentence that would allow a chance at parole.

Under Pennsylvania court orders following Miller, Boettlin was granted a resentencing hearing in 2017. In October 2017, then-forty-six-year-old Michael Boettlin Jr. returned to a Berks County courtroom to face resentencing for the murder he had committed as a teenager three decades earlier. Family members of Stanley Detweiler were present, still haunted by the memory of their loved one's fate.

Boettlin, graying and soft-spoken, addressed the court and expressed deep remorse for his actions in 1987. He didn't attempt to excuse the crime, acknowledging that no apology could undo the harm. After considering factors of Boettlin's youth at the time of the crime and his prison record, Judge Paul Yatron issued a new sentence of forty years to life in state prison.

This meant that Boettlin would become eligible for parole after serving a total of forty years. Given the time he had already spent locked up since 1987, he will first be able to petition for release in 2027, when he will be fifty-six years old.

CHAPTER 5
A STRANGE CASE

The predawn air hung still over Louisville on Sunday, May 27, 1990. Most neighborhoods slumbered peacefully on what should have been an ordinary Memorial Day weekend.

But this would be no ordinary call for the firefighters racing toward South Ninth Street. Flames had engulfed an abandoned house, sending plumes of acrid smoke into the darkness. As they battled the blaze at 2907 S. Ninth St., none could have anticipated the nightmarish discovery that awaited them.

When the last embers were quenched, and after the smoke cleared, firefighters made a horrific find. Inside the charred ruins lay the headless, burned remains of a woman. Her body was so severely damaged by the flames that immediate identification was impossible. More disturbing still was the obvious absence of her head—a calculated attempt to thwart her identification and obscure a ghastly crime. Homicide detectives soon arrived at the scene, their faces grim as they surveyed what would become one of Louisville's most disturbing crime scenes in recent memory.

As news of the headless corpse spread through the community in the following hours, a palpable anxiety gripped the city. Who was this woman? What monster could have committed such a heinous act? While these questions hung in the air, detectives were already pursuing a crucial lead: a missing persons report filed for forty-four-year-old Kathleen Strange, a beloved schoolteacher who hadn't shown up for a planned family gathering that holiday weekend.

By Monday, a meticulous search yielded the most damning piece of evidence: Kathleen's severed head, buried in the vegetable garden behind her own home. A bullet from a thirty-eight-caliber revolver was lodged in her skull, revealing the grim truth that she had been executed before her body was mutilated and burned. The discovery shifted the focus of the investigation directly to Kathleen's home—and the man with whom she shared it: her husband, John Strange.

―――――

To understand the terrible fate that befell Kathleen Strange, one must first unravel the complex web of relationships within the Strange family. Kathleen was, by all accounts, a kind and compassionate woman who had touched many lives as a teacher. The petite forty-four-year-old had even taught Sunday school, earning the respect and admiration of colleagues and students alike.

Kathleen had been married once before, and from that prior relationship came her only child, Anthony Eugene "Tony" Jones, who was twenty-two years old in 1990. Tony had shown troubling signs of a violent streak in his youth, a foreshadowing of the darkness that would eventually consume him.

Her marriage to John Strange was relatively new, having wed two years earlier. At forty-seven, John was also an educator, teaching at a local Baptist school. Their union had created a blended family that included Kathleen's son Tony, as well as John's children from his previous marriage. Among them was twenty-year-old Christine

Strange, who lived with her boyfriend, Sam Edwards, in Columbia, Kentucky, about two hours from Louisville.

On the surface, the Strange household appeared ordinary—two teachers building a quiet life together, their adult children establishing lives of their own. However, beneath this veneer of normalcy lay fault lines of tension and conflict. John and Kathleen's marriage had grown increasingly strained. As one acquaintance delicately put it, they "had their differences," though friends would later reveal that arguments had become commonplace. Financial pressures and disagreements about their children plagued the relationship, with whispers circulating that Kathleen had considered leaving John.

Tony Jones also harbored deep resentment toward his stepfather. Having dropped out of school, Tony drifted aimlessly, occasionally clashing with his mother about his lifestyle choices. In stark contrast stood Christine Strange, whose loyalty to her father was unwavering. Despite living two hours away, she maintained an intense bond with John, who had helped her and her boyfriend Sam establish themselves. Christine idolized her father, a devotion that would later prove pivotal in the aftermath of Kathleen's murder.

———

As Memorial Day weekend 1990 began, Kathleen Strange anticipated a welcome break from teaching and the chance to spend time with her family. She had spoken with relatives about gathering together, but by Saturday night, May 26, those plans took a horrific turn.

That Saturday evening, a confrontation erupted inside the Strange home. In the supposed safety of the couple's bedroom, Kathleen was shot execution-style at close range. The bullet entered the back of her head, killing her almost instantly.

What followed defies comprehension. Rather than calling for help, Kathleen's killer embarked on a cold, calculated cover-up. Her body was transported—likely under the cover of darkness—to the vacant house on Ninth Street. There, in that dilapidated building, the perpetrator decapitated her corpse with crude instruments, a ghastly act of mutilation intended to thwart identification. The head was carefully wrapped and kept separate (later to be buried in the garden at home), while her headless body was doused with an accelerant and set ablaze in the predawn hours of Sunday.

Shortly after midnight, a passerby noticed the flames and alerted the fire department. By the time firefighters arrived, portions of the old frame house were already engulfed. Upon extinguishing the fire, they then discovered the charred remains and immediately summoned police.

Investigators noted that the victim's clothing had been partially burned away, but some fabric remained. Despite the fire damage, it was evident that the body had been deliberately mutilated—the head and hands were also missing, suggesting a determined effort to prevent identification through dental records or fingerprints.

As Sunday wore on, John Strange told friends and police that Kathleen was missing. He claimed ignorance of her whereabouts, suggesting she might have gone out of town or been out late. What John failed to mention immediately was that he himself was suffering from burns on his arms and hands. He had spent part of Sunday being treated at a hospital for second-degree burns, which he explained away as an accident from a backyard barbecue grill. Of course, this explanation did little to convince detectives once they learned of it. The coincidence was too striking: a missing wife, a burned husband, and a headless body found in a fire.

By Monday, May 28—Memorial Day itself—suspicion centered squarely on John Strange. Investigators secured a search warrant for the Strange residence. In the backyard garden, under freshly turned soil, they made the crucial discovery of Kathleen's severed head wrapped in cloth. Inside the house, forensic teams detected traces of blood beneath the carpet and in the trunk of Kathleen's car. The evidence overwhelmingly indicated that Kathleen had been killed at home before her body was moved. Later that day, John R. Strange was arrested and charged with murder, abuse of a corpse, and arson.

———

In a shocking twist, police discovered that John had not acted alone in the aftermath of the murder—the investigation uncovered a family conspiracy to conceal the crime. Phone records and witness interviews placed Christine Strange and Sam Edwards at the Strange house in Louisville on the very weekend of the murder. Under questioning, both eventually admitted to helping John destroy evidence after Kathleen was killed. The two had driven from Columbia, possibly at John's urgent request, and arrived after Kathleen was already dead.

Christine and Sam were charged with tampering with physical evidence. They had washed Kathleen's blood-soaked clothing to eliminate forensic evidence and helped clean the crime scene, scrubbing bloodstains and removing any traces that might incriminate John. This calculated effort to erase evidence suggested prior planning and a clear state of mind after the murder. John had enlisted his own daughter and her boyfriend as a cleanup crew.

The notion of a daughter helping cover up the beheading and burning of her stepmother stunned investigators and the public alike. Christine was just twenty, perhaps under her father's powerful influence, while Sam, an outsider to the family, reportedly did whatever Christine asked. Both declined media interviews when their names surfaced, their exact motivations remaining unclear. Had John promised them something? Were they simply obeying him out of misguided loyalty or fear? The case had now ensnared multiple members of the Strange family in a web of criminal charges.

By early June 1990, John Strange awaited trial for his wife's murder. At a bond reduction hearing on June 28, he remained mostly silent, speaking through his attorney. Given the gruesome details and compelling evidence, the judge maintained his high bond. Christine Strange and Sam Edwards were also indicted on evidence-tampering charges. Investigators hoped one or both might cooperate in exchange for leniency, potentially providing a complete account of the plot to conceal Kathleen's murder.

————

In late August 1991, John R. Strange's murder trial began in a Louisville courtroom. The sensational details guaranteed intense media coverage, and the courthouse was packed with observers. The prosecution painted John as a cold-blooded killer who murdered his wife to escape a failing marriage and possibly claim life insurance—a motive suggested, though never fully substantiated. They presented the forensic evidence: The bullet retrieved from Kathleen's skull matched a revolver owned by John, blood spatter analysis from the Strange home matched Kathleen's blood type, and charred fabric from the burned body was consistent with a dress Kathleen had worn. Most damning was the discovery of Kathleen's head buried on John's property—something only the killer could have done. Prosecutors argued that John had killed Kathleen at home and then methodically carried out a plan to mutilate and burn her body to avoid detection.

Family drama played a crucial role in the proceedings. Christine Strange had struck a deal, agreeing to testify for the prosecution. In a tense courtroom moment, she admitted to helping her father clean up after the murder. "Daddy told me it was an accident at first," she testified softly, explaining that John had begged for her help. Christine detailed how she and Sam washed Kathleen's clothes and watched as her father loaded the body into Kathleen's car. Her testimony was a double-edged sword. While confirming John's cover-up, it also opened the door for the defense's radical new theory.

William Radigan, John's defense attorney, employed a stunning strategy. In his opening statement, he made a shocking admission and accusation: John had indeed decapitated and burned Kathleen's body, the lawyer conceded—but he hadn't killed her. Instead, Radigan told the jury that Kathleen's own son was the real murderer. Gasps rippled through the courtroom as Radigan clarified he meant Anthony "Tony" Jones, Kathleen's son from her previous marriage. According to the defense, Tony harbored deep animosity toward his mother and hatred for John. On that fateful night, the defense claimed, Tony came to the Strange house, argued with Kathleen, and shot her in the head. John supposedly discovered Kathleen's body after Tony fled. Fearing his stepson would be blamed, John panicked. In an irrational state, Radigan argued, John had decided to conceal the death by dismembering the corpse and setting the fire, hoping to make it appear as if an unknown assailant had killed Kathleen.

This claim—that a grieving husband would behead and burn his wife's body to protect the real killer—was met with obvious skepticism. Under cross-examination, John maintained, "I know how it looks, but I didn't kill Kathy." He described Tony and Kathleen's turbulent relationship, suggesting Tony might have snapped. However, there was no physical evidence placing Tony at the crime scene, and he had not been charged in connection with Kathleen's death. The prosecutor pointed out that John never called 911 upon supposedly finding his wife's body, nor did he seek medical help—instead, he embarked on a grotesque dismemberment and arson scheme. In a withering cross-examination, the prosecutor asked, "Mr. Strange, what kind of innocent man responds to his wife's murder by cutting off her head?" John had no compelling answer beyond claiming he was in shock and not thinking clearly.

Outside the jury's presence, observers noted that John remained emotionless throughout much of the trial, even when graphic forensic photos were displayed. If the defense hoped for sympathy by portraying John as a distraught protector of his stepson, it likely backfired.

After a two-week trial filled with forensic testimony, tearful statements from Kathleen's relatives, and the bizarre spectacle of the defendant essentially admitting to horrific acts while denying murder, the case went to the jury.

The verdict came swiftly. In September 1991, the jury found John R. Strange guilty on all counts: murder, abuse of a corpse, and first-degree arson. Citing the "exceptionally cruel and depraved" nature of the crime, the judge imposed a severe sentence: sixty-five years in prison. John showed little emotion as the sentence was read. Across the gallery, Kathleen's family members wept quietly, relieved that justice had been secured—at least partially.

————

Even as John Strange began serving his sentence, a question lingered: What about Tony Jones? John's trial had effectively accused him of matricide in open court. At the time, Tony was a free man; he had not been charged in connection with his mother's death and publicly denied any involvement. For a while, it seemed Tony might escape any legal consequences in the Strange case. However, Tony's own actions soon brought him infamy of a different sort.

On May 8, 1992, less than a year after John's conviction, Tony Jones committed a brutal murder that shocked Louisville anew. In Cherokee Park, a popular green space that also served as a meeting place for local gay men, Tony set out on what he chillingly described as "hunting queers." He lured thirty-six-year-old Richard Gilman into a secluded area and, in an act of hate-fueled violence, shot him to death simply because of the victim's sexual orientation. The crime was senseless and heinous—a hate crime before that term had fully entered public consciousness. Tony was quickly arrested, and Louisville prosecutors charged him with murder, seeking the death penalty for the now twenty-four-year-old.

The Richard Gilman murder trial in late 1992 dominated Louisville headlines. Not only was it a high-profile hate crime, but many noted the dark parallel: Tony was now on trial for a brutal murder just as his stepfather had been. The Strange family seemed cursed with violence. During Tony's trial, prosecutors revealed how he had bragged to acquaintances about hunting gay men in Cherokee Park. The evidence against him was overwhelming, and the jury convicted him of murder and related charges. While they stopped short of a death sentence, in October 1992, the court delivered an extraordinary punishment: Anthony "Tony" Jones was sentenced to 533 years in prison. This staggering number—essentially five centuries behind bars—sent a clear message, though news reports dryly noted that despite the massive sentence, Jones would be eligible for parole in ten years due to parole laws at the time. The jury, outraged at this possibility, publicly urged officials to deny him parole at every opportunity.

With Tony now a convicted murderer, law enforcement could not ignore the lingering questions about Kathleen Strange's death. John's defense accusations suddenly took on a different light. In December 1992, Louisville authorities announced they were reopening the investigation into Kathleen's murder, focusing on Tony's potential involvement. The community was stunned. Could both John and Tony have been involved in Kathleen's death?

Investigators reviewed old evidence and conducted new interviews. They looked for any indication that Tony might have been present during the Memorial Day 1990 crime. Some witnesses recalled seeing an unfamiliar car near the Strange home that weekend—possibly Tony's. Meanwhile, a former friend of Tony's told police that Tony had once expressed hatred for his mother and even mused about "getting rid of her," though such secondhand remarks were difficult to verify. With Tony now behind bars, prosecutors convened a grand jury to hear evidence regarding his involvement in Kathleen's case.

By January 1993, a Jefferson County grand jury indicted Tony Jones for complicity in the murder of Kathleen Strange, accusing him of participating in or orchestrating the killing alongside John. Prosecuting Tony for Kathleen's death proved to be complex. John, unsurprisingly, refused to cooperate, given that implicating Tony might undermine his future appeals. Christine's testimony had placed only John at the scene after the fact, not Tony. Lacking direct evidence tying Tony to the actual shooting, the case was largely circumstantial. Nonetheless, prosecutors moved forward, determined to hold Tony accountable if he had any role in the crime.

In mid-1993, Tony Jones was brought to Louisville to be arraigned for Kathleen's murder. In a bitter irony, he appeared in the same courthouse where he had been convicted of the Cherokee Park murder months before. Tony, now twenty-five and already serving a life term, maintained an impassive demeanor. He pleaded not guilty and, through his attorney, dismissed the charges as "retaliation for what my stepfather said." It seemed Tony and John were pointing fingers at each other: John had blamed Tony, and now Tony suggested John was lying to shift the blame. The truth, perhaps, lay somewhere in between, with each man playing a part in Kathleen's fate.

———

The second Strange murder trial—Commonwealth of Kentucky vs. Anthony Eugene Jones for the murder of Kathleen Strange—began in early 1994. This trial received less attention than John's, partly because much of the gruesome story had already been told and partly because Tony's fate (533 years in prison) was essentially sealed regardless of the outcome. Prosecutors argued that even if John had physically carried out parts of the crime, it was Tony who had the motive and vicious intent to kill his own mother. They proposed a scenario in which Tony, fueled by anger and perhaps seeking money, confronted Kathleen and pulled the trigger, after which John helped cover it up. They highlighted Tony's proven capacity for violence and hate, as evidenced by the Cherokee Park killing.

Tony's defense took the opposite approach from John's. They insisted John alone had killed Kathleen in a domestic quarrel and that John's attempt to blame Tony was a desperate lie. They reminded jurors that a prior jury had convicted John of actually committing the murder, so why revisit those facts? The defense also emphasized that Tony had no forensic ties to the crime scene. No fingerprints, no DNA—though DNA testing was rudimentary at the time—and no eyewitnesses. Essentially, Tony's team argued that the state was trying to convict him based solely on the word of John Strange, a proven murderer, and the coincidence of Tony's later crime.

The truth of Kathleen's murder may never be fully untangled. After days of testimony, the jury in Tony's trial faced a reasonable doubt conundrum. In June 1994, the verdict came: Tony Jones was acquitted of direct involvement in Kathleen Strange's murder. Lacking concrete evidence, jurors were not convinced beyond a reasonable doubt that Tony had actively participated in killing his mother. Some jurors later said that while Tony's potential involvement was suspicious, the case presented felt largely speculative. In effect, Kathleen's murder remains officially attributed to John Strange alone, who has never wavered from his story blaming Tony.

Nonetheless, Tony did not escape accountability. The legal saga concluded with Tony remaining in prison on his 533-year sentence for the Cherokee Park murder—a punishment that all but ensures he will never be released. John Strange, now in his mid-70s, likewise remains incarcerated, serving out his sixty-five-year term in a Kentucky state penitentiary. According to prison records, John will not be eligible for release until well into his 90s. Both men, once free and part of a family unit, will likely die behind bars.

As for Christine Strange and Sam Edwards, the peripheral accomplices, their fates were far less severe. In exchange for her crucial testimony against her father, Christine received a plea deal on the evidence-tampering charge. She was sentenced to probation and mandatory counseling, avoiding jail time. Sam Edwards also pleaded guilty to tampering and received a short jail sentence, partly suspended. The court acknowledged that Christine and Sam were young and influenced by John, though many still faulted them for not coming forward sooner. Their attempt to wash away the bloodstains —literally and figuratively—will haunt them for life.

———

The Strange case transfixed the Louisville community in the early 1990s. Media coverage was extensive, with local newspapers following every development from the initial fire to the trials and retrials. Local television news carried somber reports, and anchors spoke of the "decapitation murder" in tones of disbelief. It wasn't just the gore that captured public attention—it was the disturbing notion that a seemingly ordinary family could implode in such a violent, twisted way.

At Kathleen's former school and church, grief was compounded by horror. A memorial service for Kathleen was held in June 1990 once her remains were released for burial. Colleagues and students remembered her as a kind teacher taken too soon. A minister addressing the congregation warned of "the evil that can hide behind a friendly face" in reference to John Strange. Indeed, many who knew John casually— as a teacher, neighbor, or church member—were stunned that he could commit such a crime.

How could a devout Baptist schoolteacher also be a murderer who would mutilate his wife? This jarring contradiction became a talking point in Louisville. It echoed, for some, another notorious Louisville case from just two years prior: the murder of Brenda Schaefer by Mel Ignatow in 1988. Ignatow, like John Strange, had seemed unremarkable outwardly, yet he had committed unspeakable acts. The early 1990s in Louisville were marked by the realization that horrific violence could lurk behind mundane façades.

CHAPTER 6
THE VANISHING

The crisp November air settled over St. Paul, Minnesota, as the sun set on an ordinary Tuesday evening in 1981. Families across the Midway neighborhood hurried through their evening routines, with some heading to work, others to dinner, and many to local community events. Among them, the Hansen family—mother Ellen, six-year-old Cassandra "Cassie," and four-year-old Vanessa—bundled up against the chill and made their way to the Jehovah Evangelical Lutheran Church for a special family night program. The church sat like a steadfast guardian on Snelling Avenue, its warm lights beckoning parishioners inside, away from the darkening November sky.

Inside, the church basement buzzed with activity. Children darted about in excitement, parents chatted, and volunteers organized activities for the evening's festivities. Cassie, a bright, book-loving first grader with blonde hair and an eager smile, stayed close to her mother and sister as they settled in for the children's program. The church auditorium, filled with the comforting sounds of community and fellowship, was typical Tuesday night fare for this close-knit congregation. No one could have imagined that within the safe confines of this sacred space, evil lurked in the shadows, watching and waiting.

What happened next would shatter not only one family's world but also an entire community's sense of security. The events of November 10, 1981, would forever change how parents in St. Paul viewed their children's safety, even in places once considered sanctuaries from the dangers of the outside world. Tragically, this ordinary evening was the last time anyone would see little Cassie Hansen alive.

———

At approximately 6:50 p.m., as the children's scavenger hunt was about to begin, Cassie tugged at her mother's sleeve and asked for permission to use the bathroom. Ellen Hansen, seeing nothing unusual in this request within the familiar church setting, nodded and watched her daughter skip away. The church had restrooms on both the main floor and upstairs, and while Ellen expected Cassie to use the nearby facilities on the lower level, the little girl apparently decided to head upstairs instead—perhaps to the bathroom she knew better.

Those fleeting moments as Cassie walked away marked the last time her mother would see her daughter alive, a mundane parting with no opportunity for a proper goodbye.

Three witnesses later recalled seeing Cassie in the hallway and stairwell during those critical minutes. They noticed the small blonde girl making her way toward the upper level of the church. More significantly, two of those same witnesses observed something else: an unfamiliar middle-aged man lingering in the same hallway, heading up the same stairs shortly after Cassie went in that direction.

By 7:05 p.m., Ellen Hansen grew concerned. The bathroom trip was taking far too long. Rising from her seat, she went to check the restroom herself but found no sign of her daughter. What followed was a parent's worst nightmare unfolding in real time—the frantic checking of stalls, the quickening pace down hallways, the initial voice of reason saying perhaps Cassie had wandered off to explore. But as minutes stretched on and more people joined the search, a cold dread settled over the church.

Every corner of the building was searched. Cassie's coat remained behind in the auditorium—a small, poignant detail that suggested she hadn't planned to go outside. By 7:30 p.m., with the little girl nowhere to be found, the police were called. Officers Jim Groh and Rick Klein arrived promptly, young men who would later recall that even in those early moments, they sensed something deeply wrong.

Through the night, an agonizing search expanded beyond the church walls. Flashlight beams cut through the darkness as officers and volunteers combed the surrounding streets and alleys. Local television stations broadcast Cassie's photo and description, while taxi drivers and patrol officers across the city were alerted to watch for a small blonde girl, possibly in distress, possibly with a stranger. The community response was immediate and overwhelming, but as midnight came and went with no sign of Cassie, hope began to dim.

What no one realized as they searched was that Cassie was already beyond help. In those brief moments after she left her mother's side, she had encountered a diabolical predator in the stairwell. While desperate searches continued through the night, Cassie's life had already been extinguished and her small body hidden away, waiting to be discarded like refuse.

St. Paul, still reeling from a bizarre kidnapping case just the year before, when Ming Sen Shiue had not only abducted a woman and her daughter but also murdered a six-year-old boy who witnessed the crime, now faced another unthinkable tragedy involving a child. The sense of vulnerability was overwhelming, especially because, this time, the victim had vanished from inside a church—a location where most parents felt their children were safe from the evils of the world.

———

November 11, 1981, Veterans Day, dawned with the city already awake and searching. Many police officers and volunteers had been up all night looking for any trace of Cassie Hansen. The grim answer to their efforts came shortly before 11:00 a.m., when an employee behind an auto repair shop made a horrifying discovery.

Behind the Auto Clinic Garage at the corner of Grand Avenue and Grotto Street, approximately three miles from the church, the worker approached a large commercial dumpster and found the body of a small child discarded among the trash. Police were summoned immediately, and the worst fears of the community were confirmed: the body was that of Cassie Hansen.

The dumpster and surrounding area became a crime scene, cordoned off with yellow tape as detectives and crime scene technicians meticulously collected evidence. The medical examiner who arrived on the scene determined that Cassie had been killed by ligature strangulation, consistent with a belt being used as a garrote. The time of death was estimated between 8:00 p.m. and midnight the previous evening, just hours after she had disappeared from the church.

The autopsy revealed the brutality of Cassie's final moments. The child had been severely beaten, with bruises and trauma visible on her face, head, ribs, and shoulder. Marks on her face matched the pattern of a hand clamped tightly over her mouth—a stark indication of her terrified struggle as her attacker had silenced her. Though there were no signs of penetrative sexual assault, investigators discovered semen stains on Cassie's clothing, indicating a sexual motive. The killer had likely molested the child and ejaculated on her clothing even without committing rape.

This bodily fluid provided investigators with their first solid forensic lead. Though DNA profiling was still years away from becoming standard procedure, crime lab technicians could perform blood typing on the semen. Analysis showed the perpetrator had Type O blood and was a secretor, meaning his blood type antigens appeared in other bodily fluids. While this couldn't identify a specific individual, it narrowed the suspect pool to roughly thirty-six percent of the male population.

Another crucial piece of evidence came from a single foreign hair recovered from Cassie's clothing. Microscopic analysis revealed rare ring-shaped banding along the hair shaft—an unusual characteristic that experts believed could be distinctive enough to link a future suspect to the crime.

As news of Cassie's murder spread, additional evidence began surfacing in the streets of St. Paul. On the morning of November 11, a man bicycling down Milton Street had spotted a small black patent leather shoe lying in the road. He remembered seeing a car parked on that block the night before, with a man inside who seemed out of place. The cyclist turned the shoe over to police, and Cassie's family confirmed it as one she had worn to church. The matching shoe was discovered the following day in the same area. Investigators noted that both shoes were missing their metal buckles, which appeared to have been forcibly torn off. The scattered footwear, combined with the witness sighting, helped police begin to trace the killer's movements across the city.

The scattered evidence, the body in a dumpster, shoes strewn along residential streets, and signs of a sexual assault. They all painted a picture of a sexually motivated abduction that turned lethal, likely as the perpetrator attempted to silence his victim. For the investigators working the case, including veteran Ramsey County death investigator Don Gorrie, the crime scene and autopsy findings were deeply disturbing. Gorrie, who had a two-year-old daughter of his own, later admitted that the case stuck with him for years afterward. "It was just hard not to carry that case with me," he confessed.

As the police processed the crime scene, the Hansen family received the devastating news that their little girl would never come home. A community already on edge now faced the realization that a dangerous predator walked among them—one who had taken a child from what should have been one of the safest places in the neighborhood. The pressure on investigators to identify and capture the killer intensified with each passing hour.

———

While the community mourned and parents kept their children closer than ever, St. Paul's sex homicide unit was already following leads that pointed to one man—a fifty-seven-year-old taxi driver named Stuart Willis Knowlton. Even before Cassie's body was found, a tip had reached police about Knowlton from an unlikely source. Janice Rettman, an employee in the Mayor's Office, contacted WCCO-TV crime reporter Caroline Lowe with concerns about Knowlton's possible involvement based on his known behaviors around children. The reporter passed this information to investigators immediately, putting Knowlton on their radar from the earliest hours of the case.

Knowlton was a somewhat familiar figure in St. Paul's Midway neighborhood, known to loiter near places where children gathered. One acquaintance later noted that Knowlton liked to hang around playgrounds and exhibited an unsettling interest in children. His job as a cab driver provided both opportunity and cover for predatory behavior—he had a vehicle readily available and could claim to be working when questioned about his whereabouts.

As investigators dug deeper into Knowlton's activities on the night of November 10, multiple red flags emerged that could not be dismissed as coincidences.

From approximately 5:00 p.m. until 3:00 a.m. the next morning, Knowlton made no radio contact with his taxi dispatchers. He neither responded to calls nor requested fares during that entire period—highly unusual for a driver who typically maintained active communication with dispatch. This extended silence suggested he was engaged in activities he didn't want to document.

Stuart Knowlton

At approximately 7:50 p.m. on November 10, less than an hour after Cassie disappeared, a witness spotted Knowlton inside an Arthur Treacher's fish and chips restaurant located at Grand and Grotto, virtually the same corner where Cassie's body would later be found. The witness noted that Knowlton loitered there for nearly thirty minutes, appearing nervous and out of place. When the witness left, he observed Knowlton standing outside, staring intently at the Auto Clinic Garage across the street—the very location of the dumpster where Cassie would be discarded.

The witness's account placed Knowlton near the eventual dump site during the likely timeframe of the murder. It seemed plausible that Knowlton had Cassie hidden in his taxi at that very moment, perhaps restrained, as he scoped out a location to dispose of her body.

Around 3:00 a.m. on November 11, Knowlton showed up unannounced at the Comfort Massage Studio in St. Paul. Dorothy Noga, an employee at the parlor, encountered him and immediately sensed something was wrong. He was hunched over, breathing heavily, shaking, and speaking rapidly, his entire demeanor frantic and unsteady. Knowlton claimed he had stopped by just to drop off his business card, but his agitated state suggested something far more troubling. At the time, Dorothy hadn't yet heard about Cassie's disappearance, but the encounter disturbed her enough that she would remember it clearly later.

Just after leaving the massage parlor, Knowlton finally broke his radio silence—not to report any sightings of the missing girl, but to claim that a fare had stolen his briefcase containing his trip sheets, the logs that taxi drivers are required to maintain detailing all passengers. The next day, he contacted a former employer at another cab company and asked to buy blank trip sheets, falsely claiming his current employer didn't supply them. These actions strongly suggested Knowlton was attempting to cover his tracks by destroying or fabricating records of his activities that night.

Perhaps most telling was Knowlton's unusual fixation on the case after Cassie's body was found. During his next taxi shift on November 11, he twice broke protocol by using the cab radio to rant about the murder and the ongoing investigation. Each time, the dispatcher had to cut him off, reminding him that such use of the radio was inappropriate. His coworkers found it strange that he seemed so obsessed with this particular crime. Of course, criminals often insert themselves into investigations, driven by guilt or a morbid fascination with their own handiwork.

Given this constellation of suspicious circumstances, the St. Paul police quickly zeroed in on Stuart Knowlton. Police questioned Knowlton on November 12, just one day after Cassie's body was found, but released him due to a lack of physical evidence at the time. Though they didn't yet have enough evidence to arrest him, investigators quietly put him under surveillance as they continued to build their case.

Meanwhile, they sought help from those who knew Knowlton personally, hoping someone might coax out a confession or an incriminating statement. This strategy would lead to one of the most dramatic chapters in the case, involving a brave woman who risked everything to help catch a killer.

———

Dorothy Noga, a thirty-eight-year-old massage therapist and mother of four, became an unexpected hero in the Cassie Hansen investigation. On the night of November 11, moved by news of the child's murder, Dorothy called the police to report concerns about a different massage client who had made disturbing comments about children. When she spoke to investigators, however, she learned they were already looking at Stuart Knowlton as a suspect—the same man who had visited her studio in an agitated state just hours after Cassie's murder.

In that moment, Dorothy made a critical connection. Knowlton was a regular client who had shared inappropriate sexual fantasies during massage sessions, including scenarios involving children. One fantasy he had described to her bore chilling resemblance to the abduction of a child from a church—the very crime he had apparently just committed. Recognizing she might be in a unique position to help, Dorothy volunteered to assist the police by contacting Knowlton.

The police were understandably cautious about using a civilian to engage a murder suspect. They initially advised Dorothy not to get involved, as they were concerned for her safety. However, Dorothy was determined. Against police recommendations, she reached out to Knowlton on her own, beginning a dangerous cat-and-mouse interaction that would span several weeks.

On November 17 and 18, 1981, Dorothy made contact with Knowlton by phone. During their conversation on the eighteenth, Knowlton made an astonishing admission: He confessed to killing

Cassie Hansen and provided details about the murder that only the perpetrator would know. He described how he had approached the little girl in the church, lured her in with the promise of a game, and then strangled her with his belt when she began screaming. Unfortunately, this crucial confession was not recorded and existed only in Dorothy's memory.

Undeterred, Dorothy continued her dangerous liaison with the killer. On December 8, she met Knowlton in person and drove him past the Jehovah Lutheran Church. When Knowlton realized where they were, he became visibly agitated—a reaction that further convinced Dorothy of his guilt. Five days later, on December 13, they spoke again by phone, and Knowlton once more admitted to the killing. This second confession also went unrecorded due to technical issues.

The situation took a violent turn immediately after this December 13 call. Perhaps sensing that Dorothy posed a threat who could expose him, Knowlton decided to silence her permanently. He showed up at the Comfort Massage Studio in the early morning hours of December 14, 1981, and Dorothy's coworker let him in, unaware of the danger. Knowlton immediately became aggressive, pushing Dorothy into a chair and putting his face inches from hers.

"Take a look, because it's going to be your last," he snarled, then added ominously, "I'll show you what she went through"—a clear reference to Cassie. With that, Knowlton launched a frenzied knife attack on Dorothy Noga.

The assault was brutal and prolonged. For approximately twenty minutes, Knowlton tried to smother Dorothy and stabbed her thirty-two times. He slashed her throat, severed her carotid artery and jugular vein, and inflicted wounds behind her ear, on her face, and elsewhere on her body. Blood poured from Dorothy like a faucet. As her vision blurred and she began to lose consciousness, she pretended to be dead, praying for help as her life ebbed away.

In what can only be described as divine intervention, help arrived at the critical moment. Officer Pat Scott of the St. Paul Police was on a late-night break at a diner only about 125 feet from the massage parlor when the 911 call came through. He rushed to the scene and found Dorothy Noga collapsed in a pool of blood. Scott immediately grabbed a towel and applied pressure to the most serious neck wound, likely preventing her from bleeding out before paramedics arrived.

Dorothy was rushed to the hospital in critical condition. Doctors later marveled that, "there's absolutely no way in the world that this woman ever should have lived," given the severity of her injuries. The trauma and blood loss from the attack caused Dorothy to suffer memory loss, and she didn't recall Knowlton's confessions until five months later, when her memory gradually returned. Once she recovered, she was able to provide a full statement to the police about Knowlton's admissions.

While Dorothy recovered, investigators continued pursuing other angles. Janice Rettman, who had provided the initial tip, cooperated with police by speaking with Knowlton and secretly recording their conversations. Though he didn't explicitly confess to her, he made incriminating remarks, such as mentioning that Cassie had been strangled—a fact not widely known at the time. He also told Rettman he couldn't remember where he was on the night of the murder and admitted to having an explosive temper.

Another acquaintance, Janice Lloyd, reported that Knowlton had asked her to provide a false alibi for him. Three days after the murder, he called Lloyd and asked if she would say he had phoned her on the night of November 10. Lloyd knew he hadn't called then, and she refused to lie. When she directly asked if he had killed Cassie, he ambiguously replied that he wasn't sure and needed someone to talk to.

By late summer 1982, with Dorothy Noga recovered and able to testify, the case against Stuart Knowlton was ready to proceed. The physical evidence—the semen blood-type match, the distinctive ringed hair comparison that matched Knowlton's, witness sightings placing him at key locations, the shoe trail, and his pattern of suspicious behavior—when combined with Dorothy's testimony about his confessions, created a compelling case. On September 28, 1982, a Ramsey County grand jury indicted Stuart W. Knowlton on three counts of first-degree murder for the death of Cassie Hansen.

———

By the time Stuart Knowlton faced trial in April 1983, he had suffered his own misfortune. In a strange twist of fate, he had been struck by a vehicle while crossing a street in downtown St. Paul during the investigation, resulting in the amputation of his leg below the knee. This injury did not deter prosecutors, who proceeded with the case against the now-disabled defendant.

In a somewhat surprising legal strategy, Knowlton waived his right to a jury trial, opting instead to be tried by a judge alone. Perhaps his defense believed a judge might be more impartial or better able to sift through potentially prejudicial evidence than a local jury still reeling from the emotional impact of Cassie's murder.

The trial lasted three weeks and presented a wealth of damning evidence. Forensic experts testified about the semen typing that matched Knowlton's blood type, the distinctive banded hair found on Cassie's clothing that matched his, and other physical findings. Witnesses recounted seeing Knowlton at the church and near the dump site on the night of the murder. Taxi dispatchers described his unexplained radio silence during the critical hours, and acquaintances shared his incriminating remarks and behavior in the days following the crime.

Most powerful of all was Dorothy Noga's testimony. Fully recovered but bearing visible scars from Knowlton's attack, she recounted in detail what he had told her about murdering Cassie. She described how he had admitted to entering the church, approaching Cassie with the offer to play a game, leading her to his taxi, and then strangling her with his belt when she began screaming. Dorothy also testified that Knowlton had expressed a sexual fixation on young girls' shoes, specifically ones without buckles, and told her he was disappointed that Cassie's shoes had buckles. She also testified about his subsequent attempt to silence her permanently—a desperate act that further indicated his guilt.

The defense attempted to cast doubt wherever possible, suggesting other leads and pointing out limitations in the forensic evidence. They noted that hair comparison is not absolute proof of identity and emphasized the lack of direct eyewitnesses to the abduction. However, given the mountain of circumstantial evidence and Knowlton's confessions to Dorothy, these arguments gained little traction.

At the conclusion of the trial, the judge found Stuart Knowlton guilty on all three counts of first-degree murder. In June 1983, he was sentenced to life in prison for the first count: murder in the course of criminal sexual conduct. The other two counts were later vacated to avoid redundant convictions.

In Minnesota at that time, a life sentence carried the possibility of parole after serving a minimum term. When Knowlton first became eligible for parole in the late 1990s, the Hansen family mobilized to ensure he would never walk free. For nearly seventeen years after his conviction, they attended parole hearings and submitted emotional pleas to keep him incarcerated. Their advocacy succeeded; he was denied parole repeatedly, thanks in part to Cassie's family, who fought to ensure he remained behind bars.

On October 31, 2006, at the age of seventy-five, Stuart Willis Knowlton died of natural causes while still incarcerated at the Minnesota Correctional Facility – Oak Park Heights. His death came just a couple of weeks before the twenty-fifth anniversary of Cassie's murder, bringing final closure to a case that had haunted St. Paul for a quarter-century.

———

Cassie Hansen's murder left an indelible mark on St. Paul. In the immediate aftermath, there was a profound shift in how parents viewed their children's safety, even in places once considered sanctuaries. As retired officer Jim Groh recalled, "My kids were scared for years" after Cassie's case, reflecting how even families of police officers changed their habits to protect their children. Another officer noted that life was never the same for children of that era—the freedom to explore independently, to venture into public places without constant supervision, had been severely curtailed by the specter of what happened to one little girl in a church bathroom.

Churches and schools across St. Paul instituted more rigorous supervision policies. Young children were no longer allowed to go to restrooms alone, volunteer hall monitors became standard at events, and parents became hypervigilant about knowing their children's whereabouts at all times. A cousin of Cassie's later admitted that even decades after her murder, he found it impossible to let his own children use public restrooms without supervision—a direct legacy of the trauma that had affected his family.

The case also influenced law enforcement practices in Minnesota. The intensive investigation—involving hundreds of interviews and collaboration with the FBI—became a model for interagency cooperation in child abduction cases. Twenty-three members of the St. Paul Police Department's Sex Crimes Unit received a unit citation for their dedication to solving Cassie's murder.

In 2017, on the thirty-sixth anniversary of Dorothy Noga's near-fatal attack, the department held a ceremony to honor those whose contributions had gone formally unrecognized for decades. Dorothy Noga and Officers Pat Scott, Rick Klein, and Jim Groh received the Chief's Award for Merit. Without Dorothy's bravery, Knowlton might never have been convicted and may have gone on to harm others. At the ceremony, Cassie's surviving sisters, two of whom were born after her death, met and thanked these heroes for the first time. It was a poignant reminder that even though time had passed, Cassie's memory remained alive in the community.

At the Jehovah Evangelical Lutheran Church, a simple plaque was mounted in memory of Cassie Hansen as a subtle yet permanent tribute, ensuring that new generations to pass through those halls would know the history and remain vigilant.

CHAPTER 7

THE NIGHT SHIFT

T he unassuming town of Moose Lake, Minnesota, nestled against the shores of its namesake lake, embodied the idyllic peace of rural America. In the late spring of 1999, as the last remnants of winter finally released their grip on the northern landscape, the community of 2,200 residents welcomed the gentler season with a collective sigh of relief. Memorial Day weekend had just passed, and the first hint of summer was settling comfortably across the small lakeside town.

The roads running through Moose Lake served as vital arteries connecting the Twin Cities to the south with Duluth to the north, bringing travelers and truckers alike through the quiet community. Interstate 35 hummed with constant traffic, and alongside it, local businesses thrived, catering to both residents and those just passing through. Among these establishments stood D.J.'s Expressway Conoco station, a combination gas station and convenience store that served as a familiar landmark to locals.

For nineteen-year-old Katie Poirier, the station represented more than just another business—it was her workplace, a stepping stone toward the future she envisioned for herself. Katie was a familiar face to residents of Moose Lake and nearby Barnum, where she had grown up. Standing at just 5'3" with a slight build, Katie's petite frame disguised her considerable determination. Those who knew her described her as a friendly, hard-working young woman who approached life with quiet confidence and an infectious smile.

Katie had graduated from Barnum High School the previous year, a popular student with a wide circle of friends. Unlike many peers who drifted aimlessly after graduation, Katie had clear ambitions. She dreamed of building a career in criminal justice, hoping one day to become a corrections officer. The late-night shifts at D.J.'s Expressway were simply a means to an end—a way to earn money and gain experience while moving toward her goals.

The convenience store job wasn't particularly glamorous, but it suited Katie's needs. Management trusted her implicitly, often leaving her to handle the store alone during overnight hours. In a town like Moose Lake, where serious crime was virtually non-existent, such arrangements weren't considered risky. The community maintained a pervasive sense of safety, neighbors looked out for one another, and strangers were welcomed with typical Midwestern hospitality.

Nothing in Katie's upbringing or daily life would have suggested she might be in danger. Growing up in rural Minnesota had instilled in her a natural trust in others, perhaps even a certain innocence. Like countless other young adults working similar jobs across America's heartland, Katie likely never imagined that a routine shift could escalate into anything sinister.

However, as the mild evening of May 26, 1999, descended on Moose Lake, the security that Katie and her community had long taken for granted was about to be shattered in the most chilling way imaginable.

———

The evening of Wednesday, May 26, 1999, began unremarkably at D.J.'s Expressway. Katie had arrived for her shift and settled into the familiar routine of stocking shelves, assisting customers, and managing the register. The spring night was pleasant, the temperature was mild, and traffic flowed steadily along the interstate as usual. Nothing distinguished this particular evening from countless others Katie had worked at the convenience store.

As the clock approached midnight, the store had grown quieter. The late-night rush of travelers had dwindled to occasional customers stopping for fuel or coffee to ward off highway drowsiness. Alone in the store, as was typical for that time of night, Katie likely anticipated closing soon. Perhaps she was already thinking about heading home, where she would be expected by her family in neighboring Barnum.

But at precisely 11:40 p.m., the store's security camera captured a moment that would haunt the region for years to come. The grainy black-and-white footage revealed a profoundly disturbing scene: a man in jeans and a backward baseball cap escorting Katie out of the store. He wore a distinctive vintage New York Yankees jersey—number 23—and moved with deliberate purpose. Most chilling was his hand, clearly visible against the back of Katie's neck as he propelled her forward. At one point in the footage, Katie reflexively raised her own hand toward her throat in a gesture investigators would later interpret as evidence that her abductor may have looped some type of cord around her neck to maintain control.

The expressions on their faces weren't clearly visible on the grainy tape, but Katie's body language told its own story. She appeared compliant yet tense, moving under duress rather than by choice. In those few seconds of silent surveillance footage, the young woman's terror was palpable even through the primitive technology of the store's security system.

Minutes later, a customer pulled into the station and immediately sensed something was wrong. The store stood eerily empty, lights still blazing but no clerk in sight. At 12:07 a.m., the concerned patron called the police to report that the station was unattended. Moose Lake officers responded promptly, discovering Katie's personal belongings still in the store but no sign of the young woman herself. Upon reviewing the security tape, they witnessed the terrifying abduction scene unfold on the monitor before them.

The officers could discern enough from the footage to form a basic description of the suspect: A white male of average build, approximately five feet ten inches tall and around 170 pounds, wearing a backward baseball cap and a Yankees jersey. He appeared to have longer, light-colored hair, and his dress and mannerisms suggested he might be in his mid-twenties.

The realization set in quickly—they were dealing with a kidnapping. Calls went out immediately, alerting law enforcement across the region. Katie's family received the news no parent ever wants to hear: Their daughter had vanished, taken by force by an unknown assailant.

———

The news of Katie's abduction spread through Moose Lake and surrounding towns like wildfire. By dawn on May 27, the normally tranquil community had transformed into a hive of frantic activity. Katie's family, friends, neighbors, and even perfect strangers converged to assist in what would become one of the largest search operations in the region's history.

Hundreds of volunteers reported to hastily established coordination centers, ready to comb every inch of the surrounding countryside. Police K9 units attempted to track Katie's scent while helicopters swept low over the terrain, scanning the dense Minnesota woods and highway corridors of Carlton County for any sign of the missing teenager. Volunteers and officers methodically searched ditches, back roads, and forested areas, calling Katie's name into the silence.

Flyers bearing Katie's photograph and details quickly appeared in shop windows and on highway billboards throughout northeastern

Minnesota. Local radio stations interrupted regular programming with descriptions of Katie and her abductor, imploring listeners to call with information, no matter how seemingly insignificant. The community's response was immediate and overwhelming—a testament to the tight-knit nature of rural Minnesota and the collective horror felt at the brazen kidnapping of one of their own.

Meanwhile, investigators from the Carlton County Sheriff's Office and the Minnesota Bureau of Criminal Apprehension (BCA) worked around the clock, interviewing employees of nearby businesses and potential witnesses who had been near the gas station that night. Several bystanders reported seeing a black pickup truck lingering suspiciously in the vicinity of D.J.'s Expressway around the time of the abduction. One woman mentioned that the male driver had been loitering outside the Subway sandwich shop located in the same building, and his presence had made her uneasy. Crucially, at least one witness managed to recall a partial license plate from the suspicious vehicle—three numbers and a letter that would later prove vital to the investigation.

Within the first twenty-four hours, law enforcement released a composite sketch based on descriptions from four witnesses. The image depicted a young Caucasian man with light, shaggy hair and average features. This sketch, along with stills from the surveillance video and the vehicle description, was distributed to news outlets across the state. The case rapidly gained prominence in Minnesota, dominating headlines and newscasts as the public's fear and fascination grew in equal measure.

The abduction struck a nerve precisely because it undermined fundamental assumptions about safety in small-town America. The idea that a young woman could be forcibly taken from a well-lit, public place sent ripples of anxiety through communities across the region. Parents kept children closer, women avoided working alone at night, and a general unease settled over areas that had previously felt immune to such dangers.

Tips began flooding police hotlines, with over 3,500 leads eventually logged during the investigation. The FBI joined the case due to the possibility of interstate kidnapping, bringing in additional resources and expertise. Investigators checked on registered sex offenders in the region and contacted a nearby facility that housed sex offenders to confirm all inmates were accounted for. This initial sweep failed to produce obvious suspects, forcing authorities to cast a wider net and pursue creative investigative strategies.

In an unconventional twist, investigators sought help from NASA's Jet Propulsion Laboratory to enhance the surveillance footage. Using technology typically reserved for space imaging, NASA specialists worked to clarify the grainy video frames. While this high-tech effort couldn't produce a crystal-clear identification, it helped confirm certain details about the suspect's appearance, including details about the Yankees jersey.

As days stretched into weeks with no sign of Katie, hope mingled with dread. Her mother expressed a gut feeling that Katie might still be found safe, which kept volunteers motivated during the exhausting search efforts. Law enforcement, however, grew increasingly concerned that, with each passing day, the likelihood of finding Katie alive diminished significantly.

To maintain public interest and generate new leads, investigators made a unique appeal. Believing the suspect might be a baseball fan based on his Yankees jersey, they enlisted Minnesota Twins legend Paul Molitor to make a televised plea for information. Molitor's appeal, broadcast about two weeks into the search, reached viewers across the state—including one man whose suspicions would finally break the case wide open.

———

On June 18, 1999, a man named Darrel Brown contacted the tip line with information that would dramatically alter the course of the investigation. Brown, an employee at the Minnesota Veterans Home in Minneapolis, had been watching coverage of the case when something had clicked in his mind. He informed investigators that the man in the composite sketch strongly resembled a former co-worker named Donald "Don" Hutchinson, a janitor who had recently quit his job without explanation.

Brown's tip was specific and compelling. He noted that Hutchinson drove a black pickup truck that he had suddenly stopped using right after the abduction. Hutchinson had also cut his long, light-brown hair short around that same time and, most suspiciously, had failed to show up for work on May 27—the morning after Katie disappeared. Shortly thereafter, he abruptly quit his position at the Veterans Home. The timing of these actions, all occurring in the immediate aftermath of the crime, had struck Brown as too suspicious to ignore.

Investigators acted quickly, running the name "Donald Hutchinson" through their databases. Initial checks revealed no significant criminal record under that name. However, when they checked vehicle records, they discovered something crucial—Hutchinson's registered pickup truck had a license plate beginning with the very characters witnesses had recalled from the scene.

As police dug deeper, they uncovered something even more alarming: "Donald Hutchinson" was actually an alias. The man's real name was Donald Albin Blom, a registered sex offender who had a history of abducting petite, young girls just like Katie. Blom had apparently deceived his employer by using a false surname; the supervisors at the Veterans Home had been unaware of his criminal past.

Donald Blom

When investigators uncovered Blom's true identity, his violent history came into sharp focus. The fifty-year-old had multiple convictions for kidnapping and sexual assault, with a disturbing pattern of targeting young women. A quick review of his prior cases revealed that he had previously abducted victims with profiles similar to Katie —petite, young females. The investigation had finally found its prime suspect.

Authorities surveilled Blom's residence in Richfield, near Minneapolis, but discovered he wasn't home. They soon learned that Blom, under his Hutchinson alias, owned a twenty-acre rural property near Moose Lake, only about twelve miles from where Katie was abducted. This geographic connection added another compelling layer to the mounting evidence.

Neighbors near that property told police that Blom had spent considerable time there before late May, often camping or fishing on the land. However, they hadn't seen him there at all in the weeks since Katie's disappearance. It seemed that after the night of May 26, Blom had deliberately avoided returning to his Moose Lake acreage, even allowing the grass to grow tall and his chores to lapse—behavior they considered out of character for him.

With probable cause accumulating rapidly, law enforcement obtained search warrants for Blom's house, vehicles, and land. A task force was assembled to locate and apprehend him before he could potentially flee or harm anyone else.

———

On June 22, 1999, a team of agents from the Minnesota BCA and local sheriff's office tracked Donald Blom to a campground near Alexandria, Minnesota, about 140 miles from his Richfield home. Blom was staying there with his wife, Amy, and their children, apparently trying to maintain a semblance of normal family life even as the manhunt closed in. In the early morning hours, officers approached Blom at the campground, initially engaging him in casual conversation to avoid escalating the situation and potentially provoking panic. Blom quickly realized the purpose of their visit. He was polite and cooperative, neither resisting nor attempting to flee, but he immediately invoked his right to silence, declining to answer questions and requesting an attorney.

Later that day, as Blom and his family were driving back toward the Twin Cities, law enforcement moved in and formally arrested him on suspicion of kidnapping Katie Poirier. When officers got their first close look at the suspect, they noted that his formerly shoulder-length hair had indeed been cut much shorter, consistent with Darrel Brown's tip. He also appeared to have dyed out the blond highlights that witnesses had observed. Despite these alterations to his appearance, at least one eyewitness was able to identify him in a lineup.

Blom was booked and held in the Carlton County Jail while searches of his property commenced. However, he demonstrated his potential for cunning and dangerous behavior almost immediately. Within days of his detention, jail staff discovered evidence of an escape plan Blom was formulating. Maps and notes suggesting a possible jailbreak route were found in his cell, prompting authorities to place him in solitary confinement to prevent any escape attempt.

Meanwhile, Amy Blom initially provided her husband with an alibi, claiming he had been home with her the night of May 26. She claimed that Blom had returned home around 9:30 p.m., they had gone to bed together, and when she awoke the next morning, he was there making coffee, implying he could not have snuck away to commit the crime. Amy added that when she heard about Katie's disappearance on the news, she assumed he would be a suspect given his history of abducting girls, which was why she had paid attention to his where-abouts that night.

With Blom in custody, attention turned to his twenty-acre Moose Lake property. On June 30, law enforcement and volunteers conducted an exhaustive search of the land, which included a mix of meadow and woodland with an old trailer home and various outbuildings. Over 100 National Guard members were deployed to assist, alongside hundreds of civilian volunteers who had been stead-fastly looking for Katie for weeks.

The first day of searching yielded little, but a critical discovery was made on July 1, the second day of the search. In a shallow fire pit behind Blom's trailer, searchers noticed fragments mixed in with the ashes that looked suspiciously like bone. Among the charred debris, they also found a small object that resembled part of a human tooth. The fragments were carefully collected and sent to forensic labs for analysis. Initial tests confirmed that the pieces were human bone frag-ments, although they were extremely burned and broken. The larger object was determined to be a portion of a human tooth, also badly burned.

Given the state of the remains, obtaining DNA was unlikely. Any genetic material in the tooth pulp was probably destroyed by the fire's heat. However, forensic odontologist Dr. Ann Norrlander found traces of dental filling material still clinging to the tooth fragment. By analyzing the chemical composition of the filling's residue, she identified it as a very specific type of amalgam—one that had been recently introduced in dentistry and was not used by all dentists.

Investigators checked Katie's dental records and learned that she had received a filling at her dentist's office in Esko, Minnesota, just weeks before her abduction. The dentist had used the same new 3M brand dental amalgam found on the recovered tooth. Additionally, experts identified the fragment as a lower molar from a young female, consistent with Katie's age and dental history. This forensic linkage provided investigators with the grim confirmation they had dreaded: They had found evidence of Katie's fate.

The search of Blom's land also turned up other incriminating items, such as illegal firearms and pieces of wire that might have been used as a ligature. As a felon, Blom was prohibited from possessing guns. By late July 1999, authorities felt they had enough evidence to formally charge Donald Blom with kidnapping and murder, even though Katie's body was mostly unrecovered.

———

In an unexpected turn of events on September 8, 1999, Donald Blom agreed to give a full confession to authorities. Up until that point, he had maintained his silence, but now he claimed he wanted to put the matter behind him. Negotiations were made: In exchange for Blom's truthful account of what happened to Katie, prosecutors agreed not to seek the death penalty and to have him serve his time in a prison near his family. With multiple attorneys present to witness that he was acting voluntarily, Blom gave a tearful, 150-minute taped confession.

In his confession, Blom calmly recounted the events of the night of May 26, 1999. He claimed that earlier that day, he had gone fishing at his Moose Lake property before driving back home to Richfield. Later that night, restless, he drove back north toward Moose Lake. Along the way, he stopped at a bar for a drink and bought some liquor to go. He said he arrived at D.J.'s Expressway convenience store around closing time and saw Katie cleaning up inside.

According to Blom, he didn't know Katie at all—she was a random victim. He described entering the store and, on a sudden impulse, making a grab for her. Katie reacted by bolting toward the door and running outside, but Blom caught up to her in the parking lot. He forced her into his black pickup truck and restrained her. Blom claimed that Katie pleaded with him several times during the drive, asking him to let her go, but she didn't physically resist much until later.

Blom told investigators that he took Katie to his trailer on his rural Moose Lake land. There, in the darkness of the early morning hours, he said he was overcome with a mixture of guilt, panic, and feeling "stupid." As Katie begged for her life, Blom said something in him snapped. He came up behind her and wrapped his hands around her throat. "Then I choked her and killed her," he admitted on tape. He described strangling Katie from behind and said that it took approximately twenty minutes of sustained pressure before she stopped moving.

After ensuring Katie was dead, Blom set about disposing of the evidence. He carried her lifeless body out to the fire pit behind the trailer. He placed her in the pit in a fetal position, piled wood and paper on top of her, and ignited the fire. He fed the flames continuously, attempting to cremate her remains using the makeshift bonfire. By the time he was done, he believed the body had been reduced to ash and a few bone fragments. He scattered what he could and left the site.

Some aspects of Blom's confession contradicted the evidence or witness accounts. For example, he insisted that after grabbing Katie, he simply walked her out of the store with a hand on her arm or shoulder, whereas the surveillance tape clearly showed him gripping the back of her neck and likely using a ligature. He also claimed Katie only fought back once they reached his property, not at the store, which seemed at odds with her evident attempt to flee initially. Moreover, his claim of using just wood and paper to incinerate a body struck investigators as dubious; typically, such a fire would not reach temperatures high enough to cremate remains so completely.

Despite these inconsistencies, the core of his confession aligned with the evidence: He had abducted, killed, and burned Katie Poirier. After giving his statement, Blom even took the unusual step of personally calling two local television stations from jail to announce that he had confessed, wanting the media to know that he'd done what they were asking and to leave his family alone.

For Katie's family, who had held out hope that she might be alive somewhere through five agonizing weeks, the confession was devastating. They learned that Katie had cruelly lost her life on the same night she was taken, and her body had been desecrated.

Yet, even with a full confession on record, the legal journey was far from over. Not long after his dramatic admission, Donald Blom changed his story once again. He told his attorneys that the confession he gave was false—a product of psychological pressure rather than truth. Blom claimed that weeks of solitary confinement in jail, combined with being on ten different medications, had caused him to hallucinate and believe that confessing was the only way out of his oppressive situation. In Blom's new version of events, he had just told authorities what they wanted to hear to escape the stress of his cell. This about-face meant that any plea deal was off, and prosecutors prepared to take the case to trial.

———

Donald Blom's murder trial began in June 2000, a little over a year after Katie's disappearance. Due to intense publicity surrounding the case, the proceedings were moved from Carlton County to St. Louis County on Minnesota's Iron Range. Even with the change of venue, finding impartial jurors proved challenging, with jury selection alone taking five weeks.

What followed was approximately five more weeks of testimony in a courtroom packed with spectators and media. The prosecution methodically laid out a comprehensive case against Blom, while the defense attempted to cast doubt on the evidence and highlight inconsistencies.

The prosecution opened by walking the jury through the night of the crime and the subsequent investigation. The surveillance video of the abduction was played for the courtroom, creating a hushed atmosphere as jurors watched the grainy images of Katie being led away by a man in a Yankees jersey. Some of the most damning testimony came from a select few witnesses who provided crucial pieces to the puzzle.

Blom's own brother took the stand and testified that he had once given a box of old clothing to the Blom family, including a New York Yankees jersey with the number 23 on it. This directly contradicted Blom's prior claim to police that he had never owned a Yankees jersey and placed the distinctive shirt in his possession.

In a bold move, the prosecution called two women whom Blom had kidnapped in 1983, when they were teenagers, to testify about their ordeal. Normally, prior bad acts are inadmissible, but the judge allowed this testimony to show a pattern, given the striking similarities. The women recounted how Blom abducted them, tied them to a tree, threatened them with a knife, stuffed socks in their mouths, and repeatedly choked one of them unconscious, only to revive her and continue the torture. These harrowing accounts undoubtedly made a strong impression on the jury, illustrating Blom's capacity for violence.

Forensic odontologist Dr. Ann Norrlander testified about her examination of the burned tooth fragment found in Blom's fire pit. She explained how she ultimately identified it as a human tooth with a distinctive filling material. Dr. Norrlander candidly admitted that, at first, she wasn't even sure it was a tooth and that forensic odontology can be "more art than science" in some respects. However, with the aid of Katie's dental records and the chemical analysis of the filling, she was able to conclude "to a reasonable degree of dental certainty" that the tooth belonged to Katie Poirier.

Perhaps the most powerful piece of evidence was Blom's own confession tape, which the judge had allowed despite the defense's objections. The jury was given transcripts and listened to Blom speak in his own words about kidnapping and killing Katie. Hearing the defendant calmly describe the murder had a palpable effect in the courtroom. The Poirier family quietly sobbed as the tape played, and even jurors appeared shaken.

The defense, led by attorney Rodney Brodin, faced an uphill battle. With Blom's confession in evidence and even his spouse initially alibiing him, Brodin needed to create reasonable doubt wherever possible. The defense focused on challenging the reliability of identification and forensic evidence, presenting an alibi, and suggesting an alternate suspect.

Amy Blom took the stand and testified that Blom was at home with her on the night of May 26—coming home around 9:30 p.m., going to bed together, and him being there when she woke up. She explained she paid attention to that night because the news of a Moose Lake abduction caught her attention the next day, and knowing of her husband's past, she thought he might be suspected. Amy also accused the police of coercive interrogation tactics, claiming officers yelled at her, called her a liar, and threatened to take away her children if she didn't say what they wanted.

Challenging the identifications, the defense highlighted that out of six key witnesses who had seen the suspect or the truck, only one had identified Blom with certainty from a lineup. The others were unsure or chose different people. The composite sketch, while similar, was not a perfect likeness of Blom either.

In a somewhat risky move, Donald Blom himself took the stand in his own defense. By testifying, he opened himself up to cross-examination, but he likely felt he had to personally refute his confession in front of the jury. On the stand, Blom flatly denied kidnapping or killing Katie Poirier. He acknowledged making a confession earlier, but he also asserted it was a stupid mistake and false. He claimed he confessed out of desperation to get out of solitary confinement and protect his family from media harassment. Blom grew emotional on the stand, alternating between calmly giving answers and breaking down in tears, portraying himself as a victim of false accusations.

During cross-examination, the prosecution methodically went through Blom's confession point by point. When asked why he gave so many detailed facts if it was all made up, Blom mostly replied with terse yes or no answers, refusing to elaborate. At one point, Blom grew visibly irritated and even told the prosecutor he was getting upset with the questioning. The cross-examination highlighted inconsistencies and lies Blom had told during the investigation, which likely hurt his credibility with the jury.

After closing arguments, in which the prosecution asserted that all evidence pointed irrefutably to Blom and the defense warned of convicting an innocent man based on a coerced confession, the case went to the jury. The jury of twelve men and women began deliberations on August 16, 2000. Given the volume of evidence, they took their time—in total, deliberations lasted ten hours spread over two days, including about three hours spent reviewing the confession tapes again in the jury room.

On August 18, 2000, the jury returned with a verdict. They found Donald Albin Blom guilty on all counts, including first-degree murder while committing kidnapping and first-degree kidnapping. The verdict was unanimous. Jurors later indicated that the forensic evidence and Blom's own words were most convincing, and the defense's alternative theories simply didn't hold water in the face of everything. Blom himself showed little emotion as the verdict was read, though he reportedly turned and told his family that he hadn't killed Katie Poirier, even as he was led away.

Because Blom was convicted of first-degree murder in the course of kidnapping, Minnesota law mandated a sentence of life in prison without the possibility of parole under the state's Paul Antonich Law. On August 22, 2000, the judge formally imposed a life term on Blom. Additionally, for the separate charge of being a felon in possession of a firearm stemming from the guns found on his property, Blom received a nineteen-year prison sentence.

———

For Katie Poirier's family, the verdict provided some measure of justice but not full closure. Her father, Steve Poirier, told the media that it was "another step to closure. It'll probably never be closed, but it's a giant step." The knowledge that Blom would never walk free was a relief, but the loss of Katie—and the fact that her body was never recovered for a proper burial—remained an open wound.

The abduction and murder of Katie Poirier had a profound impact on her community and the state of Minnesota. The crime shattered the sense of security that had long prevailed in Moose Lake and similar small towns. Gas station owners in the region began reconsidering late-night staffing policies, and many implemented a two-clerk rule at night or installed improved security systems in the wake of Katie's case.

Perhaps the most significant legacy of this case is the reforms it spurred in Minnesota's laws regarding violent and sexual offenders. Outrage over how Blom, with five sex offense convictions, could be free to commit such a crime led to swift legislative action. In the year following the trial, Minnesota lawmakers crafted a package of measures collectively referred to as "Katie's Law." These measures, passed in 2000, aimed to tighten the supervision of repeat offenders and close the loopholes Blom had exploited.

Key components of Katie's Law included improved criminal information sharing, allowing different jurisdictions, such as police, courts, and corrections, to more readily share data on offenders. The law also strengthened predatory offender registration requirements, with more frequent address verification checks and increased penalties for failing to update one's information. Additionally, the legislation made it more difficult for felons—especially sex offenders—to change their names, addressing how Blom had used name changes to conceal his identity.

Despite maintaining his innocence, Donald Blom was transferred to a federal prison facility in Waynesburg, Pennsylvania, to serve his life term. He spent years filing unsuccessful appeals, with his final rejection by the Minnesota Supreme Court coming in December 2007. In prison, Blom remained a manipulative figure. In 2006, he tantalized investigators with an offer to confess to other unsolved crimes if authorities would transfer him to a facility closer to his family in Minnesota. However, after leading detectives on for three days without giving any real confession, he backed out of the arrangement.

On January 10, 2023, Donald Blom died in custody at the age of seventy-three. Prison officials reported that Blom had been suffering from significant health issues, and his death was due to natural causes. He died having served about twenty-three years of his life term, all the while maintaining his innocence.

CHAPTER 8
THE KILLER POET

On a crisp March morning in 2005, two plainclothes Illinois state troopers entered the Third Unitarian Church in Chicago's Austin neighborhood. They approached the church secretary with a ruse, showing her a photograph of a man they claimed to be looking for. As they spoke, a gray-haired, bearded man in his mid-60s walked into the office to pick up a business card. The officers immediately recognized him from a photo they had seen, and they casually asked his name.

"J.J. Jameson," he replied, adding a comment about how bad crime was in the neighborhood.

The officers moved in and placed him under arrest. For a split second, the man appeared shocked—the mask of J.J. Jameson shattered instantly. However, he quickly regained his composure. As they walked him out of the church in handcuffs, he sighed and said resignedly, "Well, I've had a good twenty years."

J.J. Jameson wasn't his real name. He was Norman Porter Jr., a convicted double murderer who had escaped from a Massachusetts prison twenty years earlier. Since his escape, he had completely reinvented himself as a respected poet, church historian, and beloved community figure in Chicago. Now, his double life was suddenly over.

———

Norman Arthur Porter Jr. was born on January 28, 1940, in Woburn, Massachusetts, as one of four children in a strict New England household. His father ran a well-drilling and house-moving business and instilled a strong work ethic in his children from a young age. Despite this upbringing, Porter began getting into trouble in adolescence. By age thirteen, he had started down a delinquent path, and at fifteen, he was arrested for stealing a car.

That car theft landed the teenage Porter in Lyman School for Boys, a reform school notorious for its harsh conditions. Porter later claimed the experience brutalized him. He emerged traumatized and rebellious, frequently escaping from the institution. Porter claimed he "busted out of Lyman about eighteen times," often stealing cars and joyriding until recapture. On one teenage escapade, he made it as far as Richmond, Virginia, before being caught. This pattern of escape and recapture foreshadowed the dramatic turns his adult life would take.

By age twenty in 1960, Porter was out of reform school but already an experienced petty criminal. He fell in with two other young Boston-area thieves, Theodore "Teddy" Mavor and John Deveau. Together, they embarked on a minor crime spree in the fall of 1960. Porter was actually out on bail for three pending felony charges when the trio set their sights on a clothing retailer in Saugus that night—a decision that would turn deadly.

———

On the night of September 29, 1960, Porter and Mavor entered the Robert Hall clothing store in Saugus, Massachusetts, a working-class suburb north of Boston. Both men wore blue-and-white bandannas over their faces and low-pulled hats as disguises. They expected to find only a few employees closing up for the night, but the store had stayed open late for the back-to-school shopping rush. Inside were twenty to thirty customers and staff.

Brandishing firearms, the two men herded the shoppers and employees into a back room at gunpoint. Mavor, who had worked briefly at that store months prior, carried a pistol and took charge of the store manager, forcing him toward the office to open the safe. Porter was armed with a sawed-off shotgun and had a revolver tucked in his belt. While Mavor dealt with the manager and the safe, Porter moved through the frightened crowd, demanding wallets and valuables.

One of the store clerks corralled in that back room was twenty-two-year-old John "Jackie" Pigott, who was working a part-time evening shift. Pigott was known as a friendly, hardworking young man who dug ditches by day for the gas company. Confronted by Porter's shotgun, Pigott fumbled to comply with the robber's orders. Porter thrust a raincoat at Pigott and barked, "Put your wallet in this." Pigott nervously replied that he didn't carry a wallet. "Well, put your money in it, then," Porter growled. Pigott managed to pull out two ten-dollar bills, but in his trembling state, he had difficulty sliding the cash into the raincoat pocket. A woman next to him tried to steady the coat to help. At that moment, Pigott inexplicably turned away from Porter—perhaps a reflex or a misunderstanding. Instantly, Porter raised the shotgun and blew a blast into Pigott's neck at point-blank range, killing the young clerk on the spot.

The surrounding hostages screamed and recoiled in horror. Porter coolly bent down, plucked the two ten-dollar bills from Pigott's lifeless hand, and declared, "Now you know I mean business." The robbers continued collecting cash from the others, but chaos was already unfolding: One employee grabbed a stepladder and swung it at Mavor, striking him in the head. The blow knocked Mavor into the store manager, Ralph Fabiano, and the two men scuffled. Mavor's handgun discharged during the struggle, hitting Manager Fabiano in the side. Fortunately, Fabiano survived his wound. The botched robbery was quickly falling apart.

Panicked, Mavor and Porter fled the store with only about $411. Outside, their getaway driver, John Deveau, had apparently lost his nerve; Deveau had heard the gunfire and sped off without them. Porter and Mavor escaped on foot into the night.

The senseless killing of John Pigott devastated his family. His fiancée, nineteen-year-old Claire Wilcox, later recalled that Porter's actions didn't just kill her boyfriend—they "altered the paths of many lives." In the words of Pigott's older brother Robert, "Our parents didn't live a day without my brother's memory. They were denied good things in life after he was taken from them."

———

After the Saugus robbery, Porter and Mavor were soon captured and charged with first-degree murder. While awaiting trial, Porter was held at the Middlesex County Jail in Cambridge, where security was remarkably lax. It was there, on Mother's Day 1961, that Porter made a daring bid for freedom that turned deadly.

On May 14, 1961, twenty-one-year-old Porter was being escorted back from a visit with a prison psychiatrist when he launched his escape plan. Somehow, Porter had managed to obtain a pistol—likely given to him by an accomplice through the jail's window or visiting area. As he walked down a corridor with an unarmed guard, Porter suddenly pulled out the gun and threatened the guard. He then headed to a nearby room where another inmate, Edgar Cook, was meeting with his attorney. Cook was a high-profile prisoner himself, awaiting trial for murdering a Boston police officer. Brandishing the pistol, Porter waved Cook out of the lawyer conference room, and together, the two inmates rushed for an exit.

Just before they could reach the jail's outer door, they encountered Jail Master David S. Robinson, the fifty-three-year-old head keeper of the facility. Robinson wasn't even supposed to be on duty that day; he had traded shifts so a subordinate could spend Mother's Day with his family. Now Robinson stood in the doorway, blocking the escape path of Porter and Cook. He didn't back down. The jail master ordered Porter to hand over the gun and tried to stall the escape.

Cook urged Porter to shoot Robinson, but Porter hesitated. In that split second, Robinson lunged, attempting to grab Porter and disarm him. A struggle ensued. Porter faltered, Cook snatched the gun from Porter's hand, and he fired at Robinson, shooting the jail master behind the ear at close range. Robinson fell, mortally wounded.

Porter and Cook fled the jail amid the chaos. They split up, and a massive manhunt followed. Cook was found three days later and died in a shootout with police. Porter managed to remain on the lam a bit longer. One week after the jailbreak, he turned up in New Hampshire —where, incredibly, he attempted another armed robbery of a food store. New Hampshire state troopers caught him in the act. At his arraignment, a newspaper photographed Porter smiling, his arms folded confidently, chatting with the arresting troopers as if he hadn't a care in the world.

Back in custody, Porter faced justice for both killings. In 1962, he pleaded guilty to second-degree murder in both cases (Pigott and Robinson). He received a life sentence for each killing, and the judge ordered the sentences to run consecutively, one after the other. As Porter's attorney grimly explained, "You serve life for Robinson's murder, then you die, and then you start serving life for Pigott's murder."

At age twenty-two, Norman Porter began serving what amounted to a double life term in Massachusetts prisons.

———

Porter's entry into prison coincided with a burgeoning era of prison reform in Massachusetts. In the 1960s and early 1970s, emphasis was placed on the rehabilitation and education of inmates. Porter proved to be an unusually motivated and capable beneficiary of these opportunities.

He earned his high school diploma while incarcerated and pursued college-level courses through Boston University's prison extension program. Under the mentorship of Professor Elizabeth "Ma" Barker—a noted prisoners' rights advocate who taught poetry classes in prison—Porter began exploring literature and creative writing. He discovered a talent for poetry and developed an intellectually curious persona that starkly contrasted with his earlier life as a thug.

Porter founded a prison newspaper and launched a radio program called Radio Free Norfolk, broadcasting from MCI-Norfolk over a local public radio station. The weekly half-hour show earned a 1973 United Press International Citation for Excellence in Public Service. Porter became something of a celebrity inmate, held up as proof that even a convicted murderer could be rehabilitated through education and responsibility.

His transformation into a model inmate earned him increasing privileges. He became a prison trusty and was gradually moved to lower-security facilities. By the 1970s, he had earned enough trust to receive furloughs. On furlough days, he worked as a prison system carpenter and even gave public lectures at churches and colleges about prison reform and poetry.

In 1975, after Porter had served roughly fourteen years, the Massachusetts Advisory Board of Pardons recommended commuting one of his life sentences. The focus was on the David Robinson case. Evidence had emerged indicating that Edgar Cook was the one who had actually shot Jail Master Robinson, not Porter. Combined with Porter's exemplary prison record, there was a compelling argument that at least the Robinson life term could be reduced.

Governor Michael Dukakis accepted the recommendation. On September 3, 1975, Governor Dukakis commuted Porter's life sentence for the murder of David Robinson. The sentence was reduced to thirty-six years and six months, with credit for time served, making Porter immediately eligible for parole on that count. In essence, Porter would now only have to serve out the life sentence for Pigott's murder.

The commutation was not widely publicized—notably, the Robinson family was not even notified that the man convicted of killing their patriarch had received clemency. Flush with this success, Porter turned his hopes to getting his remaining life sentence commuted as well. In 1978, he formally petitioned for a second commutation.

By then, however, the political climate was shifting. When Jackie Pigott's family learned of Porter's bid for clemency, they were outraged. Pigott's cousin, Dorothy "Dottie" Johnson, rallied opposition. Johnson obtained 5,000 signatures from Massachusetts law enforcement officers on a petition demanding no mercy for Porter. Under intense public pressure, the Governor's Council rejected Porter's second commutation request, effectively halting his path to release.

Porter took the failure of his 1978 commutation attempt hard. In April 1980, he simply walked off the grounds of a minimum-security prison—essentially an escape, though a short-lived one. Two days later, Porter returned and turned himself in, claiming that he had wandered away aimlessly due to depression. Because he surrendered so promptly, officials did not prosecute him for this escape.

By the mid-1980s, it became clear to Porter that no further commutations or clemency would be coming his way. Facing the prospect of growing old and dying in prison, Porter made a fateful decision: He would risk everything on one last escape.

———

On December 23, 1985, Norman Porter carried out one of the simplest yet most brazen prison escapes in Massachusetts history. At the time, forty-five-year-old Porter was being held at the Norfolk Pre-Release Center—essentially a halfway house on the prison grounds where trusted inmates were allowed a degree of freedom. It was an unfenced, minimum-security facility, and inmates could even sign themselves out for short periods. On that day, Porter signed the log to go out on a temporary furlough "walk" and simply never returned.

Porter's escape was clearly premeditated. Minutes before walking away, he was seen making a phone call from a prison payphone. Investigators suspect he had arranged assistance on the outside. According to Porter, he had stashed about $3,000 in cash in plastic bags in the woods near the prison—allegedly money saved from prison labor and speaking fees. After leaving the facility, he claimed he had dug up his hidden cash and caught a bus to Rhode Island. However, law enforcement believed he likely had an accomplice drive him to a distant bus or train station.

One of Porter's long-time mentors, Boston College Professor Robert Castagnola, made no secret of his support. After Porter's disappearance, Castagnola wrote a letter to a Boston newspaper stating, "I fully support Porter's escape... I will be pleased if there is anything I can do to keep Porter out of the clutches of justice and to at last be free." This shocking public endorsement highlighted how deeply some in the community believed in Porter's redemption.

By Christmas 1985, Norman Porter had virtually disappeared. It was an embarrassment for Massachusetts corrections—an inmate convicted of two murders had simply walked out. A fugitive warrant was issued, and manhunts were quietly launched, but there were few initial leads. Porter would later quip that the 1985 escape was his twenty-first successful escape, counting everything from reform school onward.

Norman Porter surfaced in Chicago a short time after his escape, arriving just before New Year's Day 1986. He was drawn to Chicago after reading Nelson Algren's Chicago: City on the Make, which paints Chicago as a haven for hustlers and underworld characters. Upon arrival, Porter checked into a flophouse hotel. Needing a new identity, he thumbed through a telephone directory and plucked a name at random. Norman Porter thus became Jacob "J.J." Jameson.

Norman Porter Jr. (J.J. Jameson)

The next few years were rough and itinerant. Jameson drifted around Chicago, grappling with alcoholism and sometimes living on the streets. He found work as a curbside newspaper vendor, standing at an on-ramp to the Eisenhower Expressway and hawking copies of local newspapers to commuters. By his account, he could make about $50 by 8:30 a.m. doing this before spending his days drinking.

Despite these struggles, Porter formed connections. David Beaton, a progressive-minded local, hired Jameson around 1986 to help renovate a building and let him crash there as a live-in handyman. They struck up a friendship, though Beaton observed that Jameson was "unpredictable and unreliable" when drinking. Beaton had no idea Jameson was a wanted killer. "I never got the sense that he was hiding something," Beaton said later. Jameson told Beaton he was from Maine and had a troubled family background, which explained his lack of ties.

A turning point came around 1988, when Porter wandered into the Third Unitarian Church in the Austin area of Chicago. The church was known for being a social-justice-oriented congregation that welcomed outcasts. Reverend Don Wheat recalled Jameson first showing up with literal "rags around his feet," looking destitute. Reverend Wheat and his church congregants took Jameson under their wing. A church member who owned property hired J.J. as a handyman and provided housing, an arrangement that would repeat many times over the next two decades. The church offered Jameson stability and a sense of belonging that he hadn't had since his prison days.

————

In Chicago, J.J. Jameson reinvented himself most visibly as a poet. By the early 1990s, he became a familiar face in the city's thriving spoken-word scene. He was in his fifties—decades older than many of the up-and-coming slam poets—but Jameson's colorful personality made him stand out. He cut a memorable figure with his grouchy-yet-humorous stage presence and eccentric outfits, often wearing a bow tie and suspenders to readings. John Starrs, who hosted readings at a local coffee shop, recalled that J.J. had "a whole persona. He would pretend to be gruff... Everybody loved him."

Jameson became a regular at open mic nights across the city. He often served as an emcee or heckler, known for barking "Read the poem!" at any poet who spent too long rambling in their intro. His poetry was described as ironic, humorous, and salty. Over the years, he honed a reputation as a kind of elder statesman of the Chicago poetry circuit —a man seemingly down-and-out yet scholarly and passionate about art.

By 1999, Jameson's work was deemed worthy of publication. A small local press published his chapbook *Lady Rutherford's Cauliflower*. Within the Third Unitarian Church, Jameson rose to be a respected member. He took on the role of church historian and regularly gave lectures or even sermons at the pulpit. J.J. was considered so trust-worthy that church friends would give him the keys to their houses and cars.

Jameson had one close call with the law during his time in Chicago. In 1993, he was arrested on minor theft charges under his alias, and his fingerprints were taken. Remarkably, they were not matched to his fugitive record at the time, and the charges were dropped, allowing him to continue his double life unchecked. Had the fingerprint match been discovered then, his time as a fugitive would have been cut short by twelve years.

By early 2005, J.J. Jameson's double life had endured for nearly twenty years. However, he had developed serious medical issues, including head tumors that affected his health. In late 2004, he underwent jaw surgery, and his appearances at poetry events became sporadic. A reading in February 2005 at a local coffee shop was something of a "comeback" after illness—it would be his final performance as a free man.

———

For two decades, Massachusetts authorities had hunted Norman Porter with little success. He remained at the very top of the state's "Most Wanted" list, but Porter's ability to blend in and the lack of digital records in the 1980s made the trail go cold.

A breakthrough came in early 2005. Acting on a tip from an informant in Massachusetts, investigators revisited old clues. They discovered that Porter's fingerprints from the 1993 Chicago arrest were sitting in an FBI file, unnoticed for twelve years. In 2005, Detective Michael Pepe received an FBI form letter indicating a fingerprint match for Norman Porter under the Jameson alias. Armed with this knowledge, Pepe simply plugged the name "J.J. Jameson" into an internet search engine. Porter's carefully constructed new life was laid bare; the search results showed Jameson as a prominent Chicago poet, even Poet of the Month on a local poetry website, complete with a photo.

Investigators were stunned that Porter had been hiding in plain sight online. They coordinated with Illinois authorities and put together a plan to apprehend him without tipping him off. On March 22, 2005, a team of officers descended on Chicago. They knew Jameson was involved with the Third Unitarian Church, so they started their search there, using a ruse of showing a random photograph and asking if anyone had seen the man in the photo.

When Jameson himself walked into the church office that morning, the officers recognized him immediately. After confirming his alias, they placed him under arrest. The guise of J.J. Jameson shattered in an instant. As they walked him out of the church in handcuffs, Porter sighed and said, "Well, I've had a good twenty years." He did not resist arrest.

The news of Norman Porter's capture made national headlines. "Escaped Killer Hid as Poet in Chicago," as one headline put it. Porter was promptly extradited back to Massachusetts under heavy guard, and reactions from Chicago friends were a mix of shock, disbelief, and retrospective clarity. C.J. Laity, a local poetry website editor who had championed Jameson, said he "broke out in goosebumps" when he learned his friend's true identity. "It was just startling—it was J.J. Jameson, a man you thought you knew," Laity told reporters. "You find out it's true: He blew a guy's head off with a shotgun, and you invited him into your home. It's very scary."

In Boston and Saugus, news of Porter's capture was met with a sense of justice long delayed. The Robinson family, who had never been notified of Porter's 1975 commutation and had spent decades grappling with the loss of David Robinson, expressed both relief and renewed grief at the news. Robinson's grandson later testified how their family had been left with only memories, a medal, and a badge to remember the jail master who died simply doing his duty. Claire Wilcox, John Pigott's former fiancée, said, "All these people have had to live forty-five years knowing this guy was out there. He's had twenty years of playtime. It's time he finished his sentence."

———

After his return to Massachusetts, Porter faced legal consequences for the 1985 escape. In October 2005, he pleaded guilty to the escape charge and received an additional three-year sentence to be served consecutively after his life term. This meant Porter's earliest parole hearing wouldn't come until 2009.

Porter was now in his mid-60s and had returned to a high-security prison environment after two decades of freedom. Unlike his earlier prison stint, Porter did not involve himself in the many institutional programs this time—perhaps due to age, or maybe a sense that he had already proven himself to be rehabilitated in the outside world.

In 2008, a documentary film titled "Killer Poet" premiered, chronicling Porter's double life and highlighting the reform vs. justice dilemma that his case embodied. The film influenced public perception as his parole hearings approached.

Porter became eligible for parole in late 2009. A group called "Friends of Norman Porter" argued that he had reformed himself during his twenty years in Chicago. They pointed to his good deeds, his role as a church leader and poet, and claimed he exemplified the ideals of rehabilitation.

On the other side stood the families of Porter's victims, who vehemently opposed parole. The Massachusetts Parole Board denied his request in November 2009, noting that Porter showed insufficient remorse and had not engaged in available prison programs since his return. They issued a five-year setback.

In January 2015, seventy-four-year-old Porter went before the parole board for the second time. Though he offered what he called a sincere apology, Porter somewhat minimized his responsibility, noting, "I didn't kill anyone," referring to not being the triggerman in Robinson's case. To the victims' families, this rang hollow. Dottie Johnson, Pigott's cousin, said bluntly: "His remorse is self-centered. He is sorry he got caught." The board again denied parole.

Porter was denied parole a third time in 2019. By then, his health was failing severely. In 2022, at age eighty-two, he applied for medical parole, a provision for terminally ill inmates. Porter was suffering from congestive heart failure, chronic lung disease, and was nearly deaf and blind. The Massachusetts Parole Board unanimously granted his request, noting the extraordinary circumstance: "We don't need to wonder whether Porter could live a relatively harmless life outside prison. He already has."

Norman Porter was released after seventeen years back inside (and forty-two total years behind bars when adding his original term). He lived quietly under parole supervision for about a year and a half. On December 27, 2023, Porter died at the age of eighty-three from natural causes.

CHAPTER 9
THE BATHTUB KILLER

The city of Arlington, Texas, sits nestled between Dallas and Fort Worth in the heart of the Metroplex. By 1996, the population had grown to nearly 300,000, making it the third-largest city in the area, and the Peartree Apartments complex was like many other suburban developments. A collection of moderately priced units populated by young professionals, students, and working-class families, with manicured lawns and tidy walkways, it projected an image of safety and normalcy.

All of that changed on September 17, 1996.

Twenty-five-year-old Christine Vu, an elementary school teacher, was preparing for her day when her long-time boyfriend, Thang Khuu, left for work. Christine had a busy schedule ahead of her, starting with her morning classes. When Khuu returned to the apartment that afternoon, he found the front door locked from the inside. After knocking several times without a response, he left briefly to call Christine's workplace and her mother, concerned by her silence. When he returned a short time later, the door was unexpectedly unlocked. He stepped inside, and what he found would haunt him forever.

Christine's nude body lay face down in the bathroom, submerged in a half-filled bathtub. In a panic, Khuu pulled her lifeless body from the water and into the living room, but it was far too late.

Police arrived to find Christine beyond help. Her body had been bound with duct tape around her wrists, ankles, and neck in a hog-tied position. Tape also covered her mouth. The autopsy would later confirm the horrific details. Christine had been raped, manually strangled, and then drowned. Her killer had held her bound body underwater until she'd stopped breathing.

Investigators initially questioned Khuu, as partners are often the first suspects in such cases. However, they quickly cleared him when forensic evidence didn't implicate him, and his timeline for the day checked out. In fact, detectives theorized that while Khuu was outside the apartment after finding the door locked, the killer had most likely been inside with Christine's body, waiting for an opportunity to slip away unnoticed.

Crime scene technicians processed the apartment meticulously. Beyond Christine's body and the tape used to bind her, they found little physical evidence. However, they did recover a single latent fingerprint from inside the apartment and collected DNA evidence from Christine's body. With no immediate suspect, the prints and DNA were entered into law enforcement databases, but in 1996, these searches yielded no matches.

The Arlington community was shocked by the brutal murder, but the horror was just beginning.

Three months later, on Christmas Eve, another tragedy struck the very same apartment complex. Twenty-year-old Wendie Prescott, a well-liked teacher's aide from nearby Mansfield, had failed to show up for a planned shopping trip with her sister. Concerned family members went to check on her at her home in Peartree Apartments— the same building as Christine Vu.

Around 11:00 p.m., Wendie's uncle, Norman Norwood, made the nightmarish discovery. Like Christine, Wendie's body lay face down in a half-filled bathtub. She was naked, bound with duct tape in the same distinctive hog-tied fashion—wrists, ankles, and neck wrapped tightly with a length of tape connecting them down her back. The medical examiner would later conclude that she had been sexually assaulted and died from manual strangulation, possibly combined with drowning from being left in the water.

The pattern was unmistakable. Two young women, both found in half-filled bathtubs, both bound with duct tape, both raped and strangled. Both lived just steps from each other in the same apartment complex. News media quickly dubbed the perpetrator the "Bathtub Killer," and residents of Peartree Apartments began moving out in droves.

"You don't have concern. You've got absolute panic," recalled Arlington Detective Tommy LeNoir of the atmosphere in late 1996.

Investigators working on Wendie's murder found one promising lead: a high-quality fingerprint impression left in dust on her TV stand. This print, along with DNA samples from her body, was carefully collected as evidence. Initial fingerprint checks in state and FBI data-bases came up empty—the print did not match any known offender on record in 1996. Similarly, the DNA from both crime scenes did not match anyone in the existing DNA indexes at the time.

With no immediate leads, both the Vu and Prescott cases went cold, frustrating detectives and terrifying the public. As months passed with no arrests, rumors swirled that a serial killer might still be lurking in Arlington.

For the next several weeks, police conducted extensive interviews with residents and maintenance staff at the Peartree Apartments. They compiled a list of male occupants who had been present during both murders, carefully checked alibis, and looked into anyone who might have had access to both victims' units. They canvassed the neighborhood, questioned known sex offenders in the area, and reviewed recent parolees—all to no avail.

Throughout 1997, the case remained at a standstill. No new murders matching the "bathtub" pattern occurred, leading some to wonder if the killer had moved on or been imprisoned for another crime. The community remained vigilant, but as time passed without new attacks, the acute fear began to wane.

While the bathtub murders had stopped after Wendie Prescott, a new pattern of violence emerged in the region. Between 1998 and 1999, a series of sexual assaults occurred across the Dallas-Fort Worth area. The attacker's method was consistent—breaking into women's apartments at night, raping and beating them, but leaving them alive.

On September 21, 1998, a woman was raped in her apartment in Grand Prairie, a city between Dallas and Arlington. The victim was ambushed at home and sexually assaulted, with DNA evidence collected from her rape kit. At the time, investigators had no suspect, but the DNA would later prove crucial.

Just eleven days later, on October 2, a Dallas police officer was attacked after returning home from her shift. The assailant surprised her in her apartment, sexually assaulted her, and fled. Notably, this officer lived only yards from the September victim, suggesting the attacker was targeting a specific area or complex. This attack on a law enforcement officer deeply rattled the police community, though her identity was protected in public reports.

Two months later, on December 18, another woman was raped in her apartment in Lancaster, Texas, south of Dallas. Again, a sexual assault forensic exam yielded DNA evidence that would later be vital to the investigation.

On February 23, 1999, twenty-two-year-old college student Chima Benson awoke in the middle of the night to find a man straddling her in her sorority house near the University of Texas at Arlington.

He said, "Don't scream, and I won't kill you," Benson later recalled.

The intruder brutally beat her and forced her to perform sexual acts. In a desperate act of resistance, Chima bit her attacker's genitals hard during the assault. Enraged, he pistol-whipped and punched her severely, then raped her again and left her for dead on the floor. Against all odds, Chima survived the attack. Her description of the rapist and the injury she inflicted would later prove pivotal in identifying her attacker.

Eight months later, on October 26, another woman in Arlington was raped in her apartment after going to sleep. Like the others, she was ambushed in the night by an intruder who seemed to know exactly when and where to strike.

All five women survived their ordeals, though they were left deeply traumatized. The attacker in each case was described as an African American male who assaulted them in the early morning hours. He subdued victims with physical force or threats of a weapon and sometimes bound or attempted to bind them, though not always with the elaborate duct tape method used in the murders.

At the time, each of these new cases was investigated in its own jurisdiction, and the connection with the Arlington murders wasn't immediately recognized.

Meanwhile, the Arlington murder cases had gone cold. Despite thorough investigations—interviewing neighbors, checking local sex offenders, and processing every piece of evidence—detectives had no name to attach to the fingerprint or DNA from the crime scenes. Detectives simply had two eerily similar murders and a nameless suspect. Investigators were stumped. The forensic evidence was solid, but it pointed to an unknown person.

In May 1999, a man named Dale Devon Scheanette was arrested for a completely unrelated crime—burglary of a car audio store in DeSoto, Texas. He was convicted of criminal mischief and sentenced to a year in jail. During this arrest, his fingerprints were taken and entered into the criminal database. At the time, no one connected this minor offender to the Arlington murders, but it planted the seed for the case breakthrough: Scheanette's prints were now on file, awaiting a match.

By mid-2000, Arlington cold-case detectives decided to re-run the fingerprints from the Wendie Prescott crime scene through the improved Automated Fingerprint Identification System (AFIS). Technology had advanced, and the database had grown substantially in the four years since the murders. This time, they got a hit.

That summer, an FBI fingerprint analyst reported back with stunning news: The unknown print from Wendie Prescott's TV stand matched the known print of Dale Devon Scheanette. The FBI's system gave the match a very high confidence score—2,500 points, significantly higher than the next possible candidate. Arlington detectives manually verified the match and agreed. After nearly four years, they finally had a name.

———

Who was Dale Devon Scheanette? Born on May 7, 1973, in Ouachita Parish, Louisiana, he relocated to Texas in the 1990s as a young adult. By all accounts, he experienced an ordinary childhood and came from what his defense attorneys later described as a "good family unit." In Texas, he held various blue-collar jobs—working as a machine operator, warehouseman, and forklift operator. By 1996, he had married and was living in Arlington.

Dale Devon Scheanette

Scheanette had no significant criminal record before his spree of violence, explaining why his fingerprints weren't in any database during the initial investigation. There was nothing in his known background—neither a troubled past nor a history of violence—that hinted at the predator he would become.

Once Scheanette was identified, Arlington Police, joined by Texas Rangers, moved quickly. Surveillance was initiated to ensure he didn't flee, and investigators gathered more information. They discovered a key detail: Scheanette had indeed lived in Peartree Apartments in 1996, placing him at the scene of both murders. He was a neighbor of the women he had killed.

With a suspect identified, detectives obtained a warrant to collect Scheanette's DNA. In September 2000, officers arrested him during a traffic stop to avoid tipping him off and took a saliva swab for genetic testing. The crime lab compared Scheanette's DNA profile to the sperm samples from Wendie Prescott's autopsy. The results were conclusive beyond any reasonable doubt: Scheanette's DNA matched the samples with astronomical certainty. It was a scientific certainty that Scheanette had raped Wendie Prescott and left his DNA behind. They ran the same comparison with Christine Vu's autopsy samples and, again, got a match to Scheanette.

Armed with his DNA profile, analysts then compared it to the backlog of unsolved sexual assault kits from 1998–99 in the area. One by one, those five cases lit up with matches. The DNA from each assault matched Dale Devon Scheanette. This conclusively tied him to seven separate attacks on women—the two murders and five rapes. Law enforcement now understood the full scope of his crime spree.

A particularly telling piece of corroborative evidence emerged thanks to Chima Benson's brave resistance. After Scheanette's arrest, investigators obtained a warrant to examine his body. They discovered a scar on his genital area consistent with a healed human bite mark, exactly where Chima had bitten her attacker months earlier. This provided a unique piece of evidence linking Scheanette to Chima's account of the assault.

Forensic science played a crucial role in solving this case. Fingerprint evidence provided the initial breakthrough, and DNA evidence sealed it shut.

Tarrant County prosecutors charged Scheanette with the death of Wendie Prescott—capital murder, because it was murder in the course of committing another felony, sexual assault. Although Scheanette was also indicted for Christine Vu's murder, the decision was made to try the Prescott case first and hold the Vu case in reserve, a common strategy in such proceedings.

The capital murder trial for Wendie Prescott's slaying began in January 2003 in Fort Worth, Texas. It had been just over six years since the crime. Media coverage was significant, with local reporters noting the community's eagerness for justice.

During opening statements, prosecutor Greg Miller outlined the forensic evidence tying Scheanette to the crime, especially the fingerprint and DNA. Surprisingly, the defense chose to defer its opening statement, offering no immediate rebuttal after the state's presentation. This suggested they had few ways to counter the hard forensic facts and would instead focus on sparing Scheanette's life.

Key witnesses included Norman Norwood, who testified about finding his niece's body on Christmas Eve 1996. His emotional account set the tone, showing the human toll of the crime. Norwood later told reporters he was relieved the trial had finally started and that he wanted to see the face of the man who killed his niece.

Crime scene technicians presented photographs of Wendie Prescott's apartment as it was found. Jurors were shown graphic crime scene photos: Wendie's body as it was discovered in the tub, the duct tape bindings, and the lifted fingerprint enlarged for comparison.

Forensic experts testified that the latent print from the scene matched Dale Scheanette's fingerprint. A DNA analyst from the state crime lab then testified about the DNA match, explaining the 1 in 763 million odds and effectively identifying Scheanette as the source of semen in Wendie's body.

Confronted with this overwhelming evidence, Scheanette's defense attorneys had a daunting task. They argued that the evidence was circumstantial and attempted to poke holes in it where possible. They questioned the handling of the fingerprint and posed the possibility that the DNA could have been contaminated. However, these arguments rang hollow given the breadth of forensic links.

After less than a day of deliberation, the jury found Dale Devon Scheanette guilty of capital murder for Wendie Prescott's death. With guilt established, the trial moved to the punishment phase, where the same jury was tasked with deciding whether Scheanette should be put to death or spend the rest of his life in prison without parole.

During the sentencing phase, the prosecution repeated the full story of Scheanette's criminal rampage to argue that he posed a future danger and deserved the death penalty.

They called five women to the stand—the survivors of Scheanette's rapes—to give heart-wrenching testimony about what he had done to them. One by one, these women recounted how Scheanette broke into their homes, beat them, threatened their lives, and sexually assaulted them. They detailed the terror of those encounters—being awakened by a stranger, the threats, and the physical injuries they sustained.

The courtroom was tense and emotional. Several jurors were seen tearing up as the victims spoke. After their testimony, the five women, who had never met one another before, cried and hugged one another outside the courtroom—a therapeutic moment of shared survival.

Their collective stories painted Scheanette as a vicious serial rapist of the worst order—one who would likely continue hurting women if ever given the chance.

Prosecutors also introduced evidence of Scheanette's behavior while in custody. They highlighted an incident where jailers found a plexi-glass shank hidden in his cell, implying he was plotting violence even behind bars. They reminded jurors that Scheanette had a prior burglary conviction—not a violent crime, per se, but something that showed a pattern of lawbreaking. All of this was meant to show that Scheanette would continue to be a danger to others, even behind bars, and should be sentenced to death instead of life in prison.

The defense tried to humanize Scheanette. They brought several of his family members to testify, who pleaded for mercy and described him in gentler terms—as a son, brother, and friend who had the potential for good. A chaplain who knew Scheanette spoke on his behalf, and a retired Texas prison employee testified about the strict security measures in prison, suggesting that Scheanette could be managed in a prison environment for life without incident. Despite these efforts, the aggravating evidence was simply too compelling.

After deliberating, the jury made its decision. In January 2003, Dale Devon Scheanette was formally sentenced to death by lethal injection for the capital murder of Wendie Prescott. As the verdict was read, Wendie's family held hands and quietly thanked the jurors. Scheanette himself showed little emotion.

The second murder charge for Christine Vu's murder remained pending, but prosecutors later announced they would not pursue a separate trial since the death sentence was secured. He was charged but never tried for the killing. This spared Christine's family the ordeal of another trial while knowing that justice had effectively been achieved.

Detectives saw in Scheanette a man who enjoyed inflicting terror and pain. The fact that he escalated to murder, then continued sexually assaulting women for years afterward, showed an unabated compulsion to dominate victims.

Yet his decision not to kill the later victims might indicate a calculating side—perhaps he knew a murder would dramatically increase police resources and media attention on his case. By "only" raping and not killing in 1998–99, he could more easily fly under the radar, as sexual assaults didn't get the same headlines as homicides.

In the years after his conviction, Scheanette's case went through the standard appeals process. The Texas Court of Criminal Appeals affirmed his conviction and death sentence in September 2004, finding no reversible error in the trial. The U.S. Supreme Court declined to review the case in 2005. Scheanette then pursued both state and federal habeas corpus relief, raising numerous claims—ineffective counsel, issues with jury instructions, etc. These were ultimately denied. In March 2007, the U.S. Fifth Circuit Court of Appeals rejected his final appeal, moving him closer to an execution date.

During his years on Texas's Death Row at the Polunsky Unit, Scheanette was mostly a silent figure. He declined interview requests from the media as his execution neared. There was no public show of remorse, nor extensive efforts to plead for clemency.

In a last-ditch move, his sister sent a handwritten motion to the U.S. Supreme Court on the day of execution asking for a stay, but it was denied within hours.

On February 10, 2009, more than twelve years after the murders, Dale Devon Scheanette was executed by lethal injection at the Texas State Penitentiary in Huntsville. He was thirty-five years old. Witnesses to the execution included six relatives of Christine Vu and Wendie Prescott, who gathered to watch the monster who had murdered their loved ones take his last breath.

Asked if he had any final statement, Scheanette paused and simply said: "My only statement is that no cases ever tried have been error-free. Those are my words. No cases are error-free."

It was an odd and defiant final statement—rather than apologizing, he seemed to suggest his trial was flawed, though courts had found otherwise. He did not acknowledge or look at the victims' family members who were present. At 6:21 p.m., Scheanette was pronounced dead. In Texas's busy execution schedule, he was the seventh person executed in the state that year.

After his death, the detectives who worked the case couldn't help but wonder if there were other victims of Scheanette out there. Given the gap between 1996 and 1998, or any period before 1996 when Scheanette was an adult, the possibility remains that he may have assaulted other women who never reported it or whose cases remain unsolved.

Two of Scheanette's surviving victims later chose to speak out publicly, turning their trauma into advocacy and personal strength. Chima Benson (later known as Chima Simone), after recovering from her injuries, went on to appear on the reality TV show Big Brother.

She used that platform to tell the world about surviving the "Bathtub Killer" and to encourage other women to fight back and report sexual violence. Adrienne Fields likewise shared her story years later, giving interviews about how she sensed the danger and how she endured the assault, hoping to help others recognize and trust their instincts in potentially dangerous situations.

The "Bathtub Killer" case became an example in law enforcement circles of the value of preserving evidence and periodically re-running prints and DNA through evolving technology. The fact that a fingerprint resubmission in 2000 solved a 1996 double murder served as a showcase of AFIS improvements. It showed how patience, persistence, and scientific advances could eventually bring justice, even when a predator seemed to have gotten away with murder.

CHAPTER 10
CHILD OF CHAOS

The coastal town of Ipswich, Suffolk, sits quietly on England's eastern shore. With a population of around 135,000, it's known for its historic waterfront, medieval churches, and as the birthplace of Cardinal Wolsey. Beneath the surface of this seemingly ordinary town, however, lies a darker reality.

Away from the tourist spots and historic sites, a different kind of life plays out in the town's rougher neighborhoods—one that most residents prefer not to acknowledge. In these forgotten pockets of Ipswich, groups gather daily in dingy flats or on street corners. They're the town's invisible residents, living day-to-day, focused primarily on where their next drink will come from. Most townsfolk simply walk past them, averting their eyes and continuing their normal lives.

But in the summer of 2009, events would unfold in this hidden community that would force all of Ipswich—and indeed all of Britain—to confront a horror they could never have imagined.

———

Born in 1994, Lorraine Thorpe had little chance of normalcy from the beginning. Her early childhood in Ipswich was marked by extreme poverty and instability. Her parents separated when she was around twelve years old, and although she initially lived with her mother, Lorraine chose to move in with her father, Desmond Thorpe, when she was thirteen.

The choice would prove fateful. Desmond was a severe alcoholic with debilitating health problems. At forty-three, he couldn't walk without assistance and required constant care. Despite his issues, there was love between father and daughter. Lorraine took on the role of care-taker for her father, a responsibility far beyond what any child should bear.

Their living situation was dire. They moved frequently between squalid flats and occasionally lived in tents. More critically, their daily life exposed Lorraine to a dangerous social circle—adults who gathered daily to drink, often engaging in petty crime and violence.

By the time she was thirteen, Lorraine had stopped attending school. She had been diagnosed with attention deficit hyperactivity disorder (ADHD) but wasn't taking her medication regularly. Suffolk Social Services were aware of her precarious situation and made multiple attempts to intervene, but Lorraine repeatedly ran away from any structure they tried to impose, always returning to her father's side.

In this dysfunctional environment, Lorraine's moral compass never properly developed. She became accustomed to seeing fights and lawlessness as everyday occurrences. By fifteen, she had become stubborn and willful beyond her years. She was known to be manipulative and quick to resort to aggression.

By 2009, Lorraine was on the run from social services, evading their attempts to place her in a safer environment. She was living full-time in an adult world where violence and chaos were the norm.

———

Among the hard-drinking crowd that Lorraine frequented was forty-one-year-old Paul Clarke. Described as a bully and the dominant figure among the group, Clarke exerted significant influence over the people around him. Despite the twenty-six-year age gap between them, Lorraine became drawn to Clarke.

Some accounts suggested Clarke was her older boyfriend, though the exact nature of their relationship remained unclear. What was evident was that Lorraine became besotted with Clarke. She craved his approval and attention, and she would do almost anything to impress him.

Their dynamic was complex. While Clarke was certainly the dominant influence, Lorraine wasn't simply a puppet. She had her own cruel streak and was capable of being highly manipulative herself.

Clarke had previously been in a relationship with a woman named Rosalyn "Rosie" Hunt, another woman in her forties who moved in the same circles. The relationship had deteriorated, and by the summer of 2009, tensions were building between Clarke and Hunt.

The catalyst appeared to be an incident involving a dog. According to court reports, Clarke became enraged because Rosalyn had allowed a dog to attack a child within their community. This dispute sparked a serious falling out.

Lorraine, fiercely loyal to Clarke and eager to prove herself, sided with him in this conflict. By early August 2009, their anger toward Rosalyn Hunt had escalated to dangerous levels, setting the stage for what would become a horrific series of events.

———

Forty-one-year-old Rosalyn Hunt was a mother of two who lived in the same world of street drinking as Lorraine and Clarke. In early August 2009, she became the target of their building rage.

After the quarrel involving Rosalyn's dog, Clarke and Lorraine decided to "teach her a lesson." In the first days of August, they went to Rosalyn's flat—the place she called home—and refused to leave.

What followed was truly horrific. Over a period of several days, Rosalyn Hunt was subjected to sustained, sadistic torture. She was held captive and brutalized in her own home.

The torture was relentless. Lorraine and Clarke beat Rosalyn mercilessly—kicking, punching, and stomping on her again and again. Autopsy findings would later reveal that Rosalyn suffered multiple broken bones, including at least nine broken ribs.

But the abuse went far beyond beating. According to court reports, the torture included grotesque, sadistic acts using various implements. They whipped her with a dog leash chain. They cruelly rubbed a cheese grater against her skin. They poured salt into her wounds to maximize her pain. At one point, they even set her hair on fire.

For days, this nightmare continued. Rosalyn was badly injured, likely incapacitated, and unable to defend herself. Neither Lorraine nor Clarke showed her mercy. In mid-August 2009, after more than a week of intermittent torture, Rosalyn Hunt succumbed to her injuries. She had been beaten to death.

A heartbreaking aspect of this case was the missed opportunity to save Rosalyn. On August 4, 2009, someone called 999 (the UK emergency number) to report a disturbance at Rosalyn's residence. Suffolk police officers responded and knocked on the door, but they received no answer. After checking around the property and seeing no obvious signs of trouble, they left without forcing entry.

At that time, Rosalyn was likely inside, possibly badly hurt and unable to call out. Whether she was still alive on August 4 remains uncertain, but the police missed a chance to intervene.

It was only five days later, on August 9, when a neighbor noticed Rosalyn hadn't been seen for days and that the authorities were contacted again. This time, officers forced their way into the flat and discovered her battered body on the floor. She had died from multiple injuries due to continuous attacks.

Far from showing remorse, Lorraine apparently boasted about the attack to friends. According to court testimony, she "gloried in it, describing to her friends how she stamped on Rosalyn's head." This chilling bravado from a schoolgirl shocked even hardened detectives.

———

With Rosalyn Hunt dead, Lorraine and Clarke now faced a problem: Desmond Thorpe, Lorraine's father, knew too much. He was aware of their social circle and could potentially implicate them in Rosalyn's death. To cover their tracks, they decided Desmond had to be eliminated as well.

Around August 9 or 10—just as Rosalyn's body was being discovered —Lorraine and Clarke carried out the second murder. The method was different this time. Instead of prolonged torture, Desmond was executed swiftly: Lorraine and Clarke suffocated him by pressing a cushion or pillow over his face until he stopped breathing.

Physically weak and dependent on his daughter for care, Desmond couldn't fight back. While Clarke likely took the lead, Lorraine was an active participant in her father's murder. After they smothered him, she assaulted his body, even striking his head, similar to what she had done to Rosalyn.

In a chilling detail, Lorraine later told police investigators that they would find the imprint of her shoe on her father's head. Just as she had said, Desmond's face bore the evidence of Lorraine's shoe tread.

The betrayal here was profound. Desmond Thorpe was so debilitated that he was unable to walk unaided or do anything for himself. He was completely defenseless, and the very person entrusted with his care—his teenage daughter—had helped kill him.

With Desmond dead, Lorraine and Clarke likely thought they had covered their tracks. However, their attempts at concealment would soon unravel, bringing the full horror of their crimes to light.

———

The discovery of Rosalyn Hunt's battered body on August 9, 2009, triggered an intensive police investigation. Within twenty-four hours, law enforcement had zeroed in on suspects. On August 10, Suffolk police arrested Lorraine Thorpe and Paul Clarke on suspicion of murder. A third man, twenty-seven-year-old John Grimwood, who was part of the same street-drinking group, was also taken into custody.

As investigators pieced together the timeline, they realized they were dealing with two homicides likely perpetrated by the same people. Physical evidence and witness statements quickly built a compelling case.

Witnesses from the drinking community came forward. Some had heard Lorraine bragging about hurting Rosalyn, while others had overheard the pair with Hunt during the days of her captivity. Forensic evidence linked the suspects to both victims. In Desmond's case, the evidence was particularly direct—the shoe impression on his face did, indeed, match Lorraine's footwear.

By late August 2009, the investigation had gathered enough evidence for formal charges. On August 25, Lorraine Thorpe and Paul Clarke were charged with two counts of murder. John Grimwood was charged specifically with Rosalyn's murder.

The UK press quickly picked up on the case, particularly noting Lorraine's young age. Headlines referred to her as potentially the youngest female involved in such crimes, drawing comparisons to rare historical cases like Mary Bell, who killed two toddlers at age eleven in 1968, and Sharon Carr, who committed murder at age twelve in 1992.

Meanwhile, police continued to investigate their earlier response to the 999 call at Rosalyn's flat. The Independent Police Complaints Commission (IPCC) launched an inquiry to determine if officers had done all they reasonably should have that night. The possibility that Rosalyn might have been saved with a more thorough response haunted the investigation.

Throughout the inquiry, Lorraine and Clarke maintained their innocence and refused to cooperate. Their strategy was simply to deny involvement and provide no testimony to counter the mounting evidence against them.

———

The trial of Lorraine Thorpe and Paul Clarke began in mid-2010 at Ipswich Crown Court, with Mr. Justice Saunders presiding. Because Lorraine was a minor, special considerations applied, including restrictions on the media naming her until conviction. Still, the proceedings drew intense interest due to the shocking nature of the crimes and the youth of one defendant.

Both Lorraine and Clarke pleaded not guilty to the murders. Throughout the trial, they denied the charges and gave no evidence in their own defense. Neither chose to testify, forcing the prosecution to prove the case solely with evidence. There was no visible remorse or explanation from the accused—just silence in the face of horrific accusations.

The prosecution laid out the horrific story of how Rosalyn Hunt had been sadistically tortured and killed and how Lorraine's father, Desmond Thorpe, was smothered days later to cover up the first crime. The jury learned of Rosalyn's broken ribs, her captivity and beatings, and how, by the end of those attacks, she was completely helpless.

When it came to the murder of Desmond Thorpe, the prosecution explained how vulnerable he had been—an immobile alcoholic killed by the daughter who should have protected him. Medical testimony described how he had died by smothering, with the added indignity of being stomped after death.

The court also heard evidence of Lorraine's disturbing attitude toward the violence. Witnesses recounted her bragging about the attacks. Unlike a frightened child coerced by an adult, the prosecution portrayed Lorraine as an eager participant who derived fun and entertainment from extreme brutality.

After hearing all the evidence, the jury returned with its verdict in August 2010. Paul Clarke and Lorraine Thorpe, now sixteen, were found guilty on all counts. The third defendant, John Grimwood, was acquitted.

———

On September 7, 2010, sentencing took place at the Old Bailey in London. Justice Saunders delivered a damning assessment of both defendants.

Paul Clarke, having already been sentenced a month earlier, received life imprisonment with a minimum term of twenty-seven years before parole eligibility. In effect, Clarke was to be locked up until at least his late sixties, if not for the rest of his life.

For Lorraine, the judge had to balance her youth against the severity of her crimes. "Her story is an appalling one, and her case is rightly described as wholly exceptional," he said. Justice Saunders acknowledged her extremely dysfunctional background but made it clear that such circumstances couldn't excuse the heinous acts she had committed.

Lorraine Thorpe was ordered to be detained for life, with a minimum tariff of fourteen years. This meant she would not even be considered for release until she had served fourteen years and demonstrated significant rehabilitation—and even then, release would depend on approval by the Parole Board.

In his sentencing remarks, Justice Saunders carefully detailed Lorraine's dual nature: a product of a terrible environment, yet also a willing perpetrator. He noted that there was "no doubt she cared for and loved her father" on some level, making her participation in his murder all the more disturbing.

He identified Paul Clarke as the instigator, calling him the dominant partner in crime, but noting Lorraine played a full part in everything that happened. She was not dragged along unwillingly; she embraced the violence. The judge highlighted how Lorraine had delighted in kicking, punching, and stomping on Rosalyn during the torture.

He also commented on how violence had become a form of entertainment for the young girl. Lorraine had become numb to the suffering of others—a likely result of having seen so much violence growing up, but also indicating a deeply disturbed mindset.

As the sentence was handed down, Lorraine Thorpe entered the annals of British crime history as the nation's youngest female double murderer. Headlines blared the news across the country, and the public reacted with horror and disgust at how a child could go so wrong.

———

Lorraine Thorpe and Paul Clarke both appealed their convictions, as was their right. In April 2011, the case went before the Court of Appeal. The exact grounds of their appeal weren't fully detailed in reports, but they likely challenged the strength of evidence, particularly for Desmond Thorpe's murder.

On April 14, 2011, the appeal was swiftly rejected. The appellate judges upheld the conviction and sentences, finding no miscarriage of justice in how the trial was conducted or in the jury's verdict.

Lorraine's life sentence remained intact, and any hope of an early release was quashed.

For Paul Clarke, prison life would be brief. On September 1, 2014, news broke that Clarke had been found dead in his cell at HMP Whitemoor, a maximum-security prison. The forty-six-year-old was discovered unresponsive early that morning. Authorities released very few details, but there were no indications of foul play. Clarke likely died by suicide or from health issues related to years of excessive alcohol abuse. He hadn't completed even a fifth of his twenty-seven-year term.

Lorraine continued to serve her sentence. Initially, she was held in a youth offenders institution until she was later transferred to an adult women's prison. Records indicate she was eventually housed at HM Prison Foston Hall, where she joined other notorious female inmates.

Behind bars, Lorraine reportedly participated in various rehabilitation programs. She engaged in courses aimed at addressing her decision-making and understanding risk factors, as well as programs dealing with substance abuse. These efforts would be crucial for any future bid for release.

After serving her fourteen-year minimum tariff, Lorraine Thorpe became eligible for parole consideration in 2023. In October of that year, the Parole Board convened to assess her case. However, Lorraine herself chose not to take part in the parole process, suggesting she either felt unready or believed her release was unlikely to be approved.

The Parole Board refused to release Lorraine or even move her to an open prison setting. In their statement, they emphasized that Lorraine was still deemed too great a risk to be released. They cited ongoing risk factors associated with her case, including her early life experiences and past substance abuse. While she had made some progress through prison programs, the board felt she needed to do more work to address these issues.

With parole denied, Lorraine Thorpe remains incarcerated today. As of the latest updates, no specific release date is on the horizon, and she continues to serve her life sentence.

———

Lorraine Thorpe's case raises pressing questions about nature, nurture, and criminal responsibility. What could drive a fifteen-year-old girl to commit such barbaric acts?

Her upbringing clearly had a profound psychological impact. From her early teens, she observed and experienced a world where physical fights and cruelty were commonplace. The adults she knew modeled dysfunctional, antisocial behavior, and over time, Lorraine became desensitized to violence. It was everyday life for her.

Lorraine also displayed traits of callousness and manipulation. She seemed to get enjoyment from violence. Multiple sources noted that she found cruelty funny and entertaining; laughing and bragging about stomping someone's head suggests a disturbing lack of empathy.

The influence of Paul Clarke was undoubtedly a significant factor. Lorraine was smitten with the man and eager to please. In the chaotic life she led, Clarke might have represented a figure of power or even affection. To gain his approval, she was willing to go to extremes.

As of this writing, Lorraine Thorpe is thirty years old—double the age she was when she committed these crimes. Whether she can ever be rehabilitated remains an open question, but the Parole Board's decision to keep her incarcerated suggests that they believe she still poses a significant threat to society.

CHAPTER 11

HE NEEDED KILLING

Skidmore, Missouri, was a typical Midwestern farming community where people tended to mind their own business and keep to themselves. With a population hovering around 435 in 1980, it was the kind of tiny town where everyone knew one another's affairs, whether they wanted to or not. Nestled among the rolling corn and soybean fields of Nodaway County in the northwest corner of the state, the town had one main street, a handful of businesses, and a quiet pace of life that rarely attracted outside attention.

For decades, the people of Skidmore had lived by an unspoken code of rural self-reliance. If someone's barn needed raising, neighbors showed up without being asked. If a family fell on hard times, food appeared on their doorstep. And when trouble came calling, folks handled it themselves whenever possible, preferring not to involve outsiders or authorities any more than necessary.

This quiet community had its fair share of good people. Hardworking farmers who rose before dawn to tend their fields, shopkeepers who extended credit during lean times, and families who had lived on the same land for generations. But amid this setting of ordinary small-town life, one man stood apart—not for his goodness, but for the cloud of fear that followed him wherever he went.

His name was Ken McElroy.

————

Ken Rex McElroy entered the world on June 1, 1934, as the fifteenth of sixteen children born to Tony and Mabel McElroy. The family lived in extreme poverty, working as migrant tenant farmers before eventually settling on the outskirts of Skidmore. From an early age, it was clear that Ken wouldn't follow the straight and narrow path. He dropped out of school in the eighth grade at age fifteen, barely literate but street-smart in ways that would serve his criminal tendencies.

Even as a teenager, McElroy's imposing physical presence made him intimidating. Standing at over six feet tall and eventually weighing around 270 pounds, he had thick, dark eyebrows that seemed perpetually furrowed in anger, piercing blue eyes, and a hair-trigger temper that could explode at the slightest provocation. Those who knew him in his youth recalled a boy who was quick to solve problems with his fists and showed little regard for rules or authority.

The young McElroy quickly discovered that his size and temperament could get him what he wanted. By his late teens, he had developed a reputation for petty theft, hunting out of season, and general mischief that gradually escalated into more serious crimes. Despite having little formal education or legitimate employment, McElroy always seemed to have cash on hand—wads of hundred-dollar bills that he carried loosely in his pocket and flashed around town.

"He never had a job that I knew of," recalled one longtime Skidmore resident. "But he always had money."

That money came from a variety of illegal enterprises that McElroy ran throughout Nodaway County and the surrounding area. Cattle rustling became his primary trade: He stole livestock under the cover of darkness and sold them quickly for profit. He also helped himself to grain, gasoline, antiques, and anything else of value that wasn't securely locked up. If something went missing in the area, locals typically had a good idea of who was responsible, though few dared to say it aloud.

As he entered adulthood, McElroy's personal life was as chaotic as his professional one. He fathered more than ten children with multiple women and cycled through a series of marriages and relationships. His treatment of women was notoriously abusive, and he seemed to view them as possessions rather than partners. By the late 1970s, he was married to a young woman named Trena McCloud, whose relationship with McElroy had begun under particularly disturbing circumstances.

————

For more than twenty years, Ken McElroy operated with near impunity in and around Skidmore. The list of crimes attributed to him grew steadily more serious as time went on: assault, arson, statutory rape, child molestation, cattle rustling, burglary, and attempted murder. Yet despite being indicted twenty-one different times for various felonies, McElroy managed to avoid conviction with remarkable consistency.

His success in evading justice stemmed from a two-pronged strategy. First, McElroy retained the services of Richard Gene McFadin, a skilled defense attorney from nearby Maryville who specialized in keeping troublesome clients out of jail. McFadin later described McElroy as the "best client I ever had," noting that he always paid in cash, showed up on time for appointments, and adamantly insisted on his innocence in every case.

McElroy and McFadin manipulated the legal system with surprising effectiveness, requesting continuances and delays that pushed court dates months or years into the future. When trials finally occurred,

McFadin aggressively attacked witness credibility or produced surprise alibis that cast just enough doubt to secure acquittals.

The second and more sinister part of McElroy's strategy involved brutal intimidation. Anyone who testified against him quickly learned the consequences. McElroy parked his distinctive red pickup outside their homes for hours, sometimes with his shotgun visibly displayed. He followed them around town, making phone calls at odd hours or simply appearing wherever they went, ensuring they understood they were being watched.

The case of farmer Romaine Henry demonstrated McElroy's methods perfectly. In July 1976, Henry accused McElroy of shooting guns on his property. McElroy responded by shooting Henry twice with a shotgun, seriously wounding him. Although Henry survived and pressed charges, McElroy launched a campaign of terror against him. By Henry's own count, McElroy parked near his home over 100 times, sometimes firing shotgun blasts into the air at night—wordless reminders of what awaited Henry if he testified.

When the trial finally occurred, McElroy's lawyer produced two surprise witnesses claiming McElroy was hunting raccoons elsewhere during the shooting. McFadin also attacked Henry's character by dredging up a decades-old minor conviction. The result was another acquittal despite clear evidence.

This pattern repeated throughout Nodaway County. People who crossed McElroy, no matter how trivially, found themselves under siege until they backed down. The few who pressed charges often recanted or refused to cooperate by trial time, too frightened of the consequences for themselves and their families.

"He knew which people to pick on. The weak people. And he followed through on his threats just often enough to make people believe he was going to do what he said," observed one local resident.

———

By the late 1970s, Skidmore existed in a state of constant anxiety. McElroy's influence had grown so pervasive that many residents felt like prisoners in their own town. They adjusted their daily routines to avoid potential encounters with him. Parents instructed children to give McElroy a wide berth, farmers who suspected him of stealing often chose silence over confrontation, and many avoided certain roads or businesses if his truck was spotted nearby.

The psychological toll on the community was immense. Even local law enforcement felt the strain. Confronting McElroy meant potentially facing down a violent man who carried multiple firearms and had shown no hesitation about using them. For the citizens of Skidmore, there seemed to be no escape from the shadow McElroy cast over their lives.

Perhaps the most disturbing aspect of McElroy's reign of terror was his relationship with his wife, Trena. Their story began when Trena was just twelve years old, a child from a poor family in the area. McElroy, then in his forties, began sexually abusing the girl, eventually making her pregnant at age fourteen. When her parents tried to intervene, McElroy responded with characteristic brutality: He burned their house down and shot their dog, then threatened to kidnap their other daughter if they didn't allow him to take Trena.

Faced with such threats and feeling abandoned by authorities, Trena's parents reluctantly consented to her marriage with McElroy, essentially handing their daughter over to her abuser. It was a calculated move on McElroy's part—by marrying Trena, he avoided potential statutory rape charges since a wife generally couldn't be compelled to testify against her husband. The arrangement was a stark illustration of how completely McElroy had managed to circumvent both the law and basic human decency.

As the 1970s gave way to the 1980s, the situation in Skidmore reached a breaking point. The legal system had proven itself utterly incapable of stopping McElroy, and the town's collective frustration was building toward an inevitable explosion. That explosion would be triggered by a seemingly minor incident at a local grocery store.

———

In 1980, the Bowenkamp family ran the grocery store in Skidmore, one of the few remaining businesses on the town's main street. Seventy-year-old Ernest "Bo" Bowenkamp and his wife Lois were known for their fair dealings and willingness to extend credit to neighbors during hard times. The couple had lived in Skidmore for decades, raising their children there and serving as pillars of the community.

One day, a clerk at the store believed one of McElroy's young daughters—a child he had with Trena—had attempted to steal candy. The situation should have been a minor one, the kind of small-town incident typically resolved with a gentle reprimand and perhaps a call to the child's parents. Lois Bowenkamp spoke to the girl, later claiming she had tried to smooth things over. However, when Trena McElroy heard about what had happened, she told Ken that their daughter had been insulted and accused of theft.

Ken McElroy

For a man like McElroy, who viewed any slight as a personal affront requiring retribution, this trivial matter became the pretext for a campaign of harassment against the older couple. In a bizarre move, he initially offered Lois money to engage in a fistfight with Trena to settle the matter—an offer she naturally refused. Rebuffed and enraged, McElroy then began a systematic intimidation campaign against the Bowenkamps that would escalate over the following months.

Almost every night, McElroy parked his truck outside the Bowenkamp home or the grocery store after closing time. He sat there for hours, watching and sometimes firing his shotgun into the air to terrorize the family. The Bowenkamps reported feeling like prisoners, never knowing what McElroy might do next. Other towns-people looked on with growing alarm; many had suffered McElroy's intimidation before, but targeting an elderly couple over candy seemed extreme even for him.

On the evening of July 8, 1980, the situation finally boiled over into violence. Bo Bowenkamp was standing on the loading dock behind his grocery store, waiting for a repairman to arrive and fix an appliance. As dusk fell, McElroy drove up to the back of the store, armed with a shotgun. In a calculated move, he first bribed two local boys to go buy sodas at a nearby vending machine, perhaps to remove potential witnesses from the immediate area.

Then, without warning or provocation, McElroy raised his shotgun and fired at the elderly grocer. The blast hit Bowenkamp in the neck, sending him crashing to the ground in a pool of blood. As Bowenkamp lay grievously wounded, McElroy calmly fled the scene in his truck. Bo's wife and others rushed to his aid, and miraculously, despite the severe injury, he survived the attack.

The community was horrified. This was different from McElroy's previous crimes—he had nearly killed a beloved seventy-year-old store owner over what amounted to a piece of candy. The shooting of Bo Bowenkamp crossed a line that even the most fearful residents of Skidmore could not ignore.

Law enforcement responded swiftly. Missouri state troopers tracked down and arrested McElroy a few hours after the shooting. He was charged with attempted murder and other offenses in connection with the attack. For once, it seemed justice might be within reach. The case against McElroy was strong, with multiple eyewitnesses and clear evidence. Even his formidable lawyer, Richard McFadin, couldn't get him off the hook entirely.

At trial in 1981, a jury found McElroy guilty of the assault charge—but, shockingly, not the attempted murder charge. This was a distinction that infuriated townspeople who had seen the viciousness of the attack. The two-year prison sentence struck many as absurdly lenient for shooting a seventy-year-old man at point-blank range. Still, it represented the first real legal consequence McElroy had ever faced, and Skidmore's residents hoped their tormentor would finally be behind bars.

But their relief evaporated almost immediately. At that time in Missouri, defendants could remain free on bail while appealing their convictions. McElroy, true to form, exploited this loophole. He posted bond and walked out of court a free man on the very same day he was sentenced, mocking the system that had failed to contain him yet again.

What happened next would push the town of Skidmore beyond its breaking point.

———

On the afternoon of July 8, 1981, exactly one year after shooting Bo Bowenkamp, Ken McElroy celebrated his temporary freedom by visiting the D&G Tavern in downtown Skidmore. The D&G was one of the town's few gathering spots, a place where farmers and townspeople stopped for a drink after work. McElroy arrived at the tavern carrying a rifle with a bayonet attached—a blatant violation of the terms of his release, which prohibited him from possessing firearms.

As he walked inside, McElroy made no attempt to hide his weapon or his intentions. In a loud voice heard by everyone present, he bragged about how he planned to finish the job on Bo Bowenkamp, describing in graphic detail how he would kill him this time. The patrons listened in stunned silence as McElroy laid out his plans for murder, brazenly unconcerned about witnesses or consequences.

For many in the tavern that day, something finally snapped. They had watched McElroy intimidate, threaten, and harm their neighbors for decades. They had seen him escape justice time and again through legal maneuvering and witness intimidation. Now, fresh from a conviction that should have put him in prison, he was openly planning his next violent crime. If the justice system couldn't protect them from Ken McElroy, they realized, no one could.

Word of McElroy's threats spread quickly through Skidmore. Within hours, concerned citizens began discussing what, if anything, they could legally do to protect Bo Bowenkamp and the community at large. Someone suggested a town meeting to address the crisis, and plans were made to gather the following morning at the American Legion Hall in downtown Skidmore.

On the morning of July 10, 1981, approximately sixty Skidmore residents assembled at the Legion Hall. Among them were the Bowenkamps and their family, local business owners, farmers, and ordinary citizens who had endured years of McElroy's terrorism. Also present was Nodaway County Sheriff Dan Estes, who had agreed to speak with the townspeople about their options.

The atmosphere in the hall was tense and emotional. People openly voiced their fears and frustrations, sharing stories of how McElroy had harassed or harmed them over the years. The central question on everyone's mind was straightforward: How could they protect themselves and their community from a man who seemed immune to legal consequences?

Sheriff Estes urged restraint. Aware of how volatile the situation had become, he recommended forming a neighborhood watch or community alert system to monitor McElroy's movements. His message was clear: Let the legal system work, and don't take matters into your own hands. However, many in the crowd felt this approach was woefully inadequate—essentially just more waiting and watching while McElroy plotted further violence.

Shortly after conveying this message, Sheriff Estes left the meeting to attend to other business outside of town. His departure meant no law enforcement presence remained in Skidmore that morning. Some later speculated that Estes had deliberately removed himself, perhaps sensing what might transpire and not wanting to witness it.

As the meeting continued, a breathless resident burst through the door with urgent news: Ken McElroy and Trena had just arrived in town and were currently sitting at the D&G Tavern, barely a block away. It was approaching noon, and McElroy was apparently following his usual routine of coming into Skidmore for a midday drink, seemingly oblivious to the charged atmosphere.

When this news reached the assembled townspeople, a collective resolve seemed to form. Without explicit planning or discussion, people began filing out of the Legion Hall and walking down Main Street toward the tavern. Some entered the tavern, while others remained outside, creating an unusual concentration of people on the typically quiet street.

Inside the D&G Tavern, McElroy sat nursing a drink with Trena beside him, suddenly surrounded by an unusually large number of townspeople. The atmosphere was thick with tension, but no confrontation took place inside the building. McElroy may have sensed the hostility, but he maintained his composure, buying a six-pack of beer to go and paying for cigarettes before standing up to leave.

As McElroy walked out of the tavern with Trena close by his side, a crowd followed them onto the main street. The time was approximately 11:30 a.m. on a bright summer day. McElroy and Trena climbed into his red Chevy pickup truck, which was parked on the street. The crowd of men and women—estimates range from thirty to forty-six people—stood in clusters nearby, watching intently as McElroy settled into the driver's seat, placed his beer on the dashboard, lit a cigarette, and put the key in the ignition. And then the silence was shattered.

———

Multiple gunshots suddenly erupted in the quiet midday air. More than twenty rounds were fired in quick succession from at least two different directions—one from behind McElroy's truck, another from down the street in front of it. Some bystanders instinctively dropped to the ground for cover. Trena, sitting beside her husband, ducked down and began screaming as bullets hit the vehicle.

Ken McElroy was struck by at least two bullets almost simultaneously. One was a heavy caliber round that smashed through the back window of the pickup, while another, smaller caliber bullet hit him from a different angle. Both rounds found their mark in McElroy's head and neck, inflicting catastrophic injuries. The shots were believed to have come from a high-powered rifle and a smaller twenty-two-caliber weapon.

McElroy slumped over the steering wheel, killed instantly or within moments by the severe wounds. Glass from the truck's windows scattered across the street, and the pickup's body was left peppered with bullet holes. The engine was still running, with McElroy's foot on the brake pedal.

The gunfire ceased as abruptly as it had begun. When the echoes faded, McElroy lay motionless in the driver's seat, bleeding from his head wounds. Trena managed to climb out of the truck, screaming hysterically and covered in her husband's blood. A man from the crowd gently took her by the arm and led her away from the gruesome scene.

In the immediate aftermath, an eerie calm fell over the street. No one called for an ambulance. No one rushed to McElroy's aid. The townspeople began to disperse quietly, many heading to their cars or back to their farms. Others lingered as if in shock. When Sheriff Estes returned to Skidmore after hearing reports of gunfire, he found McElroy's body, a distraught Trena, and dozens of shell-shocked residents—but no one claimed to have seen who fired the shots.

Investigators tried to piece together what had happened in broad daylight on Main Street. They questioned those still at the scene, asking who had fired the shots. The response, repeated over and over, was some variation of "I didn't see anything." Some claimed they ducked for cover when the shooting started. Others said they thought it was firecrackers at first and didn't catch a glimpse of the gunmen.

Only Trena McElroy provided a name. Through her tears and shock, she accused a local farmer named Del Clement of being one of the shooters, claiming he had been standing behind the truck. However, no one from the crowd corroborated her account. Clement himself never admitted involvement and was never formally charged. Apart from Trena's accusation, the wall of silence from the townspeople was nearly unanimous.

Sheriff Estes and other investigators were faced with an extraordinary situation: A murder had been committed in front of dozens of witnesses in broad daylight, yet no one was willing to identify the perpetrators. It was as if an unspoken agreement had instantly formed among the citizens of Skidmore—they would protect whoever had pulled the triggers, maintaining a code of silence that would prove impossible to break.

―――――

In the days and weeks following McElroy's death, law enforcement officials mounted an intensive investigation. The Nodaway County Prosecutor's Office, the Missouri Highway Patrol, and even the FBI were involved, given the unusual circumstances. Over one hundred interviews were conducted with residents of Skidmore and the surrounding area. Agents went door to door, asking the same questions over and over, but the results were always the same: No one saw the shooters.

The collective denial was not orchestrated in any formal way; it seemed to arise organically from a shared understanding among Skidmore's citizens. They all knew what had happened and, in many cases, likely knew who was responsible. But they considered McElroy's death a form of community justice—a fate he had brought upon himself. The attitude of many townspeople was simply that "he needed killing."

This blanket silence thwarted any attempt to build a criminal case. Without cooperative witnesses, prosecutors knew they couldn't convince a jury beyond a reasonable doubt that any specific individual had committed the crime. Eventually, both a county grand jury and a federal grand jury declined to issue any indictments. The case stalled and was eventually closed, officially leaving Ken McElroy's death unsolved.

In Skidmore, there was no appetite for second-guessing what had happened. To the townspeople, justice had been served on July 10, 1981, even if by their own hands. Many residents adopted a "don't ask, don't tell" policy. They simply didn't discuss the shooting—not with outsiders, and often not even with each other. This silence was so pervasive that it attracted national media attention. Reporters who came to Skidmore looking for answers found a community closed in on itself, with no one willing to talk about who had fired the fatal shots.

One of the few people to speak publicly was Cheryl Huston, daughter of Bo Bowenkamp. She said the town saw McElroy's death as justice for everything he had put them through, and once the decision was made to stay silent, no one broke ranks. Investigators could have questioned them endlessly and still come up empty. In the end, no one was ever arrested for the killing.

The only legal repercussion came in the form of a civil lawsuit. In July 1984, nearly three years after the shooting, Trena McElroy filed a wrongful death suit against multiple defendants: the Town of Skidmore, Nodaway County, Sheriff Dan Estes, and Del Clement, the man she had accused of firing the shots. However, the suit was settled out of court in 1985 for $17,600—a relatively small sum—with no party admitting guilt or liability.

———

With McElroy gone, the town of Skidmore experienced a profound transformation. For the first time in years, people slept soundly, no longer jumping at every creak or distant engine sound. Bo and Lois Bowenkamp could live their remaining years in peace, farmers no longer posted overnight guards for their livestock, and parents allowed their children to roam the neighborhood freely. One resident summed up the collective mood, saying, "It was like we could all breathe again."

Yet the killing left a complex legacy. Skidmore now carried a new burden: a reputation as the town that got away with murder. National media portrayed it as a vigilante community that had taken Old West-style justice into the modern era. This image persisted for decades, with articles and television news programs revisiting the case on major anniversaries, bringing unwanted attention to a community that simply wanted to move on.

For those directly involved in the case, life continued in various ways. Del Clement remained in the area until his death in 2009. He never confessed or was charged in connection with the shooting. Trena McElroy remarried and moved to Lebanon, Missouri, where she lived until her death from cancer in 2012 at the age of fifty-five. McElroy's defense attorney, Richard McFadin, continued his legal practice and occasionally spoke about his infamous client and the town that got away with murder.

The D&G Tavern eventually closed its doors. By the early 2000s, it was an empty shell—a hollow reminder of that fateful day. David Baird, the young prosecutor who had been newly appointed just before McElroy's killing, retired decades later with the case still technically open and unsolved. His successor opted not to reopen the long-dormant investigation, acknowledging that the trail was cold and the town's code of silence was unbreakable.

Even members of law enforcement, in quieter moments, seemed to accept the outcome. Richard Stratton, a retired Missouri Highway Patrol trooper who had been involved in the case, reflected years later on why the townspeople acted as they did: "Those were fathers and grandfathers on the street in Skidmore that day. Ordinary, hard-working people. They did what they did because we didn't do our job. Then they went home and kept their mouths shut."

This was a remarkable admission from a law officer: an understanding that the community felt compelled to deliver justice on their own because the legal system had failed to protect them. The county sheriff at the time of the shooting, Danny Estes, was similarly philosophical about the outcome. While he never condoned what happened, he acknowledged the systemic failures that led to it. "McElroy had terrorized that town for twenty years," Estes said years later. "He'd been charged twenty-one times and never once convicted. Tell me that isn't justice denied."

The Ken McElroy case remains one of the most widely recognized acts of vigilante justice in American history—unsolved on paper, though few believe the truth is unknown. His killing ended a reign of terror and ushered in a long-standing silence that has endured for more than four decades. It was, in every sense, a perfect crime: everybody saw it, and nobody saw it.

CHAPTER 12
THE MILLIONAIRE

B uilt in the picturesque English countryside of Shropshire, Osbaston House stood as a proud symbol of wealth and achievement. The imposing three-story mansion and its manicured grounds represented everything its owner, Christopher Foster, had worked for: success, status, and the security of a life removed from his humble beginnings. The fifteen-acre estate, with its stables, outbuildings, and sprawling gardens, was the perfect family retreat, isolated enough to provide privacy yet grand enough to impress visitors.

On the mild summer evening of August 25, 2008, neighbors would recall seeing the lights of Osbaston House glowing warmly against the darkening sky. Inside, life appeared to be continuing as normal for the Foster family. Christopher, his wife Jill, and their fifteen-year-old daughter Kirstie had returned from a neighbor's barbecue earlier that evening, where they had seemed relaxed and in good spirits. None of the party guests would later recall anything unusual about the family's behavior that day. Christopher had enjoyed the afternoon shooting clay pigeons, drinking with friends, and putting on the confident face of a successful businessman.

But behind that carefully maintained façade, Christopher Foster's world was collapsing. Unknown to most in his social circle, the millionaire businessman was just hours away from an act of destruction so complete, so meticulously executed, that investigators would later describe it as "cold and clinical"—almost like a military operation.

By sunrise the next morning, Osbaston House would be transformed into a smoldering ruin, the site of a tragedy that would shock Britain and leave a community searching for answers amid the ashes.

————

At fifty years old, Christopher Foster had the trappings of a self-made man. Born into modest circumstances in the West Midlands, he had risen through ambition and a knack for spotting business opportunities. His breakthrough came in the late 1990s, when he developed a specialized type of insulation for oil rigs that earned the highest fire safety rating possible. The product, UlvaShield, became the cornerstone of his company, Ulva Ltd, which he founded in 1998.

Business boomed quickly. By 1999, Foster had secured a £500,000 export deal for an offshore rig in Canada and was reporting an annual turnover of £1.5 million—a figure he claimed would double the following year. The money rolled in faster than Foster had ever imagined. With newfound wealth came the lifestyle he had always craved: the country mansion purchased for over £1 million and luxury cars including two Porsches, an Aston Martin, and a Range Rover. He even bought a tractor for his sprawling property, embracing the role of country gentleman with enthusiasm.

To those on the outside, Foster was living the dream. He kept horses on his estate for his equestrian-loving wife and daughter, his charisma and cash gave him social confidence, and the Foster family was often the envy of their social circle. However, Foster's spending far outpaced any long-term planning, a fact that would later prove catastrophic. An accountant who worked with him noted that Foster lived for immediate indulgence, focused on "What can I do now?" rather than preparing for the future.

This wasn't the only crack in Foster's seemingly perfect life. Behind the scenes, he maintained a string of extramarital affairs—at least eight mistresses, according to his sister-in-law. His wife, Jill, quietly tolerated these indiscretions, maintaining the outward appearance of a happy, wealthy family.

By the mid-2000s, the business empire that fueled Foster's extravagant lifestyle began to crumble. Financial records showed that by 2005, Ulva Ltd's liabilities exceeded its assets by approximately £2.8 million. The company was hemorrhaging money, largely due to Foster's lavish personal spending on homes, cars, guns, and exclusive memberships.

Desperately trying to cut costs, Foster breached an exclusive supply contract with a distributor, DRC Distribution Ltd, by sourcing materials elsewhere. This led to a legal battle that would accelerate his downfall. In July 2007, the High Court ruled that Ulva Ltd had indeed breached its contract, leaving DRC with an £800,000 damages claim.

Rather than accept the judgment, Foster attempted to evade payment through corporate maneuvers. He formed a new holding company and transferred Ulva Ltd's business to it, then put the original company into administration to dodge creditors. When the case went to the Court of Appeal in February 2008, a judge condemned Foster's conduct as "an asset stripping exercise" and described him as "bereft of the basic instincts of commercial morality...not to be trusted."

By late 2007, Ulva Ltd had entered compulsory liquidation, and the Foster family's finances were in disarray. Court orders had effectively tied up Osbaston House, prohibiting its sale without approval and ultimately transferring control to insolvency practitioners handling Ulva's collapse.

The extent of Foster's debt was staggering—approximately £2 million, including £1 million to DRC and £800,000 to the UK tax authority. Creditors were moving to repossess his beloved family home, the symbol of everything he had achieved. By the summer of 2008, Foster had lost his company, his patented invention had been seized, and he faced losing the lifestyle to which he and his family had grown accustomed.

The pressure was crushing him. Foster confided to a friend that Jill and Kirstie were accustomed to luxury and "would not be able to cope" with losing it. He hinted at external blame for his troubles, telling two friends he was owed millions by "Russians"—a claim that may have been more excuse than reality. His mental health deteriorated rapidly, and he told his doctor about suicidal thoughts and despair over his situation.

What made this situation even more dangerous was that despite his suicidal ideation, Foster possessed firearms—he was a licensed gun owner and avid shooter. The red flags were there, but the disconnect between his mental health care and firearms licensing meant that authorities were never alerted to the potential danger.

———

Bank Holiday Monday, August 25, 2008, began as a pleasant day for the Foster family. They attended a barbecue at a neighbor's house in their rural Shropshire community, which included an informal clay pigeon shoot—one of Christopher's favorite pastimes.

Witnesses later recounted that the family—Chris, Jill, and Kirstie—"all seemed completely normal" that afternoon and evening. Christopher, in particular, appeared jovial: He participated in the shooting and drank alcohol with friends. One guest noted that Chris became somewhat intoxicated by the end of the gathering, but nothing about his behavior raised concerns.

The Fosters were among the last to leave the barbecue, departing around 8:30 p.m. that evening, thanking their hosts, and heading back to Osbaston House, just a short drive away. No one at the party could have possibly imagined that within hours, Christopher Foster would enact a plan to erase his family and destroy everything he had built.

As darkness fell on August 25, Christopher set in motion a premeditated plan to annihilate everything he viewed as threatened by his failure—his wife, his child, his home, his animals, and himself.

———

In the dark early hours of Tuesday, August 26, 2008, Christopher Foster carried out a horrifying sequence of events at his estate. Sometime after midnight, as forty-nine-year-old Jill and fifteen-year-old Kirstie slept, Foster retrieved his twenty-two-caliber rifle, a weapon he legally owned. He had outfitted the rifle with a silencer, ensuring the gunshots would not be heard by neighbors—or possibly even by other occupants in the large house.

Moving quietly through the darkened rooms, Christopher first shot his wife in the back of the head at close range while she lay in bed, killing her instantly. He then went to Kirstie's room and shot his teenage daughter in the head as well. Forensic pathologists later determined that Kirstie died from a head wound consistent with a gunshot.

The shots were muffled by the silencer and the house's thick walls. Neither woman showed signs of struggle or awareness of the impending attack. It was a swift execution, carried out with an almost clinical efficiency.

With his family now lifeless in their beds, Christopher turned to the family's animals. Around 3:00 a.m., he began systematically killing the household pets. The Fosters had four dogs and several horses in their stables. Security footage from the estate's CCTV system captured Foster moving about outside, with two of the family's dogs following him across the courtyard. This was the last time those dogs were seen alive. Moments later, the CCTV showed Foster carrying what appeared to be the dead bodies of the dogs toward the stables.

Christopher Foster

Next, Foster went to the stable block and shot the three horses as they stood in their stalls. He wasn't just destroying his family; he was methodically eliminating every living creature in his care.

Having murdered his family and pets, Christopher moved to seal off the property and set it ablaze. The CCTV cameras recorded him driving a horsebox trailer down his long driveway and positioning it sideways across the main gate to block the estate's entrance. He then shot out its tires to ensure it couldn't be moved, effectively creating a barricade to prevent fire engines or anyone else from reaching the house.

Over the next thirty minutes, Foster methodically spread flammable materials and ignited multiple fires. Security footage showed him carrying his rifle over his shoulder with what investigators believed to be a battery pack on his belt. He also carried a bucket and plastic piping.

Foster had engineered a way to use the property's heating fuel as an accelerant. He cut a hole in the 2,000-liter diesel heating oil tank outside the house and attached a hose leading into the house's boiler room near the kitchen, creating an oil pipeline to flood the interiors with flammable fuel.

Inside the mansion, Foster had already staged additional accelerants. In the ground-floor library, he placed a metal drum filled with flammable liquid on its side and laid out towels soaked in fuel across the floor.

At approximately 3:45 a.m., the CCTV recorded a flash of light near the stables as Foster ignited a fire. Almost immediately, a powerful explosion erupted—likely the first drum of fuel going up in flames. This explosion disturbed the family's flock of doves and sent smoke billowing into the night sky. The stable block was soon engulfed in fire, and flames tore through the garage and outbuildings.

After starting the fires outside, Christopher returned to the mansion to finish his grim task. He likely ignited the prepared accelerants in the library, and very quickly, the ground floor was consumed by flames that spread to the upper floors.

Foster didn't attempt to flee. With the house burning around him, he positioned himself in the master bedroom suite where Jill's body lay. He lay down beside his wife's lifeless body on the floor as the toxic smoke and fire closed in. He still had his rifle with him, but he did not use the gun on himself. Instead, he chose to die by smoke inhalation.

Within minutes, the once-opulent mansion was transformed into an inferno, with flames bursting from windows and the roof and heavy smoke visible for miles.

———

Around 4:00 a.m., neighbors noticed the fire and called emergency services. Firefighters from Shropshire Fire and Rescue Service arrived to confront a towering blaze consuming Osbaston House. They were immediately impeded by the horsebox barricading the front gates, which made it impossible to drive fire engines up the long driveway.

Precious minutes were lost as crews tried to find another way in. When they finally approached the house, the heat was overwhelming. The roof had already collapsed in places, and firefighters were forced to keep a safe distance as jet streams of water were directed from afar into the inferno.

By dawn, Osbaston House was nothing more than a smoldering ruin —the skeletal brick walls were blackened, and the interior was reduced to ash. In the courtyard, the burnt-out frames of vehicles could be seen, including Christopher's Range Rover (with the personalized plate "JILL 40" that he had gifted Jill for her fortieth birthday) and one of his Porsches.

The firefighters didn't know it yet, but inside the burning house lay the bodies of Jill, Kirstie, and Christopher Foster.

At daybreak, firefighters and police faced a challenging scene. The fire was eventually extinguished after several hours, leaving unstable heaps of debris. One fire officer observed a hole cut into the heating oil tank with a pipe leading out—a clear indication that the fire had been intentionally set and fed with fuel. This was now a crime scene, not just a fire scene.

West Mercia Police opened an investigation, initially treating the Fosters as missing persons who might be victims. There was early speculation in the community—some wondered if the family had been kidnapped or if an outsider was involved. Police even put ports and airports on alert in case Christopher Foster or a suspect tried to flee the country.

Due to the structural wreckage, it took investigators time to safely enter and search the ruins. Structural engineers had to shore up parts of the house before search teams could sift through tons of debris by hand, looking for human remains and clues.

On August 27, as the rubble cooled, police confirmed the discovery of the remains of the three horses. This was a telltale sign; a random arsonist would have little reason to shoot the horses, suggesting an insider's deliberate act. Investigators also recovered spent and unspent firearm cartridges scattered around the property.

By August 30, search teams made a crucial find: two bodies in the main part of the house, the remains in poor condition due to the extreme heat. They were found near each other on the ground floor beneath what had been the master bedroom area. A twenty-two-caliber rifle was recovered lying near the bodies.

A forensic examination confirmed that it was Christopher's legally owned rifle. On August 31, dental records positively identified one body as forty-nine-year-old Jill Foster. The other was presumed to be Christopher. A post-mortem on Jill left no doubt as to the cause of death: She had died from a gunshot wound to the head prior to the fire.

It took until September 1 for searchers to locate the third body, that of young Kirstie. Her remains were found beneath collapsed debris in what had been her bedroom. Once retrieved, they were forensically identified as Kirstie.

Detective Superintendent Jon Groves, the lead investigator, summarized their conclusions: "We believe that Mr. Foster killed his wife and daughter before setting the fires which destroyed his home... We believe he then took his own life after setting the house alight."

The evidence was overwhelming. CCTV footage from the property showed Christopher Foster carrying a rifle and behaving in an "unhurried, deliberate" manner as the outbuildings burst into flames. In that footage, Foster is seen blocking the gates with the horsebox and firing a rifle at its tires.

Ballistic tests on the recovered rifle linked it to the shootings, and forensic analysts confirmed the elaborate arson setup. All the family's pets were found shot dead, and the front door had been barricaded from within.

The autopsy confirmed that Christopher Foster had died from smoke inhalation—there was no self-inflicted gunshot wound. Toxicology tests also revealed alcohol in his system, showing he had been drinking the night he carried out the murders.

————

What drove Christopher Foster to such extreme actions? The motive appears to be a combination of financial ruin, wounded pride, and a warped sense of "saving" his loved ones from a life he deemed unworthy.

It was the endgame of a man making a desperate attempt to avoid financial ruin and public humiliation. Facing bankruptcy and eviction, Foster likely saw annihilation as preferable to the shame of failure. He had told a friend that his family wouldn't cope with a backward step in lifestyle, suggesting he rationalized that killing them was better than letting them live in relative poverty or witness his disgrace.

Those who knew the Fosters struggled to reconcile the image of the devoted father with the man who murdered his family. Kirstie's headteacher said Foster had doted on his daughter.

Foster's psychological state in 2008 was fragile and depressed. He had taken steps that indicated suicidal tendencies and had told his doctor he felt like "doing himself in." The coroner's inquest revealed that he had been clinically mentally ill leading up to the event.

Pride and ego also played significant roles. Journalist Jon Ronson, who investigated the case, theorized that Foster's acts had an element of an "honor killing" of sorts—not in the cultural sense, but in that Christopher was too ashamed to face his family with his failures. He shot Jill and Kirstie in the back of the head, which Ronson interpreted as Foster being "too ashamed to look at them" as he killed them.

In his twisted logic, wiping out the family could have been his way of preserving their honor; they'd never live as the family of a disgraced man, simultaneously ending their suffering before it began. It's a pattern seen in other cases of men who kill families due to financial stress—an overidentification with one's role as a provider and an inability to accept any other outcome.

Foster also exhibited narcissistic traits. His past behavior—fraudulent business dealings, multiple affairs, and lavish excess—suggested a man focused on image and accustomed to getting his way. When the façade crumbled, rather than accept help or declare bankruptcy, he chose to erase the life he had built.

His mother perhaps encapsulated the motive best: "They were a very close, loving family unit, and I don't think he could face telling them they were going to lose everything." She added, "I can't condone what he's done," but "I've lost a dearly loved son, daughter-in-law, and beautiful granddaughter." Enid admitted the financial collapse came as a tremendous shock to the family, as Christopher had confided in nobody about it.

The motive can be seen as a toxic mix of financial desperation, fear of humiliation, distorted love, and mental illness. Foster's actions fit a narrative seen in similar cases: A middle-aged man with a history of control and success who can't countenance the loss of status and, instead of letting his family experience downward mobility or pity, decides to kill them and often himself, sometimes referred to as "extended suicide."

———

The coroner's investigation highlighted a crucial failure: Foster had told his GP he felt suicidal, yet this did not trigger any alert to authorities who had granted him a firearms license. In his recommendations, the coroner urged that medical professionals and firearms licensing authorities should share information in the future.

From the family's perspective, reactions were of profound grief and bewilderment. Jill's relatives were devastated; her sister, Ann Giddings, spoke about how Jill had tried to keep the family together despite Christopher's flaws, mentioning the affairs and how Jill played the dutiful wife.

Animal lovers were also appalled to learn that Foster had killed pets and horses. Some letters to the editor expressed outrage that he took innocent animals' lives. However, others saw it as further evidence of his mental disturbance.

———

The case of Christopher Foster stands as a devastating narrative of financial downfall turning into familial destruction. In a matter of hours, a man who once appeared to have it all—wealth, a loving family, and an estate—extinguished the lives of his wife and daughter, slaughtered his pets, and destroyed every physical trace of their affluent life before taking his own.

CHAPTER 13
BONUS CHAPTER: A FAMILIAR FACE

The winter sun was already beginning its early descent as six-year-old Randy Brown left Woodlawn Elementary School on Monday, January 26, 1976. The first-grader bundled his coat against the cool Texas Gulf breeze as he began his journey home —a route he had walked many times before through the streets of Corpus Christi. Randy was known by teachers as a "bashful and shy" boy, "not one to go with strangers." Standing at just over three feet tall with dark hair and bright eyes, the young boy was recognizable to most in the close-knit neighborhood.

What happened next would forever shatter this community.

As Randy turned onto Beatrice Street, roughly two blocks north of his school, a familiar figure approached him. Justin Bradley Fox, twenty-two, lived nearby and was a face every child knew. Fox often played with the local children, and parents thought nothing of it—he seemed harmless, if a bit immature.

It was this false sense of security that would prove fatal.

Fox convinced Randy to come with him, a task made easier by the fact that Fox wasn't a stranger at all. Several neighbors later recalled seeing the first-grader walking alongside the young man on the bicycle, an image that would later haunt them. What nobody could have known was that Randy Brown would never make it home that day. By morning, his name would be front-page news in a case that would shock the coastal Texas community to its core.

———

Randy's parents became increasingly concerned when he failed to arrive home from school that afternoon. A call to neighbors confirmed their worst fears—their son was missing. Time was slipping away with each passing moment.

The Browns immediately alerted police and organized a search. Within hours, scores of friends, neighbors, and even citizen band radio owners had fanned out across South Corpus Christi, desperately searching for the missing boy.

Radio calls crackled between volunteer searchers as they methodically combed the residential areas near Woodlawn Elementary. Police joined the effort, knocking on doors and questioning anyone who might have seen the child. Hope remained that Randy had perhaps visited a friend or gotten lost.

"We thought possibly he might have gone to a friend's house, but as searches continued, we became more and more concerned and the police became more and more concentrated in their search," said a family friend who helped coordinate the volunteer effort.

The search for Randy continued into the night. As darkness fell, the anxiety among searchers grew palpable. Many hoped for a happy resolution, but as the hours passed, a sense of dread began to settle over the neighborhood.

Police Lieutenant C.L. Wimbish had been coordinating officers in the search for Randy since the first alert went out. At approximately 11:30 p.m., nearly eight hours after Randy had disappeared, a discovery was made that would transform the missing person case into something far more sinister.

———

It was just before midnight when Justin Fox's stepmother made a gruesome discovery at their home on Rickey Street, only four blocks from Randy's usual route home. While moving through the house, she noticed something that made her blood run cold—what appeared to be a small leg protruding from beneath her stepson's bed.

Pulling back the bedding, she uncovered the nude body of a small child. In shock, she immediately contacted the authorities.

Police arrived within minutes. Randy Brown's body was found partly hidden beneath Justin's bed, carefully concealed but for the small leg that gave away the grim secret. Medical personnel at the scene confirmed the boy was deceased.

Later, an autopsy would reveal the horrifying details: Randy had been strangled to death and sexually assaulted. According to the medical examiner, the child had likely been dead for approximately eight hours before his body was discovered, placing the time of death shortly after his abduction.

The news hit the tight-knit community like a physical blow. Parents clutched their children closer, neighbors locked doors that had previously remained open, and an overwhelming sense of disbelief settled over Corpus Christi. How could something so heinous happen in their community, at the hands of someone who had lived among them?

Police quickly issued an all-points bulletin for Justin Bradley Fox. He was located and arrested just hours later, around 1:30 a.m. on January 27, at a relative's home. Fox was taken into custody without incident and transported to the Nueces County Jail, where he was charged with capital murder and kidnapping.

———

Justin Bradley Fox didn't fit the stereotype of a cold-blooded killer. Standing at an average height with dark hair and glasses, Fox was described by those who knew him as quiet and somewhat awkward. At twenty-two, he was unemployed and living with his family. His prior work experience included stints as a grocery store sacker, but nothing in his minimal employment history suggested any red flags.

Yet beneath this ordinary façade lurked something far more sinister.

Neighbors recalled Justin Fox as a "lonely boy" who often sought companionship with younger children in the area. One woman who lived nearby noted, "He played with the kids in the neighborhood. He would get down on his hands and knees, and he would play horsey with them. He roughhoused with the kids, but he never hurt them."

Those who had known Fox for years recalled a troubling shift in his behavior during his teens. According to several neighbors, he had been involved in a serious car accident that they believed had left him mentally affected. After the crash, they said, Fox was never quite the same—he withdrew socially and became noticeably more reclusive.

A former roommate from a summer camp four years prior described him as emotionally immature. "We knew Bradley needed greater self-confidence," the roommate recalled. "His emotional immaturity may have led him to seek companionship with younger people than himself."

Despite his unsettling behavior, Fox had no significant criminal record prior to Randy's murder. In fact, he was known to attend church regularly and had even distributed religious literature in the neighborhood shortly before the crime. Just days before Randy's murder, Fox had handed out church pamphlets to several homes in the area, presenting himself as a devout young man.

This double life—the churchgoing young adult who played innocently with neighborhood children versus the predator who would commit an unthinkable crime—left those who knew him reeling in confusion and disgust.

———

The case against Justin Bradley Fox was substantial from the beginning. Randy's body had been found in Fox's bedroom, and multiple witnesses had seen the boy with Fox shortly before his disappearance. Fox's own family members had discovered the crime and alerted authorities.

After his arrest, Fox gave a statement to police. While the full details of Fox's confession were never released to the public, investigators confirmed he admitted to his involvement. The physical evidence collected at the scene, combined with the autopsy findings and witness accounts, painted a disturbing picture of what had occurred. Investigators reconstructed that Randy had been abducted while walking home, taken to Fox's residence, sexually assaulted, and strangled to death.

The Assistant District Attorney took charge of the State's case against Fox. Given the heinous nature of the crime, prosecutors initially announced they would seek the death penalty. "In a case this serious, involving the murder, kidnapping, and sexual assault of a child, the state has no choice but to pursue the maximum penalty allowed by law," the prosecutor stated.

Fox's family retained an attorney for his defense. From the outset, the defense attorney requested a change of venue, concerned that the extensive pre-trial publicity would make it impossible for Fox to receive a fair trial in Corpus Christi. The prosecutor contested this motion, famously remarking to the press, "If Patty Hearst can be tried in San Francisco and Charles Manson in Los Angeles, then Justin Fox can be tried in Corpus Christi."

As the legal proceedings progressed, Fox underwent court-ordered psychological evaluations. The findings would later play a significant role in his defense strategy. Psychiatrists determined that Fox was intellectually below average—a "dullard," in their clinical assessment, indicating borderline intellectual functioning. Despite this diminished intellect, they found that Fox understood the difference between right and wrong, meaning an insanity defense would be unlikely to succeed.

———

As the legal machinery ground forward, the community of Corpus Christi grappled with the aftermath of Randy's murder. Schools implemented new safety measures, and a collective sense of innocence had been shattered.

At Woodlawn Elementary, where Randy had been a student, the administration took immediate steps to protect their pupils. The principal met with a group of concerned parents from the PTA and Woodlawn Community Advisory Committee to develop a comprehensive safety plan.

One of the initiatives was a "block mothers" program, where volunteers would place a sign in their window identifying their home as a safe haven for children in trouble. The school also planned an assembly to remind students about stranger danger—though in cruel irony, Justin Fox had not been a stranger to the children in the neighborhood. Additional measures included a new policy of verifying school absences by calling parents directly, a time-consuming but necessary precaution.

"They're all too young to realize what death is," said the school secretary, reflecting on how the students were processing the tragedy. "One little boy came in and asked if Randy got well."

For months after Randy's body was discovered, more parents than usual brought their children to school and picked them up afterward, unwilling to let them walk alone. The Brown family's grief was unimaginable. A day-long wake was held at their home, with religious overtones providing what comfort they could find. Randy was buried at Seaside Memorial Park after a moving service, where the family's pastor announced plans for a memorial fund in the boy's name.

———

As 1976 wore on, the city of Corpus Christi waited with bated breath for justice. The case against Justin Bradley Fox moved toward trial, with the evidence mounting like a dark storm cloud over the defendant's fate.

The proof was overwhelming. Several witnesses, the location of the body, and the physical evidence collected at the scene all pointed toward guilt. The autopsy findings confirming strangulation and sexual assault further strengthened the prosecution's case.

As jury selection was underway in November 1976, a dramatic turn of events occurred: Fox's defense team and the prosecution reached a plea agreement. In exchange for a guilty plea to the lesser included offense of murder, rather than capital murder, the State would withdraw its pursuit of the death penalty. This meant Fox would receive a life sentence instead of potentially facing execution.

What should have been a straightforward plea hearing on November 9, 1976, nearly collapsed when Fox hesitated during the judge's questioning. Asked if he understood what he was doing when he killed Randy, Fox claimed he was "not in my right mind at the time." This unexpected response threatened the plea agreement by calling into question Fox's legal sanity.

The courtroom held its collective breath as the proceedings paused while Fox consulted with his attorneys. When the court resumed, Fox changed course entirely. Questioned again if he knew what he was doing that January day and whether he knew it was wrong, Fox answered affirmatively to both. With these crucial admissions secured, the judge accepted his guilty plea to murder.

On December 1, 1976, a Nueces County jury formally found Justin Fox guilty of Randy Brown's murder. Even with Fox's guilty plea, Texas law at the time required a jury verdict on the issue of guilt. The punishment was fixed at life imprisonment, which was the mandatory sentence under the plea agreement.

During the sentencing phase, psychological testimony offered insights into Fox's state of mind. Fox's defense attorney reminded the court that "a life sentence in the penitentiary is not a great bargain" for a twenty-two-year-old man. A psychologist who had evaluated Fox claimed the young man "had effectively pronounced sentence on himself on the afternoon of January 26, 1976," by committing such a heinous crime.

The psychologist further testified that Fox exhibited emotional immaturity and loneliness but was not psychotic. In a statement that would prove hauntingly ironic, the expert opined that Fox was more inclined to hurt himself than anyone else.

Prosecutors, however, emphasized the brutality of the murder. They argued that for Fox, abusing and killing Randy had become "a compulsion" that he was unable to control—but that compulsion was no excuse for murder. The prosecution maintained that Fox was fully responsible for the heinous and unspeakable act against an innocent child and deserved a life term.

On January 3, 1977, Justin Bradley Fox appeared for the final time in District Court for formal sentencing. The judge confirmed the jury's verdict and imposed a life sentence. When asked if he had anything to say before sentencing, Fox replied with a simple, "No, sir."

———

After the trial concluded and Fox began serving his life sentence, the Corpus Christi community worked to ensure Randy Brown would not be forgotten. In April 1978, more than two years after the murder, the Gateway Christian Center in Corpus Christi dedicated the "Randy

Brown Memorial Children's Chapel" in his honor. Family, friends, and neighbors gathered for the ceremony, ensuring that Randy's memory would live on in a positive way.

"We lost a son, but I have great sympathy for Fox's parents—they lost a son, too," Mrs. Brown told reporters at the chapel dedication. "We feel no bitterness." Despite this remarkable display of forgiveness, the Browns continued to struggle with their loss.

The chapel, which cost approximately $16,000 to build, was dedicated debt-free, with about $3,000 of the total cost donated by friends and neighbors of the Brown family. At the dedication ceremony, a pastor offered a sermon, and the Mayor cut the ribbon, officially opening the memorial space.

As for Justin Bradley Fox, his life sentence in the Texas Department of Corrections meant he would spend decades behind bars. A life sentence in Texas in the 1970s technically allowed for the possibility of parole after serving a minimum term, typically twenty years for capital cases. However, given the severity of Fox's crime—the abduction, sexual assault, and murder of a child—it's likely he would have faced significant challenges in any parole hearing.

Fox filed no appeals of his conviction or sentence. His case concluded at the trial court level in 1977, with the life term standing as final. His quiet acceptance of his punishment—a stark contrast to the brazen nature of his crime—brought a measure of closure to a community that had been deeply wounded by his actions.

In the end, Randy Brown's legacy lived on not in the darkness of his final moments but in the light of a community's determination to protect its children and honor his memory. The chapel dedicated in his name stands as a testament to both the tragedy that befell this small Texas town and the resilience of those who refused to let evil have the final word.

355

TRUE CRIME
CASE HISTORIES

VOL. 18

12 DISTURBING TRUE CRIME STORIES
JASON NEAL

INTRODUCTION

Murder is the ultimate betrayal of trust.

Someone decides—in a moment of rage, cold calculation, or twisted obsession—that another human being's life means nothing. That their problems, desires, or fantasies matter more than someone else's right to exist.

What fascinates true crime fans isn't just the act itself, but the moment before. The split second when a person crosses the line from thinking about killing to actually committing the act. Once that boundary is shattered, there's no going back. Everything that follows is just cleanup.

The twelve cases in this book span different decades, different countries, different motives, but they all share one thing: They're about ordinary people who made extraordinary choices to destroy other ordinary people. No criminal masterminds here. Just humans who revealed what they were capable of when pushed to their breaking point—or when they simply stopped pretending to be decent.

Some of these stories will make you angry. Others will leave you unsettled for days. A few might make you look at your neighbors differently.

Each story requires extensive research through court documents, police files, autopsy reports, and eyewitness accounts. While I may occasionally change names or reconstruct dialogue, these crimes happened to real people in the real world. My goal is to give you an unfiltered look at these cases.

If you're looking for heroes and happy endings, you won't find them here. However, if you want to understand what people are really capable of when all the masks come off, keep reading.

As always, many of these stories came from readers who recalled cases from their hometowns or stumbled across forgotten newspaper clippings. Keep those suggestions coming. The best true crime stories are the ones nobody's talking about yet.

Additional photos, videos, and documents pertaining to the cases in this volume can be found on the accompanying web page at:

TrueCrimeCaseHistories.com/vol18

Welcome to the dark side of human nature.

- Jason Neal

CHAPTER 1
THE UNRAVELING

Three weeks earlier, if you had driven down East Maplewood Street in Gilbert, nothing would have caught your attention about the Harrell home. It was the kind of neighborhood where children rode bicycles on the sidewalks and neighbors waved from their driveways. The homes were modest but well-maintained, with desert landscaping and tile roofs that gleamed in the Arizona sun.

Inside the unremarkable house lived what appeared to be a typical American family. Dale Harrell, thirty-four, left for work as an air conditioner technician each morning. His colleagues knew him as reliable, hardworking, quiet, dependable, and dedicated to providing for his family. Marissa DeVault, thirty-one, stayed home with their three daughters. The girls, Rhiannon, Khiernan, and Daihnnon, attended local schools and seemed happy and well-cared for.

However, the household had an unusual addition: Stanley Cook Jr., a family friend who lived with them and helped around the house. The children called him "Uncle Stan," and he was devoted to the family. Stan was an Army veteran whose life had changed forever in 1998 when a motorcycle accident left him with a traumatic brain injury.

The damage affected his memory and cognitive abilities, but the Harrell family had welcomed him into their home, where he could contribute what he was able and feel useful.

To neighbors who occasionally chatted over backyard fences, the arrangement seemed admirable: a family helping a friend in need. Dale and Marissa appeared to have their lives together—a stable income, beautiful children, and the generosity to help someone less fortunate.

But appearances, as investigators would soon learn, could be devastatingly deceptive.

———

The lead detective handling the case had seen plenty of domestic violence scenes in her fifteen years with the Gilbert Police Department, but something about the Harrell bedroom felt different. The blood spatter told a story of extreme violence: It was not the single blow of a desperate struggle but the methodical brutality of multiple impacts.

Dale Harrell had been rushed to Scottsdale Healthcare Osborn, where trauma surgeons worked frantically to save his life. The injuries were severe: multiple skull fractures, deep lacerations, and massive brain trauma. That he was alive at all seemed miraculous.

Back at the house, detectives interviewed the other occupants. Marissa DeVault sat in the living room, still in her pajamas, her hands shaking as she clutched a cup of coffee. Red marks around her neck suggested she had been strangled, and her story came out in fragmented bursts between tears.

She had been sleeping when Dale had suddenly attacked her, she said. He had wrapped his hands around her throat and squeezed until everything went black. The next thing she remembered was waking to see Stanley hitting Dale with a hammer.

"Stan saved my life," Marissa whispered, her voice hoarse. "If he hadn't stopped Dale..."

Stanley Cook sat in the kitchen, his expression confused and distant. When investigators questioned him, his account was scattered and inconsistent. Yes, he had hit Dale with the hammer. No, he couldn't remember why exactly. His brain injury made it hard to recall details, he explained apologetically. Sometimes, events got jumbled in his mind.

But there were things about the scene that didn't add up. If Dale had been attacking Marissa, where were her defensive wounds? Why was the blood spatter concentrated around the bed rather than spread throughout the room, as it would be in a fight? And why did Stan's clothes show so little blood if he had been close enough to strike the violent blows that had created such carnage?

The detectives had been on the job long enough to trust their instincts —and those instincts were screaming that something about this story was very wrong.

———

The investigation began as most domestic cases do: with interviews of friends, family, and neighbors. What emerged was a portrait of a marriage that had grown strained over the years, but nothing that suggested the level of violence Marissa described.

Amy Dewey had been friends with the couple years earlier, even living with them briefly during the late 1990s. When detectives contacted her, she seemed genuinely shocked by the news.

"Dale was never violent," she insisted. "I mean, never. I lived in that house. I would have seen something."

Other friends echoed similar sentiments. Dale's coworkers described him as mild-mannered and professional. Neighbors had never heard shouting or fighting from the house. Teachers at the children's schools had never noticed any signs of domestic disturbance.

But as detectives dug deeper into the family's background, they began to uncover layers of secrets that no one in their circle knew existed.

The first surprise came when they examined the family's finances. Despite Dale's steady income, there were irregularities: unexplained expenses, missing money, and accounts that didn't quite balance. When they requested records from insurance companies, they discovered something startling—just two weeks before the attack, Marissa had taken out a new life insurance policy on Dale for $500,000. Combined with the existing policy, Dale's death would result in a payout of $1.25 million.

If there was one thing investigators had learned, it was that a life insurance policy taken out shortly before a suspicious death was almost never a coincidence.

But there was more. As they traced the family's financial records, investigators discovered evidence of a secret life that no one—not even Dale, apparently—had known about.

———

The trail led detectives to Allen Flores, a name that appeared on financial documents tied to Marissa but meant nothing to anyone in the Harrell family's known circle. When they tracked him down, what they learned would reshape their entire understanding of the case.

Flores was a sixty-something management consultant with an Ivy League education and considerable wealth. He had never met Dale Harrell or been to the house on East Maplewood Street, but he knew Marissa DeVault very well indeed.

In 2007, Flores explained to detectives that he had met Marissa through SeekingArrangements.com, a website where wealthy older men could connect with younger women seeking financial support.

What had begun as a sugar daddy arrangement had evolved into something more complex—and ultimately more expensive than Flores had ever anticipated.

Over the course of two years, he had loaned Marissa over $300,000. She had convinced him that she was expecting a large inheritance. Her details were always vague, but she claimed the sum was substantial enough to cover her debts and then some. All she needed was money to tide her over until the inheritance came through.

Except, as Flores had gradually come to suspect, there was no inheritance. The money he had given Marissa had simply vanished, and her excuses for why the inheritance was delayed had become increasingly elaborate and implausible.

By early 2009, their relationship had grown tense. Flores wanted his money back, and Marissa was running out of believable explanations. She had signed promissory notes for the loans, but Flores was beginning to doubt he would ever see repayment.

However, there was something else, too—something that made the investigators' blood run cold when Flores revealed it. In recent months, Marissa had begun making disturbing comments about wanting her husband "gone." She had asked Flores hypothetical questions about hiring someone to kill Dale…or whether she could kill him herself and make it look like self-defense.

Flores had assumed it was just talk—the frustrated venting of an unhappy wife. But now, with Dale lying in a hospital bed with his skull caved in, those conversations took on a sinister new meaning.

Most chilling of all was what Flores told them about January 13, the day before the attack. That afternoon, Marissa had called him with shocking news: Dale was dead. She claimed there had been a fight, Dale had attacked her, and he had been killed when she hit him with a tire iron in self-defense.

Flores had been stunned. But later that evening, he had happened to see Dale and Marissa together at a local restaurant, very much alive and apparently on a date.

The story had been a complete fabrication, but it was eerily similar to what had actually happened the next night—except with a hammer instead of a tire iron.

Had Marissa been practicing her alibi?

To verify Flores' claims, investigators obtained a warrant and seized his computer, hoping to find emails, chat logs, or financial records. What they found instead stopped them cold.

Hidden among his files were dozens of images of child pornography.

The murder investigation had just uncovered an entirely different crime.

Faced with serious felony charges unrelated to the Harrell case, Flores agreed to cooperate. Prosecutors struck a deal: In exchange for his testimony against Marissa DeVault, Flores would be granted immunity from prosecution for the illicit material discovered on his computer, but only for anything found during the murder investigation.

It was a morally queasy bargain but a legally strategic one. Flores would testify—and what he had to say next would reshape everything detectives thought they knew about Marissa's state of mind before the murder.

———

Armed with this new information, detectives returned to interview Marissa. This time, they were prepared for her lies.

When confronted with the evidence of her financial dealings with Flores and her fabricated story from January 13, Marissa's composure cracked. The tears stopped, and for a moment, investigators saw something cold and calculating in her eyes.

"Okay," Marissa said finally. "I hit him. But it was self-defense."

Her new story was different from the first. Now, she claimed that Dale had physically and sexually assaulted her that night—that she had been pushed beyond her breaking point after years of abuse. After he fell asleep, she said, she had snapped. She grabbed the hammer and began hitting him, over and over, until Stanley intervened and pulled her away.

But when pressed for details about this alleged history of abuse, Marissa's account began to fall apart. She claimed Dale had beaten her regularly, sometimes badly enough to require medical attention. Of course, when detectives requested medical records, they found nothing. No emergency room visits for suspicious injuries. No police reports of domestic disturbances. No witnesses who had ever seen evidence of abuse.

The forensic evidence also contradicted her claims. Blood spatter analysis showed that Dale had been lying prone when the attack began—likely asleep and defenseless. The pattern of wounds indicated at least seven separate blows to the head, each delivered with tremendous force. This wasn't the panicked response of an abuse victim fighting for her life. This was methodical, deliberate violence.

Most damning of all was the timeline. The new life insurance policy. The fabricated story to Flores the day before. The careful planning suggested by her actions in the days and weeks leading up to the attack.

Investigators had seen cases of domestic violence where victims finally fought back. This wasn't one of them.

———

As February arrived, Dale Harrell clung to life in the hospital's intensive care unit. He had undergone multiple surgeries to relieve pressure on his brain, but the damage was severe. He never regained consciousness enough to speak or recognize visitors. His parents maintained a vigil at his bedside, hoping against hope for any sign of improvement.

On February 9, after nearly a month of fighting, Dale's injuries proved too severe. He died surrounded by family members who had never gotten to hear his side of what happened that terrible night.

With Dale's death, the charges against Marissa were upgraded from attempted murder to first-degree murder. The stakes had just gotten much higher.

However, the case was about to take an even more bizarre turn.

At 3:47 a.m. on February 10, less than twenty-four hours after Dale's death, Gilbert Police received another emergency call. A jogger had been found beaten and left for dead on the side of a road just a few miles from the Harrell home.

That victim was Marissa DeVault.

Marissa DeVault

She was conscious but badly injured when paramedics arrived. Her jaw was broken, her ankle fractured, and she had significant bruising across her body. She told police she had been out for an early morning run when someone had attacked her from behind. She couldn't remember much about her attacker. Everything had happened so fast, and she had lost consciousness during the assault.

To most observers, it seemed like terrible timing. A grieving widow, already traumatized by her husband's death and facing murder charges, had now become the victim of a random violent crime.

But to investigators, the timing was all too convenient. The injuries, while serious, were non-life-threatening. Plus, there were aspects of Marissa's story that didn't quite ring true.

When they examined Marissa's cell phone records, they found something interesting. Someone had been calling her phone repeatedly during the time she was supposedly jogging. The calls were from Stanley Cook's number. When they asked Stanley about the calls, his explanation was halting and confused.

On February 20, after days of inconsistent statements, Stanley Cook walked into the Gilbert Police Department and confessed to a crime that stunned investigators.

He had beaten Marissa with a sledgehammer—at her request.

———

Stanley's confession revealed a plot so audacious it was almost unbelievable. According to his statement, Marissa had asked him to injure her severely enough to qualify for a disability insurance payout. She held a policy that would pay $500,000 if she became paralyzed due to a spinal injury.

The plan, as Stanley understood it, was for him to cause an injury that would paralyze Marissa but not kill her. He had initially considered shooting her in the spine, but he'd worried about causing too much damage or killing her accidentally. Instead, he decided to beat her with a sledgehammer, hoping to cause the necessary spinal damage.

However, Stanley's cognitive impairments had apparently affected his ability to carry out the plan effectively. His blows had broken Marissa's jaw and ankle but failed to achieve the paralysis that would have triggered the large insurance payout.

After the beating, Stanley carried Marissa to his car and dumped her on the roadside to make it appear she had been the victim of a random attack. The multiple phone calls during her supposed jog were meant to establish a timeline showing she had been out exercising when the attack had occurred.

Investigators struggled to process what they were hearing. In the span of less than a month, Marissa had allegedly murdered her husband for life insurance money, then conspired to have herself nearly killed for disability insurance money. The level of calculation and cold-bloodedness was staggering.

But Stanley's confession included something else that both complicated and clarified the case. He also claimed that he, not Marissa, had killed Dale Harrell.

Given everything they had learned about the forensic evidence and Marissa's own admissions, investigators didn't believe this part of Stanley's story. They concluded that he was trying to protect Marissa, either out of misplaced loyalty or because she had manipulated him into believing he was responsible.

The brain-damaged veteran who had been welcomed into the Harrell home as a friend had become an unwitting accomplice in a scheme that defied comprehension.

———

By March 2009, prosecutors had enough evidence to bring formal charges. A grand jury indicted Marissa DeVault for first-degree murder, and the Maricopa County Attorney's Office announced that it would seek the death penalty.

The aggravating factors were clear: The murder had been committed for financial gain, and it had been carried out in an especially cruel manner. The image of Dale Harrell being bludgeoned to death with a hammer while he slept would be difficult for any jury to forget.

But Marissa's case would not come to trial quickly. Legal proceedings in capital cases moved slowly, and there were complications. The same courthouse was simultaneously handling another high-profile case involving a young Arizona woman accused of killing her partner and claiming self-defense: Jodi Arias.

The parallels between the cases were striking enough that media coverage often compared them. Both involved attractive young women, both claimed to be victims of domestic abuse, and both faced the death penalty for brutal killings. The similarities were so pronounced that when Marissa was eventually housed in the same jail as Arias, reports emerged that the two became friends.

Judge Roland Steinle, who would eventually preside over Marissa's trial, was determined not to let it become the media circus that the Arias case had become. He implemented strict controls on publicity and limited the more salacious details that might turn the proceedings into entertainment.

While Marissa sat in jail awaiting trial, Dale's parents faced another heartbreaking struggle. They wanted custody of their son's cremated remains, but Marissa, still his legal next of kin, refused to release them. It was a final, bitter act of control—one that could only be resolved through a court order.

The years passed slowly. Evidence was analyzed and re-analyzed, witnesses were interviewed and re-interviewed, psychological evaluations were conducted, and the machinery of justice ground forward with methodical precision.

————

When Marissa DeVault's trial finally began in January 2014, nearly five years had passed since that terrible night on East Maplewood Street. The courtroom was packed with spectators, media, and Dale's family members, who had waited years for this moment.

Prosecutor Eric Basta laid out the state's case with clinical precision. The evidence, he argued, painted a clear picture of premeditated murder for financial gain. The timeline was damning: The new life insurance policy was taken out just weeks before the killing, there was the escalating financial pressure from Allen Flores, and the practice run with a fabricated story had occurred just the day before the actual murder.

"This was not self-defense," Basta told the jury. "This was cold-blooded murder for money."

Allen Flores took the stand to describe his relationship with Marissa and her growing desperation in the months before Dale's death. His testimony was crucial, but it came with complications. The defense seized on what investigators had found on Flores's computer, using it to challenge his credibility and paint him as someone who would say anything to avoid prosecution.

The forensic evidence was overwhelming. Blood spatter experts explained how the pattern of stains proved Dale had been lying down when the attack began. Medical examiners described the multiple skull fractures and the force required to inflict such damage. Crime scene investigators presented photographs and diagrams of the bedroom where Dale had died, pointing out details that contradicted any claim of self-defense.

The defense, led by attorney Alan Tavassoli, faced an uphill battle. They couldn't deny that Marissa had killed Dale—the evidence was too clear. Instead, they sought to explain why.

Their strategy centered on portraying Marissa as a victim of long-term domestic abuse who had finally reached a breaking point. They brought in expert witnesses to testify about battered woman syndrome and the psychological effects of chronic abuse. They argued that Marissa's actions, while extreme, were the result of years of trauma and fear.

The defense's most powerful moment came when Marissa's oldest daughter, Rhiannon, took the stand. Now eighteen and legally able to testify, she told the jury that she had witnessed Dale being violent toward her mother. It was the only direct corroboration of Marissa's abuse claims.

However, the prosecution was ready with their own psychological expert. Dr. Janeen DeMarte, who had also testified in the Jodi Arias trial, painted a very different picture of Marissa's mental state. Rather than a traumatized victim, Dr. DeMarte described someone with anti-social personality traits—a manipulator willing to lie and scheme to get what she wanted.

The trial lasted two months. Dozens of witnesses testified. Hundreds of pieces of evidence were examined. The jury heard recordings of Marissa's police interviews, saw crime scene photographs, and listened to expert testimony about everything from blood spatter patterns to insurance fraud.

After deliberating for six days, the jury reached its verdict.

———

On April 8, 2014, the jury foreman stood to read the verdict. The courtroom was silent except for the occasional sob from Dale's family members.

"We, the jury, find the defendant, Marissa-Suzanne DeVault, guilty of murder in the first degree."

The conviction was unanimous. The jury had also found an aggravating factor: The murder had been committed in an especially cruel manner. That finding made Marissa eligible for the death penalty under Arizona law.

But when it came time to decide her punishment, the same jury could not reach a unanimous decision for death. On April 22, they returned with a sentence of life in prison without the possibility of parole.

Marissa DeVault would spend the rest of her natural life behind bars.

During the penalty phase, Marissa addressed the court directly for the first time. With tears streaming down her face, she apologized to Dale's family for the pain she had caused.

"I know there is nothing I can say that will ever ease their pain," she said.

But by then, her words rang hollow. The evidence had painted a picture of someone who had methodically planned and executed her husband's murder, then attempted to manipulate and deceive her way out of the consequences. Even her remorse seemed calculated.

———

Judge Steinle formally sentenced Marissa to life without parole on June 6, 2014. As she was led away in shackles, Dale's parents told reporters they felt justice had been served, though no punishment could bring back their son.

The house on East Maplewood Street was eventually sold to new owners who had no connection to the tragedy that had unfolded there. The neighborhood moved on, though some longtime residents still remembered the shocking morning when ambulances and police cars had filled their quiet street.

Stanley Cook, whose confused loyalty to Marissa had made him an unwitting accomplice, was never charged in connection with Dale's death. The disability insurance scheme was deemed a separate matter, and his cognitive impairments were taken into account. He faded back into obscurity, another casualty of Marissa's manipulation.

Allen Flores, whose testimony had been crucial to the conviction, had his own reckoning to face. Despite his immunity deal, his involvement in the case had exposed his illegal activities to public scrutiny. The man who had thought he was buying companionship had instead become entangled in a murder plot.

Marissa DeVault was transferred to the Perryville Women's Prison, where she joined other infamous female inmates, including Jodi Arias. The woman who had once lived in a comfortable suburban home with three children and a hardworking husband now faced decades in a prison cell.

Her appeals were unsuccessful. The Arizona Court of Appeals affirmed her conviction in 2016, finding no errors in the trial proceedings. The Arizona Supreme Court declined to review the case further.

The three daughters, who had once called Dale "Daddy," were raised by relatives to grow up with the knowledge that their mother had killed their father. Rhiannon, who had testified for her mother's defense, later expressed hope that Marissa could find peace in prison. Unfortunately, the younger girls had lost both parents in one terrible sequence of events—their father to violence, their mother to her own choices.

Today, Marissa DeVault remains in prison, serving a sentence that will end only with her death.

CHAPTER 2
SHARED PSYCHOSIS

November 3, 1967. Two identical girls drew their first breaths in the small Swedish town of Sunne, in the rolling forests of Värmland. Ursula and Sabina Eriksson arrived into a world that seemed perfectly ordinary. It was a stable family home with two older siblings, parents who worked and worried like any others, and teachers who would remember them years later as unremarkable students.

Their childhood unfolded without drama. No emergency room visits for suspicious injuries. No calls to social services. No concerned teachers filed reports about disturbing behavior. The Eriksson twins were invisible in the way that healthy, normal children often are—present at school, playing with friends, growing up quietly in their corner of Sweden.

As adults, they scattered across the globe like so many young Europeans seeking their fortunes. Ursula crossed the Atlantic to America, building a life among strangers in a foreign land. Meanwhile, Sabina traveled to Ireland, where she settled in Mallow, County Cork, with a man who loved her and two children who called her mother.

For forty years, they lived lives of normalcy. Sabina never appeared on any police blotter, and Ursula never required psychiatric care. Their names appeared on no government watch lists and in no medical files flagged for concern. They were just two women among millions, living quiet lives that troubled no one.

Friday, May 16, 2008. Ursula stepped off a plane in Dublin, Ireland.

She had come to visit her sister. Whether the trip was meant as a reunion, a rescue, or a reckoning remains unknown, but within hours of Ursula's arrival in the small house in Mallow, something shifted.

Voices were raised. Words were exchanged between Sabina and her partner that cut deep enough to shatter the careful routine of their domestic life.

By 2:00 a.m. on May 17, the house stood empty save for a confused man and two sleeping children who would wake to find their mother gone.

Sabina Eriksson had vanished into the Irish night with her twin sister, leaving behind everything she had built over eight years of life in County Cork. No note. No explanation. No goodbye kiss for the children who would spend the morning asking where Mummy had gone.

The sisters boarded a ferry in Dublin as darkness gave way to dawn, crossing the Irish Sea toward England. What drove them to flee remains a mystery that neither woman has ever explained. Whatever was said in that house in Mallow had been powerful enough to make a mother abandon her children and disappear with a sister she hadn't seen in months.

At 8:30 a.m., their ferry docked in Liverpool.

One of the first places they went was St Anne Street Police Station, where Sabina told officers her children were in danger; her partner might hurt them. The officer took notes, made phone calls, and requested a welfare check from Irish authorities.

The call came back within the hour: The children were safe. Their father was bewildered but caring for them. There was no evidence of abuse, no sign of threat. Just a man trying to explain to his young children why their mother had left in the middle of the night.

Something had changed in the sisters during their night crossing. When they boarded the National Express coach to London at 11:30 a.m., the driver noticed them immediately. They clutched their bags as if their lives depended on them, refusing to let them out of their sight. Their eyes darted constantly around the bus, watching other passengers with naked suspicion.

The driver had seen nervous travelers before, but this was different. These women radiated paranoia, their bodies tense with an electric fear that made other passengers shift uncomfortably in their seats.

By the time the coach reached Keele Services on the M6, the driver had made his decision. He wanted to search their bags. When they refused, he ordered them off the bus at the service station—an unscheduled stop that left the twins stranded beside one of Britain's busiest motorways.

The service station staff watched the women with growing alarm. They stood guard over their luggage like sentries, their behavior so erratic that the manager feared they might be carrying explosives. A call went out to the police.

Two officers arrived, questioned the sisters briefly, and determined they posed no immediate threat. The women were free to go.

What the officers didn't realize was that they had just released two people who were slipping deeper into a shared delusion, walking away from help and toward a busy highway where their journey would take a terrifying turn.

———

The M6 motorway carries 120,000 vehicles daily. Trucks and cars thunder past at seventy miles per hour, their drivers focused on the road ahead, unaware of the drama unfolding in their peripheral vision.

At 3:00 p.m. on May 17, 2008, Highway Agency operators stared at their CCTV monitors in disbelief. Two figures were walking down the central reservation, the narrow strip of land that separated northbound and southbound traffic. They moved with purpose, seemingly oblivious to the tons of metal hurtling past them at deadly speeds.

Emergency calls flooded the control room. Traffic officers from the Central Motorway Police Group raced toward the scene, their patrol car cutting through traffic with sirens wailing. By sheer coincidence, a BBC television crew filming the series "Motorway Cops" was riding along with police that day, their cameras rolling as they approached what appeared to be a routine rescue operation.

The officers parked on the hard shoulder and began walking toward the two women, who stood motionless in the median strip. Standard procedure: Approach calmly, escort them to safety, and ask what had brought them onto one of England's busiest highways.

They never got the chance.

Without warning, without provocation, both women exploded into motion. They sprinted directly into the fast lane, into the path of vehicles moving at highway speed.

The first impact came almost instantly. A car struck Sabina, sending her tumbling across the asphalt in a tangle of limbs and fabric. Somehow, impossibly, she rolled to a stop and began moving. She was alive.

Ursula had made it to the far side, dodging between vehicles with seemingly impossible timing. The officers reached both women, their hearts hammering as they realized how close they had come to witnessing a double fatality.

"It's alright," one officer said, trying to calm the sisters as they guided them back to safety. "You're safe now."

They believed the crisis had passed.

From the roadside, Sabina screamed at the top of her lungs: "They're going to steal your organs!"

Before anyone could react, both sisters were running again.

This time, physics would not be kind.

Ursula ran directly into the path of a forty-ton Mercedes-Benz truck. The massive vehicle, traveling at fifty-six miles per hour, struck her and crushed her beneath its wheels. The sound of breaking bones was audible even over the noise of traffic. She lay motionless on the asphalt, her legs destroyed, blood pooling around her shattered body.

In the opposite lanes, Sabina charged into traffic with the same desperate determination. A Volkswagen Polo, traveling at full highway speed, struck her head-on. The impact launched her through the air like a discarded doll. She crashed onto the road surface and lay still for fifteen long minutes.

Both women should have died instantly. The laws of physics demanded it. The kinetic energy of the collisions should have reduced their bodies to broken fragments.

Instead, they both drew breath.

Emergency responders flooded the scene, paramedics working frantically to stabilize two people who had somehow survived the unsurvivable. Ursula lay conscious but motionless, her legs crushed beyond recognition. The medical team prepared to airlift her to the nearest trauma center.

Sabina presented a different problem entirely.

When she regained consciousness fifteen minutes after impact, her first act was violence. A policewoman approached to provide aid, and

Sabina launched herself at the officer, striking her full in the face with a closed fist. What followed defied every assumption the veteran officers held about human behavior.

Six people—trained police officers, experienced paramedics, and strong bystanders—could barely contain one injured woman. Sabina fought with inhuman fury, her strength so extraordinary that grown men were thrown aside like children. She kicked, screamed, and thrashed with such force that witnesses would later struggle to find words for what they had seen.

"Her strength was absolutely phenomenal," one officer reported. "The only time I've dealt with people with similar strength are those people that have been on drugs or under the influence of alcohol."

But when blood tests came back hours later, they revealed no trace of any substance. Sabina Eriksson was stone-cold sober.

The northbound M6 was closed for over four hours. Ursula was airlifted to a hospital for emergency surgery on her crushed legs, while Sabina was taken by ambulance to a different hospital, sedated and fully restrained.

———

What happened next would puzzle investigators for years to come. Within five hours of the motorway incident, Sabina Eriksson was deemed fit for discharge. Her injuries were minor, and her vital signs were stable. More remarkably, her aggressive behavior had completely subsided.

Sabina Erikkson

As she was processed into police custody, Sabina appeared calm and even jovial. She joked with officers and seemed entirely rational. When asked about the day's events, she made a cryptic comment that would later seem prophetic: "In Sweden, we always say that an accident rarely comes alone. Usually, one or more follows. Perhaps, two."

The transformation was so complete that it seemed impossible she was the same woman who had fought six people with superhuman strength just hours earlier.

———

On Monday, May 19, 2008, Sabina Eriksson appeared before North Staffordshire Magistrates' Court. She pleaded guilty to trespassing on the motorway and assaulting a police officer. The magistrates sentenced her to one day in custody—time she had already served while in police cells.

No comprehensive psychiatric evaluation was ordered. No mental health assessment was conducted. Sabina Eriksson was released from court that afternoon and walked free onto the streets of Stoke-on-Trent.

She was alone in an unfamiliar city, carrying her possessions in a plastic bag, with nowhere to go and no one to help her. Her twin sister lay in a hospital bed with shattered legs. Her children and partner were hundreds of miles away in Ireland. She began wandering the streets, asking strangers for directions to local hotels or bed-and-breakfasts.

As evening approached, Sabina found herself on Christchurch Street in Fenton, a district of Stoke-on-Trent. She appeared friendly but disoriented, clearly lost, and in need of assistance.

———

Glenn Hollinshead was walking his dog with his friend Peter Molloy when they encountered Sabina around 7:00 p.m. that evening. At fifty-four years old, Glenn was a self-employed welder and former Royal Air Force paramedic known throughout his neighborhood as someone always willing to help others.

Sabina approached the two men and asked if they knew of any nearby accommodations where she could spend the night. She seemed friendly enough, even stopping to pet Glenn's dog, but Peter noticed something unsettling about her demeanor. She appeared nervous, constantly looking over her shoulder as if being watched.

Glenn Hollinshead's compassionate nature overcame any reservations. This woman was clearly in distress, alone in a strange city with nowhere to sleep. Without hesitation, he offered her shelter for the night at his home on Duke Street.

The three of them walked to Glenn's house, where he prepared dinner for his unexpected guest. But as the evening progressed, Sabina's behavior became increasingly erratic. She seemed paranoid, constantly peeking through windows as if monitoring the street. At one point, she offered both men cigarettes, only to snatch them back abruptly.

"They might be poisoned," she explained.

The comment sent a chill through Peter Molloy. Something was very wrong with this woman, but he couldn't put his finger on exactly what. Around 11:40 p.m., feeling increasingly uncomfortable, Peter decided to leave.

"Are you sure about this?" he asked Glenn privately.

Glenn, with his background as a paramedic, believed he could handle whatever was troubling his guest. Perhaps his medical training made him feel responsible for someone who was clearly unwell. He assured Peter that everything would be fine.

Peter Molloy left Glenn Hollinshead alone with Sabina Eriksson for the night.

———

Tuesday, May 20, began with quiet determination. Glenn helped Sabina contact local hospitals in an attempt to locate her twin sister, Ursula, though they were unable to determine which facility she was in. At lunchtime, Glenn called his brother Paul, who worked at the University Hospital of North Staffordshire, asking if he could find out which ward Ursula was on.

Sabina remained at the house throughout the day, and Glenn

continued to show her kindness, apparently still believing he could help this troubled stranger.

At 7:40 p.m., Glenn stepped outside to ask his neighbor, Frank Booth, for some tea bags. The neighbor was washing his minibus and asked Glenn to wait a moment. Glenn chatted briefly with Frank, mentioning that his guest had hopefully calmed down since the night before.

Glenn returned to his house to make tea. Seventy-four seconds later, he staggered back outside.

"She's stabbed me," he gasped, blood spreading across his shirt.

Glenn Hollinshead collapsed on his front step. He had been stabbed five times with a kitchen knife taken from his own home. One of the wounds had pierced his heart.

Emergency services were called at 7:46 p.m., but despite the rapid response of paramedics, Glenn Hollinshead died at the scene. The fifty-four-year-old man who had spent his life helping others—first as a Royal Air Force paramedic, then as a Good Samaritan who took in strangers—had paid the ultimate price for his compassion.

Investigators would later determine that Glenn had no defensive wounds. He had been taken completely by surprise, stabbed by someone he trusted and was trying to help.

———

Sabina Eriksson fled Glenn's house immediately after the attack, running into the streets with a claw hammer she had taken from his home. Neighbors spotted her on nearby roads, apparently in a state of complete psychological breakdown.

She was hitting herself repeatedly in the head with the hammer as she ran.

Concerned witnesses called for help and attempted to intervene. A driver named Joshua Grattage stopped his car and tried to grab the hammer from Sabina to prevent her from further self-harm. During the struggle, Sabina produced a roof tile from her pocket—an object she had inexplicably been carrying—and struck the Good Samaritan on the back of the head, stunning him long enough to break free.

By now, police and paramedics were pursuing her on foot. The chase led to the Heron Cross bridge over the A50, where Sabina made one final, desperate act.

She climbed onto the railing of the forty-foot-high bridge and jumped.

Sabina Eriksson fell twelve meters onto the busy roadway below, crashing onto the median of the A50. The impact fractured her skull and broke both ankles, but incredibly, she survived. Police and medics quickly secured her at the crash site, and she was rushed to the University Hospital of North Staffordshire under armed guard.

The woman who had cheated death on the M6 motorway had done so again.

———

As Sabina lay unconscious in her hospital bed, investigators began piecing together one of the most baffling cases in British criminal history. Here was a woman with no history of violence, no criminal record, and no apparent motive for murder. She had no personal connection to Glenn Hollinshead beyond the brief kindness he had shown her.

Toxicology tests confirmed what had been established after the motorway incident: Sabina had no drugs or alcohol in her system. Her actions were not the result of substance abuse but something far more mysterious.

The focus turned to her mental state. Detectives learned about the bizarre episode on the M6 and realized they were dealing with an extraordinary situation that defied conventional explanation.

Sabina spent months recovering from her injuries while psychiatric experts evaluated her condition. When she was finally well enough to be discharged in September 2008, she was immediately arrested and charged with murder.

Throughout the investigation, Sabina maintained her silence. When questioned by police, she answered virtually every inquiry with "no comment." She gave no explanation for her actions, no insight into her state of mind, and no motive for the killing. Even her solicitors struggled to understand what had driven their client to such extreme violence.

———

When Sabina's case finally came to trial in September 2009, psychiatric experts had reached a startling conclusion. Two consultant forensic psychiatrists—one for the defense and one for the prosecution—agreed that Sabina had been suffering from a rare psychiatric disorder at the time of the offenses.

The diagnosis was folie à deux, also known as shared psychosis or induced delusional disorder. It is a condition so rare that few forensic psychiatrists encounter it in their entire careers.

In folie à deux, delusional beliefs are transmitted from one person to another within a close relationship. The experts theorized that Ursula had been the primary sufferer, experiencing an acute psychotic episode that she had somehow transmitted to her identical twin. Sabina, as the secondary sufferer, had adopted her sister's delusions and paranoid beliefs.

The evidence supported this extraordinary theory. Both women had exhibited identical bizarre behavior on the motorway. Both had shown the same paranoid delusions—Sabina's screaming about organ theft, her belief that cigarettes might be poisoned, and her constant vigilance against unseen threats. Most tellingly, once the sisters were separated by Ursula's hospitalization, Sabina's psychotic symptoms had gradually subsided.

Dr. Carol McDaniel, one of the examining psychiatrists, testified that Sabina had "heard voices but could not interpret what they were saying" during the psychotic episode. She was operating under a delusional belief system that governed all her actions, including the fatal attack on Glenn Hollinshead.

By the time of her trial, however, Sabina showed no signs of mental illness. The shared psychosis had been temporary, triggered by her proximity to her twin and resolved by their separation.

———

On September 2, 2009, Sabina Eriksson pleaded guilty to manslaughter with diminished responsibility rather than murder. Both the prosecution and defense agreed that she had been legally insane at the time of the killing but had since recovered her sanity.

The plea meant there would be no full trial by jury. Instead, the court held a sentencing hearing to determine the appropriate punishment for a woman who had killed while in the grip of a shared madness.

Mr. Justice Saunders faced an impossible task. How do you sentence someone for a crime committed while genuinely insane? How do you balance justice for the victim with mercy for a defendant who was not truly responsible for her actions?

On November 26, 2009, Justice Saunders delivered his verdict. Sabina Eriksson was sentenced to five years in prison for manslaughter.

"I understand that this sentence will seem entirely inadequate to the relatives of the deceased," the judge acknowledged. "However, I have sentenced on the basis that the reason for the killing was the mental illness and therefore the culpability of the defendant is low. It is a sentence which I hope fairly measures a truly tragic event."

The judge emphasized that Sabina had been "suffering from delusions, which she believed to be true, and they dictated her behavior." She could not have prevented the onset of her mental illness, nor could she have controlled her actions while in its grip.

————

Sabina served her sentence quietly at HM Prison Bronzefield, reportedly becoming a model inmate and finding solace in Christianity. There were no reports of psychiatric relapse or disciplinary issues. In July 2011, after serving approximately half her sentence, she was released on parole and returned to Sweden.

Glenn Hollinshead's family, while understanding the legal reasoning behind the sentence, expressed their belief that the system had failed their loved one. His brother, Garry, stated publicly that Sabina's mental disorder should have been recognized after the motorway incident, potentially preventing the tragedy that followed.

"We don't hold her responsible," Garry said, "the same as we wouldn't blame a rabid dog for biting someone. She is ill and to a large degree not responsible for her actions. But Glenn died trying to help someone who should never have been released into the community in that state."

Their anger was directed not at Sabina herself but at the authorities, who had failed to recognize the severity of her condition when they'd had the chance to intervene.

————

Ursula Eriksson recovered from her severe injuries and returned to her life in the United States. She has never spoken publicly about the events of May 2008 and has avoided all media attention. No further incidents involving her have been reported.

———

The case of the Eriksson twins raises profound questions about the nature of human consciousness and the mysterious connections between identical siblings. How could two previously stable women descend into shared madness so complete that it led to attempted suicide and murder?

Psychiatric experts have identified fewer than a hundred documented cases of folie à deux in medical literature. The condition typically occurs between spouses or family members who are isolated together for extended periods. However, the Eriksson sisters had been living on separate continents for years before their sudden reunion triggered their shared psychosis.

What caused their initial break from reality? Why did their paranoid delusions manifest so violently? How did they manage to survive collisions that should have killed them instantly?

These questions may never be fully answered. The twins themselves have offered no explanations, no insights. They remain silent about the madness they shared and the man who died because of it.

CHAPTER 3

THE STANFORD COLD CASE

"Hey, we've got a stiff in here."

The words came through the Stanford University radio at 5:45 a.m. on October 13, 1974. Security guard Stephen Crawford's voice carried an odd detachment as he reported what would become one of California's most haunting unsolved murders.

Inside Stanford Memorial Church, beneath the soaring arches and stained-glass windows, lay the body of nineteen-year-old Arlis Perry. What Crawford discovered that Sunday morning would shatter the serene academic world of Stanford University and launch a forty-four-year hunt for a killer hiding in plain sight.

———

Two months earlier, Arlis Kay Dykema had stood at the altar of Bismarck Reformed Church in North Dakota, radiant in white lace, exchanging vows with her high school sweetheart, Bruce Perry. The August 17, 1974, wedding was everything a small-town celebration should be—family, friends, and faith binding two young lives together.

Arlis had grown up as the youngest of three children in Bismarck, deeply rooted in the Presbyterian church where her father, Marvin, served as an usher and Sunday school superintendent. Her cheer-leading coach described her as "bubbly and enthusiastic but also self-contained—a girl who was easily frightened by violence and hostility." She baked cupcakes for her teammates and taught Sunday school on weekends, her faith as natural to her as breathing.

Bruce was her perfect match—a track star who'd set state records in the sprint events, bound for Stanford University on his athletic and academic merit. Like Arlis, he was deeply religious, and together they'd worked with the Fellowship of Christian Athletes and Young Life, a Christian youth organization.

After their honeymoon in a rustic log cabin owned by Arlis's parents, the newlyweds made the 1,600-mile journey to California. Bruce would continue his pre-med studies as a sophomore, while Arlis found work as a receptionist at a Palo Alto law firm. They settled into Quillen Hall in Stanford's Escondido Village, married student housing that felt like the beginning of their American dream.

However, paradise proved elusive for the young bride from North Dakota.

———

The sprawling Stanford campus, with its mission-style architecture and palm-lined roads, felt like another planet to Arlis. Where Bismarck offered a tight-knit community and familiar faces, Stanford presented endless anonymity. The sophisticated California students seemed to speak a different language, one of privilege and intellectual pretension that left her feeling isolated.

"Friends are hard to find here," she wrote to her family back home. "Many times I've been tempted to go knock on doors asking if anyone needs a friend, but I guess we just have to appreciate each other and trust the Lord for new friends."

Bruce threw himself into his studies and part-time work, leaving Arlis to navigate this new world largely alone. She found solace in long walks around campus and, increasingly, in the quiet sanctuary of Stanford Memorial Church. The ornate building, with its buff sandstone walls and colorful mosaic murals, offered the kind of spiritual refuge she'd always known.

What Arlis didn't know was that someone had been watching her during those solitary visits to the church. Someone saw her vulnerability as an opportunity.

———

Saturday, October 12, 1974, began like any other weekend evening. Bruce studied while Arlis bustled around their small apartment. The Columbus Day holiday had filled the campus with music and celebration, and students were milling about on the warm California night.

Around 11:30 p.m., Bruce agreed to accompany Arlis to the campus post office. She wanted to mail letters to her family and friends back in Bismarck—those lifelines to home that kept her tethered to who she'd been before California had changed her.

As they walked across campus, something trivial sparked an argument. Their car tire had been losing pressure, and they disagreed about who was responsible for maintaining it. Such a small thing, the kind of domestic dispute that young married couples navigate and forget.

Unfortunately, this argument would haunt Bruce Perry for the rest of his life.

By the time they'd posted the letters, it was nearly midnight. Still upset, Arlis told Bruce she wanted to visit Memorial Church alone to pray. This wasn't unusual; both of them had sought solace in the church's peaceful atmosphere when they needed guidance or simply time to think.

Bruce headed back to their apartment while Arlis walked toward the main quad, her figure disappearing into the shadows between the campus buildings. He had no way of knowing that someone else was already waiting in the church—someone who had been planning for exactly this kind of opportunity.

———

Back in their apartment, Bruce tried to focus on his studies, but worry gnawed at him as the minutes ticked by. 12:30 a.m. came and went. Then, 1:00 a.m. Arlis was never this late, never stayed out without calling.

Approaching 3:00 a.m., Bruce's concern had transformed into panic. He returned to Memorial Church but found all the doors locked tight. He searched the campus, calling her name into the empty spaces between buildings, but the night offered only silence.

At 3:00 a.m., he made the call no young husband ever wants to make. Arlis was missing, he told the Stanford campus police. She had no friends in town, and there was nowhere else she would go. Something was wrong.

Campus officers responded quickly, checking the exterior of Memorial Church. The building remained securely locked, showing no signs of disturbance. To the officers, this looked like a typical domestic dispute—a young wife cooling off after an argument with her husband. She'd return when she was ready.

They had no way of knowing that inside the locked church, something unspeakable had already happened.

———

Stephen Crawford had worked as Stanford's night security guard for three years, ever since his demotion from the university police force. The former Air Force veteran had grown bitter about the reduction in status and pay, but he dutifully made his rounds each night, checking buildings and ensuring campus security.

On Sunday morning, October 13, Crawford approached Memorial Church around 5:30 a.m. to open it for the day's visitors. As he neared the west side door, something immediately struck him as wrong. The door hung partially open, its lock apparently forced from the inside.

Crawford's first thought was burglary. He entered cautiously, moving through the nave toward the altar area. What he found in the east transept would later be described by investigators as one of the most brutal and disturbing crime scenes they'd ever encountered.

Arlis Perry lay on her back between the wooden pews, her dark brown jacket still in place, but her tan sweater pushed up to expose her chest. Her blue jeans had been removed and arranged over her lower legs in a deliberate diamond pattern—a bizarre geometric arrangement that investigators would later note spoke of cold calculation rather than frenzied violence. Her head faced toward the altar, and a kneeling pillow—the kind used for prayer—lay nearby.

But it was the other details that transformed this from a terrible murder into something far more sinister. Two three-foot altar candles had been taken from the church and used in a sexual assault that defied comprehension. One remained partially inserted in Arlis's body, while the other had been positioned between her breasts. The scene had been staged with a cold deliberation that spoke of either twisted ritual or calculated misdirection.

Most shocking of all was the ice pick protruding from behind Arlis's left ear. The wooden handle had broken off, leaving only the metal shaft embedded in her skull. This was the wound that had killed her, but the handle was nowhere to be found.

Crawford radioed his supervisors with those chilling words that would echo through Stanford lore: "Hey, we've got a stiff in here."

———

Within minutes, Stanford Memorial Church transformed from a place of worship into a crime scene. Santa Clara County Sheriff's deputies cordoned off the area while investigators began the painstaking work of documenting every detail of the horrific scene.

The medical examiner determined that Arlis had died around midnight—shortly after she'd entered the church to pray. The ice pick wound was fatal, but evidence suggested she'd also been strangled. Markings on her neck were consistent with attempted choking, and a small bone in her neck had been fractured.

Investigators found no signs of a struggle, suggesting Arlis had been caught completely off guard by her attacker. There were no drag marks leading to where her body was discovered, indicating she'd either walked to that spot willingly or been carried there after being attacked elsewhere in the church.

The forensic team processed the scene meticulously, collecting what evidence they could with 1974 technology. On one of the altar candles, they found a partial palm print that didn't belong to Arlis. Near her body, a kneeling pillow yielded traces of semen. Both pieces of evidence would prove crucial decades later, but in 1974, they offered only frustrating dead ends.

The staging of the scene immediately caught investigators' attention. The deliberate positioning of the body and the use of religious artifacts suggested either someone with a deep psychological disturbance or a killer trying to mislead police about his motives.

———

Dawn was breaking over the Stanford campus when police arrived at Bruce and Arlis's apartment. Bruce answered the door wearing a blood-stained shirt, which he quickly explained was from a nosebleed —something he was prone to during times of extreme stress.

The officers didn't immediately tell Bruce what they'd found. Instead, they asked him to come to the station to file a missing person report. For two agonizing hours, investigators questioned him about the previous night, presenting different scenarios to gauge his reactions. They asked about affairs, about pregnancy, about the argument over the tire pressure.

Bruce grew increasingly agitated, repeatedly asking, "Where's my wife?" When they suggested he might have lashed out at Arlis in anger, he became defensive, insisting he loved her and would never hurt her.

Finally, they administered a polygraph test. Only after Bruce passed did investigators deliver the devastating news: Arlis was dead, murdered in the church where she'd gone to pray.

The blood on Bruce's shirt was tested and confirmed to be his own blood type, not Arlis's. His palm print didn't match the one found on the altar candle. Most importantly, the semen found at the scene didn't match his blood type either. Within days, Bruce Perry was cleared as a suspect, but the damage to his psyche had been done already.

————

As investigators canvassed the campus, they discovered that at least seven people had been in or around Memorial Church on the night of October 12. Five were quickly identified and interviewed, their stories creating a timeline of Arlis's final hours.

Two visitors who'd been praying in the church said they saw Arlis enter around midnight. She walked to the front pews on the left side of the altar and knelt down to pray. She was still there, deep in prayer, when they left at midnight.

A passerby outside the church reported seeing a Caucasian man with sandy-colored hair near the building around this same time. The man was described as approximately twenty-five years old, medium build, and wearing a royal blue short-sleeved shirt. Despite public appeals and a police sketch, this man was never identified.

The most important witness, however, was Stephen Crawford himself. The security guard claimed he'd arrived at the church around 12:10 a.m. to lock up for the night. He said he'd entered through the rear and called out, "We're closing for the night. The church is being locked. If anyone is here, you have to leave."

When no one responded, Crawford said he'd locked all the doors and left. He also claimed he'd returned around 2:00 a.m. for a routine security check and found everything normal.

But this timeline presented immediate problems. If Arlis was killed around midnight, and Crawford locked the church at 12:10 a.m., what had happened in those crucial ten minutes? And if Crawford had truly checked the church at 2:00 a.m., how had he missed a brutal murder scene?

Some investigators began to suspect that Crawford's 2:00 a.m. security check had never happened—that he was covering up either negligence or something far worse.

———

The brutal nature of Arlis's murder, combined with the staging of her body with religious artifacts, sparked immediate speculation about satanic cults and ritual murder. This was 1974, just five years after the Manson family killings, and America was gripped by fears of occult violence.

Rumors spread that Arlis had been targeted because of her Christian faith, that she'd somehow run afoul of devil worshippers who'd followed her from North Dakota to California. The theory gained traction when people recalled that Arlis and a friend had supposedly visited a controversial religious group called the Process Church of the Final Judgment in a neighboring town, attempting to convert its members to Christianity.

Investigators pursued these leads but found no credible evidence of cult involvement, while the Process Church angle proved to be nothing more than local gossip. Still, the satanic ritual theory persisted, fueled by sensational media coverage and the public's fascination with the macabre.

The case was further complicated by its timing. Arlis's murder was the fourth unexplained death of a young person on or near Stanford's campus in just nineteen months. The previous victims included Leslie Perlov, David Levine, and Janet Taylor—all killed under mysterious circumstances that had left the Stanford community on edge.

Investigators briefly explored whether a serial killer might be responsible for all four deaths, but the connection proved elusive. Each case had distinct characteristics, and no physical evidence linked them together.

———

As months passed without an arrest, investigators cast their net wider, examining whether Arlis's killer might have been one of the notorious serial killers terrorizing California in the 1970s. The Bay Area was, in the words of one detective, "a stomping ground for murderers," with the Zodiac Killer, Ed Kemper's "Co-ed Killer" spree, and other predators creating an atmosphere of fear.

The most intriguing suspect was Ted Bundy, who had studied at Stanford in the late 1960s and was familiar with the campus. Bundy had visited the Bay Area multiple times in 1973 and 1974, during the period when several Stanford-area murders occurred. In addition, when police arrested him in Utah in 1975, his car contained an ice pick—the same type of weapon used to kill Arlis.

Investigators interviewed Bundy about Arlis's murder, but he had an airtight alibi: Credit card records showed he was filling up his Volkswagen at a gas station out of town at the time of the murder. He was also ruled out as a suspect in the other Stanford-area killings.

Ed Kemper, the "Co-ed Killer" who had terrorized the Santa Cruz area, was also investigated. Kemper had surrendered to police in April 1973, which ruled him out for Arlis's murder, but he'd been active when Leslie Perlov was killed. When questioned about the Stanford murders, the usually forthcoming Kemper denied any involvement.

Even David Berkowitz, the "Son of Sam" killer, would later insert himself into the case. In 1978, while serving life sentences in New York, Berkowitz wrote to the North Dakota Police claiming that the Process Church of the Final Judgment had hired a hitman to kill Arlis. When investigators traveled to interview him, Berkowitz became evasive and provided nothing useful, leading them to dismiss his claims as attention-seeking.

————

By 1975, with no arrests and the leads growing cold, the Arlis Perry case joined the ranks of unsolved murders that haunt law enforcement. The intensive investigation was scaled back, though the case was never officially closed; detectives would periodically review the file, hoping new technology or a fresh perspective might yield a breakthrough.

For Bruce Perry, the lack of resolution was devastating. He took leave from Stanford and spent months visiting friends across the country, trying to process the trauma of losing his wife in such a horrific manner. When he returned to his studies, the constant reminders of that terrible night proved overwhelming.

Stephen Crawford

Meanwhile, Stephen Crawford continued working at Stanford until 1976, when he left for a security job elsewhere. His colleagues in a square dance group nicknamed him "the prevaricator" for his habit of lying and exaggerating stories. In one instance, he told them his parents had died in a car crash when he was young, when in reality, they'd died in separate incidents when he was in his early twenties.

In 1992, eighteen years after the murder, Crawford's ex-wife reported him for forging a fake diploma using a blank certificate stolen from Stanford. A search of his home revealed an astonishing crime: Crawford had stolen up to three hundred rare and valuable books from the university library, including leather-bound Latin texts dating back to the sixteenth century. He'd also taken priceless artifacts from the anthropology department, including a walking cane that had belonged to university founder Leland Stanford—and a human skull.

When asked why he'd stolen the items, Crawford claimed it was retaliation for being considered a suspect in the Arlis Perry murder. He pleaded guilty to receiving stolen property and received a six-month suspended sentence with two years' probation.

The book theft revelation caused investigators to take a fresh look at Crawford as a suspect in Arlis's murder, but they still lacked physical evidence linking him to the crime. His palm print didn't match the one on the altar candle, and without DNA technology, the semen evidence couldn't definitively implicate him.

————

In 2016, forty-two years after Arlis's murder, cold-case detective Lieutenant Rick Alanis stared at the boxes of evidence that had been gathering dust in the Santa Clara County Sheriff's warehouse. The Arlis Perry case had haunted the department for decades, a constant reminder of justice denied, but new DNA technology offered hope where there had been none before.

The first shock came when Alanis and his team began meticulously reviewing the physical evidence stored since 1974. As they examined each item, cross-referencing against the original crime scene reports, a disturbing discrepancy emerged. Among the clothing evidence, a pair of pants had been labeled as belonging to Arlis Perry. However, as investigators looked more closely, they realized the terrible truth: These weren't Arlis's pants at all. They belonged to Bruce Perry.

The mix-up, likely dating back to the chaotic night of the crime when Bruce was questioned and his clothing had been collected for testing, meant that decades of forensic analysis had been conducted on the wrong evidence. Any DNA testing performed on "Arlis's pants" in previous years had been meaningless.

Alanis felt his pulse quicken as the implications became clear. Somewhere in that evidence room were Arlis's actual jeans—the ones she'd been wearing when she was murdered. The ones that might finally hold the key to identifying her killer.

The search through the warehouse became increasingly urgent. Box after box was examined, and each item was cataloged and cross-referenced. Then, in a container that had sat untouched for years, they found them: Arlis's blue jeans, carefully preserved in an evidence bag, exactly as they'd been collected from the crime scene in 1974.

The forensic lab received the jeans with instructions to conduct the most advanced DNA testing available. The technology that hadn't existed in 1974—or even in the 1990s, when the case was last actively investigated—could now extract genetic profiles from the smallest traces of biological material.

Days passed with agonizing slowness as the lab worked. Then came the call that would change everything.

The jeans contained semen stains that had yielded a complete male DNA profile. When that profile was run through CODIS—the Combined DNA Index System, which links criminal databases across the country—the computer found a match.

The name that appeared on Alanis's screen made his blood run cold: Stephen Blake Crawford.

The security guard who had "discovered" Arlis Perry's body, who had been questioned and cleared in 1974, who had lived quietly for four decades while a family grieved and a case went unsolved, was the killer.

Crawford had been hiding in plain sight all along, protected by his role as the helpful witness who'd found the victim. The very man who'd radioed, "Hey, we've got a stiff in here," had been the one who'd put her there.

―――――

The DNA match electrified the cold-case team, but they knew they had to proceed with extreme caution. Crawford was now seventy-two years old, and they had only one chance to get this right. Any misstep could compromise a case that had taken four decades to crack.

Throughout 2017 and into 2018, investigators launched a covert operation unlike anything the department had undertaken before. They quietly re-interviewed witnesses from 1974, gathering additional DNA samples to strengthen their case. Each conversation had to appear routine, part of a standard cold-case review, while secretly building the evidence needed to ensure Crawford couldn't escape justice again.

The most delicate part of the operation involved confirming the DNA match. Crawford had refused to provide voluntary DNA samples over the years, unlike Bruce Perry, who had cooperated fully. Investigators couldn't simply ask him for a sample without revealing their hand and potentially spooking him into fleeing or destroying evidence.

Instead, they obtained his genetic material from discarded items rather than asking for a voluntary sample. When the results came back, there was no doubt. The DNA matched the profile from Arlis's jeans with astronomical certainty—the odds of it being anyone else were essentially zero.

Armed with this confirmation, investigators also began discreetly monitoring Crawford's behavior. During renewed interviews in 2017, he appeared increasingly nervous and evasive. When questioned about inconsistencies in his original story from 1974, Crawford's responses seemed rehearsed, as if he'd spent decades preparing for this moment.

The surveillance revealed a man living a solitary existence in his small studio apartment, surviving on Social Security and leftover retirement funds. But beneath the façade of a lonely senior citizen, investigators sensed something darker—a man who'd been waiting for this day to come, knowing that advancing technology would eventually expose his crime.

By June 2018, the Santa Clara County District Attorney's office had reviewed all the evidence and was ready to proceed. The case against Stephen Crawford was airtight: his DNA on the victim's clothing, his inconsistent statements from 1974, his access to the church, and his opportunity to commit the crime.

A judge issued both an arrest warrant and a search warrant for Crawford's apartment.

———

Dawn was breaking over San Jose on June 28, 2018, as an unmarked convoy of sheriff's vehicles made its way through the quiet residential streets toward the Del Coronado Apartments. Detective Lieutenant Rick Alanis rode in the lead car, his heart pounding with a mixture of anticipation and dread. After forty-four years, they were finally going to arrest Arlis Perry's killer.

The team approached Crawford's ground-floor studio apartment with tactical precision. They knew they were dealing with a man who'd evaded capture for nearly half a century, someone who might be desperate enough to do anything to avoid spending his final years in prison.

At exactly 9:00 a.m., officers positioned themselves outside apartment door number 12. Alanis knocked firmly, his voice carrying the authority of four decades of waiting: "Stephen Crawford, this is the Santa Clara County Sheriff's Office. We have a warrant."

A long pause. Then Crawford's voice came through the door, sounding strangely calm: "Just give me a moment to get dressed."

Minutes ticked by. Then, more minutes. The officers exchanged glances. Something felt wrong.

"Mr. Crawford, we need you to open the door now," Alanis called out.

Silence.

The building manager, who'd been standing nervously nearby with the master key, stepped forward. Alanis made the decision: They were going in.

The key turned with a soft click. The door swung open to reveal the sparse interior of Crawford's studio apartment—a bed, a small table, and some scattered belongings. And there, sitting on the edge of the bed in full view of the doorway, was Stephen Blake Crawford holding a handgun.

"Drop the weapon! Show us your hands!" officers shouted, their own weapons drawn as they immediately backed away from the doorway. The narrow apartment offered no cover, no room to maneuver. All they could do was take defensive positions and try to talk him down.

Crawford looked up at them with what witnesses later described as an expression of resigned calm. He said nothing. He made no move to comply with their commands. For a moment that seemed to stretch into eternity, everyone froze—the officers in the hallway, Crawford on the bed, the weight of forty-four years of secrets hanging in the air between them. Then Crawford raised the gun to his head.

The gunshot was deafening in the confined space, echoing off the apartment walls and stunning the officers into momentary silence. When the ringing in their ears subsided, they could hear nothing from inside the apartment.

Stephen Blake Crawford lay slumped on his bed, killed instantly by a self-inflicted gunshot wound to the head. The man who'd carried the secret of Arlis Perry's murder for forty-four years had chosen to take that secret with him rather than face the consequences of his crime.

Building manager Laticia Gonzales, who'd been waiting down the hall, later told reporters she'd seen the deputies trying to enter the apartment moments before hearing the gunshot. Neighbor Yanet

Crisostomo described Crawford as someone who'd seemed "normal" but kept largely to himself—a description that would prove chillingly familiar to anyone who'd studied serial killers and long-term criminals.

In the immediate aftermath, as crime scene technicians processed the apartment and investigators began searching for additional evidence, one thought dominated everyone's mind: After four decades of waiting, justice for Arlis Perry would have to come without a trial, without a confession, and without the answers that might have finally explained why a young woman's prayer had ended in such unspeakable violence.

———

The search of Crawford's apartment revealed disturbing evidence of a man who'd lived for decades with the knowledge of his terrible crime. Among his possessions, investigators found the dust jacket from Maury Terry's 1987 book "The Ultimate Evil"—a discovery that sent chills through the investigation team. Terry's controversial book had spent hundreds of pages promoting the theory that Arlis's murder was the work of a satanic cult, possibly connected to the Process Church of the Final Judgment and even the Son of Sam killings in New York. The book had theorized that Arlis's deeply religious nature had made her a target for devil worshippers who'd followed her from North Dakota to California.

Terry had pointed to the staging of Arlis's body with altar candles as evidence of ritual murder, dismissing the possibility that a lone killer could have committed such a crime. The book had sent shockwaves through the Bismarck community when it was published—local bookstores had quickly sold out, the library had amassed a staggering waitlist, and when Terry came to discuss his theories in 1989, the venue had needed to be changed because the 1,000-capacity auditorium sold out with lines circling around the block.

For Crawford to have kept this book—particularly just the dust jacket, as if it were some kind of trophy—suggested a twisted pride in how successfully he'd misdirected the investigation. The satanic angle had consumed investigators' time and energy for years, sending them chasing phantoms while the real killer watched from the sidelines.

Investigators also found a suicide note. Handwritten and yellowed with age, it was dated two years earlier, when Detective Alanis had first begun the evidence review that would ultimately expose Crawford's guilt. The note was brief and deliberately vague, making no confession to Arlis's murder but clearly indicating Crawford had been contemplating taking his own life since investigators had renewed their interest in the case. The timing was no coincidence: He'd been preparing for this moment for two years, knowing that advancing DNA technology would eventually catch up with him.

The evidence painted a picture of a bitter man who'd targeted Arlis Perry to exact revenge against Stanford University following his humiliating demotion from campus police officer to night security guard. Crawford's position gave him access to the church and knowledge of its routines. He knew when it would be empty—when he could commit his crime without immediate discovery.

On October 12, 1974, when Arlis entered Memorial Church alone to pray, Crawford was ready. The young woman who'd come seeking spiritual solace instead encountered a predator who'd been watching, planning, and waiting for precisely this opportunity.

After killing Arlis and staging the scene to suggest ritual murder, Crawford forced open the west side door from the inside and exited the church. Hours later, he returned in his official capacity as a security guard to "discover" the body, playing the role of shocked witness to his own crime.

For forty-four years, Stephen Crawford had hidden his guilt behind the badge of the man who had found the victim. His intimate knowledge of the case and ability to alter his story over the years had helped him evade suspicion, even as investigators had harbored doubts about his accounts.

———

Sheriff Laurie Smith held a press conference that afternoon to announce the resolution of one of Santa Clara County's most notorious cold cases. Standing beside an enlarged photograph of Arlis Perry, Smith thanked the cold-case detectives for their relentless pursuit of justice.

"This is a case that eludes us no longer," Smith declared. "We believe we had solid evidence to arrest and even convict Stephen Crawford for the murder of Arlis Perry."

The news brought a mixture of relief and sorrow to Arlis's family. Her mother, Jean Dykema, then eighty-eight years old, expressed gratitude that the truth had finally emerged. Sadly, her husband, Marvin, had died just three months earlier, never knowing who had killed their daughter despite his desperate desire to learn the truth.

"It's about time," Jean said when informed of Crawford's identification. However, she also acknowledged the bittersweet nature of the resolution: "The question of why Arlis was killed remains as unresolved as ever."

Because Crawford had died before he could be arrested and tried, there would be no courtroom drama, no detailed confession, and no opportunity for the family to confront their daughter's killer. The case was closed through what law enforcement calls "exceptional clearance"—solved by the death of the perpetrator.

———

The resolution of Arlis Perry's case also brought clarity to the other Stanford-area murders that had terrorized the campus in the 1970s. DNA evidence definitively ruled out Crawford as the killer of Leslie

Perlov and Janet Taylor, confirming that these were separate crimes committed by different perpetrators.

In a remarkable coincidence, just five months after Crawford's suicide, investigators identified the killer of Leslie Perlov and Janet Taylor through similar DNA techniques. John Arthur Getreu, a man with a violent criminal history dating back to a 1963 rape and murder in Germany, was arrested for both crimes.

Getreu had worked as a medical technician at Stanford Hospital during the time of the murders, giving him familiarity with the area. His DNA was matched to evidence from both crime scenes after investigators obtained samples from items he'd discarded. Like Crawford, Getreu had hidden in plain sight for decades, his violent past unknown to those around him.

The identification of both killers through advanced DNA technology brought closure to three of the four Stanford-area murders from the 1970s. Only the death of David Levine remained unsolved, though investigators continued working on that case as well.

———

Bruce Perry rebuilt his life away from the public eye, generally avoiding discussion of the case that had forever changed him. He had endured intense initial scrutiny as investigators worked to clear him as a suspect, then lived for decades with the weight of unanswered questions about his wife's brutal murder. When the case was finally solved in 2018, close friends said Bruce was grateful that the truth had emerged and that he had been formally vindicated by the DNA evidence. The resolution brought him some measure of peace after forty-four years of wondering who had killed his young bride.

For law enforcement, the Arlis Perry case became a testament to the power of persistence and advancing technology. The semen sample that frustrated investigators in 1974 ultimately provided the evidence needed to solve the case more than four decades later.

CHAPTER 4
THE TRAINSPOTTER

T he phone rang at Shipways Estate Agency at 4:47 p.m. on January 22, 1992. Kevin Watts, the thirty-three-year-old branch manager, had been expecting Stephanie Slater back from her afternoon appointment for over an hour. The twenty-five-year-old had been working at the real estate agency's office in Great Barr, a suburb just outside Birmingham, England, for only six weeks, but she was punctual and professional—not the type to simply disappear without explanation.

The voice on the other end was calm, methodical, and chilling in its matter-of-fact delivery.

"I have your employee," the man said. "If you want to see her alive again, it will cost you £175,000."

Watts felt his blood turn cold. For a moment, he wondered if this was some kind of sick joke. But something in the caller's tone—the complete absence of emotion, the practiced delivery—told him this was terrifyingly real.

"Who is this?" Watts managed to ask. "What employee?"

"Stephanie Slater. The blonde girl who shows houses. She's safe for now, but that depends entirely on your cooperation."

The line went dead.

Watts stared at the phone, his hands shaking slightly. Stephanie had gone to show a property on Turnberry Road to a client who had contacted them by letter. Something about the formality of written correspondence rather than a phone call had struck him as slightly odd, but it hadn't been enough to raise any alarm. Estate agents dealt with all types of clients, and some preferred the old-fashioned approach.

Now, as he replayed the morning in his mind, that small detail took on a sinister significance.

———

Earlier that morning, Stephanie Slater had arrived at the Shipways office with her usual bright smile and cheerful disposition. She was everything an estate agency could want in an employee: attractive, articulate, and genuinely enthusiastic about helping people find homes. Her colleagues had taken to her immediately when she started six weeks earlier, charmed by her warmth and impressed by her quick grasp of the business.

Stephanie had grown up in Birmingham, living with her parents, Warren and Betty, in a comfortable semi-detached house in Handsworth. At twenty-five, she was ambitious and hardworking, seeing real estate as a stepping stone to bigger things. She'd always been good with people, able to put nervous first-time buyers at ease while maintaining the persistence needed to close deals.

The letter requesting the viewing had arrived three days earlier, written in neat handwriting on plain paper. The potential buyer had identified himself as Mr. Southall and expressed interest in the three-bedroom house on Turnberry Road—a vacant property that had been on their books for several months. He'd requested an appointment for Wednesday afternoon and provided a phone number, though when the office had tried to call to confirm, they'd gotten no answer.

Stephanie had volunteered to handle the viewing. She'd driven past the property that morning to refresh her memory of its layout and features. It was a nice house in a quiet residential street, the kind of place a young professional might want to settle down in. The fact that it was empty made it convenient for showing; there was no need to coordinate with current occupants or worry about disrupting anyone's schedule.

At 1:30 p.m., Stephanie had gathered her files, checked her appearance in the small mirror by the office door, and headed out to meet Mr. Southall. She'd told Kevin she expected to be back by 3:00 p.m. at the latest.

That was over two hours ago.

———

Detective Inspector Bob Taylor of the West Midlands Police had seen his share of missing person cases over his twenty-year career, but something about this one set off alarm bells immediately. A young woman vanishing during a routine business appointment, followed by a ransom demand within hours—this wasn't a typical disappearance.

DI Taylor arrived at the Shipways office at 6:15 p.m., less than ninety minutes after Kevin Watts had called 999. The branch manager was visibly shaken, pacing behind his desk while two uniformed officers took notes.

Taylor questioned Watts extensively about the mysterious Mr. Southall. Watts produced a thin file folder containing the original letter that had initiated the appointment.

Taylor examined the letter carefully. The handwriting was neat, almost mechanical in its precision, and the paper was ordinary, the kind you could buy at any stationery shop. There was no letterhead, no address provided beyond a phone number that apparently didn't work.

When Taylor inquired about any unusual behavior from Stephanie recently—whether she'd mentioned feeling watched, received strange calls, or had concerning interactions with clients—Watts could offer nothing. Stephanie was new to the job, but she seemed to love the work and had never mentioned any problems with anyone.

Taylor made a note to interview Stephanie's family and friends, but his instincts were already telling him this wasn't about Stephanie specifically. Someone had targeted her because of what she represented—a young woman who would be alone with strangers as part of her job. Estate agents were uniquely vulnerable, he realized. They met unknown clients in empty houses, often without anyone knowing exactly where they were or when they'd return.

As the evening wore on, Taylor's team began canvassing the Turnberry Road area. The empty house showed no signs of a struggle: no overturned furniture, no personal items left behind. Taylor felt the familiar mixture of urgency and determination that came with the start of a major investigation. Somewhere out there, a young woman was being held against her will by someone calculating enough to plan this abduction carefully. The question was, how much time did they have before the kidnapper's demands escalated to something far worse?

———

Ninety miles northeast of Birmingham, in a grimy industrial workshop in Newark-on-Trent, Stephanie Slater was learning the true meaning of terror.

The transition from showing a house to being held captive had happened with shocking speed. One moment she'd been explaining the property's central heating system to the polite Mr. Southall, the next she'd felt the cold press of a knife blade against her neck as his hand had clamped over her mouth. His voice had transformed from the mild, interested tone of a house-hunter to something flat and dangerous, threatening to slit her throat if she moved.

Now, hours later, she found herself in a nightmare that defied comprehension. Her captor had forced her into his car, driven for what felt like an eternity, and brought her to this place—a cluttered workshop that smelled of oil and metal shavings. Model trains lined shelves along the walls, locomotive nameplates hung like trophies, and the workbenches were covered with tools and mechanical parts.

But it was what sat in the corner of the room that filled her with absolute dread.

The box was roughly the size and shape of a coffin, constructed from plywood and painted dark green. Holes had been drilled in the sides for air, and the lid was hinged with heavy-duty hardware. Next to it sat a large, wheeled garbage bin, its purpose becoming horrifyingly clear as her captor, who now seemed like a completely different person from the mild-mannered Mr. Southall, began explaining her situation.

He described in the same emotionless tone he'd used during the phone call to her office how this would be her prison. The box would go inside the bin. The bin had sensors. If she tried to get out, if she so much as shifted her weight wrong, alarms would sound. He would know immediately, and he would return very angry.

Stephanie's legs nearly gave out. The man reached into a toolbox and withdrew what looked like electrical wires attached to small metal contacts. He explained that these would be attached to her leg and connected to a battery. If the alarms went off, if she tried to escape, she would be electrocuted.

Her mind was racing, trying to process what was happening to her. This couldn't be real. This kind of thing didn't happen to ordinary people in ordinary circumstances. She'd gotten up that morning, eaten breakfast with her parents, and driven to work thinking about weekend plans. Now, she was facing the possibility of being buried alive in a homemade coffin.

The man seemed to read her thoughts. He informed her that her office had been contacted. If they followed his instructions, if they paid what he'd asked for, she would be released unharmed. But that depended entirely on their cooperation and her behavior.

He gestured toward the box and ordered her inside.

For a moment, Stephanie couldn't move. Every instinct screamed against climbing into what looked like her own grave. But the knife was still in his hand, and something in his calm demeanor was more terrifying than if he'd been shouting or threatening. This was a man who had thought everything through, who was prepared for any possibility.

With shaking hands, she climbed into the wooden box.

The lid closed with a solid thunk, plunging her into absolute darkness.

———

Detective Inspector Taylor hadn't slept in thirty-six hours. The incident room at West Midlands Police headquarters buzzed with activity as officers worked phones, analyzed evidence, and coordinated with other forces. The Stephanie Slater kidnapping had become the department's top priority.

The second phone call had come eighteen hours after the first. This time, the kidnapper had been more specific about his demands and the consequences of non-compliance. He had given them one week to assemble £175,000 in used notes of various denominations, promising delivery instructions to follow. Any police involvement beyond basic coordination would result in the girl's death.

Voice analysis revealed a caller who spoke with a slight Yorkshire accent, was likely between forty and sixty years old, and showed no signs of nervousness or emotional stress. The background noise suggested he was calling from a quiet indoor location, possibly an office or workshop.

What troubled investigators most was the kidnapper's obvious familiarity with police procedure. His warning about "basic coordination" suggested he understood that the family and employer would naturally involve law enforcement, but he was drawing a line at more aggressive investigative tactics. This wasn't someone acting on impulse—this was a person who had studied how these situations typically unfolded.

———

As detectives cross-referenced unsolved cases involving ransom demands, a disturbing pattern emerged. The previous year, on July 9, 1991, eighteen-year-old Julie Dart had disappeared from a red-light district in Leeds. Her body was discovered nine days later in a field near Grantham, Lincolnshire.

The Julie Dart case bore striking similarities to Stephanie's kidnapping. Julie had been held for ransom, with letters demanding £140,000 sent to West Yorkshire Police. The kidnapper had forced Julie to write some of these communications herself, including a heartbreaking letter to her boyfriend pleading for help. When the ransom hadn't been paid, Julie had been murdered through blunt force trauma and strangulation.

Following Julie's death, the killer had continued to send taunting letters to authorities for months. He'd threatened further murders, claimed he would derail trains and bomb shops, and demanded £200,000 from British Rail to prevent railway attacks. He had actually suspended a block of sandstone from a railway bridge, apparently hoping to derail a passenger train.

The letters revealed an individual obsessed with railways and someone who viewed the entire situation as an elaborate game against the police. Every ransom instruction involved railway stations or abandoned rail lines, and the communications demonstrated meticulous planning and a disturbing sense of superiority. The killer seemed to take pleasure in outwitting authorities and maintaining control through fear.

The similarities between the cases were impossible to ignore—the methodical planning, the ransom demands directed at authorities rather than family members, the obvious intelligence behind the crimes, and most tellingly, the railway connections that appeared in both cases.

What emerged was a chilling progression. Julie Dart's murder appeared to have been a rehearsal—a way for the killer to test his methods and send a message about his seriousness. The threats that followed her death suggested someone who was studying police responses and media coverage, learning from the experience to refine his approach.

Stephanie Slater represented his real target: Someone whose kidnapping would generate the resources and media attention necessary to achieve his financial goals. Unlike Julie, a vulnerable teenage sex worker with no employer or family resources, Stephanie was a working professional whose disappearance would mobilize significant insurance funds and corporate backing.

If investigators were correct about the connection, then Stephanie was being held by a killer who had already proven his willingness to murder when his demands weren't met. But there was also hope in this analysis; if the kidnapper genuinely believed he could get his money this time, he had every incentive to keep Stephanie alive.

———

In the darkness of her wooden prison, Stephanie fought against panic with every breath. She had no idea how long she'd been in the box. It could have been hours or days. Time had ceased to have meaning in the suffocating blackness.

Her captor had kept his word about the restraints. The metal contacts were taped to her thigh, connected by thin wires to something she couldn't see but had been warned was a lethal electrical device. Whether it was real or an elaborate bluff, she couldn't risk finding out. Her hands were cuffed behind her back, her legs bound with rope. The blindfold had been so tightly secured that it pressed painfully against her eyes.

The psychological torture was perhaps worse than the physical discomfort. Every small sound made her freeze in terror—was that her captor returning? Was someone coming to hurt her? Or was it just the building settling, a train passing in the distance, or her own imagination running wild?

She'd heard trains, that much she was certain of. The distant rumble and whistle of locomotives had penetrated her wooden tomb several times, suggesting she was near a railway line. It was the only clue she had about her location, and she clung to it like a lifeline.

To keep herself sane, Stephanie began talking to herself in whispers. She recited childhood poems, sang songs under her breath, and tried to remember every detail of her life before this nightmare began. Anything to keep her mind occupied, to prevent it from dwelling on the horrific possibilities of what might happen to her.

When her captor did return—she could hear his footsteps, the jingle of keys, the sound of locks being opened—she forced herself to engage with him. It went against every instinct she had, but somehow, she knew that staying silent, becoming just an object to him, would be far more dangerous.

"Please," she would say when he briefly removed her gag to give her water or the small amounts of food he provided. "I have parents who love me. They're probably going crazy with worry."

Sometimes, he would respond, usually with instructions or warnings. But occasionally, just occasionally, she thought she detected something almost human in his voice when she talked about her family.

"Your people are cooperating," he told her during one of these brief interactions. "If they continue to follow instructions, you'll be home soon."

It was the closest thing to reassurance she'd gotten, and she seized on it desperately. Someone was working to save her. Her colleagues, her family, the police—they hadn't given up. She just had to survive long enough for them to succeed.

But as the hours stretched on in the darkness, that became increasingly difficult to believe.

———

Kevin Watts had never imagined that his job as an estate agency manager would involve carrying £175,000 in cash through the fog-shrouded countryside in the middle of the night. But as he drove his car along increasingly remote roads in South Yorkshire, following the kidnapper's cryptic instructions, he knew that Stephanie's life depended on his ability to follow orders exactly.

The money had been assembled through a combination of insurance funds and company resources, with the full cooperation of West Midlands Police. Every note had been photographed and the serial numbers recorded, though they'd been careful to ensure the bills appeared genuinely used and untraceable. The kidnapper had been explicit about the consequences of any tracking devices or marked money.

The instructions had come in stages, each one leading Watts further from civilization. First, a phone call had directed him to drive to Glossop in Derbyshire. Then, taped under a public telephone booth, was a note sending him toward Sheffield. Another call, another note, each step taking him deeper into the Pennine hills as fog rolled in to reduce visibility to mere feet.

In the back seat of his car, hidden beneath a jacket, a police radio quietly provided updates from surveillance teams trying to maintain distant contact without alerting the kidnapper. But as Watts drove through increasingly isolated terrain, those transmissions became fainter and more intermittent.

Watts felt truly alone as he navigated the narrow country roads. The kidnapper's planning was meticulous—the weather conditions, the remote location, the maze of back roads that would make police surveillance nearly impossible. This wasn't someone acting on impulse; this was a person who had anticipated every contingency.

At 11:47 p.m., Watts found what he was looking for. In the glow of his headlights, orange traffic cones marked a spot on a narrow bridle path near the village of Oxspring. Crude wooden signs had been planted in the ground, painted with the word "SHIPWAYS" in white letters—a surreal sight in the middle of nowhere.

According to the final set of instructions, Watts was to transfer the money from his duffel bag into a cloth bag that would be waiting at the site, then place the bag on a tray positioned on a low stone wall. The note emphasized that he must leave immediately afterward—the money would not be collected until after his departure.

With shaking hands, Watts made the transfer. The £175,000 in cash filled the cloth bag completely. He placed it on the metal tray as instructed, noting that the "wall" was actually the safety barrier of an old railway bridge. Below, he could hear the whisper of wind through tall grass in what appeared to be an old, unused railway cutting.

As he drove away, Watts caught a glimpse in his rearview mirror of the tray sliding off the wall, apparently pulled by a rope. Somewhere in the darkness below, the kidnapper was collecting his prize.

The question now was whether he would honor his promise to release Stephanie.

———

At 1:15 a.m. on January 30, 1992, Stephanie Slater stumbled down a residential street in Handsworth, Birmingham, barely able to see through the damaged vision caused by eight days of tight blindfolding. Her legs could hardly support her after the prolonged confinement, and she was missing her shoes, but she was alive and free.

Her captor had spoken to her one final time before the release, his voice carrying what might have been genuine regret: "I'm sorry about everything. You were the innocent victim." Then, after warning her not to look back at his car, he had pushed her out onto the pavement and disappeared into the night.

The reunion with her parents was emotional and chaotic. Warren and Betty Slater had endured eight days of unimaginable anguish, and the sight of their daughter, alive but traumatized, left them sobbing with relief. The family liaison officer who had been stationed at their home initially didn't recognize the disheveled woman at the door, but Warren Slater's cry of "It's Stephanie! Stephanie's back!" brought the nightmare to an end.

Within hours, however, a new challenge emerged. The media attention was overwhelming, and perhaps misjudging the situation, police arranged for Stephanie to appear at a press conference less than twelve hours after her release. Still pale, shaken, and under sedation, she faced a battery of cameras and reporters—an ordeal that added to her trauma rather than providing the closure for which authorities had hoped.

However, Stephanie's survival had provided police with something invaluable: a living witness who could describe her captor in detail. Despite the blindfold and her damaged eyesight, she had formed clear impressions of the man who had held her. She described his voice, his mannerisms, and even fragments of conversation that revealed details about his personality and possible background.

Most importantly, she confirmed the railway connection. Throughout her captivity, she had heard the distant sound of trains, and her captor had made several references to locomotives and railway terminology that suggested a deep familiarity with that world.

————

The decision to broadcast the kidnapper's voice on BBC Crimewatch was a calculated risk. Police had obtained clear audio recordings of the ransom calls, and they believed that someone, somewhere, would recognize the distinctive Yorkshire accent and measured speaking style.

The Crimewatch episode aired on February 4, 1992, featuring dramatic reconstructions of both the Stephanie Slater kidnapping and the Julie Dart murder, which police had now definitively linked to the same perpetrator. The voice recording was played multiple times, accompanied by an artist's sketch based on witness descriptions and Stephanie's account.

In the village of Sutton-on-Trent, Nottinghamshire, a woman named Susan Oake was watching with growing unease. The voice was familiar—terrifyingly familiar. It belonged to her ex-husband, Michael Sams, a man she had divorced more than a decade earlier but whose distinctive speech patterns she could never forget.

Susan had kept in touch with Michael's criminal history through mutual acquaintances, and she knew that he had served time for fraud in the late 1970s. She also knew about his obsession with railways—his home was filled with model trains, locomotive photographs, and railway memorabilia. Most disturbing of all, she knew he was capable of violence and manipulation.

Without hesitation, Susan contacted the police.

At the same time, Michael Sams was watching the broadcast with his current wife, Teena, at their home in Sutton-on-Trent. When the sketch appeared on screen, Teena remarked on its resemblance to her husband. Sams brushed off her comment with characteristic arrogance, apparently confident that his elaborate planning had covered all possible angles.

He was wrong.

———

The surveillance began immediately. Officers positioned themselves around the quiet village of Sutton-on-Trent, watching the modest house where Michael Sams lived with his third wife. What they observed was a man who appeared perfectly ordinary—a fifty-year-old toolmaker who walked with a limp due to a prosthetic leg, tended to his garden, and spent long hours in his converted workshop.

But when detectives obtained a warrant to search that workshop in nearby Newark-on-Trent, they discovered a chamber of horrors that confirmed their worst suspicions.

Michael Sams

The green garbage bin was still there, along with the wooden box that had served as Stephanie's prison. Tool marks on the workbench matched implements found at the crime scenes. Most damning of all, forensic specialists found traces of blood that would later be confirmed as belonging to Julie Dart—evidence that both victims had been held in the same location.

Michael Sams was arrested at his home on February 5, 1992, just one day after the Crimewatch broadcast. During initial questioning, he made a tactical decision that revealed both his arrogance and his desperation: He confessed to kidnapping Stephanie Slater but vehemently denied any involvement in Julie Dart's murder.

Instead, Sams spun an elaborate lie about a mysterious accomplice—a shadowy figure who had supposedly borrowed his workshop and carried out the Julie Dart kidnapping independently. According to Sams's story, he had merely provided assistance with the ransom letters but had never met Julie, and he claimed he knew nothing about her death until his "friend" confessed to accidentally killing her during a botched escape attempt.

It was a masterful piece of fiction, carefully crafted to admit to the crime they could prove while denying the one that carried a murder charge. Of course, it fell apart under forensic scrutiny. The evidence was overwhelming: Handwriting analysis confirmed that Sams had written all the ransom letters, fiber analysis linked him to both crime scenes, and most importantly, the methodical planning revealed in his computer files showed that both crimes were the work of a single, obsessively organized mind.

————

Nottingham Crown Court had rarely seen a case that generated such public interest. When Michael Sams's trial began in May 1993, the public gallery was packed with journalists, victim advocates, and ordinary citizens who had been transfixed by the story of survival and justice.

Stephanie Slater's testimony was the emotional centerpiece of the prosecution's case. Despite the trauma she had endured, she spoke with remarkable composure and detail about her eight-day ordeal. She described the terror of being confined in the wooden box, the constant fear of electrocution, and her conscious decision to humanize herself to her captor as a survival strategy.

"I talked to him about my family, my life, anything I could think of," she told the jury. "I wanted him to see me as a real person, not just an object. I was terrified every time I spoke to him, but I knew that staying silent might be more dangerous."

Her account of the kidnapper's behavior provided crucial insights into Sams's personality. She described a man who was methodical and controlled, but also someone who seemed to take genuine pleasure in the elaborate nature of his scheme. There were moments when he appeared almost proud of his planning, explaining the intricacies of his security systems and ransom drop procedures as if demonstrating a particularly clever puzzle.

When Michael Sams took the stand in his own defense, he maintained his story about the mysterious accomplice with remarkable consistency. He admitted to planning a kidnapping scheme and carrying it out with Stephanie, but he insisted that Julie Dart's murder was the work of another person who had used his ideas and equipment without permission.

Under cross-examination, however, the prosecution systematically demolished his alibi. How could he explain the blood evidence in his workshop? Why were all the ransom letters in his handwriting? How could a supposed accomplice have accessed his personal computer to input the detailed planning documents that investigators had recovered?

Sams's answers grew increasingly implausible. He claimed the accomplice had been a trusted friend with keys to his workshop. He suggested that similarities in handwriting could be explained by the friend attempting to copy his style. When confronted with the computer evidence, he insisted that the accomplice was familiar with his equipment and had input the files himself.

The jury wasn't convinced. After just three and a half hours of deliberation, they returned with guilty verdicts on all counts: the kidnapping and murder of Julie Dart, the kidnapping and extortion involving Stephanie Slater, and four separate counts of blackmail.

As the verdicts were read, emotions erupted in the courtroom. Julie Dart's mother, Lynn, stood up and shouted, "You bastard!" at Sams before collapsing in tears. Stephanie Slater wept with relief and silently mouthed "thank you" to the jurors.

Mr. Justice David Judge sentenced Sams to life imprisonment, calling him "an extremely dangerous and evil man" who had shown "no qualms, no remorse." The judge imposed four concurrent life sentences, ensuring that Sams would spend the rest of his natural life behind bars.

————

Three days after his conviction, Michael Sams finally told the truth. In a private meeting with Detective Chief Superintendent Bob Taylor, he confessed to murdering Julie Dart, providing details that only the killer could know. He claimed he was doing it for the sake of Julie's grieving mother, saying, "It's only fair that she knows I did it."

The confession was recorded but kept secret for thirty years, only being publicly revealed in a 2022 documentary. By then, it served mainly as historical confirmation of what the evidence had already proven.

————

Stephanie Slater never fully recovered from her ordeal. She was unable to return to her career as an estate agent, moving away from the Midlands to start fresh on the Isle of Wight. For years, she battled PTSD symptoms and struggled with the trauma of her experience. However, she found purpose in her pain, working with police forces across the country to improve their handling of kidnapping cases and victim support.

Her advocacy led to significant changes in police procedures, particularly in how victims are treated in the immediate aftermath of their release. The hasty press conference that Stephanie had endured just hours after her freedom became a cautionary tale in police training programs.

In her initial interviews and statements to police, Stephanie did not disclose the full extent of her ordeal. Years later, in her 1995 book *Beyond Fear: My Will to Survive*, she revealed that Sams had raped her on the first night of her imprisonment. She had originally chosen not to reveal this assault to spare her mother, who had a heart condition, from additional anguish. Adding insult to injury, Michael Sams denied the rape, claimed the sex was consensual, and unsuccessfully attempted to sue her for libel.

Stephanie Slater died of cancer in 2017 at the age of 50, remembered by colleagues and friends as a woman who had transformed her trauma into a force for positive change.

Michael Sams is still in prison at the time of writing and is set to remain there for the rest of his life, becoming one of Britain's longest-serving inmates. He has continued to file frivolous lawsuits and complaints from behind bars, winning £4,000 in compensation when the prison service lost his prosthetic leg, a payout that outraged the public. His attempts at parole have been denied repeatedly, with authorities consistently ruling that he remains too dangerous for release.

Julie Dart was not forgotten. Her mother, Lynn, established a memorial fund to help other vulnerable young women, ensuring that her daughter's brief life would have lasting meaning beyond the circumstances of her death.

Police eventually used ground-penetrating radar to locate £150,000 of the ransom money buried in a field. The remaining £25,000 was never recovered, likely spent or hidden by Sams before his capture.

The case became a landmark in British criminal history, studied by law enforcement agencies around the world as an example of how meticulous police work, forensic science, and media cooperation could bring even the most calculating predator to justice. But perhaps more importantly, it demonstrated the extraordinary courage of ordinary people—from Kevin Watts driving through the fog with a bag of ransom money to Stephanie Slater talking to her captor about her family in a desperate bid to stay alive.

In the end, Michael Sams's elaborate game of cat and mouse with the authorities had a simple outcome: Justice prevailed, and the innocent survived to tell their stories.

CHAPTER 5
THE DARK WEB
ASSASSIN

Detective Sergeant Randy McAlister had grown comfortable with the quiet streets of Cottage Grove, Minnesota. Twenty years on the force in this sleepy community of thirty-six thousand, nestled along the Mississippi River's north bank, had taught him to appreciate predictability. Serious violent crime was almost unheard of—just two murders in the past four years.

The monotony suited him just fine.

But on the evening of November 13, 2016, a single phone call would change everything, pulling him into the most complex case of his career.

———

The 911 dispatcher's voice cut through the radio static like a blade. "Cottage Grove units, we have a possible suicide at 7624 110th Street South. Caller reports his wife has shot herself."

Just another tragedy in suburbia. Or so it seemed.

Sergeant Gwen Martin arrived first, her patrol car's headlights sweeping across the modest prefab home. She had worked these streets for years and had seen her share of domestic calls and weekend disturbances. However, nothing had prepared her for what waited inside that quiet house on 110th Street.

Amy Allwine lay motionless on the bedroom floor, her body forming a grotesque scene beside the neatly made bed. Blood pooled beneath her head in the soft glow of the bedside lamp. A 9mm Springfield handgun rested near her left elbow, cold and silent.

In the garage, Amy's husband, Stephen, stood with their nine-year-old son, his voice eerily steady as he continued his conversation with the 911 operator.

"She's not breathing," Stephen said, his tone flat, almost conversational. "I can't tell where she's shot. I don't know."

Martin stared at the scene, her trained instincts screaming that something was terribly wrong. The pieces didn't fit. They never fit when evil wore the mask of the ordinary.

When Martin's voice came through Detective Sergeant McAlister's phone, he could tell immediately that something was wrong. She was shaken—really shaken—and that wasn't like Gwen Martin at all.

"There's an apparent suicide," she managed, her voice thick with concern. "But you need to get down here. Right now. Her name is Amy Allwine."

The name stopped him cold. Amy Allwine.

The memories came flooding back—the FBI visit, the dark web threats, the murder-for-hire plot that had seemed almost surreal. The woman someone had paid thousands of dollars to kill was now lying dead in her own bedroom.

McAlister had been a cop too long to believe in coincidences.

———

To understand the horror of what had happened that November evening, you need to understand what Amy Allwine represented: Everything good and pure about small-town America. She was forty-three years old and devoted to three things that defined her existence: her family, her church, and her dogs.

But appearances, as Detective McAlister was about to learn, can be the most dangerous deception of all.

Amy had grown up in a strict religious household, adhering to the fundamentalist faith that shaped her life within the United Church of God. She had met Stephen Allwine at Ambassador College in Big Sandy, Texas. It was more a training ground for church service than a typical college, where young men and women were groomed for future leadership roles within the church.

They had married on August 11, 1996, in Cottage Grove. Amy's father had placed her hand in Stephen's and said, "Take good care of my little girl."

The Allwines were the kind of family that made neighbors feel safe and made communities proud. Stephen worked as an IT specialist from their home, his basement office filled with the latest technology. Amy had transformed her love of dogs into Active Dog Sports Training, drawing clients from across the Twin Cities to their twenty-eight-acre property.

They were pillars of their church, the United Church of God. Stephen had risen to the role of elder, counseling troubled marriages and delivering sermons. Amy was beloved in the dog training community for her sunny disposition and positive approach.

They had even adopted a son as an infant. On the surface, they embodied everything the American dream promised.

But beneath that perfect surface, something dark was stirring. Something that would turn their quiet Sunday afternoon into a nightmare that would haunt Cottage Grove forever.

———

When McAlister arrived at the Allwine home, the first thing that struck him was how ordinary it all seemed. The smell of roasting pumpkin drifted from the kitchen—Amy had been preparing Sunday dinner when death came calling.

He found Stephen in the garage with his son, both waiting with an eerie patience. There was something unsettling about Stephen's demeanor. The man was too calm, too controlled for someone who had just discovered his wife's body.

In the bedroom, McAlister's experienced eyes began cataloging the inconsistencies. Amy lay spread-eagled beside her bed, arms splayed in an unnatural position. Her pants were undone, her sweater pulled up—details that felt wrong, staged.

The 9mm handgun by her left elbow was the first obvious problem; Amy's family would later confirm she was right-handed. But there were others, too—more subtle signs that told McAlister he was looking at a crime scene, not a suicide.

There was no blood on Amy's hands. No gunshot residue. None of the telltale signs that scream "suicide" to a trained investigator.

What really caught McAlister's attention wasn't just the blood—it was what was missing. There was a large pool beneath Amy's head, consistent with where she was found. However, to the left, he noticed a series of small blood drops that didn't make sense. These weren't the fine mist of high-velocity spatter you'd expect from a close-range gunshot. Instead, they looked like drip stains—round droplets that had fallen straight down from something held above the floor. It suggested that something, or someone, had been over Amy's body, dripping blood after the fact. That pointed to a staged scene, not a suicide.

Also, blood from her nose and mouth had dried along the left side of her face despite her lying flat on her back. It was clear someone repositioned her after her death.

Another unsettling detail was the clean patch on the hardwood floor just outside the bedroom door. In a house where dog hair clung to every surface, where the messiness of family life was inescapable, this one area stood out, gleaming as though it had been meticulously scrubbed clean.

McAlister felt the familiar chill that came when a case shifted from routine to sinister. He reached for his phone to call the Minnesota Bureau of Criminal Apprehension.

He knew Amy Allwine hadn't killed herself. Someone had murdered her and tried very hard to make it look like suicide. The question was, who?

———

As the crime scene team worked through the night, McAlister found himself thinking back to the bizarre case that had first brought Amy Allwine to his attention. It was a story so strange it seemed like fiction.

It had begun on a warm spring day in May 2016, when FBI Special Agent Asher Sukey walked into the Cottage Grove Police Department with news that would disturb any small-town cop. The FBI had intercepted a threat against a local resident—but this wasn't your typical stalking case.

This threat had come from the dark web.

Sukey explained that the dark web was like a hidden version of the internet, accessible only through special software that promised complete anonymity. It was home to the worst humanity had to offer: black markets trafficking in weapons, drugs, stolen identities, and human misery.

Among its most disturbing offerings were murder-for-hire services.

The most notorious was called Besa Mafia, a professional operation that had opened for business in December 2015. Unlike other sites that tried to maintain some veneer of sophistication, Besa Mafia was brutally honest about what they sold: the services of gang members and drug addicts willing to kill strangers for money.

However, on April 25, 2016, a hacker breached Besa Mafia's servers, exposing a database that kept FBI agents working late into the night. Among the files was order number 30312, with a target name that made McAlister's stomach turn: Amy Allwine.

Someone calling themselves "dogdayGod" had paid $13,000 worth of Bitcoin to have Amy murdered, providing her photograph, detailed travel plans, and specific instructions about how they wanted her killed.

———

On June 1, 2016, Stephen and Amy Allwine sat across from FBI agents in the sterile environment of the Cottage Grove Police Department, about to hear something that would shatter their understanding of their safe, predictable world.

Someone wanted Amy dead. Someone with money, technical sophistication, and intimate knowledge of her daily life.

Amy's reaction was exactly what you'd expect from an innocent woman: shock, confusion, and genuine fear. She insisted she had no enemies, had never been unfaithful, and couldn't imagine who would harbor such murderous hatred toward her.

Stephen's response seemed equally appropriate. He appeared mystified, concerned, and protective. He suggested maybe someone had confused his wife with another Amy, or perhaps a business rival was behind the threat. His demeanor was that of a loving husband grappling with an incomprehensible nightmare.

But appearances, as McAlister was learning, could be the most dangerous lie of all.

The FBI delivered what seemed like good news: Amy wasn't in immediate danger. The hack had revealed that Besa Mafia was actually an elaborate scam. No hits were ever carried out, and the site existed solely to steal money from would-be killers.

Still, the fact remained that someone had paid a small fortune to have Amy murdered—someone who knew details about her life that only a close acquaintance could possess.

The invisible enemy was still out there, nursing their deadly obsession in the shadows of the dark web.

The FBI's advice was straightforward: install better security, stay vigilant, and report anything suspicious. Stephen threw himself into the task with apparent dedication to his wife's safety. He upgraded their home security system, installed motion detection cameras, and even obtained a permit to purchase a 9mm handgun for protection.

The same gun that now lay beside Amy's lifeless body.

But the torment didn't end with better locks and security cameras. On July 31, 2016, Amy's phone buzzed with an email that would push her terror to new heights.

The sender called themselves "Jane," and their message was a calculated exercise in psychological torture: "Amy, your family is in danger. Last Sunday you received an email with the solution to this problem and you have not done anything about it yet. Are you so selfish that you will put your family's lives at risk?"

Amy frantically checked her spam folder and found the earlier message—a venomous screed that accused her of destroying someone's marriage and demanded the ultimate price: "Commit suicide. By the time I am done you will want to end it anyway, so why not do it now?"

The emails contained details that terrified Amy. The sender knew which pink shirt her son had worn the previous week. They knew the exact locations of the gas meters at her home and her parents' house. They knew intimate details about her family's routines and vulnerabilities.

Most chillingly, they promised to target everyone Amy loved unless she took her own life.

Amy called the FBI immediately, her voice shaking as she read the threats aloud. Agent Sukey tried to reassure her, explaining that the move from hiring a killer to demanding suicide was actually a de-escalation. However, Amy found little comfort in his words. Someone out there hated her enough to orchestrate an elaborate campaign of terror, and she had no idea who it could be.

———

November 13, 2016, dawned like any other Sunday in the Allwine household. However, beneath the veneer of suburban normalcy, something sinister was already in motion.

Stephen worked from his basement office, surrounded by the sophisticated computer equipment that had made him the family's tech expert. Amy, feeling unwell after lunch, retreated to the bedroom with complaints of dizziness, a dry mouth, and lightheadedness—symptoms that would later take on a far more ominous significance.

Around 1:00 p.m., Amy's father, Charles, arrived to finish installing a new dog door, part of the many weekend projects with which he regularly helped. He was a frequent visitor, always eager to assist his daughter and son-in-law. Since Amy was resting and feeling poorly, Charles worked quietly, not wanting to disturb her. He finished around 2:00 p.m. and drove away, unaware that the next few minutes would change everything.

He had barely made it five minutes down the road when his phone rang.

It was Stephen, and there was an urgency in his voice that hadn't been there an hour earlier. Amy's condition had worsened, he explained. Could Charles return to pick up Joe? Stephen might need to rush Amy to urgent care.

Charles, being a devoted father and grandfather, didn't hesitate. He turned his car around and returned to collect his grandson, who was waiting outside as if the pickup had been carefully orchestrated. By 2:30 p.m., Charles was driving away again, this time with Joe buckled safely in the backseat.

The house on 110th Street was now empty except for Stephen and Amy.

What happened in the next few hours would remain Stephen's secret, but the evidence would tell its own story—a story of cold-blooded calculation, of a husband who had finally decided to finish what the dark web killers had failed to start.

At 5:00 p.m., Stephen made another call to Charles—casual, unhurried, almost conversational. He was running a bit late to pick up Joe, Stephen explained. He needed to stop for gas and had some errands to run. There was no urgency in his voice now, no mention of hospitals or medical emergencies.

When Stephen finally arrived at Charles's house at 5:30, he delivered news that should have been cause for celebration: Amy had "decided not to go to the clinic after all." She was feeling better, he said, resting comfortably at home.

Charles was relieved. Stephen seemed relaxed, even taking the time to chat before collecting Joe and heading out for dinner at Culver's restaurant. Just a normal Sunday evening for a father and son.

But nothing about this Sunday was normal.

When they returned home around 7:00 p.m., Stephen let Joe run ahead into the house while he unpacked the car—a decision that would traumatize the nine-year-old forever.

"Why's Mommy lying on the floor?" Joe's voice cut through the evening air, high and confused and heartbreaking.

———

Later, when detectives sat in the conference room reviewing the 911 recording, that moment would become a crucial piece of evidence. As Stephen spoke to the dispatcher about his wife's apparent suicide, his nine-year-old son's voice cut through the background with heartbreaking innocence: "Are you going to remarry?"

What came next was deeply disturbing. Stephen actually chuckled—a sound so inappropriate in the context of the scene that investigators had to replay it multiple times. "I don't know, bud," he replied with casual indifference, as if he were discussing weekend plans rather than responding to his traumatized child, who had just discovered his mother's body. For Detective McAlister, that chuckle became the moment he knew they were no longer dealing with a grieving husband.

———

As the investigation deepened, McAlister felt like he was peeling back layers of deception, each revelation more disturbing than the last. The home's security system told a story that demolished Stephen's claims of innocence: No one had entered through any monitored door after Stephen left to collect Joe. There were no signs of forced entry. Even the family dogs, who normally roamed the backyard as natural guardians, had been locked in their kennels, rendering them useless as witnesses or protectors.

Stephen Allwine

When Stephen submitted to testing for gunshot residue, the results were damning: His hands tested positive for the telltale particles that indicated the recent firing of a weapon. Amy's hands, by contrast, were clean.

However, it was the medical examiner's report that transformed the case from suspicious death to calculated murder. Amy's blood contained Scopolamine—the so-called "devil's drug"—at levels twenty to forty times higher than any therapeutic dose. The drug, typically used for motion sickness, becomes something far more sinister in large quantities: a chemical straitjacket that renders victims helpless, disoriented, and completely compliant.

Amy had no prescription for Scopolamine. There was no legitimate reason for the drug to be in her system at such catastrophic levels.

Someone had drugged Amy Allwine into helplessness before putting a bullet in her head. And that someone had access to her food, her home, and her trust.

Amy hadn't just been murdered. She had been chemically paralyzed first, turned into a victim who couldn't fight back, couldn't run, and couldn't even understand what was happening to her.

————

The Cottage Grove Police Department was woefully unprepared for a case involving cryptocurrency, dark web communications, and sophisticated digital forensics. This wasn't the kind of crime that happened in their quiet suburb—this was something out of a cyber-punk nightmare.

They called in the specialists, including digital forensics expert Mark Lanterman, who would prove to be Stephen's ultimate downfall. Lanterman began the meticulous process of dissecting Stephen's extensive collection of electronic devices, searching for the digital breadcrumbs that modern killers always leave behind.

What he found was a textbook case of self-incrimination.

Stephen had told investigators he'd never heard of the dark web before the FBI's visit—a lie that crumbled the moment Lanterman fired up his computers. Stephen's MacBook Pro revealed searches for Tor browser software dating back to early 2016, right around the time dogdayGod first made contact with Besa Mafia.

But the real smoking gun came from the most unexpected place: a routine backup of Stephen's iPhone. Hidden in the cloud storage, preserved despite Stephen's best efforts to delete it, was a single note containing thirty-four seemingly random characters and numbers.

It was a Bitcoin wallet address—the exact same address dogdayGod had used to pay Besa Mafia for Amy's murder.

The timestamp on the note was devastating: It had been created just twenty seconds before the payment message was sent to the murder-for-hire site. Stephen had literally copied and pasted the wallet address from his phone to the dark web communication.

For Lanterman, it was the Holy Grail of digital evidence. "For forensic evidence, it doesn't get any better," he would later testify, his voice filled with the quiet satisfaction of a hunter who had finally cornered his prey.

The digital breadcrumbs told an inescapable story: Stephen Allwine and dogdayGod were the same person. The loving husband and the would-be killer were one and the same.

But Lanterman wasn't finished. As he dug deeper into Stephen's digital life, a pattern emerged that was as methodical as it was damning. Every Google search Stephen had performed was mirrored in the dark web communications. Photos he had accessed from the family server appeared in messages to Besa Mafia within hours. His installation of Tor browser software coincided exactly with dogdayGod's first contact with the murder site.

The most chilling discovery came when Lanterman traced Stephen's post-Besa Mafia activity. After the murder-for-hire scam collapsed, dogdayGod had moved to another dark web marketplace called Dream Market, desperately seeking the drug that would eventually incapacitate Amy: Scopolamine.

The digital timeline was precise. In over seventy distinct data points, Lanterman had reconstructed the parallel lives of Stephen Allwine and dogdayGod—two identities that moved in perfect synchronization, planning Amy's death with the methodical precision of a man who believed technology would be his perfect alibi.

He had been wrong. Dead wrong.

————

The final betrayal was yet to come. As investigators dug deeper into Stephen's life, they uncovered a secret that would shatter any remaining illusions about the grieving widower and devoted church elder.

Stephen Allwine had been living a double life that would have made a Hollywood screenwriter blush.

While counseling troubled marriages at church, preaching about the sanctity of marital vows, and presenting himself as the model Christian husband, Stephen had been secretly frequenting AshleyMadison.com—a website designed specifically to facilitate extramarital affairs.

The irony was staggering. Stephen had learned about Ashley Madison while counseling church couples about infidelity. Rather than using that knowledge to help strengthen marriages, he had used it to destroy his own.

For over a year, he had conducted multiple affairs, meeting women for coffee, dinner, and sex while Amy attended dog shows or church events. He had even brought one woman, Michelle, to their family home when Amy was out of town, showing her through the house where he and Amy had built their life together before having sex with her in their bed.

His motive was brutally clear. Stephen wanted out of his marriage, but divorce wasn't an option for a man in his position. The United Church of God viewed marriage as a lifelong commitment, and a church elder who got divorced would lose everything that mattered to him—his position, his reputation, and his standing in the community.

Murder, however, would solve all his problems. He would be free to pursue his extramarital interests, maintain his religious standing, and collect on Amy's $700,000 life insurance policy.

Amy had been worth more to Stephen dead than alive—a calculation that revealed the true depths of his depravity.

———

On January 17, 2017, the charade finally ended. Stephen Allwine was arrested at a routine traffic stop on his way home from dropping Joe at school—a mundane moment that marked the beginning of the end for a man who had thought himself untouchable.

The charges were initially second-degree murder, but as prosecutors reviewed the mountain of evidence—the year-long planning, the dark web plotting, the systematic deception—they realized they were dealing with much more than just a crime of passion.

This was premeditated murder in its purest form, calculated and cold-blooded in its execution.

Stephen posted $500,000 in bail and returned to the very house where he had murdered his wife, a development that horrified Amy's family and the community that had once trusted him. However, his freedom was short-lived. Within weeks, he was arrested again after violating the terms of his bail by attempting to contact his son through his smartwatch.

The judge raised his bail to $2,000,000—an amount Stephen couldn't meet. For the first time since Amy's death, Stephen Allwine found himself behind bars, where he would remain until trial.

Justice was finally closing in on the man who had believed he could commit the perfect digital-age murder.

———

The trial began on January 23, 2018, in Washington County District Court, and from the first day, it was clear that this was no ordinary murder case. The courtroom was packed with an unlikely mix of spectators: church members struggling to reconcile their faith with the evil that had lurked among them, dog trainers who had loved Amy like family, and digital forensics experts who had never seen evidence quite this damning.

For six days, prosecutors methodically constructed their case. They didn't just prove Stephen was guilty—they painted a portrait of calculation and cruelty that left court observers shaken.

The digital evidence alone was overwhelming. Lanterman took the jury on a journey through Stephen's electronic devices, showing them the parallel timelines that proved beyond any doubt that Stephen Allwine and dogdayGod were the same person. Seventy distinct data points, each one a nail in Stephen's coffin.

However, it was the physical evidence that truly horrified the jury. The Scopolamine levels that had turned Amy into a helpless victim. The staged crime scene. The cleaned blood evidence. The gun placed near the wrong hand.

Most damning of all was Stephen's own behavior—the eerily calm 911 call, the chuckle when his son asked about remarriage, and the complete absence of the grief and shock that any innocent husband would have displayed.

Stephen's defense attorney fought an impossible case. He suggested unknown intruders, claimed Stephen's devices might have been hacked, and pointed to inconsistencies in the timeline, but he could provide no credible alternative suspect. There was no evidence of digital tampering, no explanation for the mountain of evidence pointing directly at his client.

Stephen never took the stand in his own defense—a decision that spoke volumes about the weakness of his position.

After just eight hours of deliberation, the jury returned with a verdict that surprised no one who had followed the evidence: guilty of first-degree premeditated murder.

The man who had thought himself clever enough to commit the perfect digital-age murder had been undone by the very technology he had trusted to conceal his crimes.

————

At his sentencing hearing, Stephen Allwine finally broke his silence—and revealed himself to be every bit as delusional as the evidence had suggested.

In a rambling eight-minute statement that left courtroom observers stunned, Stephen maintained his innocence while simultaneously positioning himself as some sort of jailhouse missionary. He spoke of his love for Amy, claiming he never went to sleep without kissing her —a statement that rang hollow given the mountain of evidence proving he had drugged and murdered her.

Most bizarrely, he bragged about converting fellow inmates to Christianity, as if his time behind bars had been some sort of evangelical success story rather than the natural consequence of his murderous actions.

He offered no apology to Amy's family. No acknowledgment of the evidence against him. No explanation for how someone else could have orchestrated the elaborate digital deception that bore his fingerprints at every turn.

Judge William Eckstrom had heard enough. Addressing Stephen directly, he delivered a scathing rebuke that cut to the heart of the man's character: "I believe you are a hypocrite and great actor who could turn tears on and off."

The sentence was inevitable: life in prison without the possibility of parole. Stephen Allwine would die behind bars, his dreams of freedom and new relationships crushed by the weight of his own digital arrogance. Stephen had used his technical expertise and religious standing to attempt what he believed would be the perfect crime—but the same digital tools that enabled his deception ultimately ensured his destruction. In the end, justice prevailed, ensuring that Amy's killer would spend eternity paying for his betrayal of everything she had believed their marriage represented.

CHAPTER 6

THE WATERBED

E ight-year-old Maddie Clifton bounced through the front door of her Jacksonville home, her red YMCA basketball shirt bright against the Florida afternoon sun. November 3, 1998, was shaping up to be a perfect day for outdoor play—warm but not too hot, with enough daylight left for at least an hour of neighborhood games.

First things first: piano practice. Maddie dutifully sat at the family piano for her required twenty minutes, her small fingers dancing across the keys. Her reddish-brown hair caught the light streaming in through the window as she worked through her exercises, eager to finish so she could get outside, where the real fun waited.

The Lakewood neighborhood in Jacksonville's Southside, Florida, was exactly the kind of place where eight-year-olds could safely roam. Tree-lined streets wound through modest homes with carefully maintained lawns, and parents felt comfortable letting their children venture outside alone. Maddie embodied everything that made this community special. She was energetic, fearless, and magnetic, the kind of child who could transform an ordinary Tuesday afternoon into an adventure.

After finishing her practice, Maddie changed into play clothes and headed out to round up friends. This was her usual routine: knock on doors, see who was available, and organize whatever game struck her fancy. Unfortunately, most of her regular playmates were busy that afternoon with homework, family obligations, and the usual weekday complications that frustrated active children.

Undeterred, Maddie decided to make her own entertainment. She found some golf clubs and balls in the garage and set up an impromptu golf game in the street. Soon, she was joined by a couple of neighbors: Justin, a boy slightly older than herself, and Larry Grissom, a forty-five-year-old man who often kept a friendly eye on the neighborhood children while they played.

The three took turns hitting balls down the street, with the adults offering tips on Maddie's swing and cheering for her good shots. It was exactly the kind of innocent, community-minded activity that defined life in their neighborhood—children playing safely under the watchful eyes of caring adults.

As the afternoon progressed, they began running low on golf balls. Several had rolled into storm drains or been hit into yards, and they needed more to keep the game interesting. Maddie immediately volunteered to run home and grab additional balls from her family's collection.

"I'll be right back," she called, already jogging toward her house. "I know right where they are."

Justin offered to walk with her, and the two set off together. The Clifton house was only three doors down—a distance that took no more than a couple of minutes to cover.

When they reached the house, Maddie ran inside while Justin waited downstairs, chatting briefly with her sister Jessie, who was practicing piano. Maddie searched her room thoroughly, looking in closets and under her bed for the golf balls she was certain were stored somewhere. The search took longer than expected, creating enough noise to disrupt Jessie's practice.

After several minutes, Justin grew impatient. He called up to Maddie that he was going to head back and continue playing with Larry—she should join them when she found the balls.

Maddie eventually gave up her search. She hadn't found any additional golf balls, but she figured they could continue playing with what they had. She left the house and began walking back toward where Justin and Larry were waiting.

She never arrived.

———

When 5:00 p.m. approached and dinner was ready, Sheila Clifton sent Jessie outside to find her younger sister. This was standard family routine—Jessie would hop on her bicycle and make a quick circuit of the neighborhood, calling Maddie's name and checking the usual spots where children congregated.

But this time was different. Jessie rode through the streets, her voice echoing off silent houses as she called out. The other children who had been playing earlier had vanished inside their own homes for dinner, and there was no answering call, no flash of red shirt, no sound of Maddie's distinctive laughter. Nothing.

Jessie returned home with growing dread twisting in her stomach. She told her parents that she couldn't find Maddie anywhere, that the streets seemed unnaturally quiet, and that none of the neighbors she'd spoken to had seen her sister in the past hour.

Steve and Sheila Clifton felt the first cold fingers of panic. They immediately went outside themselves, splitting up to cover more ground and calling Maddie's name with increasing desperation. Their voices carried through the twilight air, urgent and raw. The sound drew neighbors out of their houses like a fire alarm, and within minutes, an informal search party had formed.

As the minutes ticked by with no response, no glimpse of their daughter, the terrible reality began to sink in. Eight-year-old girls don't simply vanish from familiar neighborhoods. They don't disappear between one house and another on a route they've walked a hundred times.

By 6:33 p.m., with darkness swallowing the last traces of daylight and no sign of Maddie anywhere, Sheila Clifton's hands trembled as she dialed 911.

"Yes sir. Hi, this is Sheila Clifton. My daughter went out to play this afternoon. I thought she was with her friends, and now she's missing. She's eight years old."

The words came out in a rush, breathless and desperate. In the background, the dispatcher could hear shuffling, other voices, the sound of a family's world collapsing in real time.

Within minutes, patrol cars were slicing through the neighborhood with their lights painting the darkness in urgent reds and blues. Officers were taking statements from family members and neighbors, their radios crackling with coded urgency. What had started as a family's private crisis was now a race against time.

———

Word of Maddie's disappearance spread through Jacksonville like wildfire. By the morning of November 4, local news stations were running breaking updates every hour, and the story was attracting attention from across Florida and beyond.

But the real response came from ordinary people who felt the primal pull to help find a missing child. Within twenty-four hours of Maddie's disappearance, hundreds of volunteers had joined what was becoming one of the largest search efforts in Jacksonville's history.

They came with flashlights and determination: parents who couldn't bear the thought of losing a child, retirees who had time to contribute, teenagers who wanted to help, and complete strangers driven by something deeper than curiosity.

The search took on the intensity of a military operation. Police set up a command post in the neighborhood and began coordinating systematic searches of ever-widening areas. Teams of volunteers combed through wooded areas behind housing developments, checked abandoned buildings and construction sites, and peered into storm drains and drainage ditches. Divers plunged into ponds and retention basins throughout the area. Police helicopters circled over-head like mechanical vultures, their searchlights cutting white scars through the darkness.

Among the volunteers was fourteen-year-old Josh Phillips, who lived directly across the street from the Cliftons. Josh helped print and distribute missing person flyers, canvassed assigned search areas, and appeared genuinely concerned about Maddie's welfare. His family had always maintained friendly relations with the Cliftons. It was the kind of casual neighborly relationship that develops when families live across the street from each other for years.

The Clifton family threw themselves into the search with the despera-tion of people who knew that time was their enemy. Steve and Sheila barely slept, spending every available moment either actively searching or coordinating with the growing band of law enforcement and volunteers. They gave interviews to local television stations, their faces etched with exhaustion and barely controlled terror. Their message was simple and heartbreaking: Please help us bring our daughter home.

———

While volunteers scoured the physical landscape, law enforcement was conducting a more focused hunt for answers. Jacksonville Sheriff's Office detectives began the methodical process of interviewing everyone who'd had contact with Maddie in the hours before she vanished into thin air.

The investigation quickly zeroed in on Larry Grissom, the adult neighbor who had been playing golf with Maddie and Justin. A routine background check revealed that Larry had been accused of sexual assault almost twenty years earlier. The charges had been dropped and were unrelated to children, but in a case involving a missing eight-year-old girl, any red flag demanded immediate attention.

Larry was brought in for questioning and willingly submitted to a polygraph test. The results sent a chill through the investigation team: The test indicated he was being deceptive when asked about his knowledge of Maddie's disappearance, yet his alibi was rock solid. Multiple witnesses confirmed his whereabouts both during and after the golf game, leaving no window of opportunity for him to have harmed the child.

The contradiction between the failed polygraph and the ironclad alibi created a maddening puzzle for investigators. They obtained search warrants and tore through Larry's house, looking for any shred of evidence that might connect him to Maddie's disappearance. They found nothing. Eventually, despite the polygraph results that continued to nag at them, they were forced to conclude that Larry Grissom was not their man.

With their most promising lead evaporating, investigators faced the terrifying possibility that Maddie had been taken by a complete stranger—someone who had snatched her in broad daylight from a busy neighborhood and vanished without leaving a trace. The FBI was called in to assist, bringing additional resources and expertise to bear on what was becoming a nightmare scenario.

As part of their standard procedure, investigators conducted routine interviews with all neighborhood residents, including the Phillips family. Josh Phillips was interviewed along with his mother, since he was a minor. The teenager explained that he had seen Maddie outside that afternoon but hadn't played with her. His father didn't approve of him having friends over when adults weren't present, he said. Josh claimed he had been inside his house for most of the afternoon and evening, seeing nothing unusual.

The detective found Josh's responses reasonable and consistent. Officers also conducted a cursory search of the Phillips property with the family's permission, checking the garage, shed, and main areas of the house. Nothing they observed raised any red flags.

———

As November 10 dawned, the Clifton family faced a milestone that no parent should ever have to endure: one full week without their daughter. In missing child cases, statistics become the enemy. The vast majority of children who are recovered alive are found within the first few hours of their disappearance. With each passing day, hope doesn't just diminish; it withers.

But Jacksonville refused to give up. The number of volunteers had swelled to over a thousand, and the search had evolved into something resembling a small army. Professional search and rescue teams had joined the effort, bringing specialized equipment and techniques to areas that volunteers couldn't access safely. The reward for information leading to Maddie's safe return had grown to $50,000, funded by donations from individuals and businesses across the region.

The media coverage had exploded beyond local news to regional and national outlets. Maddie's face, captured in a school photo that showed her bright smile and sparkling eyes, had become familiar to people across the country. Her image stared out from television screens and newspaper front pages, a reminder that somewhere, somehow, an eight-year-old girl was in desperate need of rescue.

For the Clifton family, each day brought a fresh cycle of agony. Every phone call might be the one with news. Every knock on the door might be an investigator with a breakthrough. However, as each lead proved fruitless and each search area came up empty, the weight of uncertainty grew unbearable.

Steve and Sheila Clifton had aged years in just seven days. The strain of constant worry, minimal sleep, and the emotional rollercoaster of false hopes and crushing disappointments had carved lines into their faces that hadn't been there a week before. They held onto each other and their faith, but privately, both were beginning to confront the possibility that they might never see their daughter again.

Josh Phillips continued to participate in the search effort, showing up for volunteer assignments and helping wherever he was needed. To those around him, he appeared to be holding up well under the stress of the situation, though he seemed somewhat withdrawn and quiet— entirely understandable, given the anxiety that gripped the entire neighborhood like a fever.

The community itself had taken on a surreal quality. Streets that had once been filled with children playing were now patrolled by law enforcement and searched by volunteers carrying flashlights and wearing grim expressions. Houses that had always felt safe and welcoming now seemed to harbor potential secrets. The very fabric of neighborhood life had been altered by Maddie's absence.

———

On the morning of November 10, exactly one week after Maddie's disappearance, Missy Phillips noticed something that made her stomach turn. An increasingly powerful odor was emanating from her son's bedroom. It was a smell that had been growing stronger each day—despite both Josh's claims that it was from his pet birds and his attempts to mask it with air fresheners.

Josh had already left for school when Missy decided she couldn't ignore the smell any longer. It was far worse than anything the birds had ever produced, and it was making the entire house nearly unin-habitable.

As she looked around Josh's room, trying to identify the source, she noticed a wet spot on the floor near his waterbed. Her first thought was that the waterbed had sprung a leak, which would explain both the moisture and the worsening smell—standing water could create exactly this kind of problem.

Looking more closely, she could see that someone had attempted to repair the bed by taping the corner of the frame. She could also see what appeared to be a white sock caught in the tape, probably stuck there accidentally during the repair process.

Missy tried to pull the sock free, but it wouldn't budge. She peeled away some of the tape and tried again, but the sock seemed to be snagged on something inside the bed frame. Puzzled and increasingly concerned, she lifted the mattress slightly, but the interior was too dark to see clearly.

She went to get a flashlight, her hands already shaking with a dread she couldn't name. When she returned and lifted the mattress again, shining the light into the bed frame, the beam illuminated something that shattered her world.

The white sock belonged to a small foot. And that foot belonged to a child.

Missy Phillips ran from the house screaming, her mind unable to fully process what she had just discovered. She ran directly to the Clifton house, where she knew police officers were stationed. The first officer she encountered could see immediately that something catastrophic had happened. Missy was hysterical, barely able to form coherent words.

"Something's in Josh's bed!" she gasped. "Oh God, something's in Josh's bed!"

Josh Phillips

The officer called for immediate backup and followed Missy back to the Phillips house. What he found in Josh's bedroom would haunt him for the rest of his career, changing the trajectory of the investigation forever.

Hidden inside the base of the waterbed, wrapped in blood-soaked bedding, was the decomposing body of Maddie Clifton.

———

Fourteen-year-old Josh Phillips was sitting in his high school classroom when police arrived to arrest him. He was called to the principal's office, where detectives were waiting with handcuffs and questions that would unravel an unbelievable deception.

The detectives informed Josh that they had found Maddie Clifton's body in his bedroom and that he was under arrest for her murder. Josh's reaction was not shock or denial but something that looked almost like relief—as if a weight he had been carrying for seven days had finally been lifted.

Within hours of his arrest, Josh Phillips confessed to killing Maddie Clifton. His story revealed a cascade of poor decisions and panic that had led to an unthinkable outcome.

According to Josh's confession, the events of November 3 had begun innocently: Maddie had come to his house asking him to play baseball in his backyard. Despite his father's strict rules about having friends over when adults weren't present, Josh had agreed to play with her.

Unfortunately, Steve Phillips was not a man you wanted to cross. A drug addict and alcoholic who ruled his household through intimidation and violence, he had made it explicitly clear that Josh was never to have friends over when he wasn't home—especially young girls. Both Josh and his mother lived in constant fear of Steve's explosive outbursts and brutal punishments.

While they were playing, Josh claimed he had accidentally hit a baseball that struck Maddie in the eye. The impact caused her to bleed and cry loudly, and Josh immediately panicked. His father was due home soon, and Josh knew the consequences of being caught with a crying, injured child—in direct violation of the household rules—would be severe.

In his terror, Josh made a decision that would destroy multiple lives. Instead of seeking help for Maddie or calling for medical attention, he dragged her inside the house and into his bedroom, desperately trying to quiet her cries before his father arrived. When she wouldn't stop crying, Josh grabbed his baseball bat and struck her in the head, fracturing her skull and causing life-threatening injuries.

Josh then hid Maddie's body under his waterbed. However, his nightmare was far from over. When his father arrived home, Josh discovered that Maddie was still alive under the bed, moaning weakly from her injuries. Terrified that the sounds would be heard and his secret would be discovered, Josh removed her from the bed and cut her throat with a knife from a Leatherman multi-tool. Then, to ensure she was dead, he stabbed her multiple times in the chest.

The confession was as disturbing for what it revealed about Josh's mindset as it was for the brutal details of the crime itself. This was not a moment of blind rage or a single terrible decision, but rather a series of escalating choices made over an extended period of time. Josh had multiple opportunities to seek help, to stop the violence, and to do the right thing. Instead, he had continued down a path that led to murder.

———

As investigators processed the crime scene and analyzed the evidence, the full scope of Josh's week-long deception became horrifyingly clear. The physical evidence painted a picture of someone who had gone to extraordinary lengths to conceal his crime while maintaining a façade of normalcy that fooled an entire community.

Josh had used duct tape to seal the waterbed frame, desperately trying to contain both the body and the increasingly powerful smell of decomposition. He had strategically placed air fresheners throughout his room and burned incense, claiming to anyone who asked that he was just trying to deal with odors from his pet birds.

The medical examiner's autopsy revealed the savage nature of the attack. Maddie had been struck repeatedly in the head with a blunt object consistent with the baseball bat found hidden in Josh's room. Her throat had been cut so deeply it nearly severed her windpipe, and she had been stabbed numerous times in the chest and abdomen.

Many of the stab wounds appeared to have been inflicted after she was already dead or dying.

However, troubling inconsistencies emerged between Josh's version of events and the physical evidence. He claimed that Maddie had been accidentally hit in the eye with a baseball, but the autopsy showed no bruising or injury consistent with being struck by a ball. No blood was found in the backyard where Josh claimed the accident had occurred, and the baseball he said he had used showed no traces of blood.

Perhaps most disturbing was the evidence of how Josh had maintained his elaborate deception. For seven entire days, while a community searched desperately for Maddie, Josh had helped print and distribute missing person flyers bearing her photograph despite knowing she would never be found alive. He had participated in organized search efforts while knowing exactly where she was. Investigators even found one of Maddie's missing person flyers in his bedroom, placed prominently on a bookshelf where he would see it every day.

The realization that Josh had been sleeping directly above Maddie's decomposing body for an entire week—climbing into his bed each night knowing that his victim's remains were just inches below—suggested a level of psychological compartmentalization that chilled homicide detectives.

———

The revelation that Josh Phillips was responsible for Maddie's murder sent shockwaves through Jacksonville that reverberated far beyond the immediate neighborhood. For seven agonizing days, hundreds of people had searched tirelessly for a missing child, holding on to hope that she might be found alive and returned to her family.

The discovery that she had been dead the entire time—murdered on the very first day and hidden just yards from where volunteers had established their command post—was a betrayal of trust that defied comprehension.

For the volunteers who had spent days combing through wooded areas and drainage ditches, the news was devastating. Many had formed deep emotional connections to the case, driven by their own parental instincts and genuine desire to help bring a child home safely. Learning that their efforts had been futile from the very beginning—and that they had been unknowingly manipulated by the very person responsible for the crime—left many feeling violated and betrayed.

The Phillips family found themselves in an impossible position. Missy Phillips, who had discovered Maddie's body and immediately reported it to police, was simultaneously a hero for ending the community's agony and a mother whose son had committed an unthinkable crime. The family faced not only the legal consequences of Josh's actions but also the social ostracism that inevitably accompanies such cases.

Neighbors who had known Josh as a quiet, polite teenager struggled to reconcile that image with the brutal reality of what he had done. Parents throughout the community began questioning their own judgment, wondering how they could have so completely misjudged someone their children had played with regularly. The sense of safety that had defined the neighborhood was not just damaged; it was obliterated.

———

Josh Phillips was tried as an adult despite being only fourteen at the time of the murder, a decision that sparked intense debate about juvenile justice and the appropriate punishment for children who commit adult crimes. Due to extensive media coverage that had saturated Jacksonville, the trial was moved to Polk County in an attempt to find an impartial jury.

The prosecution's case was devastating in its simplicity. They presented Josh's detailed confession, the overwhelming physical evidence from the crime scene, and testimony from medical experts about the savage nature of Maddie's injuries. The evidence spoke for itself—Josh Phillips had brutally murdered an innocent child and then deceived an entire community while they searched desperately for her.

The defense faced a nearly impossible task. Josh's attorney made the controversial decision not to call any witnesses on behalf of his client, instead focusing his efforts on a closing argument that attempted to portray the crime as an act that "began as an accident and deteriorated through panic that bordered on madness."

The trial lasted only two days—an unusually brief duration that reflected both the overwhelming strength of the prosecution's evidence and the defense's strategic decision not to present witnesses. Josh himself never testified, leaving the jury without any personal sense of remorse or explanation beyond his initial confession.

The jury deliberated for just over two hours before returning with a verdict that surprised no one: guilty of first-degree murder. The speed of their decision suggested they found the evidence overwhelming and the defense arguments unconvincing.

Josh Phillips was sentenced to life imprisonment without the possibility of parole, making him one of the youngest people in Florida history to receive such a sentence. At fifteen years old, he was destined to spend the rest of his life behind bars, paying for seven days of deception that had followed a few moments of unthinkable violence.

———

Josh Phillips entered the Florida correctional system as a teenager serving a life sentence, a situation that presented unique challenges for both him and prison administrators. Remarkably, he became what corrections officials consistently described as a model prisoner. He completed his GED, pursued college courses through correspondence programs, and eventually trained as a paralegal to assist other inmates with their legal appeals.

His disciplinary record was extraordinarily clean, with only minor infractions in his first few years and none at all after 2005. This transformation from troubled teenager to apparently rehabilitated adult raised profound questions about the justice system's approach to juvenile offenders and whether true rehabilitation was possible even in cases involving the most serious violent crimes.

In 2012, the United States Supreme Court issued a landmark ruling in Miller v. Alabama that declared mandatory life sentences without parole for juvenile offenders unconstitutional. The court found that such sentences violated the Eighth Amendment when applied to defendants who were under eighteen at the time of their crimes, recognizing that children are fundamentally different from adults in their capacity for change and rehabilitation.

This ruling opened the door for Josh Phillips and hundreds of other juvenile lifers across the country to seek new sentencing hearings. For Josh, who had spent nearly two decades in prison by this point, the Miller decision represented the first real hope for eventual release that he had experienced since his conviction.

In 2017, Josh was granted a re-sentencing hearing that became as emotionally charged as his original trial. The defense presented extensive evidence of his rehabilitation and transformation, while the prosecution argued that some crimes are so heinous they warrant life imprisonment regardless of the offender's age.

Perhaps most remarkably, Harry Shorstein, the prosecutor who had originally sought Josh's life sentence, testified that his understanding of juvenile brain development had evolved over the years and that he regretted not offering a plea to second-degree murder.

Josh himself addressed the court, offering a detailed apology to the Clifton family and expressing what appeared to be genuine remorse for his actions. However, Judge Waddell Wallace III ultimately concluded that the nature of the crime warranted continued imprisonment, though he included the possibility of future review after twenty-five years from the original conviction.

———

More than two decades later, the case of Joshua Phillips and Maddie Clifton continues to haunt Jacksonville. For the Clifton family, it represents an irreplaceable loss that has shaped every day since November 1998. For the community, it shattered the illusion that watchful neighbors could protect children from all harm; Maddie fell victim to someone they had trusted completely.

As Josh became eligible for his twenty-five-year review in 2023, the case returned to public attention. After a review, the court declined to modify his life sentence, determining that continued incarceration was appropriate.

CHAPTER 7
THE SECOND CHANCE

The fluorescent lights hummed overhead in the Ottawa-Carleton Regional Police Headquarters as Constable Robert Cross settled into another quiet Monday night shift at the public information desk. It was nearly midnight on April 24, 1995, when he noticed a man approaching across the polished floor. Mid-forties, graying hair, bushy mustache—the stranger moved with the measured gait of someone carrying heavy news.

"I need to report a missing person," the man said, his voice steady but strained.

Brett Morgan explained that his partner, forty-six-year-old Louise Ellis, had vanished more than two days earlier. She'd left their Ottawa home on Saturday afternoon, excited about a weekend getaway to visit an old friend's cottage in Quebec's Gatineau Hills. It was just a thirty-minute drive through forested countryside. She'd packed an overnight bag and a wrapped birthday gift for her friend's young daughter, but Louise had never arrived.

Constable Cross listened as Brett recounted the timeline. Louise had left around 2:00 p.m. on Saturday. When she failed to show up by

Sunday, her friend, John, called Brett out of concern. Brett hadn't worried initially—Louise had mentioned possibly visiting another friend in the area. But by Monday evening, with still no word, panic set in.

Brett had started making calls. One went to Brenda Missen, Louise's colleague from Canada Post, who lived near Wakefield. Brenda's memory was sharp—earlier that day, she'd noticed a yellow and white Suzuki Sidekick parked on a rural roadside. The same make and model as Louise's car.

Brett rushed to meet Brenda at the location. The license plates confirmed their fears. Louise's distinctive vehicle sat abandoned on the shoulder of Highway 105, doors locked, seemingly untouched. Inside, everything remained exactly as Louise had left it—her overnight bag in the back seat, the wrapped gift for John's daughter, and her purse on the front passenger seat with wallet, cash, and bank cards intact. Everything except Louise herself.

As Brett recounted these details to Constable Cross, filling out the missing person report, something unexpected happened. Mid-conversation, Brett suddenly volunteered information the officer hadn't requested.

"I need you to know," Brett said, his voice dropping, "I was previously convicted of killing a woman."

The words hung in the air. Constable Cross felt his pulse quicken. Here was a man reporting his partner missing, appearing genuinely concerned and cooperative, casually admitting to homicide.

Brett explained it had happened seventeen years earlier—a manslaughter conviction for strangling a twenty-one-year-old woman named Gwen Telford during his younger, more troubled days. He'd served ten years, been released, and then been convicted again on fraud and theft charges before serving his second sentence.

"I understand this makes me a suspect," Brett said, meeting the officer's eyes. "But I didn't harm Louise. She's my soulmate. She saved my life."

———

Their love story, Brett explained, began three years earlier in the most unlikely of places—a Supreme Court hearing. Louise Ellis was a freelance journalist covering what would become one of Canada's most notorious wrongful conviction cases. David Milgaard had been imprisoned for decades for a murder he didn't commit, and Brett Morgan—then an inmate himself—was testifying against his former cellmate, the real killer.

Louise had been struck by Brett's courage; few prisoners would risk testifying against another inmate. After Brett finished his testimony, while he was being escorted away in shackles, Louise followed him to the elevator.

"I think what you did was really brave," she told him.

That moment sparked a correspondence that grew into something deeper. Letters became phone calls, and phone calls became prison visits. Louise saw in Brett Morgan a story of redemption—a man paying his debt to society, ready to change. She believed he deserved a second chance at life, so she hired lawyers to help with his parole application and advocated tirelessly for his release.

In May 1994, Louise had been waiting outside the prison gates when Brett walked free. She drove him home in her yellow Suzuki Sidekick, stopping to buy him an ice cream cake to celebrate his freedom. Brett moved into her house in Ottawa's Old South neighborhood, and Louise helped him start a home renovation business. Neighbors often saw them sitting together on the front porch, holding hands.

Constable Cross found Brett's openness about his criminal past disarming. Most guilty parties didn't volunteer damaging information. Brett seemed genuinely distraught about Louise's disappearance, cooperative in every way. Still, the officer knew what had to happen next.

"If something has happened to Louise," Cross told him, "your record means you'll naturally be a suspect."

"I understand," Brett replied. "I expected that."

Within hours, Brett found himself in the Criminal Investigation Department, repeating his story to detectives who listened intently, taking careful notes. They asked him to return the next day with photographs of Louise so they could put together a missing persons poster.

When Brett arrived on Tuesday morning with a friend and an armload of photos, the detectives wanted to interview him again. The ninety-minute session felt more intense than the previous night's questioning. Brett emerged looking shaken, telling his friend the detectives had "put quite a bit of heat" on him, demanding detailed accounts of his recent movements.

But he remained cooperative. When detectives asked to see Louise's will, Brett obliged. It revealed he was her sole beneficiary, though he wouldn't inherit anything for seven years unless she was confirmed dead. He handed over Louise's financial records and something more intimate—her private diaries, filled with her thoughts and fears in her own handwriting.

However, the diary entries painted a troubling picture of their relationship. Louise had documented arguments and moments of tension, writing about fights that left her drained and despondent. While the entries suggested turmoil, they weren't explicit enough to immediately brand Brett a killer—especially given his cooperative demeanor and apparent transparency about his criminal past.

The search began in earnest on Wednesday morning. A diverse group assembled outside a Wakefield restaurant—Ottawa detectives, Quebec police officers, Brett Morgan, and members of Louise's family. They spread out from River Road, where her vehicle had been found, to comb through dense woods made muddy by spring rains.

The area was unforgiving terrain. Thick brush, fallen logs, scattered boulders, and a derelict car provided countless hiding places. A couple living nearby confirmed they'd first noticed the abandoned Suzuki on Saturday—the same day Louise had disappeared. The vehicle itself offered no clues. Nothing was wrong with it mechanically, the gas tank was full, and when officers dusted for prints, they found nothing suspicious.

For days, volunteers tramped through the cold forest, and divers searched the nearby Gatineau River. Every lead turned up empty.

While official search efforts scaled back, Brett Morgan pressed on alone. He printed homemade posters featuring Louise's photo and a plea for witnesses. He gave interviews to local media, speaking frankly about his past.

"I was convicted of manslaughter and it involved a woman," he told the Ottawa Citizen. "I understand the implications of that. I have to be a suspect—it's obvious. But I would never harm the woman who gave me a life free from crime."

A week after Louise vanished, Brett spent Saturday standing at the spot where her car was found, flagging down passing motorists with his stack of posters. "I can't rely on the police," he told reporters. "It's hard living at home not knowing where she is."

The authorities seemed strangely reluctant to treat the case as anything more than a missing person. "People go missing every day," one Ottawa detective told the media. "She may have just gotten tired of this world and walked away."

Quebec investigators were equally dismissive, noting there was nothing to indicate Louise had even been on their side of the border— despite her car being found there.

Rumors swirled through Ottawa's tight-knit community. Some pointed to a small ad Louise had placed in a Wakefield newspaper: "Responsible nature lover seeks comfortable quiet cottage." Friends confirmed she'd been looking to lease a summer retreat. Perhaps she had wandered off while viewing rental properties. Others whispered about suicide or a random abduction.

Brett dismissed such theories. "She's my sweetheart," he told reporters. "She wouldn't give up on me and I am not going to give up on her."

But privately, Brett had a different theory. He suspected Louise's ex-boyfriend, John Maisonneuve.

Louise and John's relationship had been complicated. They'd met four years earlier at a jazz festival and moved in together within months, but their romance had proved volatile—a cycle of passionate reconciliations and bitter separations. When Louise became enchanted by Brett Morgan in that Supreme Court hearing, it marked the end of her relationship with John. He took the breakup badly, refusing to speak to Louise for over a year.

It was only in the summer of 1994, after Brett's release from prison, that John and Louise had reconnected as friends. The romantic element was gone, but Louise had grown fond of John's daughter from a previous relationship. It was this girl's twelfth birthday that Louise had been planning to celebrate when she vanished, the wrapped book about horses still sitting in her abandoned car.

Detectives knew they had to interview John Maisonneuve. They found him at his workplace, the University of Ottawa, where he worked as a researcher. John's account was straightforward: He'd last spoken to Louise on Friday evening, April 21, when he'd invited her to dinner at his cottage that night. She had declined the invitation.

But John's story contained a puzzling contradiction. He claimed he hadn't been expecting Louise to visit on Saturday—yet both Brett and

Louise's friends knew she had planned to spend the weekend at John's cottage for his daughter's birthday. Even more suspicious, John had called his ex-wife on Sunday, expressing concern that Louise "hadn't arrived." Investigators wondered: Why would he be worried about someone not showing up if he hadn't been expecting them in the first place?

John's alibi appeared solid—he told detectives he'd spent Saturday with his daughter after picking her up from horseback riding. Investigators had no immediate reason to doubt him. Still, they brought in sniffer dogs to search a secluded area of land he owned near his cottage, although the search turned up nothing.

With no physical evidence and no clear suspect, the investigation stalled. Detectives explored other possibilities. Could Louise have been targeted by Larry Fisher, the convicted killer Brett had testified against? Fisher was free at the time of Louise's disappearance, not yet charged with the murder Brett had exposed. What if this was revenge?

But when investigators checked, they found Fisher had been stopped by police in Saskatchewan on April 22, 3,000 kilometers from where Louise's car was discovered. Another dead end.

By early May, Brett had hired two private investigators to follow up on leads the police couldn't pursue. He told reporters that the local force was understaffed and overwhelmed. When a television news crew asked how he was feeling, Brett's composure cracked slightly.

"Increasingly terrified," he admitted.

———

Meanwhile, twenty-five minutes away in St. Pierre, Quebec, a businesswoman named Marie Parent was following the case with growing interest. Originally from Scotland, Marie had moved to Canada in 1990 to reconnect with her estranged French-Canadian father. She'd tried running a restaurant and video store, but neither venture had fulfilled her true passion—detective work.

In February 1995, Marie enrolled in a three-month private investigator course. As the program neared completion, Louise Ellis's disappearance captured her attention. There was a missing woman, an abandoned car, and a distraught partner making public pleas for help. It seemed like the perfect opportunity to apply her newly learned skills.

On May 17, Marie called Brett Morgan's home number, leaving a message on his answering machine with an offer of her assistance. Brett returned the call within two hours, but he explained he already had two private investigators working the case and couldn't afford a third.

Marie assured him she didn't want payment—just the experience of working a real case. Brett agreed to meet her.

Two days later, Marie drove to the red brick house in Old Ottawa South where Louise and Brett lived. She brought a tape recorder and asked Brett's permission to record their conversation. He agreed without hesitation.

Sitting at the kitchen table where Louise had once eaten breakfast, they discussed various theories about her disappearance. Stranger abduction seemed unlikely—why would Louise have locked her car if she'd only stepped out briefly to help someone? Brett eventually shared his strongest suspicion: John Maisonneuve had to be involved. Louise's ex-boyfriend's cottage wasn't far from where her car was found, yet police seemed uninterested in pursuing this lead.

Over the following weeks, Marie conducted her own investigation. She met with Brett several more times, spoke with him regularly by phone, and tried contacting Louise's other friends and family members. Most wouldn't talk to her—they'd already formed their own opinions about what had happened to Louise.

Marie began to notice things that troubled her. During one of their recorded conversations, Brett made a slip that caught her attention later. They'd been discussing Louise's abandoned car when Marie had asked whether the driver's seat was still positioned for someone of Louise's height or if it had been pushed back for a taller person.

"Exactly the way I left…" Brett began, then abruptly stopped and corrected himself. "Exactly the way Louise left it."

Marie rewound the tape several times, studying Brett's voice and the pause. Something felt wrong.

Other details nagged at her. When she visited Brett's house, all traces of Louise seemed to have vanished. No women's toiletries in the bathroom, none of Louise's jewelry or clothing visible anywhere. It was as if she'd never lived there at all.

By mid-June, Marie had reached a disturbing conclusion. She called Ottawa Police and asked to speak with someone about the Louise Ellis case.

Detective Bob Pulfer had already been watching Marie's involvement with growing interest. Police wiretaps on Brett's phone had intercepted his regular conversations with the aspiring private investigator from Quebec. When Marie called requesting a meeting, Pulfer was intrigued.

Marie arrived at police headquarters carrying her tape recordings and a heavy suspicion. When Detective Pulfer asked what she thought had happened to Louise Ellis, Marie's answer was direct.

"I think Brett Morgan murdered her."

Pulfer exchanged glances with his partner, Detective John Savage. It was exactly what they'd begun to suspect. Brett's seemingly helpful behavior had been masking deeper deceptions. A review of his bank statements revealed significant discrepancies in his timeline for April 22: Brett claimed he'd deposited a check for Louise at noon, then stopped at a 7-Eleven to withdraw money for himself before arriving home around 1:00 p.m. to give Louise her bank card back before she left.

But the bank records told a different story. The deposit was made at 1:32 p.m., and Brett withdrew the $250 at 2:53 p.m.—after Louise should have already left for her weekend trip.

The detectives had another question for Marie: Would she be willing to go undercover?

"What would you need me to do?" Marie asked.

"Perhaps you could find out what Brett Morgan knows about the disappearance of Louise Ellis," Detective Pulfer replied.

Detective Savage looked at Marie with a half-smile. "Maybe you could find the body, too."

Marie agreed without hesitation. From that moment, she became a double agent.

Following police instructions, Marie Parent fed Brett a carefully crafted lie. She told him she'd interviewed John Maisonneuve and found discrepancies in his story. She claimed John and Louise had argued because John wanted Louise to leave Brett, but she'd refused.

Brett appeared stunned by this information. Marie pressed her advantage, suggesting they needed to find Louise's remains so they could build a case against John. Without a body, police couldn't lay charges, and any inheritance Brett was entitled to would remain tied up indefinitely.

Brett quickly speculated about where Louise might be buried. He wouldn't have taken the body far, he reasoned—carrying dead weight would be like hauling a sack of potatoes. Probably just fifty or sixty feet into the woods from where her car was found.

Marie suggested they search together. On June 24, she and Brett drove to the Wakefield area and spent five hours combing through wooded country roads. They found nothing, but Marie noticed that Brett's searching seemed halfhearted—more like a casual nature walk than a serious investigation.

A few days later, Marie fed Brett another lie: John Maisonneuve had failed a polygraph test. Brett remained convinced that Louise's body was somewhere near John's cottage and agreed to search again.

However, Brett's behavior was becoming increasingly erratic. He canceled their next planned search at the last minute, claiming he'd been too distraught to sleep, kept awake by the thought of finding Louise's remains. He canceled again a few days later.

Frustrated, Marie confronted Brett about his lack of cooperation, accusing him of leaving all the work to her. Brett apologized and suggested they meet at a local restaurant to discuss the case over drinks.

During their conversation, something deeply unsettling happened. Brett pulled out a bandanna and, without warning, wrapped it around Marie's neck. Given what she knew about his history of strangling women, the gesture terrified her. She pushed his hands away immediately.

"It's just a gift," Brett said casually. "To keep you cool during our searches."

The incident left Marie shaken, but she maintained her cover. They made plans to search together the following day, July 6.

Unknown to Brett, police had been busy during his restaurant meeting with Marie. While she kept him occupied, technicians had slipped a listening device into his pickup truck. Every word he spoke while driving would now be recorded.

Thursday morning, July 6, dawned clear and warm. Marie met Brett in Wakefield, and they headed into the wooded backcountry of Sainte-Cécile-de-Masham. Brett drove along various dirt roads, sometimes backtracking as if lost or uncertain of his direction.

Finally, they reached Irwin Road—an obscure dead-end track about ten kilometers west of Wakefield. Dense trees separated the road from the deeper forest beyond. Brett led Marie through the wooded area, pushing back branches as they walked in single file.

They emerged into a small clearing dominated by a large pine tree. Dead branches and needles carpeted the forest floor, and as Marie's eyes swept the area, she caught sight of something that didn't belong.

"Look," she said, pointing. "There's something over there."

Scattered clothing lay among the pine needles—a blue coat, a sweater, and two running shoes. What appeared to be bone protruded from the sweater. Dark brown hair was visible on a nearby mossy patch, and beside the coat, unmistakably human, was a skull.

"It's Louise," Brett said immediately before bursting into tears.

Marie watched Brett's performance with cold calculation. The tears seemed genuine, but his instant identification of remains that were barely recognizable struck her as impossible—unless he already knew what they would find.

Brett Morgan

Brett's emotions swung wildly. One moment, he was sobbing incon-solably; the next, his eyes would glaze over, and he'd stare at Marie in a way that felt threatening. Worried that he might be regretting having led her to the body, Marie played her part, touching his face comfortingly and whispering soothing words.

They took photographs of the scene, and then Brett announced he wanted to check how far they were from John Maisonneuve's cottage. They drove to Wakefield's city hall to examine a map. Brett calculated the distance at roughly two miles.

"That's pretty close, you know," he said with satisfaction.

Brett wanted to call the police immediately, but Marie suggested they phone in an anonymous tip instead. After they parted ways, Marie contacted Detective Pulfer and guided him to the location.

Dental records confirmed the remains belonged to Louise Ellis. After more than ten weeks in the elements, decomposition was advanced, but the medical examiner was able to determine that she had died from strangulation.

Brett Morgan was arrested that same day and charged with first-degree murder.

As investigators pieced together the crime, the full extent of Louise Ellis's suffering became clear. A deeper examination of her private diaries revealed details that had been overlooked in the initial investigation—months of documented physical abuse that went far beyond the turmoil first noted. Louise had written of Brett shoving her, gripping her arms, pouring beer over her head, punching holes in walls, and making verbal threats.

"This relationship is either going to kill me or cure me," Louise had written just weeks before her death.

The financial motive was equally clear. Brett had systematically drained Louise's accounts, forging checks totaling over $12,000. Louise had discovered the theft and was demanding repayment. Friends confirmed that by April 1995, Louise had decided to end the relationship regardless of whether Brett repaid the money.

"She was sick of him controlling and using her," one friend testified.

The timeline investigators reconstructed was chilling in its calculation. On April 22, Louise had called her bank twice to check whether money from Brett's friend "Bob" had arrived to repay her loans. It hadn't. That afternoon, as Louise prepared to leave for Wakefield, a confrontation likely erupted over the missing money.

Police believed Brett killed Louise in the bathroom of her home—the only room with no windows and no escape route. He'd used the shower curtain to wrap her body, explaining why it was missing when police searched the house. Brett had then loaded Louise's corpse into the trunk of her own Jeep and driven to the remote forest near John's cottage, hoping to frame her ex-boyfriend for the crime.

His plan was clever but flawed. Brett had dumped the body on Crown land, not John's property as he'd intended. Still, he'd positioned Louise's remains close enough to John's cottage to cast suspicion his way.

After abandoning Louise's car on Highway 105, Brett had likely bicycled back to Ottawa under the cover of darkness. The next day, he began his performance as the grieving partner, giving interviews and organizing search parties while knowing exactly where Louise lay decomposing in the Quebec woods.

Brett Morgan's trial began in September 1997 and lasted six months— a marathon proceeding that featured more than ninety witnesses. Marie Parent took the stand to describe her dangerous undercover work, detailing Brett's suspicious behavior and the chilling moment he had wrapped a bandanna around her neck.

The defense argued police had "tunnel vision," focusing solely on Brett because of his criminal record while ignoring other suspects like John Maisonneuve. They claimed Brett had no motive to kill Louise— she'd supported him financially and helped secure his parole.

However, the prosecution painted a different picture. Louise's growing insistence on being repaid, her plans to end their relationship, and her discovery of Brett's ongoing theft had backed him into a corner. Witnesses testified to Louise's anxiety about money in her final days and her open discussions about Brett's violence.

The jury deliberated for three days before returning their verdict: guilty.

Louise's family and friends wept, shouted, applauded, and embraced each other in the courtroom. Brett Morgan remained expressionless.

"I didn't do this, your honor," he stated flatly.

The judge's response was withering.

"You planned and deliberated upon the killing of Louise Ellis, a young woman in the prime of her life, who gave everything she had in an attempt to assist you in your reintegration into society. She was an intelligent, vibrant, highly creative, fiercely loyal, and loving human being who shall be sadly missed by her family and those who loved her."

The judge noted something particularly damning about Brett's character: "Implicit in the jury's verdict is that you wrongfully accused an innocent man, John Maisonneuve, of being responsible. That treacherous act speaks very poorly about your moral fiber."

Brett Morgan was sentenced to life in prison with no possibility of parole for twenty-five years.

The story had one final twist. Two months into his sentence, Brett Morgan died in prison from hepatitis C. It was April 24, 1998— exactly three years to the day since he had reported Louise Ellis missing.

For her role in solving the case, police awarded Marie Parent $4,600. She later told reporters the reward felt "like a slap in the face after all I had done over the years." Marie has since appeared in multiple documentaries about the case and continues working on a memoir about her time as a private investigator.

At Louise's funeral, 200 mourners packed into Glebe St. James United Church in Ottawa. She was remembered as a passionate, artistic woman of great integrity, an excellent cook, a talented writer, and a fierce advocate for justice. In 1976, she wrote and illustrated a children's book called "The AlphaVegetaBet," teaching children about letters and vegetables through whimsical drawings.

Louise's father, Allan Ellis, showed remarkable grace in the aftermath of his daughter's murder. When asked about Brett Morgan, he said simply: "Never return evil for evil. Never."

Louise's name is now engraved on Ottawa's Enclave Memorial, commemorating women murdered by men.

CHAPTER 8

THE GREEK PILOT

The helicopter circled low over the schoolyard on the Greek island of Alonnisos, its rotors whipping dust across the courtyard where students had gathered for their midday break. Fifteen-year-old Caroline Crouch looked up from her conversation with friends, shielding her eyes against the Mediterranean sun as the aircraft made another pass overhead.

The pilot was showing off, and everyone knew it.

Caroline had grown up on this idyllic island since she was eight years old, when her British father, David, and Filipina mother, Susan, had fallen in love with its pristine beaches and crystal-clear waters. The family had relocated from England, seeking the peaceful island life that Alonnisos offered. Caroline embraced her new home completely, developing a passion for scuba diving and swimming in the surrounding Aegean Sea.

She was a popular student—bright, athletic, and known for the infectious smile that seemed permanently etched on her face. Friends described her as someone you immediately wanted to befriend, a girl who brought light into every room she entered. Caroline had even earned a black belt in kickboxing, demonstrating the determination and strength that would define much of her life.

The helicopter pilot's name was Haralambos Anagnostopoulos, though everyone called him Babis. At twenty-seven, he was charismatic and successful, working as a commercial helicopter pilot and flight instructor. His mother lived on Alonnisos and worked at Caroline's school, which was how he'd learned about the beautiful British teenager who had captured the attention of half the island's young men.

But Babis had advantages that they didn't. He was older, financially secure, and possessed an easy confidence that came from success. When he finally introduced himself to Caroline during a Good Friday parade in 2017, the twelve-year age gap seemed to disappear in the face of his charm and attention.

Caroline was smitten. Here was a handsome, accomplished man who owned his own helicopter and seemed to offer her a world far beyond the quiet island life she'd known. To her teenage eyes, Babis represented adventure, sophistication, and romantic possibility all rolled into one irresistible package.

Their courtship was swift and intense. Within eighteen months, Babis had proposed to the seventeen-year-old Caroline, presenting her with an engagement ring and promises of a fairy-tale future together. Caroline believed she'd found her perfect match, the love story she'd dreamed about since childhood.

Three days after Caroline's eighteenth birthday in July 2019, the couple exchanged vows in a small ceremony in Portugal. It was an intimate affair, far from the elaborate Greek wedding traditions that typically brought together extended families and entire communities. Instead, Babis and Caroline kept their celebration private, just the two of them beginning what she hoped would be a lifetime of happiness.

They settled in Glyka Nera, an affluent suburb on the outskirts of Athens, where Babis continued his work as a pilot while Caroline enrolled at a university in the city. Their social media accounts painted a picture of blissful young love—romantic dinners, beach vacations, and tender moments captured in carefully staged photographs. To the outside world, they appeared to be living the perfect life.

Caroline gave birth to their daughter Lydia in June 2020, completing what seemed to be their ideal family. The new mother doted on her baby girl, sharing videos of tender moments between them on Instagram. In one post, Caroline was captured on a beach near her childhood home, joyfully lifting Lydia into the air before planting a gentle kiss on her cheek.

But behind the carefully curated images of domestic bliss, cracks were beginning to show.

The transformation began slowly, almost imperceptibly. What had initially seemed like Babis's protective nature gradually revealed itself as something more controlling. As Caroline focused on her studies and adjusted to motherhood, she found herself increasingly isolated from friends and family. Money became a source of tension—Caroline had none of her own, making her completely dependent on her husband's income.

The couple's non-traditional wedding had been an early sign of Babis's desire to keep Caroline separated from potential support systems. Now, living in Athens, far from her childhood home, Caroline discovered that her movements were being monitored and restricted in ways that left her feeling trapped.

Still, to their neighbors in Glyka Nera, the Anagnostopoulos family appeared perfectly normal. Babis continued his work as a pilot while Caroline cared for their baby daughter in their comfortable two-story townhouse. They seemed like any other young family navigating the challenges of new parenthood and building their future together.

―――――

The emergency call came in at 4:30 a.m. on May 11, 2021. Through the phone, dispatchers could barely make out the muffled words of a man in desperate distress.

"Help… help… ambulance… ambulance…"

The voice was strained, terrified, obscured by what sounded like tape covering the caller's mouth. When the operator pressed for details, the response sent chills through the emergency dispatch center in Athens.

"Robbers came in."

The caller managed to gasp out an address in Glyka Nera before the line went quiet, except for the sound of a baby crying somewhere in the background.

First responders raced through the pre-dawn darkness, their sirens piercing the stillness of the affluent suburb. By 6:00 a.m., police cars and ambulances surrounded the townhouse where the Anagnos-topoulos family lived.

What officers found inside would haunt them for years to come.

The living room looked like a tornado had torn through it. Drawers hung open, their contents scattered across hardwood floors. Clothing and personal belongings were strewn everywhere in what appeared to be a frantic search for valuables. A Monopoly board game box lay upended, and a small security camera had been ripped from the wall and discarded behind a couch, its memory card conspicuously missing.

But nothing—absolutely nothing—could have prepared the responding officers for what awaited them throughout the rest of the house.

Hanging from the banister was a brown and white husky puppy, barely seven months old, suspended by her own leash. The sight of the dead animal—innocent and defenseless—sent waves of revulsion through investigators. In their years of police work, they had seen violence directed at humans, but the deliberate killing of a family pet suggested a level of cruelty that defied comprehension.

Upstairs, they discovered the human casualties of whatever nightmare had unfolded in this house.

On the bedroom floor lay a man, hands and feet bound tightly behind his back with rope. Duct tape circled his head multiple times, covering his eyes and mouth and extending down to his neck in what appeared to be a methodical restraint job. When officers carefully removed the bindings, they revealed Babis Anagnostopoulos gasping and disoriented from his ordeal.

Face down on the bed nearby lay nineteen-year-old Caroline Crouch. Her skin had turned a pale, waxy color that immediately told the responding officers everything they needed to know. Beside her, eleven-month-old Lydia was crying inconsolably, clapping her tiny hands and desperately trying to wake her mother by hitting and pushing her lifeless body.

The baby's distress was heartbreaking to witness—a child too young to understand death but old enough to know something was terribly wrong.

When Babis was freed and saw his wife's condition, his legs buckled beneath him. The sound that escaped his throat was barely human—a wail of anguish that echoed through the house and would stay with the officers long after they left the scene.

Once baby Lydia was safely in the arms of a female officer, Babis struggled to piece together the horror that had shattered his family. His account emerged in fragments, interrupted by sobs and moments where he seemed to lose the ability to speak entirely.

Three hooded men had burst into their bedroom around 4:30 a.m., he explained through his tears. They wore motorcycle balaclavas and carried weapons—a silver Colt pistol and a black handgun that he'd glimpsed during those first terrifying seconds of the attack. The intruders spoke broken Greek with what sounded like Albanian accents, barking demands for money as they quickly overpowered him.

The attackers knew exactly what they were looking for. Just days earlier, Babis and Caroline had purchased a plot of land where they planned to build their dream family home. Caroline's parents had gifted them fifty thousand euros to help with the purchase, and the couple had kept additional cash in the house—over ten thousand euros hidden inside the Monopoly game box for construction costs.

It was common practice in Greece at the time, where banks remained unreliable: Citizens often preferred to keep significant amounts of cash at home rather than risk institutional failure.

When the robbers found the money, they weren't satisfied. They ransacked the house, moving from room to room in search of jewelry and other valuables. Their demands became increasingly aggressive as they tore through the couple's belongings, and then the situation escalated beyond mere robbery.

According to Babis, the men held a gun directly against baby Lydia's head.

Caroline began screaming in absolute terror—the sound of a mother watching her child's life hang in the balance. Babis was helpless, bound, and blindfolded, able to hear his wife's panic but unable to see what was happening just feet away from him. Then Caroline's screams stopped.

"I kept losing consciousness from the tape around my neck," Babis told investigators, his voice hollow with trauma. "Every time I passed out, I thought I was going to die. When I finally came to and realized they were gone, all I could hear was my daughter crying."

The physical evidence seemed to support his harrowing account. The house showed clear signs of a violent break-in and systematic search. Valuable items were missing, including cash and jewelry. The intruders had apparently entered through a basement window after failing to force their way through a back door, then moved through the house with the confidence of experienced criminals.

The coroner's preliminary examination of Caroline's body revealed she had been suffocated, most likely with a pillow pressed over her face. The attack had lasted several agonizing minutes, and evidence suggested she had fought desperately for her life. Bruising on her lips and tongue indicated the use of a sharp object, while other marks across her body showed she had struggled against her attacker until the very end.

Most disturbing was the killing of seven-month-old Roxy, the family's beloved husky. The deliberate murder of the innocent animal served no practical purpose in a robbery—it was an act of pure cruelty that suggested the perpetrators were either under the influence of drugs or possessed a level of sadistic brutality that went far beyond typical criminal behavior.

A police spokesperson struggled to find adequate words to describe the scene. "We've seen several other ugly murders throughout the years, but this was extremely brutal and violent. It took someone with a strong antisocial personality and a distinct lack of emotion to carry out such a heinous act."

The question that haunted investigators from the very beginning was why Caroline had been killed at all. As one detective put it, "In a robbery, the motive is money. It was not necessary to kill to achieve this goal. Therefore, the question on everyone's mind was: why was Caroline Crouch killed?"

Several theories emerged during those first crucial hours. Perhaps the intruders had been high on drugs and lost control of the situation. Maybe Caroline had gotten a good enough look at their faces that she could have identified them later. Given her background in kickboxing, she might have fought back with unexpected skill and strength, forcing them to use deadly force to subdue her.

The most chilling possibility was that her frantic screaming after the gun was placed against her daughter's head had simply been too loud —that the killers had silenced her to prevent neighbors from hearing and calling for help.

What investigators knew with certainty was that this had been no random crime. The attackers knew about the money hidden in the house, understood the family's routines, and had planned their approach carefully. Someone in the couple's inner circle had either participated in the crime or provided crucial information to the perpetrators.

The case sent immediate shockwaves through Greek society. Here was a young British mother, barely out of her teens, brutally murdered in her own home while her infant daughter slept beside her. The image of baby Lydia trying desperately to wake her dead mother became seared into the public consciousness, a symbol of innocence destroyed by unthinkable violence.

News outlets across Europe picked up the story within hours. Public outrage grew by the minute as details of the crime spread through social media and traditional news channels. The Greek government, recognizing the international attention the case was receiving, posted a substantial reward of three hundred thousand euros for information leading to the capture of the killers.

At the center of this media storm stood Babis Anagnostopoulos—a grieving widower whose world had been shattered in a single night of terror. He became the human face of the tragedy, appearing on television with red-rimmed eyes and a voice that broke when he spoke about his murdered wife.

"I hope what happened to me and my family and my wife's family never happens again," he told reporters gathered outside his home. "The police know how to do their job, and they will find them."

Five days after Caroline's murder, Babis posted a heart-wrenching tribute on his Instagram account. It was their wedding photo—an image of pure joy and hope from just two years earlier, accompanied by a simple message that brought tears to thousands of eyes: "Always together. Farewell my love."

The investigation began immediately, spearheaded by the elite Crimes Against Life Department of the Hellenic Police. Based on Babis's detailed account and their analysis of the crime scene, investigators concluded they were hunting for a highly organized gang of professional criminals.

The perpetrators had clearly conducted surveillance on the Anagnostopoulos family, learning their daily routines and identifying the optimal time to strike. They had studied the house's layout, located potential entry points, and possessed inside knowledge about the cash stored within. This level of preparation suggested experienced criminals rather than opportunistic thieves.

Working around the clock, detectives began the painstaking process of investigating every known criminal in the Athens area with a history of violent break-ins. They focused particularly on Albanian and Georgian crime syndicates, which were known to operate sophisticated robbery operations targeting wealthy suburban families.

A composite sketch was created based on Babis's brief glimpse of one attacker during the initial struggle—a tall, dark-skinned, overweight male under thirty years old. The image was distributed to every police station in Greece and shared with international law enforcement agencies in case the perpetrators had fled the country.

The breakthrough seemed to come just three days later, on the very day Caroline was laid to rest.

The funeral took place on Alonnisos, the island where Caroline had spent her teenage years and where her parents still lived. It was a heartbreaking scene—a young woman who should have had her entire life ahead of her being lowered into the ground while her husband held their now-motherless baby.

Hundreds of mourners gathered to pay their respects to Caroline, whose radiant smile and generous spirit had touched so many lives during her brief time on Earth. Friends spoke of her kindness, her devotion to her daughter, and the dreams she'd harbored for the future that would never be realized.

As the funeral concluded, police at a routine checkpoint near the Bulgarian border were pulling over a suspicious vehicle. The driver, a middle-aged Georgian man, handed over identification papers that were quickly determined to be forged.

The man was Harod Zish Whey, a career criminal with a violent past that read like a blueprint for the attack on the Anagnostopoulos home. His record included multiple convictions for break-ins around Athens, and investigators discovered he had been involved in at least twelve similar crimes in recent months. Three of those break-ins had occurred in Caroline's neighborhood of Glyka Nera.

The pattern was unmistakable. Harod and his accomplices would target affluent homes, break in through rear windows when front entrances proved too difficult, and use extreme violence to control their victims. In one case, they had dragged a female resident by her hair before threatening to slit her throat. In another, they had tied up an elderly couple and their cleaning lady during a home invasion that netted substantial cash and valuables.

Most compelling of all, Harod bore a striking resemblance to the composite sketch that Babis had helped create. His physical description matched perfectly—tall, dark-skinned, overweight, and within the estimated age range.

Greek police were convinced they had found Caroline's killer.

For four straight days, Harod was subjected to intense interrogation. Officers worked in shifts, maintaining constant pressure as they demanded answers to the same questions over and over: "How did you get in the house? How did you kill her? Where are your accomplices?"

The interrogation methods were brutal by any standard. Harod was physically restrained and beaten during questioning, treatment that left him concussed and disoriented. But despite the abuse he endured, he maintained his innocence throughout. He had never heard of Caroline Crouch, he insisted. He knew nothing about any murder in Glyka Nera.

When forensic evidence failed to connect Harod to the crime scene, investigators were forced to release him. Three officers were subsequently demoted for their treatment of the suspect, but the investigation continued with renewed urgency.

The case was becoming a national obsession. Media coverage intensified daily as the Greek public demanded answers about who had committed such a heinous crime. The reward money attracted dozens of tips, but none led to viable suspects. Fear spread through affluent neighborhoods as residents realized that if this could happen to the Anagnostopoulos family, it could happen to anyone.

Police expanded their investigation, eventually compiling a list of one hundred potential suspects before narrowing it down to ten hardcore criminals of various nationalities. These were men known for particularly brutal methods—what detectives called the "Red List" of criminals capable of the level of violence seen at the crime scene.

———

Weeks stretched into a month, and still the case remained unsolved. The €300,000 reward went unclaimed despite massive publicity. Public patience began to wear thin as other robberies and burglaries continued throughout Athens, leaving residents terrified that another family would soon face the same nightmare.

A criminologist expressed what many were thinking: "If this was an ordinary burglary, it would have been solved by now. We read that there is no DNA, no fingerprints, that there is little evidence, and yet they seem like amateurs. Something is not right."

But while investigators struggled publicly to identify the killers, they were privately growing suspicious of inconsistencies in the case that didn't fit the profile of a professional robbery gone wrong.

———

The basement window that the intruders had allegedly used to enter the house was extremely small—too small, several investigators believed, for multiple grown men to pass through easily, especially considering Babis's description of one attacker as tall and overweight. The logistics simply didn't make sense.

More puzzling was the complete absence of forensic evidence from the crime scene. Professional criminals might be careful about finger-prints, but the total lack of DNA, hair fibers, or any biological traces was unprecedented in the experience of veteran investigators.

Investigators determined her attack occurred over six minutes. Yet during those minutes of struggle with her attacker, not a single piece of physical evidence was left behind.

Also suspicious was the home security camera, which had been found damaged in the living room. While criminals often steal surveillance equipment entirely, in this case, someone had simply removed the memory card while leaving the device behind. It suggested intimate knowledge of how the system worked—the kind of familiarity that came from living in the house rather than breaking into it.

Digital analysis revealed that the memory card had been removed at 1:20 a.m. on May 11—more than three hours before Babis claimed the break-in had occurred at 4:30 a.m. The timeline made no sense if unknown intruders were responsible.

The most damning evidence came from an unexpected source: Caroline's Apple Watch.

The device had been monitoring her vital signs throughout the night, creating an electronic record of her final hours that told a story dramatically different from her husband's account. At 3:58 a.m., Caroline's heart rate indicated she was in a deep sleep. At 4:05 a.m., her pulse suddenly spiked by more than fifty percent, showing she had awakened in extreme distress. At 4:11 a.m., Caroline Crouch's heart stopped beating forever.

All of this had happened before the time Babis claimed the intruders had even entered their home.

Analysis of Babis's smartphone revealed equally troubling contradictions. A fitness app that automatically tracked physical movement showed he had been active and mobile throughout the house during the exact period when he claimed to be bound, blindfolded, and helpless on the bedroom floor.

Haralambos "Babis" Anagnostopoulos

Furthermore, when investigators attempted to recreate Babis's account of using his nose to dial emergency services while completely restrained, none of them could successfully complete the call. The physical mechanics of the story simply didn't work.

Perhaps most revealing were text messages and digital communications that painted a picture of the Anagnostopoulos marriage that was far different from the fairy tale romance portrayed on social media.

———

On the night of her murder, Caroline had been attempting to book herself and baby Lydia into a hotel room. Messages to friends revealed growing desperation and fear. The perfect couple that had charmed

Greece with their love story was fracturing behind closed doors, and Caroline had been planning to escape.

Thirty-seven days after Caroline Crouch was found dead in her bed, police finally decided to confront the inconsistencies directly.

————

A small memorial service was being held on Alonnisos to mark the completion of traditional Greek mourning periods. As family and friends gathered to remember Caroline one final time, police helicopters appeared on the horizon like mechanical vultures circling the island.

Detectives waited respectfully for the service to conclude before approaching Babis with news that would change everything. Important new information had emerged in the investigation, they told him. A suspect had been identified, and they needed Babis to come to Athens immediately to help with the identification process.

Babis agreed without hesitation. He approached Caroline's mother, Susan, embracing her tearfully as he explained that he needed to leave to help catch his wife's killers. The image of the grieving widower comforting his mother-in-law before boarding a police helicopter would soon become one of the most chilling photographs in Greek criminal history. He had no idea he was flying toward his own reckoning.

At police headquarters in Athens, investigators systematically dismantled the elaborate fiction that had consumed the nation for over a month. For eight hours, they presented evidence piece by piece: the security camera timeline that made no sense, Caroline's Apple Watch data that contradicted every element of his story, his phone's movement records that proved he'd been active when he claimed to be restrained, the complete absence of any forensic evidence from mysterious intruders.

The digital evidence was overwhelming and irrefutable. Every electronic device in the house told the same story—one that bore no resemblance to the home invasion narrative that had captivated Greece and fooled millions of people.

Confronted with this mountain of technological proof, Babis Anagnostopoulos finally broke.

In the early hours of June 18, 2021, the man who had played the grieving widower for thirty-seven days confessed to murdering his nineteen-year-old wife.

The truth was more shocking than anyone could have imagined. There had been no Albanian gang, no professional criminals, no break-in at all. Caroline Crouch had been killed by the man who had promised to love and protect her until death do us part.

The confession revealed a marriage that had been disintegrating for months behind the carefully maintained social media façade. According to Babis, he and Caroline had been fighting constantly as her desire to leave him became increasingly obvious. She had been making plans to escape with their daughter, threatening to destroy the perfect family image he had worked so hard to create.

In his signed statement to police, Babis described the events that led to Caroline's death with chilling matter-of-factness. "That night, we had been fighting since early in the day," he confessed. "At one point, she threw the baby into its bassinet and told me to get up and leave the house. She pushed me and punched me. I blurred and suffocated her, and then I staged the crime scene." His clinical recounting of the murder revealed a man who had crossed an unthinkable line during what he characterized as a domestic dispute, then immediately began calculating how to escape the consequences.

———

As the full scope of Babis's deception became clear, investigators realized they had been witnesses to one of the most elaborate and convincing performances in criminal history. For over a month, he had maintained his role as the traumatized survivor, appearing in media interviews, posting tributes on social media, and even comforting Caroline's grieving parents—all while knowing he was the one responsible for their daughter's death.

The revelation sent shockwaves through Greek society and beyond. Television programming was interrupted to report the stunning confession. Social media exploded with expressions of outrage, disbelief, and betrayal from a public that had invested their sympathy and support in a man who had been lying to them from the very beginning.

———

As investigators pieced together the real story of Caroline's final hours, they uncovered evidence of a young woman who had been trapped in a controlling relationship, desperately seeking escape, and ultimately killed by the man who claimed to love her more than life itself.

During his confession, thirty-three-year-old Babis revealed the calculated steps he had taken to create his elaborate deception. After suffocating Caroline with a pillow as she slept—an attack that lasted nearly five agonizing minutes while their baby lay nearby—he had panicked and constructed an intricate cover-up designed to fool the world.

He had strangled the family's beloved husky, Roxy, with her own leash, hanging her from the banister to make the scene appear more convincing. He had methodically ransacked his own home, scattering belongings to simulate a robbery. Most chillingly, he had placed his crying infant daughter next to her mother's lifeless body before binding himself with rope and duct tape to complete the illusion.

His stated motive for the elaborate charade was protecting their child. He claimed he didn't want his daughter to grow up without either parent, preferring to be seen as a victim rather than to face the consequences of his actions.

———

When Babis Anagnostopoulos finally stood trial in May 2022, nearly a year after Caroline's murder, the courtroom was packed with reporters and members of the public who had followed every twist of the case. He faced charges of premeditated murder, animal abuse, filing false reports, and providing false testimony to authorities.

The prosecution painted a devastating portrait of calculated cruelty. They argued that Babis's actions before, during, and after the murder demonstrated a man in complete control of his faculties—someone who had planned Caroline's death and executed an elaborate cover-up with chilling precision. The removal of the security camera's memory card hours before the killing, the methodical staging of the crime scene, and his ability to maintain the deception for thirty-seven days all pointed to premeditation rather than a crime of passion.

Evidence presented during the trial revealed the true nature of the Anagnostopoulos marriage for the first time. Caroline's private diary entries were read aloud, documenting years of escalating control and manipulation. Her therapist testified that Caroline had confided her desperate desire to escape the relationship, describing Babis as extremely controlling and manipulative—a man who monitored her every movement and kept her financially dependent and isolated.

The most damning testimony came from the couple's counselor, who had met with Caroline and Babis in late 2020. She painted a devastating picture of financial and psychological control that went far beyond typical marital problems. "Her mother would send her money, and he would take it," she testified. "She didn't even have five euros on her." Caroline had dreamed of attending pastry school, but she couldn't afford the tuition because Babis controlled every aspect of their finances. Even her movements outside the house were monitored through a trusted taxi driver friend of Babis, ensuring he always knew her whereabouts. The counselor revealed that from their very first session, Caroline had confided her desperate desire to take baby Lydia and leave the marriage, describing a woman who felt utterly trapped by the man who claimed to love her.

Perhaps most damning was expert psychiatric testimony that diagnosed Babis with severe antisocial personality disorder. The psychiatrist described his complete lack of empathy and his narcissistic inability to understand how his actions affected others, particularly his own daughter.

Babis testified in his own defense for ten hours, showing remarkably little emotion as he recounted the details of killing his wife and staging the elaborate cover-up. He maintained that the murder had not been premeditated, claiming he had acted in a "blurred state of mind" during a heated argument. He portrayed Caroline as unstable and aggressive since becoming a mother, attempting to shift blame even as he sought the court's mercy.

The only crack in Babis's composed demeanor came when Caroline's diary entries were read aloud in court. As the prosecutor recited her words—"I fought with Babi again. This time it was serious. I hit him, I cursed at him and he broke down the door. All I wanted was for him to ask how I am when I woke up. I woke up so weak and tired."—tears finally appeared in his eyes. For a brief moment, the calculating performance faltered, revealing perhaps genuine remorse or simply the recognition that Caroline's own words were damning him from beyond the grave. The tears seemed to validate what the court already knew: Caroline had been desperate, trapped, and afraid in the final months of her life, while the man now crying had been the source of her suffering.

The jury wasn't convinced by his performance. After deliberating, they returned a unanimous verdict of guilty on all charges.

The sentence was severe, reflecting both the brutality of the crimes and the calculated deception that followed. Babis was condemned to life imprisonment for Caroline's murder, with an additional ten years for killing the family dog and eleven years and six months for misleading authorities. Under Greek law, he would not be eligible for parole for at least sixteen years.

He attempted to appeal the conviction in 2023, claiming the murder was not premeditated, but Babis ultimately abandoned the effort and accepted his fate. The appeals court unanimously affirmed the original verdict, ensuring that he would remain imprisoned until at least 2048.

Caroline's parents were awarded custody of little Lydia, who had been found crying beside her mother's body that terrible morning in May 2021. They relocated to the Philippines, where the child could grow up far from the shadow of her father's crimes. Her surname was legally changed from Anagnostopoulos to Crouch, severing the final official link to the man who had destroyed her family.

The murder of Caroline Crouch became a watershed moment in Greek society's understanding of domestic violence and femicide. She was one of seventeen women killed by their romantic partners in Greece that year, and her case sparked national conversations about the hidden epidemic of abuse that too often ended in tragedy.

CHAPTER 9
COUNT TO THREE

The security camera captured it all in grainy black and white—a teenage girl slipping through her bedroom window at 12:30 in the morning, moving across the parking lot with the easy confidence of someone who had done this before. Skylar Neese paused at the edge of the frame, her slight figure illuminated by the apartment complex's dim lighting, before disappearing into the back seat of a waiting sedan.

Within hours, that thirty-second piece of footage would become the most important piece of evidence in a case that would shatter a small West Virginia community and leave investigators grappling with questions they never thought they'd have to ask.

———

July 5, 2012, had been just another summer evening for Skylar Neese. The sixteen-year-old honor student finished her shift at the local Wendy's and returned to the modest apartment she shared with her parents, Dave and Mary, in Star City, just outside Morgantown. At five feet tall with shoulder-length brown hair and an infectious smile,

Skylar was the kind of teenager who lit up a room—bubbly, outgoing, and fiercely loyal to her friends.

Her parents knew their daughter well. She was responsible, never missed work, and despite the typical teenage desire for independence, she rarely stayed out past curfew. When Skylar said goodnight and went to her room that Friday evening, Dave and Mary Neese had no reason to expect anything other than a peaceful night's sleep. They were wrong.

Somewhere around midnight, Skylar's phone buzzed with a text message. The conversation was brief—a friend wanting to meet up for a late-night drive, the kind of spontaneous adventure that seemed perfectly reasonable to a sixteen-year-old on summer break. Skylar had done this before, sneaking out to meet friends for innocent escapades around Morgantown. Her parents, sound asleep in the next room, never heard her quietly push open her bedroom window.

The apartment complex's security camera recorded her descent—Skylar lowering herself carefully from the window, her feet touching the ground with practiced ease. She walked across the parking lot toward a light-colored sedan idling at the edge of the complex. The car's occupants were hidden in shadow, but Skylar moved toward the vehicle without hesitation. These were people she trusted.

She climbed into the back seat, and the car pulled away into the West Virginia night.

It was the last time anyone would see Skylar Neese alive.

———

Saturday morning brought panic. Mary Neese woke to find Skylar's bed empty, her daughter nowhere to be found. The window stood open, screen pushed aside—clear evidence of how Skylar had left. However, this wasn't like her. This wasn't like her at all.

Skylar had left behind her contact lenses, something she never would have done if she'd planned to stay out. Her phone charger sat plugged into the wall. Her work uniform hung ready for her Saturday shift—a shift she would never miss without calling.

Dave Neese's heart sank as the implications hit him. His daughter, his only child, was gone.

The family immediately began calling Skylar's friends, starting with the two girls she was closest to—Shelia Eddy and Rachel Shoaf. The trio had been inseparable for years, calling themselves "The Three Musketeers." If anyone knew where Skylar was, it would be them.

Shelia answered Mary's frantic call with apparent confusion and concern. No, she hadn't seen Skylar since the previous day. She had no idea where she might be. Then she paused as if suddenly remembering something. "Oh wait," Shelia said, "we did pick her up last night around 11:00 p.m. for a drive, but we dropped her off before midnight. I thought she went home after that."

Rachel, reached later that morning, echoed the same story with identical details. Both girls promised to help search for their missing friend.

By evening, when Skylar still hadn't returned home and hadn't contacted anyone, the Neeses made the call that would launch one of West Virginia's most baffling missing person cases.

———

Star City Police responded to the Neeses' frantic call with routine questions and frustrating protocol. Because Skylar had left voluntarily through her bedroom window—caught on camera meeting people she clearly knew—officers classified her as a probable runaway. The designation carried devastating implications: No Amber Alert would be issued. No immediate statewide search would be launched.

"You need to wait forty-eight hours," they told Dave and Mary. "Most teenagers come home on their own."

The Neeses protested vehemently. This wasn't their daughter. Skylar was a responsible girl scheduled to work the next day, and she would never disappear without a word. She had left behind essentials she couldn't function without. Something was terribly wrong.

But policy was policy. Without clear evidence of abduction or immediate danger, law enforcement would treat this as a routine runaway case. The precious first hours—when missing persons are most likely to be found—ticked away while bureaucratic wheels turned slowly.

Dave and Mary refused to wait. They printed missing person flyers and began canvassing the community themselves, showing Skylar's photo to anyone who would look. The security footage confirmed their worst fears—their daughter had gotten into a car with someone, and no one knew who.

————

The security footage became the investigation's first real clue. The grainy video showed Skylar walking confidently toward a waiting sedan, climbing into the back seat without apparent coercion. Police began interviewing her friends and classmates, trying to identify the car and its occupants.

Shelia Eddy and Rachel Shoaf were among the first to be questioned, and their story was detailed and consistent. They had picked up Skylar around 11:00 p.m. for a drive around Morgantown, smoking marijuana and talking about their friendship, which had grown strained in recent weeks. After about an hour, they had dropped her off at the end of her street, watching as she walked back toward her apartment building.

Both girls seemed genuinely distraught about their friend's disappearance. Shelia, who had been close to Skylar since they were eight years old, broke down crying during conversations with Mary Neese. She helped distribute missing person flyers around town, her face etched with worry and grief.

"How could someone do this to Skylar?" Shelia asked through tears, sitting in Skylar's bedroom with Mary. "She's the sweetest person I know."

Rachel appeared more composed but equally concerned. She had Broadway aspirations and was known for her dramatic flair, but her worry seemed genuine. Both girls threw themselves into the search effort, posting on social media and reaching out to classmates for any information about Skylar's whereabouts.

———

As days turned to weeks, investigators began noticing troubling inconsistencies. The surveillance footage clearly showed Skylar leaving at 12:30 a.m., not 11:00 p.m. as the girls claimed. When confronted with this timeline discrepancy, Shelia and Rachel seemed confused but adjusted their story—perhaps they had misremembered the exact time, but their basic account remained the same.

Cell phone records painted a different picture. While the girls claimed they had stayed in the Morgantown area, phone tower data showed their devices had pinged off a tower in Blacksville, nearly thirty miles away, in the early morning hours of July 6. The data placed them in a remote area near the Pennsylvania border—nowhere near where they claimed to have driven.

When confronted with this evidence, both girls initially denied traveling that far from town. Their denials were firm and seemingly sincere, but the digital evidence was irrefutable. Something didn't add up.

The investigation expanded beyond Star City's small police force. In September 2012, the FBI and West Virginia State Police joined the case, bringing additional resources and expertise. The missing person case had grown cold, but investigators refused to give up hope.

State Police Corporal Ronnie Gaskins took a personal interest in the case, promising the Neese family he would not stop searching for their daughter. His persistence would prove crucial in the months ahead as he worked methodically to unravel the web of lies surrounding Skylar's disappearance.

———

As autumn arrived, the pressure on Skylar's two closest friends intensified. Classmates at University High School began whispering about the inconsistencies in their stories. Some students recalled overhearing strange conversations between Shelia and Rachel in the weeks before Skylar's disappearance—offhand comments about "getting rid of" people that had seemed like typical teenage dark humor at the time.

One science teacher even remembered sending the girls to the office after overhearing them discussing something that sounded threatening, though the context hadn't been clear then. Now, those half-remembered conversations took on a more sinister meaning.

The community was divided. Some residents supported the two girls, viewing them as victims of overzealous police work and unfair suspicion. Others whispered darker theories, wondering if Shelia and Rachel knew more than they were admitting. The constant scrutiny was taking its toll on both teenagers.

Rachel, in particular, seemed increasingly stressed. Friends noticed she had grown withdrawn and anxious, jumping at unexpected sounds and avoiding large social gatherings. She continued to post occasionally on social media about missing Skylar, but her messages seemed forced and hollow compared to her earlier desperate pleas for information.

Shelia Eddy & Rachel Shoaf

Shelia, by contrast, appeared remarkably composed for someone whose childhood best friend had vanished. She maintained an active social media presence, posting about schoolwork, television shows, and daily life as if nothing had changed. To investigators, her apparent normalcy seemed almost unnatural, given the circumstances.

———

By late November 2012, the weight of physical evidence was becoming impossible to ignore. Cell phone tower data, surveillance footage from gas stations along their route, and witness statements were building a case that contradicted the girls' story at multiple points.

Under mounting pressure during another police interview, Rachel Shoaf finally broke down and admitted they had lied about their route that night. Yes, she confessed, they had driven to a remote location near Brave, Pennsylvania. But their reason for lying was innocent—

they were afraid of getting in trouble for taking Skylar so far from home to smoke pot.

In this revised version of events, they claimed they had dropped Skylar off at the county line and watched her get into another car with people they didn't recognize. It was a story that explained the cell phone data while maintaining their innocence, but investigators still weren't satisfied.

Too many details continued not to add up. The girls' behavior during questioning struck investigators as rehearsed rather than natural. They seemed more concerned with keeping their stories consistent than with finding their missing friend.

————

December 28, 2012, brought a dramatic and terrifying turn in the case. Rachel Shoaf experienced a severe emotional breakdown at her home, becoming violent and hysterical in a way that shocked her family. She screamed uncontrollably, threatened to harm herself, and appeared to be suffering from a complete psychological collapse.

Her mother, terrified by her daughter's behavior and unable to calm her, called 911. Emergency responders found Rachel in an agitated state, requiring immediate psychiatric intervention. She was transported to a mental health facility, where she remained for several days under professional care.

The hospitalization marked the beginning of the end for the carefully constructed lie that had held for nearly six months. Something had finally broken inside Rachel Shoaf, and the pressure of maintaining her secret was literally driving her to madness.

Upon her release on January 3, 2013, Rachel made a decision that would shock everyone who knew her. Instead of going home to recover, she asked her parents to take her directly to an attorney's office. From there, she contacted Monongalia County authorities and requested an immediate meeting.

———

Corporal Gaskins and other investigators gathered in the attorney's office that January afternoon, expecting another round of revised statements and partial truths. Rachel sat across from them, looking fragile and exhausted from her recent hospitalization. When she spoke, her voice was barely above a whisper.

"We stabbed her."

Her words hung in the air. After months of searching, following false leads, and investigating theories about runaway teenagers and drug-related disappearances, the truth was simpler yet more horrifying than anyone had imagined.

Rachel's story poured out in chilling detail. She and Shelia had planned Skylar's murder for months, driven by a motive that seemed incomprehensible at the time—they simply didn't want to be friends with her anymore. The friendship had grown strained, and rather than dealing with the conflict like normal teenagers, they had chosen a permanent solution.

The confession revealed a level of premeditation that stunned investigators. This wasn't a crime of passion or a tragic accident. It was cold-blooded murder, planned and executed by two sixteen-year-old girls against their supposed best friend.

———

According to Rachel's detailed confession, the murder plot had been brewing for months. The two girls had grown tired of Skylar, viewing her as an obstacle to their own closer friendship. They had discussed various methods of "getting rid of" her, eventually settling on a plan that seemed both simple and foolproof.

They chose a location they knew well—a remote wooded area just across the Pennsylvania state line, where they had gone before to smoke pot with Skylar. It was isolated enough that no one would hear screams, and the interstate boundary would complicate any investigation.

In the days leading up to July 6, Shelia and Rachel prepared meticulously for their crime, putting together what they referred to as a "murder kit." Each girl stole a large kitchen knife from her home, selecting weapons that could be easily concealed. They packed cleaning supplies—paper towels, wet wipes, and bleach—to eliminate evidence. They brought changes of clothes, anticipating they would be covered in blood.

The girls searched the internet for ways to get rid of a body, including the idea of feeding her body to pigs. Instead, they brought a shovel, planning to bury Skylar's body where it would never be found.

The night of July 5, they put their plan into motion. Shelia texted Skylar around midnight, suggesting a late-night drive to talk through their friendship problems. It was exactly the kind of impulsive adventure that appealed to Skylar, and she agreed immediately.

———

The drive to Pennsylvania was tense with anticipation. Skylar, unaware of her friend's intentions, chatted normally as they made their way through the dark country roads. She was excited about the prospect of repairing their strained relationship and had no idea she was traveling to her own execution.

When they reached the wooded area near Blacksville, all three girls got out of the car under the pretense of hanging out and smoking marijuana. The location was perfect for their purposes—completely isolated, surrounded by dense trees, with no chance of being seen or heard.

As they stood in the darkness, Shelia and Rachel positioned themselves on either side of their unsuspecting friend. They had agreed on a signal earlier—a count to three. When Rachel reached "three," they planned to strike simultaneously, giving Skylar no chance to escape or defend herself.

The moment stretched endlessly. Skylar stood between her two best friends, trusting them completely, having no idea that knives were hidden in their clothing just inches away.

"One," Rachel began counting, her voice steady despite her racing heart.

"Two."

Skylar turned slightly, perhaps sensing something wrong in her friend's tone.

"Three."

————

The assault was swift and vicious. Both girls pulled their concealed knives from beneath their hoodies and began stabbing Skylar repeatedly. In her confession, Rachel told detectives they lost count after they had stabbed her at least fifty times. Their months of planning culminated in an intense explosion of violence. Their friend, caught completely off guard, stumbled backward with the first blows, crying out in pain and confusion.

"Why?" Skylar gasped, the single word cutting through the night air as she realized what was happening to her.

Despite being outnumbered and caught by surprise, Skylar fought desperately for her life. In the struggle, she managed to wrest one knife away from Rachel and wounded her attacker in the leg, drawing blood and proving that she wouldn't die without a fight.

But two against one in the darkness were hopeless odds. The attack continued with relentless brutality as Skylar's strength faded. Her cries for help echoed uselessly through the empty woods, heard by no one except her killers.

When it was over, silence returned to the Pennsylvania forest. Two sixteen-year-old girls stood over the body of their friend, breathing heavily, covered in blood, and facing the reality of what they had just done.

————

With Skylar dead at their feet, Shelia and Rachel immediately set about concealing their crime. They had planned for this moment, bringing supplies they hoped would eliminate any evidence linking them to the murder.

They had intended to bury the body, but the rocky Pennsylvania soil proved impossible to dig in the darkness. After several futile attempts that left them exhausted and frustrated, they abandoned the burial plan and opted for a simpler solution.

Working together, they dragged Skylar's body deeper into the woods, away from the road where it might be discovered by passing motorists. They found a fallen log and positioned the corpse beside it, then covered it with branches, leaves, and debris they gathered from the forest floor. In the darkness, their camouflage work seemed adequate—the body was hidden from casual view.

Using the cleaning supplies they had packed, they methodically wiped down their murder weapons and cleaned blood from their hands and faces. They shed their blood-soaked clothes and stuffed them into garbage bags, changing into the fresh outfits they had brought for this purpose. The transformation was remarkable—within hours, they looked like normal teenagers again.

The cleanup took most of the night. They wiped any fingerprints from the car's interior, disposed of the murder weapons and bloody clothing in separate locations during the drive home, and rehearsed their alibi story until it sounded natural and believable.

As dawn broke on July 6, Shelia Eddy and Rachel Shoaf drove back to Star City. They had committed what they believed was the perfect crime. Their friend was dead, hidden in the Pennsylvania woods where she would never be found, and they had an explanation for Skylar's disappearance that would satisfy any investigation.

———

What followed was a six-month masterclass in deception that would have impressed career criminals. Both girls threw themselves into the search effort with apparent dedication and genuine emotion. They distributed flyers, comforted Skylar's distraught parents, and maintained active social media profiles that showed no hint of guilt or knowledge about their friend's fate.

Shelia's performance was particularly chilling in its authenticity. She cried with Mary Neese in Skylar's bedroom, asking how anyone could hurt such a sweet person. She attended vigils and search parties, her face a mask of concern and grief. She even helped organize fundraising efforts for the search, appearing on local television to plead for information about her missing friend.

On social media, Shelia posted regular messages about missing Skylar and hoping for her safe return. Her tweets seemed heartfelt and desperate, peppered with inside jokes and memories that demonstrated their close friendship. To anyone monitoring her accounts, she appeared to be a devoted friend desperate for answers.

Rachel, though more visibly affected by stress, also maintained the pretense convincingly. She attended church camp shortly after the murder, apparently able to compartmentalize what she had done enough to function normally around other teenagers and adult counselors. When questioned by investigators, she displayed appropriate emotion and provided consistent details about their last night with Skylar.

Both girls returned to their normal teenage routines—attending school, hanging out with friends, and posting on social media as if nothing had changed in their lives. Their ability to maintain normalcy while hiding such a devastating secret spoke to a level of psychological detachment that disturbed investigators.

———

Rachel's January confession gave investigators exactly what they needed—not just an admission of guilt, but specific information about where to find Skylar's body. On January 16, 2013, a team of state police and FBI agents followed Rachel's detailed directions to the remote woods in Wayne Township, Pennsylvania.

Six months of exposure to Pennsylvania weather had taken a devastating toll. What investigators found bore little resemblance to the vibrant teenager who had climbed out of her bedroom window the previous July. Skylar's remains lay exactly where Rachel said they would be, still covered by the same branches and leaves her killers had used to conceal their crime.

The medical examiner's report would later reveal the full extent of the violence inflicted on Skylar Neese. Her body bore more than fifty separate stab wounds, many of them inflicted after she was already dying or dead. The sheer number of injuries spoke to a frenzy of violence that went far beyond what was necessary to kill their victim.

Many of the wounds were defensive, showing that Skylar had fought desperately for her life despite being outnumbered and caught by surprise. The medical examiner determined that she had lived for several minutes after the initial attack, conscious and aware as her life ebbed away in the Pennsylvania woods.

The discovery brought a devastating end to the Neese family's hope that their daughter might still be alive somewhere. It took two months for forensic analysis to officially confirm the identity of the remains through DNA testing, finally giving Dave and Mary Neese the closure they had desperately sought, despite confirming their worst fears.

———

The most disturbing glimpse into Shelia's psyche came in the form of a Twitter post that would later send chills down investigators' spines. On March 30, 2013—just weeks after Skylar's body had been discovered and identified—Shelia posted a cryptic message that seemed to mock the very crime she had committed: "we really did go on three." To casual observers, the tweet appeared meaningless, perhaps referencing some inside joke or teenage drama. But investigators who knew the details of Rachel's confession understood its sinister meaning. It was an apparent reference to the countdown that had preceded Skylar's murder—the signal that had marked the beginning of the end for their unsuspecting friend. The fact that Shelia would brazenly reference their crime on social media, even in coded language, demonstrated a level of callousness that shocked investigators. It was as if she couldn't resist leaving a breadcrumb trail of her guilt, confident that no one would understand the true meaning behind her words.

———

With Rachel's confession and the discovery of Skylar's body, law enforcement moved quickly to close the case. On May 1, 2013, Rachel Shoaf formally pleaded guilty to second-degree murder in exchange for her cooperation with prosecutors. That same day, Shelia Eddy was arrested in the parking lot of a Cracker Barrel restaurant in Morgantown, finally ending her months-long charade of innocence.

The arrests sent shockwaves through the University High School community and beyond. Students and teachers struggled to process the reality that two popular, seemingly normal classmates had murdered a third in cold blood. The case challenged every assumption about teenage behavior and female violence.

Shelia initially pleaded not guilty to first-degree murder charges, maintaining her innocence even after Rachel's confession had exposed their plot. However, as her trial date approached in early 2014, the weight of evidence became impossible to deny. On January 24, 2014, she changed her plea to guilty, accepting a sentence of life in prison with the possibility of parole after fifteen years.

Rachel Shoaf received thirty years in prison for second-degree murder, with eligibility for parole after ten years. Her cooperation with investigators and apparent remorse earned her the lesser charge, though both girls would spend their young adult years behind bars for their inexplicable crime.

———

For years, the question of why two teenagers would murder their friend remained largely unanswered. Rachel's initial explanation—that they "didn't want to be friends with her anymore"—seemed woefully inadequate to explain such brutal premeditation.

The truth emerged only in 2023, during Rachel's first parole hearing. After more than a decade of speculation, she finally revealed the deeper motive that had driven her and Shelia to murder. Rachel and Shelia had been involved in a romantic relationship, a secret they desperately wanted to keep hidden in their conservative West Virginia community.

Skylar had discovered their relationship during a sleepover in 2011, witnessing intimate behavior between her two friends. As their friendship deteriorated in 2012, Skylar had threatened to expose their secret, creating what felt like an impossible situation for the two teenagers.

Rather than face potential ostracism, family rejection, or social humiliation, they chose murder as their solution. It was a decision that destroyed not just Skylar's life, but their own futures and countless other lives in the process.

———

For Dave and Mary Neese, the resolution of their daughter's case brought justice but no peace. They had lost their only child to people they had trusted most—girls they had considered part of their family. The betrayal cut almost as deeply as the loss itself.

The couple channeled their grief into advocacy work, determined that Skylar's death would serve a purpose in protecting other children. Their efforts led to the passage of "Skylar's Law" in West Virginia, which requires law enforcement to issue Amber Alerts for missing children even when they are initially suspected of being runaways.

They also established "Skylar's Promise," an initiative encouraging young people to speak up when they see or hear something wrong. Through school visits and speaking engagements, they share their daughter's story and emphasize the importance of breaking the code of silence when someone's safety is at risk.

CHAPTER 10
THE PINK NOTEBOOK

The 911 call came in at 10:43 p.m. on December 13, 2001. The voice on the other end was breathless, shaking.

"I need help. I shot someone. There were two men in my house."

Tracey Richter's words tumbled over each other as she spoke to the dispatcher from her home in Early, Iowa—a town so small that everyone knew everyone, and where the biggest excitement usually centered around Friday night football games and the annual corn festival. Tonight was different.

"Ma'am, are you injured? Are the intruders still in the house?"

"No, one of them ran. The other one... he's dead. I had to shoot him. He was trying to kill me and my children."

When Deputy Sheriff Randy Weise arrived at the modest two-story house on Highway 20, he found Tracey sitting on her front steps, a gun still in her hand. Red marks circled her neck like a crude necklace. Her wrists showed similar markings. Three small children huddled behind her—an eleven-year-old boy, a toddler, and a baby still in diapers.

"He strangled me with pantyhose," Tracey told the deputy, her voice hoarse. "I passed out. When I came to, I had to get to my gun safe. I had to protect my babies."

Inside the house, Deputy Weise found a haunting scene. In the master bedroom, a young man lay motionless on the carpeted floor, surrounded by a constellation of blood spatter. Nine bullet wounds marked his body. Three of them were clustered at the back of his head and neck.

The dead man was twenty-year-old Dustin Wehde, a neighbor who lived just down the road with his mother, Mona. Everyone in Early knew Dustin—the quiet, awkward boy who spent his days tinkering with computers and struggling to fit in as part of a world that seemed to move too fast around him.

But what was Dustin Wehde doing in Tracey Richter's bedroom at nearly eleven o'clock at night?

————

Three years earlier, Tracey Ann Richter had arrived in Early like a breath of fresh air in the stagnant Iowa town. She was beautiful, sophisticated, and carried herself with the confidence of someone who had seen more of the world than most locals ever would. With her second husband, Michael Roberts, she had purchased a house and started a small computer business.

Tracey brought complexity to a simple place. She had already been married once before to Dr. John Pitman III, a plastic surgeon from Virginia. That marriage had ended in 1996 with the kind of bitter custody battle that left scars on everyone involved. Tracey had accused Pitman of sexually abusing their son, Bert—allegations that were later discredited, but which poisoned their relationship permanently.

The divorce proceedings had been particularly nasty. During one heated argument in Colorado in 1992, Tracey had actually fired a gun at Pitman. No one was hurt, but Pitman's attorney described her as diabolical.

Now, in 2001, Tracey was locked in another custody dispute with her ex-husband. A court hearing was scheduled for early 2002, with Pitman seeking custody of eleven-year-old Bert while paying $1,000 monthly in child support. The legal bills were mounting, and Tracey needed every advantage she could get.

Michael Roberts had tried to help by befriending some of the local young men, including Dustin Wehde. Michael occasionally hired Dustin for odd jobs around their computer business, mostly out of kindness. Dustin's mother, Mona, had been the real estate agent who helped them find their house, and the families had developed a neighborly relationship.

Tracey, however, was less enthusiastic about Dustin's visits. She found him socially awkward and preferred that Michael be present whenever the young man came around. There was something about Dustin that made her uncomfortable, though she could never quite articulate what.

———

On the evening of December 13, Michael Roberts was out of town on business, leaving Tracey alone with their three children. The house felt different when Michael was away—larger somehow, full of shadows and unfamiliar sounds.

Tracey was upstairs giving Mason, her one-year-old daughter, a bath when she heard the first sound. A door opening. Footsteps on the hardwood floor below.

"Hello?" she called out. "Michael?"

No answer.

She wrapped Mason in a towel and stepped onto the landing. The house was dark except for the bathroom light behind her. She could hear voices now—two men talking in low, urgent tones.

Her heart began to race. She thrust Mason into the arms of eleven-year-old Bert and whispered, "Stay in your room. Lock the door."

According to Tracey's account to the police, what happened next was a parent's worst nightmare. Two men appeared at the bottom of the stairs. One of them, whom she recognized as Dustin Wehde, was carrying a baseball bat. The other man remained in the shadows.

"Where's the safe?" one of them demanded.

Tracey tried to reason with them, but Dustin allegedly lunged forward with a pair of pantyhose, looping them around her neck. The nylon bit into her skin as he pulled tight. The world began to go gray around the edges.

She fought back, clawing at his hands, gasping for air. Somehow, she managed to break free and stumble toward her bedroom. Behind her, she could hear one of the men threatening Bert through his locked door.

The gun safe was in her bedroom closet. Tracey fumbled with the combination. The numbers seemed to dance before her eyes, but muscle memory guided her fingers. The heavy door swung open, revealing her husband's collection of firearms.

She grabbed the first gun she could reach—a .22 caliber revolver—and spun around just as Dustin appeared in the doorway. In the darkness, she could barely make out his silhouette.

"Please don't hurt my children," she whispered.

The shot was deafeningly loud in the enclosed space. Then another. And another.

When the gunfire stopped, Dustin Wehde lay motionless on her bedroom floor. The second intruder had vanished.

———

In the immediate aftermath, Tracey Richter was hailed as a hero. Local newspapers praised the brave mother who had defended her children against armed intruders. The story resonated across Iowa and beyond—here was a woman who had done what any parent would do when faced with the unthinkable.

She appeared on The Montel Williams Show in 2002, receiving applause as she recounted the harrowing incident. The audience was captivated by her composure and strength in the face of trauma.

But beneath the surface, questions began to emerge.

———

Lieutenant Dennis Cessford of the Sac County Sheriff's Department was one of the first investigators on the scene. He had seen plenty of break-ins in his career, but something about this one didn't sit right. There were no signs of forced entry, no broken windows, and no splintered door frames. The house was undisturbed except for the bedroom where Dustin had died.

Most puzzling was what they found in Dustin's car, parked boldly in the Roberts' driveway. On the front seat sat an old desktop computer —a clunky model that Mona Wehde would later describe as "a piece of junk"—and a pink spiral notebook.

The notebook contained entries written in Dustin's distinctive hand-writing. As investigators read through the pages, their confusion deepened. The entries described a bizarre plot: A mysterious man named "JP" had allegedly hired Dustin to kill Tracey and her son Bert, making their murders look like a murder-suicide.

Tracey Richter

The initials "JP" corresponded to John Pitman—Tracey's ex-husband. The notebook even contained Pitman's phone number and the name of his attorney.

The discovery should have been the break investigators needed. Here was evidence of a murder-for-hire plot, a motive that explained everything. However, instead of providing answers, the notebook only raised more questions.

How had Dustin Wehde—a socially awkward young man with no criminal history—gotten involved with Tracey's ex-husband? Why would a successful plastic surgeon who lived more than 1,000 miles away in Virginia recruit a small-town Iowa boy for such a scheme? And perhaps most troubling of all, why did the notebook's contents seem almost too convenient?

Detective Randy Weise made a crucial decision. The contents of the pink notebook would remain secret, known only to a handful of investigators. As he explained to his colleagues, "Whoever knew about this notebook was involved in what happened here."

————

Dr. John Pitman III learned about the shooting from a phone call that came in the middle of his workday. His ex-wife had killed someone in Iowa, and he was implicated in a murder plot.

Pitman was stunned. He had never even heard of Dustin Wehde, let alone hired him to kill anyone. Phone records, travel logs, and multiple witnesses confirmed that Pitman had been in Virginia on December 13, working at his practice, nowhere near Iowa.

When investigators interviewed him, Pitman's bewilderment seemed genuine. His attorney, Stephen Komie, was more direct: "This has Tracey's fingerprints all over it. She's done this kind of thing before."

The investigation stalled. With Pitman cleared and no evidence of a second intruder, the case grew cold. The small-town sheriff's department lacked the resources to pursue the complex forensic analysis that might have provided answers. In the shadow of 9/11, priorities had shifted, and the Dustin Wehde case gradually faded from active investigation.

For Mona Wehde, the mother of the dead boy, the official story never made sense. She knew her son. Dustin was shy, gentle, and more interested in computer programming than violence. He had never owned a gun, never been in trouble with the law. The idea that he would attempt a home invasion—especially against someone he knew —was absurd.

"Dustin parked right in their driveway," she told anyone who would listen. "What kind of burglar does that?"

But her voice was just one among many, and in the months that followed, some believed that Tracey Richter had gotten away with the perfect crime.

———

Years passed. Tracey's marriage to Michael Roberts began to deteriorate under the strain of the shooting and its aftermath. The couple separated in 2004, launching another bitter custody battle— this time over their two young children.

It was during this period that cracks began to appear in Tracey's carefully constructed narrative.

———

Mary Higgins had been a friend of Tracey's, someone she trusted with her deepest secrets. In early 2002, just months after the shooting, Tracey had mentioned something that made Higgins uncomfortable.

"The police found a notebook in Dustin's car," Tracey had said casually, as if discussing the weather. "It proves my ex-husband was behind everything. John's going to be arrested soon."

Higgins was puzzled. She hadn't heard anything about a notebook.

But it was a conversation a few months later that truly alarmed Mary Higgins. Tracey had called her out of the blue with an urgent warning.

"Forget everything I told you about that pink notebook," Tracey said. "Just forget it ever existed."

The call left Higgins shaken. Why would Tracey want her to forget about evidence that supposedly proved her innocence?

———

Michael Roberts was having his own doubts. As he reflected on the events of December 13, 2001, troubling details emerged. It had been his idea to take the business trip that night—a trip that conveniently placed him far from Early when the shooting occurred. However, the timing now seemed too perfect, too convenient. Had Tracey somehow influenced his decision without him realizing it?

Other actions from that period also took on new meaning under scrutiny. Shortly after Dustin's death, Michael had given his employee, Ray Friedman, a $5,000 bonus and a $20,000 raise. At the time, it had seemed like a generous gesture for a job well done during a difficult period. Now, Michael wondered: Had Tracey manipulated him into making those payments as well? Was there some purpose he hadn't understood?

The more Michael examined his wife's behavior, the more convinced he became that he had been used as an unwitting pawn in a larger scheme. Had Tracey orchestrated not just Dustin's death but every detail surrounding it, including ensuring Michael's convenient absence? In 2005, Michael contacted law enforcement with his concerns. The man who had once stood by his wife's story was now urging investigators to take another look at the evidence.

———

In 2008, Special Agent Trent Vileta of Iowa's Division of Criminal Investigation received an assignment that would change everything. He was tasked with taking a fresh look at the Dustin Wehde case, applying new forensic techniques and investigative methods to evidence that had sat dormant for seven years.

Vileta was immediately troubled by what he found. The original investigation had accepted Tracey's account largely at face value, but a more skeptical examination revealed disturbing inconsistencies.

The crime scene itself told a story that contradicted Tracey's version of events. Despite her claims of a violent struggle, furniture remained undisturbed. The pantyhose allegedly used to strangle her showed no signs of the wear and tear that would be expected from a life-or-death fight.

Most damning was the forensic analysis of the shooting itself. Using advanced ballistics and blood spatter techniques, investigators recreated the sequence of events in Tracey's bedroom. The results were shocking.

The trajectory of the bullets and the pattern of blood evidence indicated that Dustin had been shot while lying face-down on the floor, not while lunging at Tracey in the dark. Congealed blood on his face suggested that some of the wounds had been inflicted after a significant delay—possibly several minutes.

Rod Englert, a renowned bloodstain pattern expert, examined the evidence and reached a chilling conclusion: This was not self-defense; this was an execution.

"The last shots were fired into the back of his head while he was already down," Englert explained. "The blood patterns show he was motionless when those final bullets entered his skull."

The forensic evidence painted a picture of cold-blooded murder, but investigators still needed to connect Tracey to the fabricated notebook directly. That connection came from an unexpected source.

———

In 2009, investigators re-interviewed Mary Higgins, pressing her for details about her conversations with Tracey. This time, Higgins was ready to tell the complete truth.

She described how Tracey had displayed an unsettling lack of emotion when discussing Dustin's death, recounting the shooting "like she was reading a grocery list." But most importantly, Higgins revealed Tracey's detailed knowledge of the pink notebook's contents —information that had never been made public.

"She knew exactly what was in that diary," Higgins told investigators. "She described the murder-for-hire plot, mentioned John Pitman by name, even knew about the phone numbers. The only way she could know those details was if she had written them herself—or forced Dustin to write them."

For the first time, investigators had direct evidence linking Tracey to the notebook. The case that had seemed impossible to solve was finally coming together.

Ben Smith, the newly elected Sac County Attorney, made the decision to convene a grand jury. On August 5, 2011—nearly ten years after Dustin Wehde's death—Tracey Ann Richter was formally charged with first-degree murder.

————

The trial began on October 26, 2011, in Webster County District Court. Due to pretrial publicity in the small community of Early, the proceedings had been moved to Fort Dodge, where a jury of six men and six women would decide Tracey's fate.

Prosecutor Douglas Hammerand presented the state's case with methodical precision. This was not self-defense, he argued, but a carefully orchestrated murder designed to frame an innocent man.

"Tracey Richter lured Dustin Wehde to her home on the night of December 13, 2001," Hammerand told the jury. "She forced him to write entries in that pink notebook, creating a fake murder-for-hire plot. When her plan was interrupted by an unexpected visitor, she killed Dustin to keep him quiet."

The prosecution's timeline was compelling. Marie Friedman, a family friend, had arrived at Tracey's house unexpectedly around 6:30 p.m. on December 13. She found Dustin leaving the house at the same time, which contradicted Tracey's claim that he had arrived unan-nounced later that evening.

Marie had stayed for about an hour, during which time Tracey had seemed nervous and distracted. When Marie left around 7:30 p.m., prosecutors argued, Tracey called Dustin back to finish what they had started, then killed him to ensure his silence.

The forensic evidence was devastating to Tracey's defense. Ballistics expert Rod Englert testified that the blood patterns and bullet trajec-tories proved Dustin had been shot execution-style, not during a struggle. The nine shots that hit him—out of only ten fired—demon-strated an accuracy that would be nearly impossible for someone firing "blindly in the dark," as Tracey claimed.

Perhaps most powerfully, prosecutors presented the pink notebook itself. Reading from its pages, they showed how the entries were clearly fabricated—too convenient, too detailed, containing informa-tion that only someone close to Tracey would know.

"This notebook is a work of fiction," Hammerand declared. "It was created for one purpose: to destroy John Pitman and win Tracey's custody battle."

———

Scott Bandstra, Tracey's defense attorney, faced an uphill battle. His strategy was to convince the jury that the original story was true—that Dustin Wehde and an unknown accomplice had indeed invaded Tracey's home with violent intent.

The defense portrayed Dustin as a troubled young man with mental health issues and a capacity for unpredictable behavior. Ray Friedman testified that he had found Dustin "deeply disturbed" during their limited interactions, even warning others to stay away from him.

But the defense's most dramatic moment came when Bert Pitman, now twenty-one years old, took the stand to support his mother's account. Bert had been eleven at the time of the shooting, and his testimony was emotional and detailed.

He described hearing his mother scream for help, the awful choking sounds from the hallway, and a man threatening him through his bedroom door. According to Bert, when his mother finally opened his door after the shooting, she had guns in both hands and pantyhose around her wrists.

"I saw Dustin start to move," Bert testified. "Mom told him to stay down, but he kept moving. That's when she fired the last shots."

Under cross-examination, however, prosecutors revealed that Bert's 2011 testimony contained details that had been absent from his 2001 police interview as an eleven-year-old boy. The implication was clear: His memory had been influenced by years of hearing his mother's version of events.

The defense also attempted to cast suspicion on Michael Roberts, suggesting that Tracey's second husband might have orchestrated the attack. They pointed to the suspicious timing of his business trip and the generous bonuses he had given to employees shortly after the shooting.

But these alternative theories felt desperate, lacking the evidence needed to create reasonable doubt.

———

After nearly two weeks of testimony, the case went to the jury on November 4, 2011. The twelve jurors deliberated for hours, weighing Tracey's claims of self-defense against the prosecution's allegations of premeditated murder.

On November 7, they reached their verdict. Guilty.

Tracey Richter buried her face in her arms and sobbed as the words echoed through the courtroom. The woman who had once been hailed as a hero was now a convicted murderer, facing life in prison without the possibility of parole.

For Mona Wehde, who had fought for years to clear her son's name, the verdict brought a measure of peace. Dustin was no longer remembered as an intruder but as a victim. A young man whose life had been cut short by someone he trusted.

"My son was not a criminal," she said outside the courthouse. "He was just a boy who got caught up in someone else's lies."

———

On December 5, 2011, Tracey Ann Richter was sentenced to life in prison without the possibility of parole. The judge noted her "years of fraudulent and dangerous behavior," referencing not just Dustin's murder but the pattern of deception that had characterized her adult life.

Tracey's appeals were unsuccessful. The Iowa Court of Appeals upheld her conviction in 2013, finding that the evidence overwhelmingly supported the jury's verdict. The court noted that there was "substantial evidence" proving the killing was not justified self-defense but premeditated murder.

The case had taken nearly a decade to resolve, but finally, justice had been served. Dustin Wehde's name was cleared, John Pitman was vindicated, and Tracey Richter was behind bars, where she could no longer manipulate and deceive.

———

The small town of Early, Iowa, struggled to come to terms with what had happened in their midst. For years, they had celebrated Tracey Richter as a hero, never suspecting that the real monster was hiding in plain sight.

But perhaps the most profound impact was on the families involved. Dustin Wehde's memory was restored. His mother could finally grieve for her son without the stigma of believing he had been a criminal. The truth, however painful, was better than living with a lie.

Michael Roberts, who had unknowingly been married to a killer, gained custody of his children and tried to rebuild their lives away from the shadow of their mother's crimes. He spoke of forgiveness, even for Tracey, hoping that she might someday find redemption behind prison walls.

As for Tracey Richter herself, she continues to maintain her innocence from her cell in an Iowa correctional facility. She insists that she was the victim of a home invasion, that she acted in self-defense, and that the justice system failed her.

CHAPTER 11
BAIL GRANTED

Andrew David Bagby had finally found his calling. At twenty-eight, the California-born doctor was thriving in his family medicine residency at Latrobe Area Hospital in Pennsylvania. Just four months into the program, he'd already made an indelible impression on colleagues and patients alike. His infectious laugh echoed through the hospital corridors, and his genuine compassion for patients set him apart from other residents.

The path to Latrobe hadn't been straightforward. After earning his medical degree at Memorial University in St. John's, Newfoundland, Andrew initially pursued a residency in surgery in Syracuse, New York. However, something about surgery felt wrong—too detached, too clinical. He craved the personal connections that family medicine offered.

His parents, David and Kathleen Bagby, had watched their only son struggle with that decision from their home in Sunnyvale, California. When Andrew called to tell them about the family medicine opportunity in Latrobe, they could hear the excitement in his voice for the first time in months. Pennsylvania felt like a fresh start.

The small town of Latrobe welcomed Andrew immediately. He rented a modest apartment, bought a black Toyota Corolla, and threw himself into his work. His supervisors marveled at how quickly he'd adapted, how naturally he connected with patients who often requested him specifically for follow-up appointments.

However, beneath Andrew's professional success lay a personal struggle of which few of his new colleagues were aware. His romantic life had been turbulent for the past two years, dominated by a complicated relationship with a woman from his medical school days—a relationship that was becoming increasingly difficult to escape.

———

Shirley Jane Turner entered Andrew's life during his third year at Memorial University in 1998. Nearly twelve years his senior, she was a fellow medical student who carried herself with an intensity that both attracted and unsettled those around her. Born in Newfoundland but raised partly in Kansas, Shirley had a complex history that included two failed marriages and three children she'd largely left in the care of others while pursuing her medical degree.

At first, Andrew had been drawn to Shirley's intelligence and ambition. However, as their relationship deepened, troubling patterns emerged. Shirley demanded constant attention, became jealous of Andrew's friendships, and flew into rages when she felt he wasn't giving her enough focus.

Friends who knew Andrew before Shirley noticed changes in him. The carefree young man who'd once been the center of every social gathering became more withdrawn, more anxious. Phone calls from Shirley could derail his entire day, leaving him emotionally drained and distracted.

The relationship continued even after Andrew graduated and moved to Syracuse, New York, for his surgical residency. Shirley remained in Newfoundland to complete her degree, and the distance seemed to intensify her possessiveness rather than diminish it. She would call him at all hours, demanding to know where and with whom he was.

After completing her medical degree in 1998, Shirley struggled to find her professional footing. Her residency supervisors in Newfoundland noted concerning behavior—she became hostile when criticized, manipulative when caught in lies, and showed an alarming lack of empathy in patient interactions.

By 2000, Shirley had secured a position in Council Bluffs, Iowa, putting even more distance between her and Andrew. Unfortunately, distance only seemed to fuel her obsession. She would drive or fly to see him during his residency, showing up unannounced and creating scenes that embarrassed Andrew in front of his colleagues.

When Andrew made the decision to switch to family medicine and move to Pennsylvania in 2001, Shirley's behavior escalated dramatically. She saw his new start as a threat to their relationship and began calling him multiple times a day, often screaming accusations and demands through the phone.

As autumn arrived in Latrobe, Andrew was beginning to flourish professionally and personally. He'd made new friends among the hospital staff and had grown close to a female colleague who appreciated his humor and dedication. For the first time in months, he seemed genuinely happy.

Shirley Turner was watching from afar, and she didn't like what she saw.

————

In Council Bluffs, Iowa, Shirley Turner was spiraling. Her medical practice was struggling, her colleagues found her difficult to work with, and her long-distance relationship with Andrew was clearly deteriorating. She could sense him pulling away, building a new life that didn't include her.

In October 2001, Shirley made a series of decisions that would later take on chilling significance. She purchased a Phoenix Arms .22 caliber pistol, claiming she needed protection as a single woman living alone. She enrolled in shooting lessons at a local gun range, spending hours learning to handle the weapon with increasing proficiency.

Her behavior became more erratic as the month progressed. She called Andrew at work, disrupting his patient care with emotional outbursts and accusations. She'd discovered that Andrew had been spending time with a female colleague, and her jealousy consumed her thoughts.

Shirley began researching Andrew's new life in Pennsylvania with obsessive detail. She found his home address, learned his work schedule, and even identified the woman she viewed as her romantic rival. She printed out driving directions from Iowa to Pennsylvania and studied maps of the Latrobe area.

As October turned to November, Shirley made a desperate decision. She decided to fly to Pennsylvania to confront Andrew in person, to force him to choose between his new life and their relationship. The visit was a disaster from the start. They fought constantly—about his new friends, his female colleague, and his apparent happiness without her.

Finally, Andrew reached his breaking point. On November 3, 2001, he formally ended their relationship. The conversation was painful but necessary. He told Shirley that he couldn't continue living under the constant stress and emotional manipulation.

To ensure a clean break, Andrew drove Shirley to the airport on November 4 and personally escorted her to her flight back to Iowa. As he watched her plane taxi away from the gate, he felt a weight lifting from his shoulders for the first time in months.

That night, Andrew slept better than he had in weeks.

———

Shirley Turner's flight back to Iowa landed in the early afternoon of November 4, 2001. She was seething with rage and humiliation. Andrew had actually gone through with it—he'd ended their relationship and literally put her on a plane like an unwanted visitor.

From the airport, she drove to her apartment in Council Bluffs and immediately began calling Andrew's number. Each time the call went to voicemail, her fury intensified. Around 1:00 p.m., Shirley made a decision that would seal both their fates. She loaded her .22 caliber pistol and a full case of ammunition into her Toyota RAV4. She grabbed the printed MapQuest directions from Iowa to Pennsylvania that she'd prepared weeks earlier, and she began driving east.

The journey from Council Bluffs to Latrobe spanned nearly 950 miles —driving straight through would take approximately sixteen hours, but Shirley wasn't planning to stop for rest.

———

Andrew Bagby was getting ready for work on the morning of November 5 when he heard a knock at his door. Looking through the peephole, he was stunned to see Shirley Turner standing on his doorstep. She looked disheveled and exhausted, her eyes red-rimmed from crying and a lack of sleep.

She was agitated, speaking rapidly about their relationship and demanding another chance. Andrew tried to remain calm while mentally calculating his options. After several tense minutes, Shirley seemed to calm down slightly. She begged Andrew to meet with her that evening after his shift, pleading for one final conversation. Against every instinct screaming at him to refuse, Andrew agreed.

When Andrew arrived at Latrobe Hospital that morning, his distress was obvious to everyone around him. Dr. Clark Simpson, the chief resident and one of Andrew's closest friends, pulled him aside to ask what was wrong.

Andrew explained that Shirley had returned unexpectedly and that he'd agreed to meet with her after work. Simpson was immediately alarmed.

"Don't meet her alone," Simpson urged. "Something's not right about this."

But Andrew shook his head. He believed he could handle Shirley, that his compassion and reason could reach whatever part of her was still rational. He promised Simpson that he'd be careful and that he'd stop by Simpson's house later that evening after the meeting.

"I'll call you when it's over," Andrew assured his friend. "Don't worry. I can handle this."

At 5:30 p.m., Andrew finished his shift and walked to his car in the hospital parking lot, steeling himself for what he hoped would be his final conversation with Shirley Turner.

———

While Andrew worked his shift on November 5, Shirley Turner spent the day in his apartment. Using his computer, she logged into her personal email accounts and even made a phone call to her workplace in Iowa to report herself sick. She was methodically covering her tracks while preparing for the evening ahead.

As evening approached, Shirley drove to Keystone State Park in nearby Derry Township. The park, about fifteen miles from Latrobe, offered secluded areas around a small lake. In November, with the weather growing cold and the daylight hours shortened, the park would be largely deserted after sunset.

When Andrew arrived at the meeting location, he found Shirley waiting beside her RAV4 in the parking area near Keystone Lake. A local resident driving through the area around 6:00 p.m. noticed Andrew's black Toyota Corolla parked next to a Toyota RAV4 in the otherwise empty lot.

What happened next unfolded with shocking brutality. At some point during their encounter, Shirley Turner drew her .22 caliber pistol and opened fire on Andrew at close range. She shot him five times—once in the face, once in the chest, once in the back of the head, and twice in the buttocks. She also pistol-whipped him with the gun itself, causing severe blunt-force trauma to his head.

Andrew fell behind his car, his body coming to rest face down on the cold asphalt. He was still wearing his blue hospital scrubs and ID badge from his shift that day. During the violence, Shirley's pistol ejected a live .22 caliber cartridge—the same malfunction her shooting instructor had observed weeks earlier. The unspent round fell near Andrew's body, providing crucial evidence that would later link her to the crime scene.

After confirming that Andrew was dead, Shirley got back into her vehicle and drove away, leaving his body in the park's remote parking area. By the time early morning dog walkers discovered Andrew's remains on November 6, she was already hundreds of miles away, racing back toward Iowa.

———

The discovery of Andrew Bagby's body sent shockwaves through the Latrobe medical community. When he failed to show up for his morning shift on November 6, colleagues knew immediately that something was terribly wrong.

Pennsylvania State Police investigators arrived at Keystone State Park to find a crime scene that told a story of intimate violence. The location of Andrew's body, the close-range nature of the gunshot wounds, and the isolated setting all suggested this was a crime of passion committed by someone who knew him well.

Within hours, they'd heard multiple accounts of his troubled relationship with Shirley Turner and her recent visit to Latrobe. When investigators called Shirley's number in Iowa that same day, she answered with what seemed like practiced calm. She expressed shock and grief at the news and claimed she'd been home sick in bed all day on November 5.

But investigators were already gathering evidence that would systematically destroy her alibi. The first crack came from cell phone records. Rather than being home sick in Iowa, as she claimed, Shirley's phone had been pinging cell towers along the route from Council Bluffs to Pennsylvania throughout November 4 and 5.

Even more damning evidence emerged from Andrew's apartment. Computer logs showed that someone had accessed his personal desktop on November 5, logging into Shirley's accounts. A phone call had also been made from Andrew's landline to Shirley's workplace, reporting her absence due to illness.

———

When Pennsylvania State Police executed search warrants at Shirley's Council Bluffs apartment, they discovered a trail of evidence that painted her as a methodical killer. Hidden among her belongings were printed MapQuest directions from Iowa to Latrobe, Pennsylvania. They also found a box of condoms that carried the same lot number as a box Andrew had purchased in Latrobe on November 3, the night of their final breakup.

Shirley had already told her firearms instructor that her .22 caliber pistol had been "stolen"—an obvious lie to explain why she no longer possessed the weapon. The unspent cartridge found near Andrew's body was consistent with the ammunition she'd purchased and the type of malfunction her gun was known to have.

When confronted with this mountain of evidence, Shirley changed her story. She admitted to being in Pennsylvania on November 5 and even acknowledged meeting Andrew at Keystone State Park. However, she offered an absurd explanation: She claimed Andrew had somehow taken her gun and placed it in his car trunk.

Phone records also revealed that Shirley had been calling not only Andrew obsessively but also his female colleague, apparently trying to gather information about Andrew's new relationship.

By November 12, 2001, exactly one week after Andrew's murder, Pennsylvania authorities issued an arrest warrant charging Shirley with first-degree murder.

But when they moved to arrest her, they discovered she was gone.

————

While Pennsylvania investigators were building their case, Shirley Turner was executing an escape plan. Immediately after returning to Iowa from her murderous trip to Pennsylvania, she began liquidating her assets and preparing to flee the country.

Shirley Turner

On November 11, Shirley abandoned her Council Bluffs apartment and drove to Missouri. From there, she caught a flight to Toronto, then continued on to St. John's, Newfoundland. By returning to Canada, Shirley had effectively placed herself beyond the immediate reach of U.S. law enforcement.

What made the situation even more complex was a discovery investigators made while searching through Shirley's belongings. Among the items she'd left behind were ultrasound printouts indicating that she was pregnant with Andrew Bagby's child. The baby had been conceived in late October 2001, just days before the murder.

On December 12, Royal Newfoundland Constabulary officers arrested Shirley Turner in St. John's at the request of U.S. authorities.

At the time of her arrest, Shirley was approximately six weeks pregnant.

Canadian authorities initially held Shirley at the Clarenville Correctional Centre for Women while extradition proceedings began. Given the serious nature of the charges against her, most observers expected she would remain in custody throughout the lengthy legal process.

––––––

However, in January 2002, Newfoundland Supreme Court Justice Gale Welsh made a decision that would haunt the case for years to come. Despite the fact that Shirley Turner was charged with first-degree murder, despite the substantial evidence against her, and despite warnings from U.S. prosecutors about her potential for violence, Justice Welsh granted her bail.

The judge's reasoning defied common sense. Welsh concluded that Shirley was not a danger to the general public because her alleged crime was directed at a specific individual rather than random victims. In Welsh's view, since Shirley's violence was targeted rather than indiscriminate, she posed no significant threat to society.

The bail conditions required Shirley to post CAD 75,000 in cash, surrender her passport, remain within Newfoundland, report weekly to police, and have no contact with the Bagby family. Dr. John Doucet, a psychiatrist who had worked with Shirley previously, posted the substantial bond money to secure her release.

By February 2002, Shirley Turner was free to walk the streets of St. John's while pregnant with the child of the man she was accused of murdering.

––––––

When David and Kate Bagby learned that their son's accused killer was not only free on bail but also carrying their grandchild, they faced the most difficult decision of their lives. They could remain in California, safe from the painful proximity to Shirley Turner, but forever cut off from Andrew's son—or they could uproot their entire existence and move to Newfoundland to be near the child.

For the Bagbys, there was no real choice. In 2002, they sold their home in California, left their careers behind, and moved to St. John's to begin one of the most psychologically devastating ordeals imaginable.

The arrangement forced them into a grotesque charade of civility with Shirley Turner. To maintain access to their grandson, they had to suppress their grief and rage, smile politely at the woman they believed had killed Andrew, and pretend their interactions were normal family visits.

On July 18, 2002, Zachary Andrew Turner was born at a St. John's hospital. The baby was beautiful and healthy, bearing a striking resemblance to his father. For the Bagbys, holding their grandson for the first time was both a moment of profound joy and devastating sorrow.

Shirley initially refused to allow the Bagbys regular access to Zachary, paranoid that they might try to kidnap him. Thus, the Bagbys were forced to work through Newfoundland's family court system just to secure basic visitation rights with their own grandson.

———

Those who observed Shirley with baby Zachary during this period noticed disturbing patterns. Social workers and family friends remarked that the infant seemed poorly bonded with his mother and often appeared more comfortable with other caregivers.

At Zachary's first birthday party in July 2003, held at a McDonald's restaurant in St. John's, the baby's behavior spoke volumes. When given the choice, Zachary consistently gravitated toward his grandparents, crying when Shirley tried to hold him and calming immediately when the Bagbys took him back.

During one particularly telling moment, Shirley snapped at Kate Bagby in frustration: "He obviously loves you more than me, so why don't you take him?"

Meanwhile, the extradition process crawled forward with agonizing slowness. In June 2002, a Newfoundland judge ruled that Shirley Turner could be extradited to the United States. Shirley immediately appealed. By November 2002, she was briefly taken back into custody pending a final decision.

Two months later, Justice Welsh intervened once again, making the inexplicable decision to release Shirley on bail for a second time. Welsh reiterated her position that Shirley's alleged crime was specific rather than random, making her supposedly safe for the general public.

———

In June 2003, Canada's federal Justice Minister finally approved Shirley Turner's extradition to Pennsylvania. After nearly two years of legal maneuvering, it appeared that justice for Andrew Bagby might finally be served. But Shirley's legal team immediately launched another appeal, and she remained free on bail.

During these final months, Shirley's behavior became increasingly erratic. In July 2003, she met a man at a bar in St. John's and began what would be her final romantic entanglement. After a few dates, the man learned about her background and decided to end their brief relationship. Shirley's response was predictably obsessive—over the following month, she called him approximately 200 times.

On the night of August 17, 2003, Shirley's harassment escalated to a chilling and calculated level. Around midnight, she drove her adult son's car to the area near the man's residence, bringing thirteen-month-old Zachary with her. After stopping to ask for directions to his street, she made her way to his home and began leaving disturbing evidence in a pattern that suggested she was planning to frame him for what was to come.

She placed a photograph between the door frame of a nearby ambulance at his workplace, then drove to his residence, where she left two photographs in the driveway—one of herself with Zachary, another of herself in revealing clothing—along with a used tampon on the ground beside them. When her car slipped into a ditch as she tried to position it near his home, she was unable to free it. She gathered Zachary from the vehicle, locked the doors with her belongings still inside, and walked away into the night.

That night, Shirley Turner began making the final preparations for an act that would shock even those who knew her capacity for violence.

———

August 18 began like any other day in St. John's. Shirley Turner was scheduled to have custody of Zachary as part of the interim arrangement with the Bagbys—but Shirley had already made other plans.

That morning, she drove to a pharmacy and filled a prescription for lorazepam, a powerful sedative. Shirley picked up Zachary from the Bagbys as scheduled. The happy, healthy toddler had just learned to walk and was beginning to say his first words.

At some point during the day, Shirley administered a heavy dose of lorazepam to Zachary, likely mixing the sedative into his formula bottle. She also consumed a substantial quantity of the medication herself. The drug would have made the baby drowsy and eventually unconscious.

As evening approached, Shirley loaded the drugged infant into her car and drove to Foxtrap Marina in Conception Bay South, a remote coastal area. There, beside the dark waters of the Atlantic Ocean,

Shirley Turner committed an act of devastating cruelty. She tied her sweater around herself and Zachary, securing the unconscious child to her chest, and then stepped off the end of a fishing wharf into the frigid Atlantic waters below.

————

Just after 7:00 p.m. on August 18, 2003, a couple walking their dog along the shoreline made a discovery that would haunt them forever. They spotted the body of a woman in the surf. When police arrived, they found the body of baby Zachary just meters away from his mother's remains.

The scene left no doubt about what had occurred. Shirley's abandoned car was found about a kilometer away, providing investigators with a clear timeline of her final movements. This was a planned murder-suicide, the final desperate act of a woman who had chosen to kill her innocent son rather than face justice.

Autopsies conducted the following day confirmed the horrific details. Zachary had drowned, but the medical examiner found significant amounts of lorazepam in his system. The sedative had likely rendered him unconscious before he was submerged, meaning the innocent child didn't suffer during his final moments.

The deaths ended all legal proceedings. The extradition case became moot with Shirley's death. Andrew Bagby's killer would never face trial for his murder, and his son had paid the ultimate price for the failures of a justice system that had prioritized the rights of an accused murderer over the safety of an innocent child.

————

The case exposed catastrophic failures in multiple systems that were supposed to protect the innocent. Within days, public outrage began building across Canada. The provincial government of Newfoundland and Labrador ordered a comprehensive review.

Dr. Peter Markesteyn, a respected pediatric forensic pathologist, led the investigation. The resulting Turner Review and Investigation, released in October 2006, was a scathing 450-page indictment of institutional failures. Markesteyn's findings were unequivocal: Zachary Turner's death had been entirely preventable.

The report revealed a pattern of deference and assumption that proved deadly. Social workers had assumed that if a judge granted Shirley bail, she couldn't be that dangerous. Throughout the entire ordeal, officials had consistently prioritized Shirley Turner's rights over Zachary's safety.

"Nowhere did I find any ongoing assessment of the safety needs of the children," Markesteyn wrote. The child welfare system had become more concerned with the accused murderer's parental rights than with protecting an innocent infant.

————

Despite their unimaginable grief, David and Kate Bagby refused to let their losses be meaningless. They channeled their pain into a determined campaign for legislative change that would prevent other families from enduring similar tragedies.

Working with Canadian Member of Parliament Scott Andrews, the Bagbys began advocating for changes to Canada's bail laws. The current system contained a dangerous loophole that failed to consider the safety of an accused person's minor children when making bail decisions.

On October 23, 2009, MP Andrews introduced Bill C-464 in the Canadian House of Commons. The legislation, which became known as "Zachary's Bill," explicitly added provisions allowing bail to be denied when an accused person might pose a threat to children under eighteen years of age.

The bill moved through Parliament with unprecedented speed and unanimous support. On December 16, 2010, it became law. For the first time in Canadian legal history, the safety of children was explicitly recognized as grounds for denying bail to accused violent offenders.

CHAPTER 12
THE HUDSON MURDERS

The St. Croix County medical examiner pulled into the parking lot of O'Connell Family Funeral Home expecting a routine pickup. It was a crisp February afternoon in Hudson, Wisconsin, and he needed to collect a death certificate before heading home.

The front door was unlocked. This was strange—out of the ordinary. Dan O'Connell was meticulous about security.

"Dan?" he called out, stepping into the hushed interior.

No answer.

He made his way toward the office, his footsteps echoing in the silence. What he found there would shatter this peaceful river town's sense of safety.

Dan O'Connell lay slumped over his desk, blood pooling beneath his head. Across the room, a young man lay motionless on the floor, his face turned toward the doorway as if he'd been trying to escape.

The examiner quickly reached for his phone to call 911. In twenty-four years, there hadn't been a murder in Hudson. Now, there were two bodies and no explanation for why anyone would want these men dead.

———

Six hours earlier, Dan O'Connell had been very much alive, going about his morning routine in the town where his family had operated their funeral home for generations. At thirty-nine, Dan was a fixture in Hudson—the kind of man who knew everyone's name and never missed a community event.

That morning, he'd stopped at Walmart for supplies. The encounter there would later prove crucial, though at the time, it seemed like just another conversation with a fellow parishioner from St. Patrick's Catholic Church.

Mary Pagel was selecting groceries when Dan approached her with an unusual question.

"Have you ever seen anything inappropriate happen at church? I mean…with the children?" he asked, his voice lower than usual.

Mary was taken aback. Dan seemed agitated, not his usual cheerful self.

He explained that he'd received disturbing information—an allegation involving someone at their parish. He planned to address it that afternoon in a face-to-face meeting.

"Maybe you should call the police," Mary suggested.

Dan shook his head. "No, no. I can handle it."

Those would be among the last words Dan O'Connell ever spoke to anyone outside of his funeral home.

———

When Hudson Police arrived at the funeral home, they found a crime scene unlike anything they'd encountered in this quiet Mississippi River town. Chief Richard Trende surveyed the carnage with the grim realization that his small department was facing something entirely beyond their experience.

Dan O'Connell had been shot once in the head at close range while seated at his desk. The violence was precise, execution-style.

The second victim lay near the office doorway. James Ellison, twenty-two, was a mortuary science student from Barron, Wisconsin, working as an intern at the funeral home. He'd been shot in the back while apparently trying to flee—the bullet had entered his skull and killed him instantly.

Three shell casings from a .22 caliber weapon littered the floor. Investigators believed the killer had fired three times, missing once as Ellison ran for his life.

Nothing was stolen. Dan's wallet remained in his pocket, and cash sat untouched in the petty cash box. This wasn't a robbery gone wrong.

But if money wasn't the motive, what was?

Detective work began immediately, but the physical evidence was limited. No fingerprints on surfaces the killer might have touched. No witnesses to the actual shooting. No signs of forced entry.

The crime scene told investigators one crucial fact: Dan O'Connell had been the primary target. He'd been killed deliberately, professionally. James Ellison had died simply because he was there—a horrific case of being in the wrong place at the wrong time.

But who would want Dan O'Connell dead?

———

Hudson hadn't seen violence like this in a generation. The last murder occurred in 1978, and now two respected men had been gunned down in broad daylight at a local business.

Fear rippled through the community. If someone could kill the town's beloved funeral director and a college student in the middle of the afternoon, who was safe?

Chief Trende and his investigators began with the fundamentals. They interviewed Dan's family, friends, and business associates. They examined his financial records, looking for debts or disputes. They traced James Ellison's movements, searching for any connection that might explain why he'd become a victim.

During their interviews, they learned about Dan's conversation with Mary Pagel at Walmart that morning. She mentioned he'd seemed agitated about confronting someone over inappropriate behavior, but Dan hadn't provided specifics about who or what exactly he planned to discuss. Without more details, investigators had no clear direction to pursue. The lead seemed to evaporate into the same dead end as everything else.

Dan O'Connell emerged as exactly what everyone believed him to be: a decent man with no enemies. He was married with two young children, active in his church, and volunteered as an ambulance attendant. He helped organize community festivals and coached Little League. His funeral home served grieving families with compassion and integrity.

James Ellison was equally blameless—a student pursuing his career, well-liked by professors and peers. His connection to Hudson extended only to his internship at the funeral home.

The investigators explored increasingly disparate theories. Could the murders be connected to a fringe religious group that opposed modern burial practices? They tracked down members of a cult called "Rest of Jesus" that had written letters protesting embalming, but they found them to be harmless cranks with no connection to Hudson.

Perhaps drug users had broken into the funeral home seeking embalming fluid to use as an intoxicant? But embalming chemicals were cheap, easily obtainable, and legally available. Why risk a violent break-in?

As weeks passed without answers, rumors spread throughout the town. Some whispered that the victims had interrupted someone desecrating bodies in the mortuary. Others suggested the killings were connected to a September 11th charity fundraiser Dan had helped organize—perhaps someone had been stealing donations, and they'd killed to cover their tracks.

All of these theories would prove false, but they reflected the community's desperate need to understand how such violence could occur in their peaceful town.

———

Months turned to years. The case file grew thick with dead ends and false leads. Chief Trende felt the weight of two unsolved murders pressing down on his small department.

The families of Dan O'Connell and James Ellison lived with the unbearable reality that their loved ones' killer walked free. Dan's widow struggled to raise two children while wondering if the murderer might return. James's parents grieved their son's promising future, cut short by random violence.

In 2003, more than a year after the murders, an investigator named Jeffrey Knopps was assigned to review the cold case. He approached it with fresh eyes, methodically examining every piece of evidence, every interview, every theory that had been explored and discarded.

Knopps understood that the key to solving old cases often lay not in the physical evidence but in recognizing patterns that earlier investigators might have missed. He began reinterviewing witnesses, looking for connections that hadn't been apparent in the immediate aftermath of the killings.

One name kept appearing in his notes: Thomas Smith, a young man from North Dakota who had called the police with what seemed like an unrelated complaint about a Catholic priest providing alcohol to minors.

———

In March 2003, Thomas Smith contacted police in Bismarck with what appeared to be a minor allegation. A Catholic priest had given him alcohol when he was underage, during the time Smith lived in Wisconsin.

The Bismarck Police forwarded Smith's complaint to Hudson authorities in April 2003, where it landed on Detective Knopps's desk as he worked the cold murder case.

Initially, it seemed like another dead end. However, when Knopps reinterviewed Smith in April 2004, something in the young man's demeanor suggested there was more to the story.

Smith, now in his early twenties, seemed nervous and troubled. He spoke carefully about his time in Hudson, describing regular visits to a Catholic rectory where he'd been supervised for community service work.

"He would give me beer," Smith said. "A lot of beer. And hard liquor."

When Knopps pressed for more details, Smith's account became disturbing. The drinking sessions weren't casual. They were elaborate games where Smith would inevitably lose and be forced to consume more alcohol. He estimated drinking about twelve hundred beers and twelve hundred shots over a two-year period, often vomiting or passing out.

"We would lie in bed together," Smith admitted quietly. "His hands would end up in places they shouldn't have been."

Smith described approximately ten incidents of inappropriate sexual contact while he was intoxicated, often too drunk to remember everything that happened the next morning.

The priest had discouraged Smith from dating girls and repeatedly suggested he consider joining the priesthood—classic grooming behavior designed to isolate a victim and maintain control.

For the first time since the murders, Detective Knopps had a potential motive. Dan O'Connell's conversation with Mary Pagel suddenly took on new significance. Dan had planned to confront someone about inappropriate behavior with children on the day he was killed.

The priest Thomas Smith described had been stationed at St. Patrick's Catholic Church in Hudson during the period when the murders occurred. His name was Father Ryan Erickson.

————

Father Ryan Erickson had arrived at St. Patrick's Church in Hudson shortly after his ordination in June 2000. At twenty-seven, he was young for a parish assignment, but he brought enthusiasm and strong conservative convictions to his ministry.

To most parishioners, he seemed like a dedicated priest. He encouraged traditional practices like kneeling during Mass and even offered Latin-language liturgy. His sermons were passionate, often focusing on moral purity and the dangers of secular culture.

But Father Erickson was also a divisive figure. His rigid approach to doctrine and his dramatic preaching style alienated some church members. He seemed to relish being the center of attention, cultivating devoted followers while dismissing critics as "lukewarm" Catholics.

Some parishioners, including Dan O'Connell, had grown uncomfortable with what they saw as a developing "cult of personality" around the young priest.

Father Erickson also had unusual interests for a cleric. He was an avid gun collector who owned at least sixteen firearms. Parishioners had given him a 9mm semiautomatic pistol, and he was known to carry weapons both under his cassock and even beneath his vestments during Mass.

More troubling were his relationships with teenage boys. He would take groups of young men fishing and invite them to watch violent R-rated movies. Parishioners noticed odd behavior—he would massage boys' backs with mud at retreat centers and was once observed in what a witness later described as inappropriate physical contact with a young man outside the rectory.

After the murders, Father Erickson had participated in Dan O'Connell's funeral Mass, appearing somber and subdued as he presided over the service. No one suspected that the priest offering prayers for the dead might be their killer.

———

As Detective Knopps dug deeper into Father Erickson's background, he uncovered a disturbing pattern that church officials had known about for years.

In 1992, as Ryan Erickson prepared to attend seminary, investigators in Vilas County, Wisconsin, received a troubling report. A fourteen-year-old boy claimed that Erickson, then nineteen, had invited him to his trailer at Eagle Lake Resort, told him scary stories, and then massaged him while naked before fondling his genitals and offering oral sex.

The boy had refused Erickson's advances and reported the incident to authorities. However, the district attorney declined to file charges, citing insufficient corroboration. Remarkably, the investigator wrote that while he couldn't prove the case beyond a reasonable doubt, he was "not totally convinced that Ryan is totally innocent of some impropriety."

Even more remarkably, the investigator decided to give Erickson the "benefit of any doubt," specifically because he was entering a seminary.

The Diocese of Superior received this report in 1994. Bishop Raphael Fliss was made aware of the allegations, along with other concerning incidents from Erickson's youth—including admitted sexual contact with his four-year-old male cousin when Erickson was six years old.

Father Ryan Erickson

Despite these red flags, the diocese allowed Erickson to continue toward ordination. They removed him from responsibilities involving young people and required psychological evaluations, but multiple assessments produced conflicting results. Some psychologists found him suitable for the priesthood, while others expressed serious reservations.

At St. Paul Seminary, faculty members noted additional troubling behaviors. Erickson was disciplined for heresy, showed an inability to control his impulses, and was reported for drinking heavily. One professor voted against his ordination due to character concerns.

Nevertheless, Bishop Fliss ordained Ryan Erickson on June 4, 2000, and assigned him to St. Patrick's Church in Hudson.

————

Armed with Thomas Smith's allegations and the new information about Father Erickson's history, Detectives Knopps and Shawn Pettee drove to Hurley, Wisconsin, in November 2004. The priest had been transferred there the previous August to serve St. Mary of the Seven Dolors Parish.

The interview began with questions about Smith's allegations. Father Erickson admitted to providing alcohol to minors and acknowledged lying in bed with a teenage boy, though he denied sexual contact.

Then, the detectives shifted to the real purpose of their visit.

"Do you know how Dan O'Connell and James Ellison were killed?" Knopps asked.

Father Erickson's response sent chills through both investigators.

"I think James was going through a door," he said without hesitation. "Dan was behind his desk."

The detectives exchanged glances. This information had never been released to the public. The specific positions of the victims were details known only to investigators—and the killer.

"How do you know that?" Pettee pressed.

Father Erickson seemed to realize his mistake. He stumbled through inconsistent explanations—first claiming he'd heard it from another priest, then suggesting it had come from news reports or church gossip.

But the detectives knew that such specific crime scene details had been deliberately withheld from all media coverage. There was only one way Father Erickson could know exactly where the victims had been when they'd died. He had been there.

———

Following the November interview, Father Erickson's behavior became increasingly erratic. He confided in Deacon Russell Lundgren at St. Mary's Parish, making a shocking admission.

"I done it and they were going to catch me," he told Lundgren.

He expressed terror about prison, asking, "Do you know what they do with young guys in prison, especially priests?"

Lundgren was stunned but didn't immediately report the confession to authorities—a decision that would later raise serious questions about his judgment.

As police pressure intensified, Father Erickson began making frantic phone calls to friends in Hudson, desperately seeking alibis for the time of the murders. He claimed he had been buying cigars when the killings occurred, but his panicked attempts to construct a retroactive defense suggested he knew his story wouldn't withstand scrutiny.

On December 7, detectives conducted a follow-up interview. This time, they confronted Father Erickson directly about the inconsistencies in his statements and the mounting evidence against him.

The priest's responses became increasingly incoherent. He suggested the mafia might be responsible for the murders, a theory so absurd it only reinforced investigators' certainty about his guilt.

Two days later, police executed a search warrant at St. Mary's rectory. On Father Erickson's computer, hidden in buried folders, they discovered more than forty explicit images of prepubescent and teenage boys engaged in sexual acts. Some images showed bondage scenarios. The computer also contained photographs of boys sleeping in rectories where Erickson had served.

The child pornography discovery corroborated everything Thomas Smith had reported and more. Combined with Father Erickson's unexplained knowledge of the crime scene, investigators were convinced they had identified James Ellison and Dan O'Connell's killer.

————

By mid-December 2004, Father Erickson knew his time was running out. Police had confiscated his computer and his extensive gun collection. He had retained a public defender who advised him not to take the polygraph test he had previously agreed to undergo.

On December 16, Hurley Police Chief Daniel Erspamer visited Father Erickson at the rectory. He was concerned about the priest's mental state, especially after discovering that Erickson had written what appeared to be his last will and testament.

When asked about suicidal thoughts, Father Erickson assured Chief Erspamer that he was coping and had support from friends and fellow clergy. He even seemed to regain some composure over the following days, performing his regular parish duties and interacting normally with parishioners.

Friends Richard Reams and Tom Burns visited him on Saturday night, December 18, finding him upset but not distraught. He told them he had "lived more life than most eighty-year-olds"—a statement that would later seem ominous.

None of them realized it would be their last conversation.

Early Sunday morning, December 19, the church janitor made a horrific discovery. Father Ryan Erickson hung from the iron fire escape behind the rectory, dressed in his black clerical cassock, dead by his own hand at age thirty-one.

———

Reams and Burns, who had stayed overnight, found three suicide letters along with the priest's body. In the notes, Father Erickson denied committing the murders, writing, "I NEVER killed anyone." However, he acknowledged deep personal failings: "My ego, my pride, my lust, my envy have always stopped me from being the best person I could be. I am tired."

He also wrote cryptically about being "tormented for years, ever since I was twelve years old" and admitted, "I have preached truth, but I found myself unable to live it in its entirety."

With Father Erickson's death, the immediate criminal investigation ended abruptly. But the victims' families deserved an official resolution.

At the request of the O'Connell family, St. Croix County District Attorney Eric Johnson convened a "John Doe hearing"—a judicial proceeding to determine whether a crime occurred and who likely committed it.

On October 3, 2005, fifteen witnesses testified before Judge Eric Lundell. Thomas Smith described the sexual abuse he had suffered. Mary Pagel recounted Dan O'Connell's plans to confront Father Erickson about child abuse allegations. Investigators detailed the priest's impossible knowledge of crime scene facts that had never been made public.

After hearing all the evidence, Judge Lundell issued his finding.

"On a scale of one to ten as far as strength of evidence, I would consider this ten," he said. "It is a very strong case for circumstantial evidence."

The judge formally concluded that Ryan Erickson "probably committed these crimes in question."

————

The judicial finding brought mixed emotions to Hudson. Dan O'Connell's and James Ellison's families finally had official confirmation of their killer's identity, but there was little satisfaction in the resolution.

"There aren't any winners here," said Sally Ellison, James's mother. Both families had lost their sons to violence, and even the Erickson family had lost a child to his own destructive actions.

The case raised serious questions about institutional failures. Church officials had known about Father Erickson's history of sexual misconduct with minors, yet they had ordained him anyway and assigned him to work with families and children.

The O'Connell and Ellison families pursued civil litigation seeking accountability from diocesan officials, arguing that proper screening would have prevented the tragedy. While the lawsuits didn't achieve all their goals, they led to the establishment of the James Ellison Foundation for the Protection of Children.

Today, a memorial garden at the O'Connell Family Funeral Home honors both victims. Hudson has rebuilt its sense of security, but the scars remain visible.

Dan O'Connell died trying to protect children from a predator who had successfully deceived an entire community. His courage in confronting evil cost him his life, but it ultimately helped expose the truth about Father Ryan Erickson.

CHAPTER 13
BONUS CHAPTER: THE CALDWELL FARMHOUSE

Nadja Medley stood in the middle of the sprawling horse paddock, her smartphone in hand, filming a video tour for her friends back in Utah. "Well folks, here's my new back-yard," the forty-eight-year-old said with obvious pleasure in her voice. She slowly panned the camera, capturing overgrown grass and wild-flowers that surrounded her under a cloudless blue sky.

"Kind of liking this just a little bit," Nadja remarked as she focused on a rundown fence that needed repair. At her feet, one of her three dogs sniffed and chewed on grass. "Dogs are the only thing that's grazing now," she joked, "but that will change."

The land had so many trees that the farmhouse wasn't visible from where she stood. The pleasure she took in this peaceful country setting was evident as she narrated her video tour, eventually pausing on a small building in the distance. "This is our hay shed," she explained simply. "Yep baby, we're loving it."

It was Wednesday, May 10, 2017, and Nadja had moved to the Cald-well, Idaho, farm just one week earlier from her previous home in Ogden, Utah. She kept her friends updated on her new life through

Facebook, where they could watch videos of her exploring the property. "It looks right down your alley," commented one friend. "That's so pretty," wrote another.

"It's a ton of work," Nadja admitted, "but I'm loving Idaho already."

The move represented a fresh start for Nadja and her fourteen-year-old daughter, Payton. Originally from Germany, Nadja had immigrated to the United States alone, where she met and married an American man named Todd Medley. Together, they had worked in a pet store and bred small animals to make extra money. In 2002, they welcomed their daughter Payton. Almost a decade later, Nadja gave birth to a second child who died shortly after birth. Then, in 2014, tragedy struck again when Todd suffered a fatal heart attack.

With no other family in the United States apart from Todd's relatives who lived out of state, Nadja and Payton had grown extremely close. They bonded over their shared love of animals and enjoyed activities like swimming and picnicking together. Nadja described Payton as one of her favorite people.

Despite her deep connection with her daughter, Nadja had struggled in Utah. As a staunch atheist, she found the state's overwhelmingly religious culture foreign and uncomfortable. Finances were also difficult. Todd hadn't left behind any money when he'd died, and now Nadja was the sole provider. She began working as a massage therapist at an Ogden spa to make ends meet.

———

One day in 2015, a man in his late fifties arrived at the spa for an appointment. His name was Gerald "Mike" Bullinger, and despite the age difference, Nadja felt an immediate spark. Mike was warm and charming, with a wide smile. Both loved hiking and exploring the great outdoors. Mike was also an atheist, and his values seemed to align perfectly with Nadja's.

The two soon began dating, and Nadja's friends were thrilled for her. It was clear that Mike had brought happiness back into her life after years of grief and struggle. He was also wonderful with Payton, sometimes picking her up from school or taking her out for lunch. He became something of a father figure, teaching Payton outdoor skills like shooting and playing with her in the autumn leaves. Payton seemed to adore Mike almost as much as her mother did, and soon, she had started calling him "dad."

Mike, Nadja, and Payton attended concerts and festivals together, went to baseball games, and hiked and camped in Yellowstone National Park. Because Mike worked as a pilot, he often had to travel for several days at a time, but he made up for his absences by taking Nadja and Payton on vacations and adventures, which Nadja documented enthusiastically on her Facebook page.

By the beginning of 2017, Nadja and Mike had been together for almost eighteen months. Things were going so well that Nadja felt ready to ask Mike an awkward but necessary question. Her single income wasn't substantial, and she was having trouble making her mortgage payments. She had seen Mike's paychecks, and she knew he made more than ten thousand dollars a month, so she wondered if he might be able to help her out financially.

Mike, however, was troubled by the question. He told Nadja he had divorced his wife a decade earlier, and she was the first woman he'd been involved with since then. Becoming financially entangled with another person seemed far too serious for him, and he worried that the relationship was moving more quickly than he was ready for. After several heated conversations about the matter, the couple broke up.

———

Mike had recently been offered more consistent work based out of Boise, Idaho's capital city. He had purchased a rundown farm in the city of Caldwell, about twenty-eight miles west of Boise. The property was around five acres and featured a fully equipped farmhouse built in 1964. From the outside, it looked like a modest weatherboard home, but it had four bedrooms and two bathrooms, as well as a spacious kitchen. As he was nearing retirement age, Mike thought the property would be a scenic spot to live out his golden years.

Yet, not having Nadja in his life made Mike realize what he'd be giving up. Despite no longer being a couple, they had stayed in touch and spoke regularly. Both of them missed each other desperately and found being apart unbearable. Within a few weeks, they decided to get back together.

Proving how serious he was about their relationship, Mike asked Nadja and Payton to come live in Caldwell with him. Nadja accepted his offer eagerly. She looked forward to settling in the countryside and starting a new phase of their lives as a family. The setting also suited the animal-loving Payton, who would have plenty of room for all her pets, which included dogs, cats, rabbits, chickens, birds, fish, and one snake. Nadja planned to raise livestock and keep horses on the land.

In late March 2017, Nadja shared the news of her upcoming interstate move on Facebook, posting, "Here we come!" Just over a month later, on Thursday, May 4, 2017, Nadja and Payton headed north to join Mike in Idaho. With spring in full bloom, the Caldwell farm was green and covered in wildflowers. Nadja and Payton loved it from the moment they arrived.

The three of them spent considerable time outdoors working on repairs that needed to be done around the property. Nadja posted photos and videos of her country life online while encouraging her friends to visit anytime. In one Facebook survey, which she completed a month after moving, question twenty-five asked: "Are you where you want to be in life?" Nadja's answer was simply: "Yes."

———

What Nadja didn't know was that Mike Bullinger was living a carefully constructed lie. Far from being the divorced pilot he claimed to be, Mike was married to another woman—a woman who believed she was planning a retirement with her devoted husband on that very same Caldwell farm.

————

Cheryl Baker was in her mid-forties when she caught a flight to Alaska and found herself seated next to the engaging Mike Bullinger. He was warm and friendly, and the two hit it off immediately. They wound up exchanging phone numbers and began dating when they were both back home in Utah.

In 2010, when Cheryl was fifty and Mike was fifty-three, they married. Cheryl, who was artistic and creative, made her own wedding dress. The couple had a lot in common—both enjoyed traveling, hiking, and horseback riding. Cheryl practiced Hinduism and attended the Sri Ganesha Temple of Utah. Mike took an interest in the faith and would accompany her to the temple. He even learned Sanskrit, a classical language of South Asia, so he could better understand the Hindu texts.

Mike was an experienced outdoorsman who would sometimes act as a guide for hunting parties. Cheryl hated guns and would have to leave the room whenever Mike returned from one of these trips, unable to stomach being in the same space while he cleaned his firearms.

Overall, though, the couple's friends and family were struck by how happy they seemed. In 2016, six years after their wedding, Cheryl and Mike went on a rafting vacation together. When they returned, Cheryl was glowing as though she'd just been on her honeymoon. She raved about what a wonderful time she and Mike had shared.

————

Around this time, Cheryl was in her late fifties and had been a teacher for almost four decades. In 2017, she worked at Greenwood Charter School in Harrisville, a city just a few miles north of her home in Ogden. Mike worked as a charter pilot, which provided the perfect cover for his double life—he was sometimes away for days at a time, rotating between his two worlds without either woman suspecting the other existed.

To Cheryl's family, Mike appeared to be a devoted husband. He would join his in-laws for holidays and take Cheryl on outdoor adventure trips as a loving partner. Cheryl's brother would describe how she thought her marriage was perfect, with Mike showing no obvious signs of pulling away.

———

Simultaneously, to Nadja's friends, he presented himself as a caring boyfriend, as well as a father figure to Payton. Mike ingratiated himself with Nadja and her daughter, even talking about a future together. He had supposedly proposed to Nadja—friends believed she was engaged to him in 2017.

Mike's double life was so expertly orchestrated that even though both women lived in Ogden, Utah, they never crossed paths. Neither woman knew of the other's existence. Close friends of Nadja and relatives of Cheryl had all believed Mike's lies and assumed he was wholly committed to their respective loved one.

———

The couple—Cheryl and Mike—began to think about their future and what they wanted their retirement to look like. They decided to buy a rural property together—fixing it up would be a fun project after Cheryl left her teaching position in Utah. On May 3, 2017, the couple purchased the farm in the small town of Caldwell. Cheryl's assets helped fund this purchase; she and Mike took out a loan against her Ogden house to finance the Idaho property.

The plan, as Cheryl understood it, was for Mike to move there right away and start working on things that needed fixing, such as plumbing and painting, while she stayed in Ogden to get their house ready to be sold. However, Mike had a far more sinister plan in mind. The same day their farm purchase was finalized, he brought Nadja and Payton Medley to Caldwell with him, establishing a new household in what Cheryl believed was their future retirement home.

Mike had convinced Nadja and Payton to abandon their Utah life and move to Idaho, promising them a fresh start on the farm. Meanwhile, he told Cheryl he needed time alone to fix up the property before she joined him.

By early June 2017, the stage was set for disaster: Mike had both his wife and his girlfriend believing they would each be the lady of the Caldwell farmhouse.

———

On Friday, June 9, 2017, Nadja was scheduled to drive back to Utah to pick up some horses for the farm. She never arrived. The horse sellers tried calling her cell phone when she didn't show up, but there was no answer. It seemed strange, but since the sellers didn't know Nadja well, they didn't think much of it initially.

However, something felt terribly wrong. As an enthusiastic social media user, Nadja was normally reliable about replying to messages quickly. When her friends stopped hearing from her, alarm bells began ringing. Payton's friends noticed that she had fallen silent, too. The last time she had replied to a text message was on Thursday, June 8. Since she was ordinarily glued to her phone, this sudden silence felt ominous.

Mike's family hadn't heard from him either. He had two sons from a previous marriage, and neither had spoken to him in days. The silence from the Caldwell farm was deafening. When more than a week passed with no word from anyone, panic began to set in among the families.

Cheryl's loved ones were equally concerned. Several days after June 6, when fifty-six-year-old Cheryl worked her final day at Greenwood Charter School, one of her friends received a strange text message from Cheryl's phone. It read: "Take care of my dogs. I don't know if I'm coming back."

The message sent chills down her friend's spine. When Cheryl's brother heard about it, he tried to rationalize it—Cheryl and Mike loved to travel, so perhaps they had gone on a last-minute camping trip somewhere. But as days stretched into more than a week with no word from anyone, authorities were asked to perform welfare checks.

———

As the deputy pulled into the gravel driveway of 216 South Kcid Road, his radio sprang to life. It was Monday, June 19, 2017, and Canyon County Sheriff's Deputy had been dispatched for what seemed like a routine welfare check. A concerned friend in Utah had called about three people who had suddenly gone silent—no phone calls, no text messages, no social media posts for over ten days.

The farmhouse sat on five acres of rural Idaho countryside, just outside the small city of Caldwell. As the deputy stepped out of his patrol car, an oppressive quiet settled around him. No dogs barking, no sounds of daily farm life—just an eerie stillness that made the hair on his neck stand up.

The deputy approached the modest weatherboard house and knocked firmly on the front door. "Sheriff's department!" he called out. No response. He tried again, louder this time. Still nothing. Walking around the perimeter of the house, he peered through windows and called out repeatedly, but the farmhouse remained disturbingly silent.

Inside the house, deputies found the bodies of several dead dogs, cats, and pet birds. The animals appeared to have starved to death. Other pets, including some rabbits and a snake, were still alive outside but showed signs of neglect. The deputies checked the hen house and found it full of dead chickens that had also apparently died of starvation.

Then the deputy caught it—a smell that every experienced law enforcement officer recognizes immediately. The deputy's stomach tightened as he followed his nose toward a small storage shed at the back of the property. The closer he got, the stronger the odor became. Flies buzzed in unusual numbers around the shed door.

Inside the shed, a blue tarp covered something large on the floor. The deputy pulled back the covering and immediately radioed for backup. Under the tarp lay three decomposed bodies—two adult women and one teenage girl. The summer heat had accelerated decomposition to the point where the victims were unrecognizable.

What had started as a simple welfare check had just become a triple homicide investigation.

———

As investigators delved into the case, a disturbing picture emerged of Mike Bullinger's past. Born in Wyoming in 1957, he had grown up surrounded by wilderness, which had fostered his interest in the outdoors. His family belonged to the Church of Jesus Christ of Latter-day Saints (commonly known as the Mormon Church), and in 1976, when he was nineteen, Mike traveled to Manila in the Philippines for his LDS mission.

Mike Bullinger

When Mike returned to the United States, he began studying at an LDS college in Idaho, where he met another young church member named Jacqueline Garcia, who went by Jackie. The pair married at the LDS Temple in Salt Lake City, Utah, in 1978.

Almost immediately, Jackie knew she had made a terrible mistake.

The newlyweds argued constantly, and during one particularly violent fight, Jackie found herself sprawled across the floor while Mike loomed over her. Jackie saw the rage burning in his eyes and asked, "You wanted to hit me, didn't you?"

Mike simply replied, "Yes."

Eventually, he began acting on this desire, and he beat Jackie regularly. At times, she feared Mike was going to kill her. He also regularly cheated on her and lied constantly about everything, from where he'd been to how much money he was spending.

Jackie tried everything she could think of to fix the marriage. She contacted Mike's parents, called a domestic violence hotline, sought couples counseling through the church, and sent Mike to therapy aimed at abusive men. But Mike refused to change his behavior. He seemed incapable of accepting responsibility for his actions, always finding ways to blame Jackie for provoking him.

Eventually, Jackie went to her church bishop and asked for help getting a divorce. The divorce was granted in 2007, after nearly twenty-nine years of marriage. Jackie was granted sole custody of their two sons, but they still visited their father occasionally.

When the boys returned home after a stay with their father, the younger one told his mother that Mike had hit him. Jackie called Mike and told him he was not to strike their children. Mike said nothing, but the next time his sons visited, he sat them both down and warned them that whatever happened at his house was to stay at his house.

After his divorce from Jackie, Mike remarried briefly, but that marriage also ended in divorce. Years later, when he met Cheryl Baker on that Alaska flight, she had no idea about his violent past, and they began dating.

———

The bodies appeared to have been covered hastily and left with minimal attempts at concealment beyond the tarp. Alongside the three human victims were the bodies of three dogs that had clearly been shot execution-style. Someone had systematically killed everything living on the property before fleeing.

Investigators immediately treated the area as a crime scene and launched a triple homicide investigation. The coroner estimated that the three victims had been dead for ten to twelve days by the time they were found on June 19, which placed their time of death around June 7–9.

Identifying the badly decomposed bodies proved challenging. One victim was quickly suspected to be a woman who'd been reported missing by concerned relatives in Utah. On June 30, 2017, the Canyon County coroner announced that the first body had been positively identified through dental records as fifty-six-year-old Cheryl Baker of Ogden, Utah.

This confirmation sent shockwaves through both investigation circles and the victims' communities. If one body was Cheryl Baker, and investigators suspected the other two were Nadja and Payton Medley, then where was Mike Bullinger?

Due to the advanced state of decomposition, formal identification of the remaining two victims took considerable time. It wasn't until early August 2017—more than six weeks after the grisly discovery—that the coroner positively identified the other two victims as forty-eight-year-old Nadja Medley and her fourteen-year-old daughter Payton Medley.

Autopsies revealed that each victim had died from a single gunshot wound to the head, executed with clinical precision, just like the three dogs that were found alongside them.

———

Investigators believe that when Cheryl arrived at the Caldwell property on that Thursday, June 8, she discovered the truth about Mike's double life. She likely found Nadja and Payton living in what she believed was her retirement home. Canyon County Sheriff Sergeant Charles Gentry stated, "I don't believe that Cheryl had been to this property before, and that she wanted to come here and see it."

A confrontation must have ensued between the three adults, with fourteen-year-old Payton possibly present during the argument.

Neighbors later reported hearing what sounded like a woman screaming in the middle of the night sometime between June 6 and June 10, though they couldn't be sure if it was a person or an animal. Others thought they heard gunshots on or around June 10 but hadn't thought anything of it at the time, as shooting wasn't unusual in the rural area.

Investigators wondered if Mike's plan had been to kill Cheryl after using her to buy the Caldwell property so he could form a full-time family with Nadja and Payton. Perhaps, when Cheryl decided to make an unannounced visit, this plan had been foiled. Maybe Cheryl had threatened to divorce him, leaving him with no assets since both property deeds were in her name.

The precision of the executions—including the murder of a teenage girl who was an innocent bystander—showed a chilling level of resolve to eliminate all witnesses to the confrontation.

———

The next confirmed sighting of Mike Bullinger was on Saturday, June 10, when he had breakfast in Nampa, a city just ten miles southeast of Caldwell. After that, he drove his pickup truck all the way back to Ogden, Utah, where he went to a local dealership to pick up a 2007 Ford Focus that he and Cheryl had owned and was being serviced. Mike retrieved the car and began driving it instead of his truck.

On either June 11 or June 12, a surveillance camera in Swan Valley, Idaho, captured Mike entering the city—he had driven back to the state he had fled. The day after that, another surveillance camera caught Mike paying an entrance fee to the Bridger-Teton National Forest, located east of Idaho in Wyoming.

Investigators believed Mike had sent that strange text message from Cheryl's phone as part of his escape plan, trying to buy himself more time before anyone became suspicious.

———

From the moment the bodies were discovered, Mike Bullinger was the primary suspect in the triple homicide, and investigators began attempting to locate him for questioning. When initial checks revealed that Mike had apparently fled and was missing, law enforcement became convinced he was the perpetrator. Within days, a warrant was obtained for Mike's arrest on the charge of failure to report a death.

On August 8, 2017, after positively identifying all victims and gathering more evidence from the crime scene, the Canyon County Prosecutor's Office filed three counts of first-degree murder against Mike Bullinger. Sheriff Kieran Donahue emphasized that only Mike knew "why he committed this heinous crime."

Mike's photograph was shared widely throughout Idaho and Utah in the hope he might be recognized. He was sixty years old, 240 pounds, and six feet one inch tall, with gray hair and brown eyes. Soon, tips were flooding in from people who thought they had seen him, but Mike had a significant head start—he'd had over ten days to disappear before the bodies were even discovered.

———

The Bridger-Teton National Forest is a 3.4-million-acre wilderness that sprawls across western Wyoming. It sits adjacent to Grand Teton and Yellowstone National Parks and serves as a haven for outdoor enthusiasts who love camping and hiking. On Wednesday, July 12, approximately one month after the triple homicide, Mike Bullinger's 2007 Ford Focus was discovered parked at the forest's Pacific Creek Campground. It was a remote campsite, and the car appeared to have been abandoned for some time.

Investigators were aware that Mike was a competent outdoorsman who would have no trouble trekking into the nearby wilderness. His experience as a pilot might have meant he was also familiar with the forest from aerial views. Law enforcement used police dogs, infrared technology, and helicopters to scour the area. The terrain was difficult to navigate on foot due to rocky ground and thick vegetation. Because Mike was considered armed and dangerous, searchers remained on high alert the entire time, prepared for the possibility that he might try to ambush them.

Local communities and subdivisions were checked, as were abandoned farmhouses, but no trace of Mike Bullinger was found.

————

One week after the Ford Focus was discovered, park rangers in nearby Yellowstone National Park spotted an SUV being driven by a light-haired man. Two rangers pursued the SUV in separate vehicles, forcing the driver to pull over.

Also in the car were a woman and a seven-year-old girl. The rangers blocked in the vehicle, and soon, more law enforcement officers arrived. After about an hour of tense questioning, they permitted the driver to show them his identification. His name was Brett, and the passengers were his wife and daughter—they were on vacation from Missouri. The officers explained that they were looking for a wanted killer and showed Brett a photograph of Mike Bullinger. Brett couldn't see any resemblance except that they both had light gray hair.

The family was permitted to leave, though they later filed a lawsuit against the officers, alleging that they had been held at gunpoint for an hour with no proper explanation. The mistake underscored the intensity of the manhunt—law enforcement was on edge, desperate to apprehend Mike.

Other sightings of the wanted fugitive continued to trickle in. Someone thought they had seen Mike driving in Salt Lake City after his Ford was found. A river guide in Idaho spotted men by Henry's Fork, a tributary of the Snake River. The guide thought the men were behaving suspiciously, and one of them looked like Mike. None of these sightings could be confirmed.

————

Investigators considered multiple possibilities for Mike's fate. Had he taken his own life somewhere deep in the forest? If so, why would he travel so far from home in the days after the murders if he had planned on killing himself? Why not do so at the farm back in Caldwell?

Perhaps he had hitched a ride out of the forest with another car, leaving his Ford Focus abandoned there to throw police off his trail. Mike was described as a chameleon who could mold himself to be whatever a particular woman wanted. Some wondered if he had found another woman to manipulate and was living in hiding with her somewhere. Others speculated that maybe Mike had used his pilot's license to fly out of the country and start a new life overseas.

In an interview with the Idaho Statesman, Mike's first wife, Jackie Garcia, described Mike as a prolific liar and possibly a sociopathic personality. Another person who knew Mike but wished to remain anonymous agreed: "If you know about sociopaths, you know they're unlikely to kill themselves. He would have to feel guilty, and he doesn't have a conscience."

In late 2017, a family was hiking in Bridger-Teton National Forest near the Pacific Creek Campground when they came across a junction where two trails met. Standing there was a disheveled man who looked to be in his early sixties. He was alone and appeared ill-equipped to be hiking in winter—he had no backpack, water, or safety protection, and his face was very weathered. The man passed by the family and kept his head down the entire time.

When investigators heard about this interaction, they suspected the man could have been Mike Bullinger, but the sighting led nowhere.

———

More than a year after the murders, in August 2018, authorities regrouped and carried out another extensive search of the Bridger-Teton Forest. Roughly twenty investigators from multiple agencies split into four groups to cover a four-mile radius of wilderness north of the Pacific Creek Campground.

Cadaver dogs accompanied the search teams. If Mike was still in the forest, investigators doubted he was still alive. It had snowed toward the end of 2017, and the snow line was right by the Pacific Creek Campground. Mike would have had to survive a bitterly cold winter without proper gear or provisions. Even for an experienced hunter and guide like him, that would have been extremely difficult.

The forest was also home to grizzly bears, wolves, and mountain lions. If Mike hadn't taken his own life or died from the elements, there was every possibility that he had been killed by a predatory animal.

Police searchers didn't recover Mike's remains. However, they did find some evidence that they wouldn't disclose publicly. They told the media it indicated Mike had never left the forest and had died there. They put out a bulletin advising people visiting the forest throughout the summer and fall to keep an eye out for anything that looked like scattered clothing or human remains.

If Mike had died during the winter, wildlife would have scavenged his remains when the snow thawed. Nothing of significance was ever recovered.

———

Enough evidence was found in Mike's abandoned Ford Focus and at both of his properties to confirm he was responsible for killing Cheryl, Nadja, and Payton. Detectives have not publicly disclosed what that evidence is, but it was sufficient to file formal charges against him.

Mike Bullinger has been charged with three counts of first-degree murder, yet as of 2025, law enforcement remains confident that he is no longer alive. Canyon County Sheriff Kieran Donahue has repeatedly stated that they will not close the case until Mike is found, one way or another.

Whether he died in the Wyoming wilderness or somehow escaped to begin yet another deceptive life elsewhere, the families of Cheryl Baker, Nadja Medley, and Payton Medley continue to wait for the closure that only finding him can bring. The Caldwell farmhouse stands empty now, a silent witness to the three lives cut short by one man's web of lies—lies that finally collapsed under the weight of their own deception.

Online Appendix

Visit my website for additional photos and videos pertaining to the cases in this book:

http://TrueCrimeCaseHistories.com/vol16/

http://TrueCrimeCaseHistories.com/vol17/

http://TrueCrimeCaseHistories.com/vol18/

———

Thank you for reading these volumes of True Crime Case Histories. I truly hope you enjoyed them. If you did, I would be sincerely grateful if you would take a few minutes to write a review for me on Amazon using the link below.

https://geni.us/TrueCrimeBox6

I'd also like to encourage you to sign up for my email list for updates, discounts, and freebies on future books! I promise I'll make it worth your while with future freebies.

http://truecrimecasehistories.com

And please take a moment and follow me on Amazon.

One last thing. As I mentioned previously, many of the stories in this series were suggested to me by readers like you. I like to feature stories that many true crime fans haven't heard of, so if there's a story that you remember from the past that you haven't seen covered by other true crime sources, please send me any details you can remember, and I will do my best to research it. Or if you'd like to contact me for any other reason, feel free to email me at:

jasonnealbooks@gmail.com

Thanks so much,

Jason Neal

More books by Jason Neal

Looking for more?? I am constantly adding new volumes of True Crime Case Histories. The series **can be read in any order,** and all books are available in paperback, hardcover, and audiobook.

Check out the complete series at:

https://amazon.com/author/jason-neal

All Jason Neal books are also available in **AudioBook format at Audible.com.** Enjoy a **Free Audiobook** when you signup for a 30-Day trial using this link:

https://geni.us/AudibleTrueCrime

FREE BONUS EBOOK
FOR MY READERS

As my way of saying "Thank you" for downloading, I'm giving away a FREE True Crime e-book I think you'll enjoy.

https://TrueCrimeCaseHistories.com

Just visit the link above to let me know where to send your free book!

ABOUT THE AUTHOR

Jason Neal is a Best-Selling American True Crime Author living in Hawaii with his Turkish-British wife. Jason started his writing career in the late eighties as a music industry publisher and wrote his first true crime collection in 2019.

As a boy growing up in the eighties just south of Seattle, Jason became interested in true crime stories after hearing the news of the Green River Killer so close to his home. Over the subsequent years, he would read everything he could get his hands on about true crime and serial killers.

As he approached 50, Jason began to assemble stories of the crimes that have fascinated him most throughout his life. He's especially obsessed by cases solved by sheer luck, amazing police work, and groundbreaking technology like early DNA cases and, more recently, reverse genealogy.

Printed in Dunstable, United Kingdom